O9-ABE-651

Essentials of Artificial Intelligence

MATT GINSBERG

MORGAN KAUFMANN PUBLISHERS
San Francisco, California

Sponsoring Editor: Michael B. Morgan
Production Manager: Yonie Overton
Production Editor: Carol Leyba
Editorial Coordinator: Douglas Sery
Cover Design: Ross Carron Design
Cover Photo: Mary Jo Dowling
Back Cover Photo (Terminator): Merie Weismiller Wallace
Text Design: Rebecca Evans and Associates
Composition: Maryland Composition, Inc.
Illustration: Alexander Teshin Associates
Photography: Tom Paiva
Copyeditor: John Hammett
Proofreader: Judy Weiss
Printer: R R Donnelley & Sons

Morgan Kaufman Publishers, Inc.
Editorial Office:
340 Pine Street, Sixth Floor
San Francisco, CA 94104

97 96 95 94 5 4 3 2

Library of Congress Cataloging-in-Publication Data
Ginsberg, Matthew L., 1955-
Essentials of artificial intelligence / Matt Ginsberg.
p. cm.
Includes bibliographical references and index.
ISBN 1-55860-221-6
1. Artificial intelligence. I. Title.
Q335.G55 1993
006.3—dc20 92-46106
CIP

About the Cover: The robot on the front cover is *Dante*, developed by Red Whittaker of Carnegie Mellon University with support from NASA and NSF. Dante has visited the Mt. Erebus volcano in Antarctica. The robot on the back cover is a Cyberdyne Systems series 800 *Terminator*, created by James Cameron. The Terminator has visited movie theaters throughout the world.

Figure Credits: Figure 16.2 was reprinted from "Computer Vision," by Y. Aloimonos and A. Rosenfeld, *Science* 253 (5025), September 13, 1991, by permission of the publisher and authors. • Figures 16.3a and 16.6 were reprinted from "A Computational Approach to Edge Detection," by John Canny, *IEEE PAMI*, copyright 1986 IEEE, by permission of publisher and author. • Figures 16.5 and 16.21 were generated by Donald F. Geddis. • Figure 16.19 was reprinted from *Fun with Unicorns* by Jim Razzi by permission of Scholastic Inc. • Figure 16.20 was digitized by Rebecca Evans and Associates. • Figure 18.1 and 18.2 were reprinted from "The Structure of the MYCIN System," by William van Melle, in *Rule-Based Expert Systems: The MYCIN Experiments of the Stanford Heuristic Programming Project*, edited by Bruce G. Buchanan and Edward H. Shortliffe, with permission of the author.

About the Type: Text has been typeset in Melior; display heads in Gill Sans; computer code in Clarendon Typewriter; symbols in Universal Math, all of the Merganthaler Type Library.

To my students

Acknowledgement

There are many people who helped and supported me both as I learned the material that I am about to share with you and as I wrote the book itself, and I would like to take this opportunity to thank them.

First, my thanks to my students, who showed tremendous patience as I learned the art of teaching and advising. I am indebted to all of them, but especially to Andrew Baker, Adnan Darwiche, Don Geddis, Will Harvey, Hugh Holbrook, Ari Jonsson, Eunok Paek, and Scott Roy. I only hope that you all have profited as much from our interactions as I have.

Thanks to Nils Nilsson, who provided me with a wonderful environment in which to work at Stanford, and supported my efforts to pursue my own research ideas, however baroque they may have seemed to him at the time. John McCarthy first encouraged me to become involved with AI and provided crucial guidance at a variety of points early in my career.

Mike Morgan, Carol Leyba, and the rest of the gang at Morgan Kaufmann have been a pleasure to work with as ever. Their professionalism has given my words a polish that surprises me. My thanks also to those who helped with the cover: Reid Simmons and Mary Jo Dowling, who provided the photograph of the Dante robot, Geoff Burdick and Van Ling of Lightstorm Entertainment, who helped with the photograph of the *Terminator* endoskeleton on the back, and Wallace Todd, who provided my photograph, also on the back.

My mother introduced me to science when she taught me to add fractions almost a full lifetime ago. Science and mathematics have been a source of never-ending pleasure for me ever since, and I owe it to her. Thanks, Mom.

Various people commented on drafts of this book; I may have disagreed with their suggestions at times, but have agreed and profited from their remarks far more frequently. Special thanks are due to Venu Dasigi, Ernie Davis, Tom Dean, Rina Dechter, Jon Doyle, Charles Dyer, Michele Evard, Don Geddis, Gil Harman, Will Harvey, Jim Hendler, Chris Hutchison, Jugal Kalita, Rich Korf, Deepak Kumar, Jean-Claude Latombe, Steven Lytinen, Jalal Maleki, Nils Nilsson, Peter Norvig, Judea Pearl, Martha Pollack, John Rager, Scott Roy, Stuart Russell, Haim Schvaytser, Jude Shavlik, Devika Subramanian, Peter Szolovits, Marco Valtorta, and Mike Wellman. Any remaining errors, of course, are mine alone.

I am also indebted to the agencies that funded my work during the period that this book was written: DARPA, Rome Labs, the Air Force Office of Scientific Research, and the National Science Foundation. Needless to say, the opinions expressed here are mine and not those of the United States government.

Finally, to my wife. She sees me through the good times and bad and gives my life a clarity that I would never have dreamed possible. Without her help, neither this book nor its author would be what we are. Pam, my thanks and my love as always. As soon as this manuscript goes off to the printer I promise to write a play that you'll like more than the last one.

Preface

Imagine what it must have been like to be a physicist in Newton's day. I mean it. Close this book, set it aside, and think about it.

From a modern point of view, they didn't know *anything*. The problems and challenges faced by a physicist in the sixteenth century weren't any easier than those faced today, but they were tremendously more *accessible*—it's a lot easier to explain $F = ma$ to a person on the street than it is to explain the intricacies of quantum field theory. It was an age of scientific romanticism; the accessibility of the problems meant that revolutions in thinking could—and typically did—rest on the shoulders of individual researchers of exceptional insight and imagination.

Artificial intelligence (or AI, as I shall refer to it) is like this today. It is a science in its infancy, and that makes it special. Sciences in their infancy are not like more established disciplines, and I have tried in writing this textbook to honor this distinction and the ways in which it makes AI unique.

Perhaps the most important way in which AI's newness as an enterprise makes it different is the fact that it shares an excitement with the physics of four hundred years ago. Newton described himself as a child playing on a beach, making progress simply by picking up interesting-looking stones and examining them; one has the feeling, reading his description, that physics was so full of exciting problems that he found it difficult to know where to start.

AI is the same. In this book, I have tried both to touch on the shiniest pebbles on our particular beach and to give you some sense for the layout of the shore itself by drawing the problems I discuss into a (somewhat) uniform whole.

You should be careful, however, not to confuse the accessibility of AI's central problems with simplicity. AI is a mixture of longstanding problems from more established fields, including philosophy, linguistics, psychology, mathematics, physics, statistics, decision theory, biophysics, and neuroscience. We bring to these fields the power of the computer, both as a tool and as a method of inquiry, and that gives us a unique perspective on some established questions—but it doesn't make the questions themselves any easier!

Especially in a new science, it is all too easy to lose sight of this, since the novelty of one's investigative techniques and the scarcity of established results make it *seem* that tremendous progress is being made at all times.

Progress is made no more quickly in AI than in any other discipline. As with other sciences, at least 90 percent of the research that is reported will be forgotten as the field develops and changes the problems on which it is focused. Many other AI texts present a careful view of the field in its entirety, trusting either their readers or the fullness of time to determine precisely what should be preserved from one edition to the next.

This book isn't like that. Instead, I have tried to present those ideas that are most central to the AI enterprise itself. You typically won't find AI's newest ideas here, but its oldest. Rather than present specific research results from the past decade, I have tried to distill out the understanding that underlies those results, in the hope that this understanding will be longer-lasting than the results themselves. If you want to know the specific differences between two of the latest approaches to knowledge representation, find another book. But if you want to know what knowledge representation is *about*, what the problems are and where the solutions might lie, keep reading.

Of course, just as it would be inappropriate for me to present *all* of AI's newest work, it would also be unwise for me to present none of it. I have tried to select among recent results, choosing to describe those that are the most likely both to survive the test of time and to remain central to the field. By making these selections, I am able to do you the service of presenting a coherent description of AI as a whole, although this service is inevitably at the cost of subjecting you to my own views about what is likely to remain important as time passes.

In a physics text, this would be inappropriate. But in a field as new as ours, coherence of description is both valuable and hard to come by; I hope that my identity as an active researcher in a variety of AI subfields has given me the perspective to choose wisely.

This book is written as a one-semester or one-quarter textbook in introductory artificial intelligence. It is a text for both undergraduates and graduate students, since in a new field, there isn't really all that much difference. AI's ideas are just as accessible to an undergraduate as they are to a graduate student. They're just as hard, too. A course in data structures is a useful prerequisite but not an essential one; most of what follows should be sensible without it.

Finally, I've tried to select a range of exercises, some of which are little more than busywork and others of which are intended to really stretch you and get you to look at the material in new ways. I haven't indicated which are which with asterisks or some such; no one ever tells a practicing scientist which problems are easy and which are hard, and you might as well get used to it.

Enough, already. I hope you find AI as much fun as I do.

MATT GINSBERG
Palo Alto, California
November, 1992

Contents

PART I

INTRODUCTION AND OVERVIEW

CHAPTER

1

INTRODUCTION: WHAT IS AI?

It seems that all introductory books on AI begin by telling you what AI is, and this one is no exception. I don't want to stop there, though, because there's a lot more to introducing AI than simply presenting a definition of it.

This is partly a consequence of how new the field is—it's premature for me to try to present a truly crisp definition. But it's also a consequence of the fact that there are a variety of things about AI that make it unique, and these aren't obvious from the definition alone. So what I'd like to do here is to define AI and then to give you a flavor for it by describing two more things—what AI is *about*, in the sense that I'd like to describe the sorts of things that AI researchers work on and worry over, and what AI is *like*, in the sense that I'd like to describe how they feel as they're working.

1.1 DEFINING ARTIFICIAL INTELLIGENCE

Let me start with a fairly simplistic definition of what AI is and then work on refining it. Here's the simple definition:

> *Artificial intelligence is the enterprise of constructing an intelligent artifact.*

The problem is that this doesn't really say anything: If I want the definition to be of any use, I'll have to tell you what I mean by *intelligence* and by *artifact*.

1.1.1 Intelligence

So what is intelligence? As a first cut, let me take the rather egotistical view that tasks demonstrating intelligence are those that people do well. As we will see throughout this book, many things that we take completely for granted are actually extremely subtle.

Vision is a good example. My ability to recognize a particular friend or landscape is something that strikes me as trivial, but the computational problems encountered in getting a machine to do this are immense. As this book is being written, it's possible to write a program that recognizes people by examining frontal photographs of them (like the ones appearing in passports) but if the people turn sideways, the computer isn't able to identify them any more.

Recognizing voices is similar. We can write programs that are extremely efficient at identifying speakers by listening to them speak; such programs obviously have tremendous potential applications in privacy-sensitive domains from banking to the military. Unfortunately, if the speaker being identified has a cold, the machine won't recognize the voice any more.

Think about the assumptions you will make when you turn the page in this book. What will you find? You *expect* to find a continuation of this introduction, but that's because you've made all sorts of assumptions about my intentions as an author, about the intentions of the publisher, and about our abilities to honor those intentions and get you a coherent textbook. But these assumptions might be wrong—the publisher or printer may have made a mistake, or I might have put a picture of the Eiffel tower on the next page simply because I was in that sort of a mood. You have no trouble making these assumptions (and revising them when they turn out to be in error); our computer programs are not yet able to do this.

All of these examples share a common feature, and it appears to be ubiquitous in AI work thus far. Our "intelligent" programs are in fact extremely brittle in that they can function only in the domains and conditions for which they are written. Any attempt to extend their abilities—by turning a photograph sideways, giving a speaker a cold, or changing the assumptions underlying a commonsense inference—wreaks havoc with their performance.

Note, however, that not all things people do well are part of AI. What about eating? Surely getting machines to prefer Big Macs to lima beans isn't part of what AI is all about. And there are other bodily functions that it would also be a shame to duplicate! Woody Allen tells a story about his father, saying that he at some point lost his job because some company came out with a machine that could do everything his dad could do, only better. That wasn't so bad, Allen reports; the really sad part came when his *mother* bought one of the machines.[1]

1 I should take a moment here and make a confession. Throughout this book, you will find a variety of stories, some of which have a lot to do with AI and some of which are purely anecdotal. One of the entertaining things about working in a field as new as AI is that there are a great many such stories floating around, and I can think of no reason not to share them with you. At the very least, they will make the material I'm presenting more enjoyable; they will also—I hope—help to capture some of the attitudes underlying AI and the problems with which it is concerned.

There is something else outside the scope of AI that people are good at. People are good at being people.

This may seem trivial, but it isn't; consider Woody Allen's story once again. The goal of AI is to create an artificial intelligence—a machine that may well be smarter than we are. What will become of us if we do so? Here is what Edward Fredkin has to say about this:

> Humans are okay. I'm glad to be one. I like them in general, but they're only human. It's nothing to complain about. Humans aren't the best ditch diggers in the world, machines are. And humans can't lift as much as a crane. They can't fly at all without an airplane. And they can't carry as much as a truck. It doesn't make me feel bad. There were people whose thing in life was completely physical—John Henry and the steam hammer. Now we're up against the intellectual steam hammer. The intellectual doesn't like the idea of this machine doing it better than he does, but it's no different from the guy who was surpassed physically. So the intellectuals are threatened, but they needn't be—we should only worry about what we can do ourselves. The mere idea that we have to be the best in the universe is kind of farfetched. We certainly aren't physically.
>
> The fact is, I think we'll be enormously happier once our niche has limits to it. We won't have to worry about carrying the burden of the universe on our shoulders as we do today. We can enjoy life as human beings without worrying about it. And I think that will be a great thing. [Quoted in McCorduck 1979, page 352]

Think about turtles. What are they good at? Not much of anything—except being turtles. But turtles aren't a melancholy species; that's enough for them. And Fredkin would argue that being people should be enough for us. However AI proceeds, that is our niche. And it will remain ours.

But let me return to the question of defining intelligence. Many things (such as playing a good game of chess) that used to be considered hallmarks of intelligence have turned out to be too specific to be relevant to our definition of AI. Because of the brittleness mentioned earlier, good chess-playing programs can hardly be thought of as "intelligent" simply because they are good at chess; they are completely hopeless at everything else.

This doesn't mean that work on chess playing has no relevance to AI; by focusing on a specific *aspect* of intelligence, this work has an important role to play indeed. We are simply saying that playing a good game of chess, in and of itself, is not an indication that a computer program has an intellect.

The definition of general intelligent behavior that I find the most acceptable is one due to Alan Turing, a British mathematician of the 1940s. Turing proposed the following:

Imagine that you are typing into a computer terminal. At the other end of the line is either another person or an artificial system of some sort. You have thirty minutes to ask whatever you want; if, at the end of that time, you cannot reliably distinguish the human from the artificial respondent,

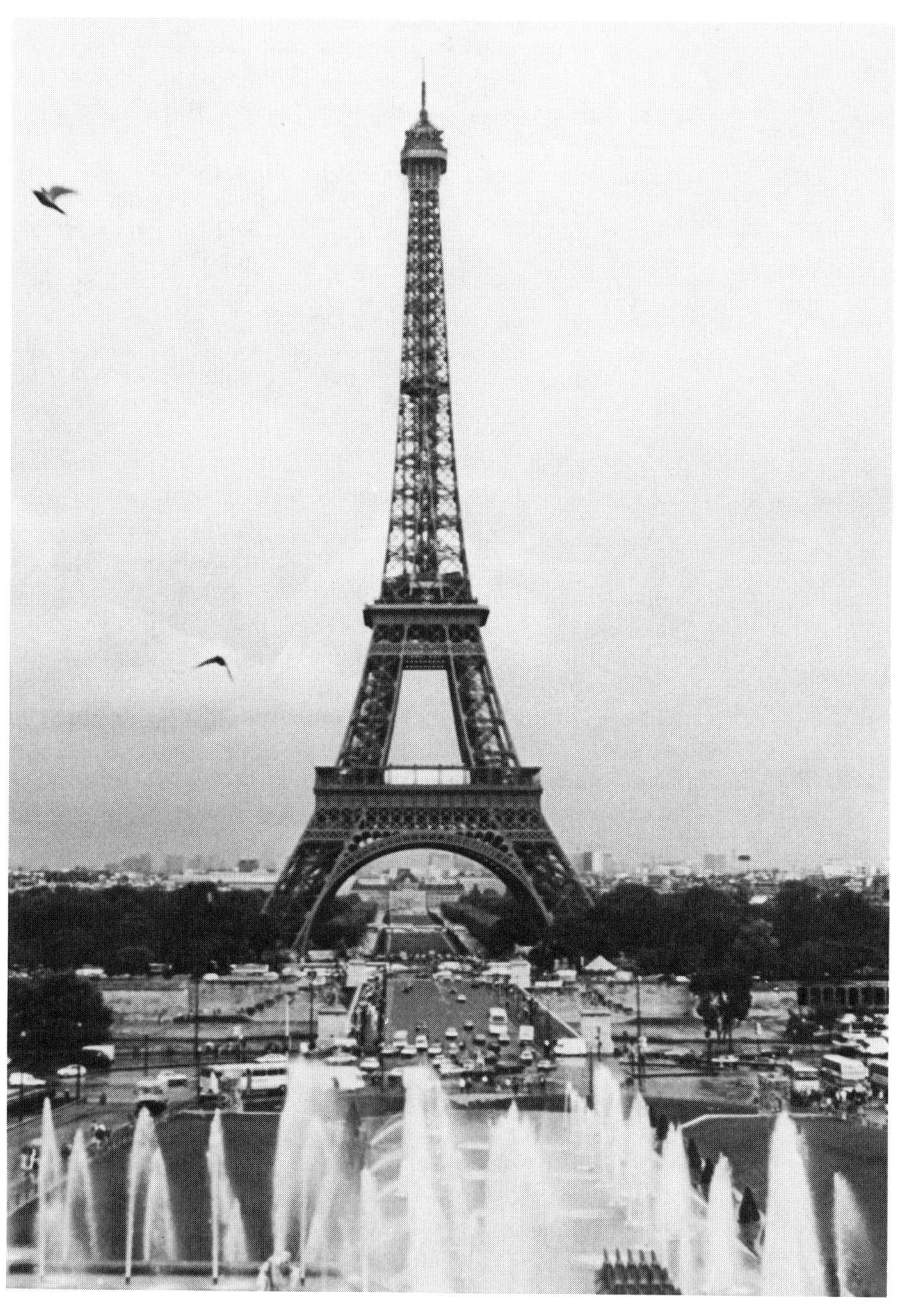

FIGURE 1.1
The Eiffel tower

the artificial system is deemed to be generally intelligent. This is known as the *Turing test.*

The Turing test is extraordinarily difficult. The machine on the other end needs to be able to discuss a tremendous range of topics, since there is no way to know in advance if you will want to discuss baseball or the weather, philosophy or poetry. And things may be even trickier if you decide to ask about mathematics. If, for example, you ask the computer to multiply two twelve-digit numbers, its most "intelligent" response is probably to take five minutes before answering—and then give the wrong answer!

In the face of observations such as this, the Turing test may seem a bit too difficult, but it retains the advantage of being a reasonably sharp description of intelligence. Our definition of AI has now become:

> *Artificial intelligence is the enterprise of constructing an artifact that can reliably pass the Turing test.*

Objections There are a couple of objections to the above definition that we should discuss before turning to other issues. As a start, it is possible for a machine to pass the Turing test simply because the human interrogator is too lazy to ask any questions! The program will have demonstrated as much intelligence as it can in quite limited circumstances, but should this count as intelligence? Presumably not; this is why the above definition requires that our artifact be able to pass the Turing test not just once, but *reliably.*

A more serious objection is the following: Since the interaction takes place over a computer terminal, and people can type at a maximum of perhaps 10 characters per second, the computer will have to respond to at most 18,000 characters during the half hour. Would a machine that stored all possible sequences of up to 18,000 characters together with appropriate responses be intelligent?

The easy response to this is simply that you can't do it; there are too many such sequences to hope to store responses to each of them. But this avoids the serious issue: Any computer program is, at some fundamental level, simply manipulating bits, 1s and 0s. Can it ever be reasonable to say that such a machine is intelligent or that it understands what it is doing?

I would argue that it can be, that intelligence is not a matter of design but of function. When something acts intelligently, we call it intelligent independent of how it comes to act as it does. After all, our brains are also manipulators of electric signals, and we certainly are prepared to call ourselves intelligent even though no individual neuron has any notion of the larger machine of which it is a part.

By adopting this functional definition of intelligence—the ability to pass the Turing test and nothing more—we are taking a strong philosophical position. We are taking the view that a machine that responds effectively to queries simply by finding the answers in a huge table *is* intelligent. There's nothing wrong with taking this view, of course, but we need to be aware of the nature of the commitment being made.

1.1.2 Artifacts

Artificial intelligence is the enterprise of constructing an artifact that can reliably pass the Turing test. But what is an artifact? If we fertilize a human egg in a test tube, is the child that is eventually born an artifact?

At the very least, by *artifact* we mean an inorganic object. In fact, though, I will take a rather different tack, taking an artifact to be what Allen Newell and Herb Simon have called a *physical-symbol system*.

> A physical symbol system consists of a set of entities, called symbols, which are physical patterns that can occur as components of another type of entity called an expression (or symbol structure). Thus, a symbol structure is composed of a number of instances (or tokens) of symbols related in some physical way (such as one token being next to another). At any instant of time the system will contain a collection of these symbol structures. Besides these structures, the system also contains a collection of processes that operate on expressions to produce other expressions: processes of creation, modification, reproduction and destruction. A physical symbol system is a machine that produces through time an evolving collection of symbol structures. Such a system exists in a world of objects wider than just these symbolic expressions themselves. [Newell and Simon 1976]

This is very expensive language, but what Newell and Simon are basically doing is defining a physical-symbol system to be a symbol-manipulating entity. The symbols could be bits in a computer, letters on a piece of paper, marks on the tape of a Turing machine, or what have you. Newell and Simon also require that the physical-symbol system be embedded in an external environment of some sort in order that it be possible for its behavior to be evaluated against this external framework.

Here, then, is our definition of artificial intelligence:

> *Artificial intelligence is the enterprise of constructing a physical-symbol system that can reliably pass the Turing test.*

There is one additional assumption that is often made about physical-symbol systems, and that is that the symbols they manipulate correspond to objects in their environments. A computer program thinking about restaurants should have identifiable symbols for concepts in this domain: food, drink, service, and so on.

This assumption is known as *declarativism* and is subscribed to by most—but by no means all—AI scientists. A system that responds to queries by looking them up in a table may be intelligent, but it is not declarative. Most of the people working in the declarative framework believe that it is the only way to construct an intelligent artifact; they feel that AI is so difficult that progress cannot be made without frequent appeals to our understanding of how humans solve problems, and these introspective appeals are typically declarative in nature.

With one exception, this book adopts the declarativist assumption; as mentioned above, it appears to be the prevailing view in the AI community as a whole. In addition (or perhaps as a result), most of the material that belongs in an introductory textbook is declarative in nature. As in Section 1.1.1, there is nothing wrong with our making the declarativist assumption—provided that we are clear about making it.

The place in this book where we deal with nondeclarative notions is where we discuss *neural networks*. The idea here is to interconnect a large number of small processors in a way that duplicates the neural firings in the brain. Because the signals being propagated by a neural network do not correspond to objects in our world, neural networks are outside the boundaries of declarative AI. Nevertheless, there has been a great deal of interest in them recently, and we will return to them in Chapter 15.

1.1.3 Construction

Artificial intelligence is the enterprise of constructing a physical-symbol system that can reliably pass the Turing test. Let me also spend a few moments discussing the impact of the appearance of the word *construction* in this definition. What it says is that AI is fundamentally an engineering discipline, since our fundamental goal is that of building something.

This does not mean to say that there is no place for science in AI; there is. All good engineering rests on a solid scientific foundation, and AI is no exception. It's possible, though, that the scientific foundation of AI has already been laid, and that the work that remains is engineering in nature.

Many respected members of the AI community believe this; Ed Feigenbaum is probably one of the best-known examples. Feigenbaum and his followers believe that if you take a system that exhibits intelligence in a restricted domain and give that system a great deal of additional knowledge, the system will come to display general intelligent behavior. If this view is correct, the interesting problems are the engineering ones involved in developing the large body of knowledge to be supplied to the program.

At the other end of the philosophical spectrum are people who believe that AI has many fundamental *scientific* problems still to be solved; that the goal of constructing an intelligent artifact today is not dissimilar to the goal of building a nuclear reactor in 1920—there is still a great deal of science left to be done. John McCarthy is a typical advocate of this position, saying that, "Fundamental progress [in AI] cannot be achieved through incremental advances in existing technology."

Who's right? There is no way to tell. If Feigenbaum and his followers succeed in creating a computer program that behaves intelligently, they will have been right. If they fail and instead need to apply scientific results that have not yet been discovered, McCarthy will have been right. I personally hope that McCarthy turns out to be right, but that's only because I'm committed to doing AI and find science more fun than engineering!

1.2 WHAT AI IS ABOUT

The material in the previous section describes the long-range goals of AI. But the basic problem of constructing an intelligent artifact is far too difficult to have much impact on the day-to-day activities of individual AI researchers, who need to identify more tractable problems on which to focus their efforts. This brings us to the question of what AI is *about*.

As it turns out, AI is about three separate things: search, knowledge representation, and, to a somewhat lesser extent, applications of these ideas. Let us discuss each of them in turn.

1.2.1 The Subfields of AI

By *search*, we mean solving a problem where the basic technique being used involves examining a large number of possibilities while looking for a solution.

The problem of generating crossword puzzles is typical. You are given a frame into which letters must be entered; the problem is to do so in a way that is a legal crossword, since the letters making up each slot need to spell an English word.

In the small puzzle in Figure 1.2, there are nineteen places into which letters must be placed; as a result, there are 26^{19} ways in which we might do so. But only a few of these are legal crosswords, since there are ten combinations of letters (five going across, and five going down) that need to be English words. Finding a legal crossword among these possibilities is a search problem.

FIGURE 1.2
A search problem

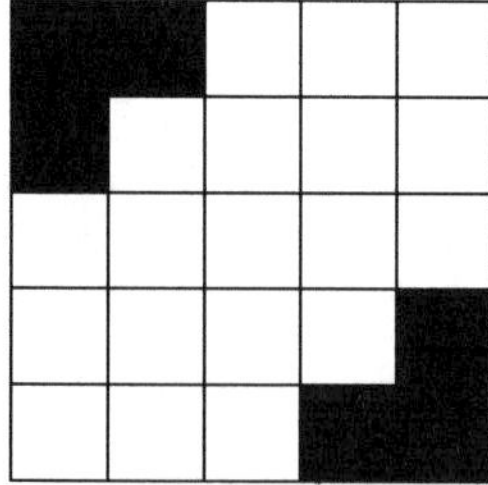

Note, incidentally, that there is an alternative way to view this problem. Instead of filling the nineteen spaces with letters and hoping to do so in a way that produces legal words, we can fill the ten word slots with words and hope to do so in a way that doesn't produce conflicts in the nineteen squares. Thus the first letter of the top word across has to match the first letter of the middle word down, and so on. Many search problems admit alternative representations of this sort.

Chess can also be viewed as a search problem. In principle, one could play a perfect game of chess by expanding all legal sequences of moves from the opening position, and deciding on this basis what to do; in practice, there are far too many possible chess games (on the order of 10^{160}) for this approach to be viable. Computer chess programs expand only a small portion of the complete game tree and then try to make an informed decision about what move to select based on the results of searching through this partial information.

Planning problems also involve search. Consider the goal of planning a Christmas vacation—should I visit my family, my wife's family, or take some time off and go to Tahiti? After I decide to go to Tahiti, I have to select a flight, a hotel, maybe a rental car, and so on. The overall problem is that of making an intelligent selection from the multitude of possible trips I could take over the holidays.

The reason search problems are hard is that they tend to be computationally intractable, since the size of the space being searched often grows exponentially with the size of the problem. There will be only $26^4 = 4.6 \times 10^5$ ways in which to enter letters into a 2×2 crossword; the puzzle in Figure 1.2 admits $26^{19} = 7.7 \times 10^{26}$ possibilities. For a typical *New York Times* puzzle, the number might easily be $26^{190} = 6.9 \times 10^{268}$. There is clearly no way to examine the search space in its entirety, just as there is no way to completely examine the search space associated with chess. Much of the work on AI has to do with the problem of finding ways to attack search problems such as these with the limited computational resources available in practice. Instead of searching blindly, we can use some sort of *heuristics*, or rules of thumb, to focus our efforts. In chess, for example, we might choose to focus on moves that have some purpose, such as attacking or capturing our opponent's pieces. There are also sophisticated techniques for improving the performance of search algorithms in the absence of heuristic information.

The other main theoretical thrust of AI involves *knowledge representation*. Any intelligent declarative system will need to know an awful lot about the environment in which it is situated; knowledge representation research studies the problem of finding a language in which to encode that knowledge so that the machine can use it.

A common view in the 1970s was that first-order logic was the "solution" to the knowledge representation problem; the idea was that any particular fact could be recorded simply by translating it into a sentence in first-order logic. A computer program could prove theorems using the supplied information as premises, thereby drawing conclusions in an intelligent way.

This approach has many attractive features. First-order logic is well-understood by mathematicians; its syntax (the rules by which legal sentences in the language are formed) and semantics (the rules by which these sentences are interpreted and used to derive other sentences) are both precisely defined and well understood. In addition, it can be shown that first-order logic is *universal* in the sense that if it is possible to capture some bit of knowledge in any formal system at all, it is possible to capture it using first-order logic.

Although this view still retains a few adherents, it has been generally abandoned by the knowledge representation community. The reason is that although it's always *possible* to axiomatize any piece of knowledge using first-order logic, it is typically extremely awkward to do so.

As an example, consider the sentence, "The probability that this coin will come up heads is 0.5," which we could write using some sort of probabilistic language as

$$p(\texttt{heads}) = 0.5$$

In first-order logic, however, we can only say that things are true or false, not that they have some intermediate probability. So if we want to express the same information using logic, we have to say something like

$$\text{The sentence, ``}p(\texttt{heads}) = 0.5\text{,'' is true.} \tag{1.1}$$

The problem is that we now also have to present axioms telling us how to manipulate sentences like the one appearing in (1.1); we need, for example, an axiom telling us that the probability of a conjunction of independent events is the product of the probabilities of the individual events, and so on. Performing a simple probabilistic calculation now involves deriving the rules of probabilistic manipulation from first principles—surely a lot harder than simply using a system that understood probabilities in the first place!

Logic's requirement that we label sentences as either "true" or "false" is an overly restrictive one; much of the work in knowledge representation over the past decade is an outgrowth of this realization. Many applications use labels that convey useful additional information; probabilities are just one example. As another, if we want to tell a user *why* we believe a particular statement, we can label it with a reason of some sort; this idea underlies what are known as *truth-maintenance systems*, a topic to which we return in Chapter 10.

In other cases, we have a sentence that is almost true, but not quite; the most famous example is the statement that birds fly. This isn't really true—after all, not all birds fly. But it's a good rule of thumb; if you see a bird about which you have no additional information, it's a reasonable bet that it flies. Once again, it is inappropriate to label sentences such as "Birds fly" as either true or false; understanding examples such as this will be the focus of Chapter 11.

Knowledge representation doesn't stop here, of course; it isn't enough to simply assign sentences all sorts of labels unless we go on to say what those labels mean, in the sense that we can derive labels for new sentences given the labels for old ones.

Suppose I make a bet with a friend that a certain coin will come up heads. There is presumably a 50 percent chance that the coin will fall as I have predicted; let's say that the chances that I manage to collect from my friend if it does so are 90 percent. Now the chance that I actually get paid off is 45 percent—the product of these two figures. When we use probabilities to assign values to sentences, we also commit to using the rules of probability theory to manipulate these values.

Other examples are similar; truth-maintenance systems include sophisticated mechanisms to manipulate the reasons that sentences are believed, and systems that reason with default sentences like "Birds fly" are similar. In addition to representing knowledge, we have to be able to reason with it; knowledge representation work involves both of these issues.

While search and knowledge representation form the "core" of AI, there is also a great deal of effort aimed at solving the other problems of intelligence—vision, natural language processing, and so on. The last part of this book covers these areas, which are typically applications of the more basic results that we discuss first. Because of the increased engineering focus in these application areas, it is often not clear which of their results will survive as AI matures; as a result, I focus somewhat on core AI in this book. This is not to say that the applications aren't important or that the progress being made is not exciting—only that it is difficult to tell now what ideas from these application areas will pass the test of time.

1.2.2 The Role of Examples in AI

In the previous section, I described AI in terms of search, knowledge representation, and applications. But there is a very different way to look at it also: AI is about examples.

AI is like any other science; the idea is to make falsifiable claims. Thus, when I say about some new idea, "This is a good search procedure," or "This is a good evaluation function for chess positions," I'm making a falsifiable claim. You can compare one search algorithm against others; my algorithm will either perform well or it won't. The purpose of the examples is to give you something on which to compare the procedures; the examples make sure that the people making the claims stay honest.

Of course, a good example for one argument may be a bad example for another; often, what distinguishes a good AI researcher from a bad one is the ability to think up new examples that highlight the differences between competing approaches. There shouldn't be anything hard about doing this; it's mostly a matter of introspection. If you understand a search algorithm (for example) well enough to be able to characterize its strengths and weaknesses, you understand it well enough to generate examples that display these strengths and weaknesses. What seems to make the process difficult is that the examples really do keep you honest—if your latest and most exciting idea is in fact rubbish, they'll make it clear. You need to avoid the trap of examining only those examples that validate the theory you're trying to test.

As an example, I once had a discussion with a colleague of mine about a particular form of commonsense reasoning known as *inheritance*. This small subfield of AI has to do with reasoning about conditions under which members of one class inherit properties from another class. Thus since birds typically fly and canaries are birds, we can conclude that canaries typically fly. But ostriches are birds that don't fly, so there are clearly some exceptions. The problem of deciding just when it's legitimate to pass a property down from a class to a subclass turns out to be quite a subtle one.

This particular domain has a lot of "standard" examples that illustrate most of the difficulties; we'll see some of them in Chapter 11. I once went to a talk in which this colleague presented a theory that seemed (at least to me) to have no intuitive grounding; the only thing it had going for it was that it solved these standard examples correctly.

Since the method was so nonintuitive, it wasn't hard to think about it for a while and find an example on which it produced the wrong answer (saying that a particular ostrich *did* fly, only somewhat more complicated). I showed this example to my colleague; he disappeared for a while and returned with his theory modified in a way that handled my new example.

The new theory was no more intuitive than its predecessor, and I generated another counterexample. Shortly thereafter, my colleague returned with a newly modified theory, and I generated *another* counterexample. We went through this a few times until he finally asked me to simply list all of my examples in advance so that he wouldn't be tricked into presenting all of these wrong approaches!

Needless to say, this misses the point entirely. The role of examples in AI is to test our theories, and it is the responsibility of individual researchers to conduct an honest search for examples that test their theories as critically as possible. After all, if you don't do it, you can be sure that someone listening to your results will! It really is like physics in the sixteenth century; the principal difference is that our experiments are introspective instead of material. The best AI researchers are invariably skilled at producing interesting examples—not because this makes them any smarter than their colleagues, but because it gives them more experimental evidence on which to base their views.

1.3 WHAT AI IS LIKE

Finally, let me end this chapter by telling you not what AI is or what it is about, but what it's *like*. How does it feel to "do" AI?

The bottom line is that like physics in Newton's day, it's both very easy and very hard. The problems really are accessible; if an intelligent person goes to a talk at one of the national AI conferences held each summer, he is more likely than not to understand a good part of it.[2] If you pick up the proceedings of one of these conferences, many of the articles will make sense. The bottom line is that we haven't yet had a chance to build a foundation of accepted results upon which more current authors are expected to build.[3]

As easy as it is to understand the problems of AI, it's remarkably hard to make progress on those problems. AI is no easier than any of its academic siblings—philosophy, psychology, and so on. Although the problems are accessible, they are also subtle; progress is (and doubtless will continue to be) slow. Robots like R2-D2 are still probably hundreds of years in our future.

To my mind, this is what makes AI interesting. It's what makes it exciting, and what makes it fun. How can such simple things turn out to be so complicated? Perhaps more than any other academic discipline, AI rewards the ability to think deeply about simple things.

1.4 FURTHER READING

There are a variety of books on the philosophical underpinnings of AI; two of the best are McCorduck [1979] and Haugeland [1985]. The first is a layman's introduction to AI generally; the second is a more sophisticated investigation of specific philosophical issues.

The description of the Turing test given in the text is not faithful to Turing's original description in Turing [1950]. There, it was suggested that the human interrogator try to determine which of *two* respondents was a man and which was a woman. If either the man or the woman could be

2 I have tried to use gender-neutral language throughout this book, but there are points where it is awkward to express things without the use of a personal pronoun. In these cases I have chosen to use *he* or *his* because the text reads more smoothly as a result. No specific gender choice is intended.

3 As an example of this, I finished graduate school with a degree in an obscure branch of physics called *twistor theory*. Although beautiful mathematics, twistor theory had very little to do with physical reality, and I decided to change disciplines to either quantum chromodynamics (mainstream physics, basically) or to AI. Changing to mainstream physics involved going back to graduate school for another six years; changing to AI involved little more than saying, "I am doing AI now." You can see which one I chose.

replaced by a computer without affecting the tester's ability to distinguish between them, the program would have passed the test.

An excellent biography of Turing is Hodges's *Alan Turing: The Enigma* [1983]. Whitemore's play *Breaking the Code* is a dramatized version of Turing's life based on Hodges's book.

The objection that we have described to the Turing test is related to Searle's "Chinese room" [Searle, 1980]. Imagine that someone is sitting in a room; people pass him questions written in Chinese and he is expected to pass out answers.

Unfortunately, the person in the room doesn't understand Chinese; all he has is a set of rules that tell him how to turn the questions into answers. Can we possibly say that the man understands Chinese based only on his ability to answer questions? How can we say that a machine is intelligent when it isn't really doing anything different from the man in the room?

Our answer is that the combination of the man and the room *does* understand Chinese, at least in any measurable sense. Understanding is a matter of function, not design.

There is a substantial literature on nondeclarative approaches to AI, and I should at least give you some pointers to it here. An early version of neural networks was developed in the 1960s, but shown in Minsky and Papert [1969] to have very limited expressive power. The recent resurgence of this approach is a consequence of the fact that modern neural networks avoid the expressive limitations of the earlier work. We return to this issue in Chapter 15.

Neural nets aren't the only nondeclarative method; another is due to Rod Brooks. Roughly speaking, Brooks suggests that the idea that intelligence can be split "vertically" into tasks like knowledge representation and search is simply misguided; a more suitable split is "horizontal" and based on function. According to Brooks, AI should proceed as evolution did, beginning by constructing primitive but self-contained artificial "insects" and progressing from there to more sophisticated mechanisms. Brooks summarizes his approach in Kirsh [1991]; this issue of the journal *Artificial Intelligence* contains a variety of articles describing the declarativist debate in AI.

There are many good sources of introductory material on artificial intelligence. The three most popular textbooks (other than this one, of course) are probably by Charniak and McDermott [1985], Rich and Knight [1991], and Winston [1992]; interesting perspectives on the field as a whole can also be found in Bobrow and Hayes [1985] and Marr [1977]. Schrobe [1988] contains a variety of survey articles on subfields of AI such as search, natural language processing, and so on. The series of readings books published by Morgan Kaufmann is also an excellent source (including Allen *et al.* [1990], Bond and Gasser [1988], Brachman and Levesque [1985], Fischler and Firschein [1987], Ginsberg [1987], Grosz *et al.* [1986], and

Rich and Waters [1986]). The collection of papers edited by Webber and Nilsson [1981] is especially valuable.

1.5 EXERCISES

Unlike the exercises in most chapters, the first two exercises here are more "term projects" than they are things to be done at this point in the text.

1. Find two papers that disagree from recent proceedings of either the national meeting of the American Association of Artificial Intelligence (AAAI) or the International Joint Conference on Artificial Intelligence (IJCAI). Explain the disagreement, pick a side, and explain why one of the authors is right and the other wrong.
2. Write a program that accepts as input a blank frame such as that appearing in Figure 1.2 and generates a legal crossword puzzle using this frame. I will refer to this particular problem at a variety of points throughout this text, calling it the *crossword-puzzle problem.*
3. What is the most intelligent thing you did in the past week? Why?

CHAPTER

2

OVERVIEW

The rest of this book follows the description of AI presented in Section 1.2 of the last chapter. Chapters 3 through 5 deal with search, Chapters 6 through 13 deal with knowledge representation, and the remainder of the book deals with applications of these ideas. Before examining these ideas in detail, however, I would like to devote a bit more space to a high-level discussion of them. The purpose of this discussion is both to introduce search and knowledge representation and to defend the position that I took in the last chapter, where I said that AI was fundamentally an investigation into knowledge representation and search. What do these topics have to do with intelligence?

2.1 INTELLIGENT ACTION

It's December 24, and I have just decided to start my Christmas shopping. What mental processes will underlie my actions for the next twenty-four hours?

First, I have to decide what to get my friends and relatives. My mom is a tremendous football fan; I decide to go to a local sports outlet and get her a sweatshirt with her home team's logo. My father, meanwhile, owns a boat and has said he needs to learn more about maintaining the teak woodwork; I can presumably find a suitable book in a local bookstore. I'm not sure what to get my wife, but trust that a visit to a jeweler will turn up something. My friends will have to make do with what I come across during my travels.

What has gone into my reasoning thus far? A great deal of knowledge about the world, for one thing. I used the fact that my dad wants a book on maintaining his boat, so I must have somehow *recorded* that fact in a way that allows me subsequent access to it. My decision to get my mom sports attire is a bit more subtle; here, I used both specific information about her interests and general information about sports fans, their likes and dislikes, and the extent to which sports outlet stores cater to these wishes. My wife's gift is more subtle still, since I've used knowledge about what she is likely to enjoy and where I am likely to find it even though I have no precise gift in mind.

Now what? Which bookstore should I visit? Which jeweler? There are doubtless many possibilities for each, and I have to select among them. Perhaps the closest sports outlet is in a mall a few miles south of my house; there's a bookstore there as well, so that's where I'll look for the woodworking book. There's a jeweler in the mall also, but I know that my wife has a special fondness for the work of a different jeweler, and I decide to try there first.

Of course, my wife's gift is rather a hit-and-miss affair; if the first jeweler doesn't have something suitable, I'll have to look elsewhere. This is why I decide to visit my wife's favorite jeweler first; if I can't find something there, I'll go to the jeweler in the mall where I'm getting something for Mom and Dad.

If I want to describe this reasoning precisely enough for a machine to duplicate it, what sort of facilities will I need?

First, I need to capture the knowledge that entered into my decisions. That means that I need a precise language in which to encode this knowledge—just as I need to use a programming language for programming purposes, I need a knowledge representation language for knowledge encoding. Even in our simple example, note that there are at least two kinds of knowledge involved: *certain* (or nearly certain) knowledge, such as my belief that my father will be happy with a book on woodworking, and *probable*, or *default* knowledge, such as my expectation that I can likely find my wife a suitable gift at a jewelry store.

Of course, simply finding a language in which to represent my knowledge is hardly enough—I have to encode my knowledge in that language as well! Just as the bulk of work in solving programming problems involves coding and not simply the selection of a language, the bulk of work in "knowledge engineering" involves not the selection of a suitable language, but deciding what to say in that language.

Unfortunately, knowledge representation isn't as advanced as programming language technology; most knowledge representation languages are woefully inadequate for dealing with realistic problems. For that reason, current work in this area tends to focus not on *what* to say, but on the more basic issue of how to say it. As we will see in Chapter 11, simply understanding the difference between the default and certain information in our Christmas example involves subtle and unsolved questions.

After using our knowledge to decide to visit a sports store, a bookstore, and a jeweler's, we needed to select specific stores to visit. This is a *search* problem—there is a variety of possible stores from which to choose, and we need to find the choice that will allow us to complete our shopping as effectively as possible.

There are several ways in which we might go about this. We might, for example, enumerate every combination of a sports store, a bookstore, and a jeweler's and see which choice allows us to shop the most sensibly. More effective, however, is to use additional information about the locations of the stores to narrow our search, first picking the sports store (since one is much closer than the others) and then using this choice to select a bookstore. Our choice of jeweler is governed by other concerns, and we decide to visit the jeweler first because that will give us a convenient chance to try a second shop if necessary.

Here, too, we see something to which we will return on many occasions: Unconstrained search is hard. A hallmark of intelligence is the use of knowledge to make search problems more tractable.

In any event, what we have seen here is typical; problem solving can commonly be reduced to knowledge representation and to search. Some problems highlight search and others knowledge representation, but much of AI can be reduced to one or the other.

2.2 SEARCH

We will often describe search problems using diagrams similar to that in Figure 2.1. There is an initial node i, which is where the search starts, and a goal node g. The object is to find a path through the search space that connects the initial node to the goal.

A search space is not in general stored in its entirety by the computer; instead, we have available some procedure that takes a node in the space as input and produces its successors. In the figure, the successors of the initial node are the three nodes c_1, c_2, and c_3; these are the nodes that can be reached from i in a single step. So the *input* to a search problem is a description of the initial and goal nodes and a procedure that produces the successors of an arbitrary node; the output should be a legal sequence of nodes starting with the given initial node and ending with the goal node.

A very small portion of the search space involved in the crossword-puzzle problem is shown in Figure 2.2. Here, the nodes correspond to partially completed crosswords; the description in the figure corresponds

FIGURE 2.1
A search problem

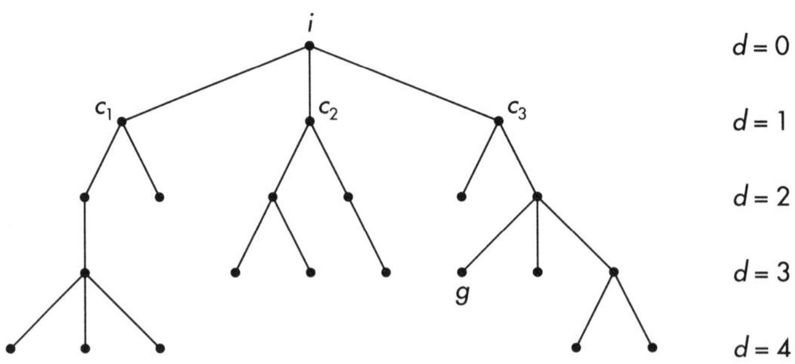

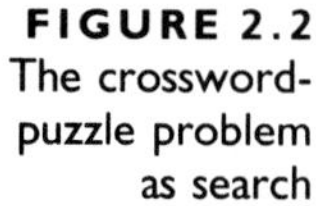

FIGURE 2.2 The crossword-puzzle problem as search

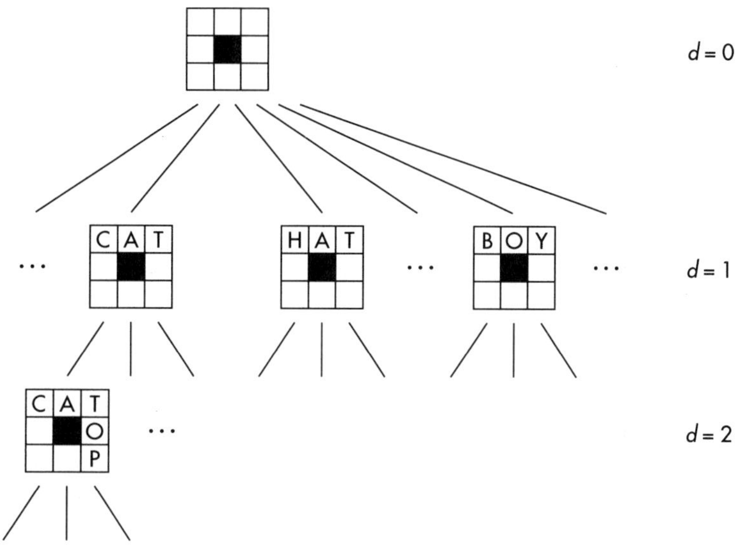

to the approach in which the crossword is developed a word at a time. Figure 2.3 shows a portion of the search space using the letter-by-letter approach.

In this case, there will be more than a single goal node—any completed crossword is acceptable. There are also search problems containing a variety of initial nodes; consider a problem where you have a group of crossword frames and must fill any one of them. In these problems with multiple goal and initial nodes, the task may be to find any path from an initial to

FIGURE 2.3 One letter at a time

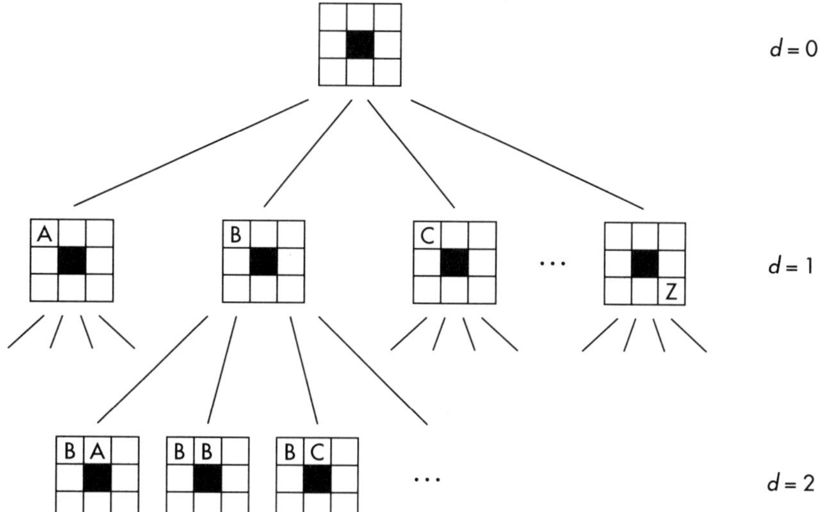

a goal node (as in the crossword-puzzle problem), to find all such paths, or to find the *best* path.

As an example, suppose that I am searching a map to find a route from my house in Palo Alto to a theater in San Francisco. An "acceptable" solution is to drive to Los Angeles and then return to my house before proceeding to the theater, but that is certainly not the route that I would want to take! Planning problems in domains where one's resources are constrained in some way typically exhibit this requirement that one find not just *any* plan to achieve a goal, but a plan that is either optimal or nearly so.

In our example search problems, we have labelled each node with a *depth* that indicates the number of steps needed to reach that node from the initial node. Thus the goal node in Figure 2.1 is at depth 3; the search space itself runs as deep as depth 4. In the crossword search in Figure 2.2, all of the goal nodes are at depth 4, since there are four words to fill in the crossword. In addition, *every* depth 4 node is a goal node.

Search problems are often described in terms of their *branching factor*. This refers to the number of children possessed by a node that isn't a terminal node (that is, a node that *has* children). In Figure 2.1, the branching factor varies between 1 and 3.

The branching factor in the crossword-puzzle problem is much higher; consider the initial node in Figure 2.3. Here, there are eight squares to fill and twenty-six letters that can be put in each, so the branching factor at the initial node is $8 \cdot 26 = 208$. Each of the 208 nodes at depth 1 has $7 \cdot 26 = 182$ successors, and so on. Not every depth 2 node has $6 \cdot 26$ successors, since some of these successors would include a completed "word" that was in fact illegal. The branching factor in this problem varies from node to node, but obviously remains much higher than that in Figure 2.1. Since there are typically many more than twenty-six possible choices for an entire *word* in a crossword, the branching factor in Figure 2.2 is higher still.

Except for the large number of nodes that typically need to be explored, solving search problems is easy. Provided that the branching factor is finite, the following procedure works:

PROCEDURE 2.2.1

To solve a search problem:

1. *Set* L *to be a list of the initial nodes in the problem. At any given point in time,* L *is a list of nodes that have not yet been examined by the program.*
2. *If* L *is empty, fail. Otherwise, pick a node* n *from* L.
3. *If* n *is a goal node, stop and return it and the path from the initial node to* n.
4. *Otherwise, remove* n *from* L *and add to* L *all of* n*'s children, labelling each with its path from the initial node. Return to step 2.*

In this particular procedure, we check the nodes to see if they are solutions to the original search problem at the point when we expand them to generate their children; it is somewhat more efficient to do this when the nodes are generated. The reason we have made the choice in Procedure 2.2.1 is that it simplifies the analysis in the next chapter considerably.

Up to fairly insignificant modifications like the one in the previous paragraph, all search programs proceed as described in Procedure 2.2.1. What distinguishes one search algorithm from another is the choice made in step 2—how do we pick the node to be expanded next?

As we will see in the next two chapters, there are two ways that this choice can be made. In *blind* search techniques, the choice is made in a way that depends only on the node's position in the search tree, and not on any other features. In our problem of planning a route from Palo Alto to a theater in San Francisco, we could not use the fact that Los Angeles is in the wrong direction, since this makes use of "domain-specific" information that blind search techniques are not permitted to exploit. In *heuristic* search, such domain-specific information is used to help decide what to do next.

2.2.1 Blind Search

There are a wide variety of blind search techniques; we introduce two of them here and two more in Chapter 3. The two we discuss here are called *depth-first* and *breadth-first* search.

The simplest way to think of depth-first search is as expanding a search tree such as that in Figure 2.1 so that the terminal nodes are examined from left to right, the nodes being explored in the order shown in Figure 2.4. You always explore a child of the most recently expanded node; if this node has no children, the procedure backs up a minimum amount before choosing another node to examine. We stop the search when we select the goal node g. Depth-first search can be implemented by pushing the children of a given node onto the *front* of the list L in step 4 of Procedure 2.2.1, and always choosing the first node on L as the one to expand:

FIGURE 2.4 Depth-first search

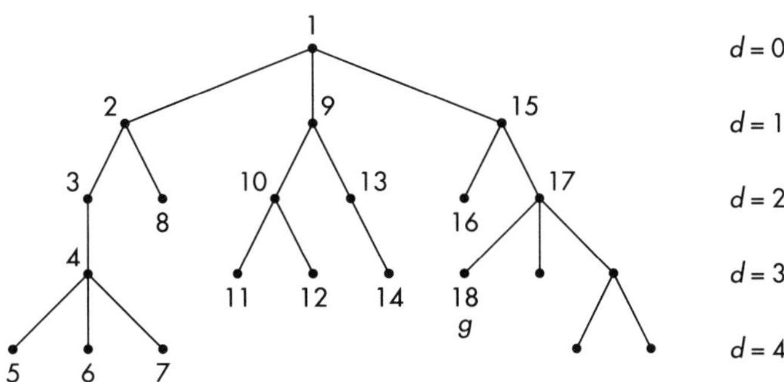

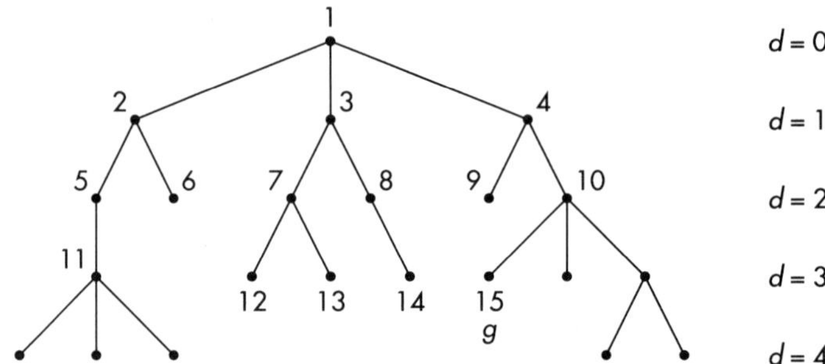

FIGURE 2.5 Breadth-first search

PROCEDURE 2.2.2

Depth-first Search *To solve a search problem using depth-first search:*

1. *Set* L *to be a list of the initial nodes in the problem.*
2. *Let* n *be the first node on* L*. If* L *is empty, fail.*
3. *If* n *is a goal node, stop and return it and the path from the initial node to* n*.*
4. *Otherwise, remove* n *from* L *and add to the front of* L *all of* n*'s children, labelling each with its path from the initial node. Return to step 2.*

In *breadth-first* search, the tree is examined from the top down, so that every node at depth d is examined before *any* node at depth $d + 1$ is. Figure 2.5 shows the tree in Figure 2.1 being searched in a breadth-first order; we can implement breadth-first search by adding the new nodes to the *end* of the list maintained in Procedure 2.2.1:

PROCEDURE 2.2.3

Breadth-first Search *To solve a search problem using breadth-first search:*

1. *Set* L *to be a list of the initial nodes in the problem.*
2. *Let* n *be the first node on* L*. If* L *is empty, fail.*
3. *If* n *is a goal node, stop and return it and the path from the initial node to* n*.*
4. *Otherwise, remove* n *from* L *and add to the end of* L *all of* n*'s children, labelling each with its path from the initial node. Return to step 2.*

Note that deciding to search a tree depth-first does not mean that we will search it in a *specific* order; it only commits us to the idea of always expanding a node as deep in the search tree as possible. Thus a search from right to left is also depth-first, as is the search in Figure 2.6, where we have chosen among the successors to each node in a fairly random way.

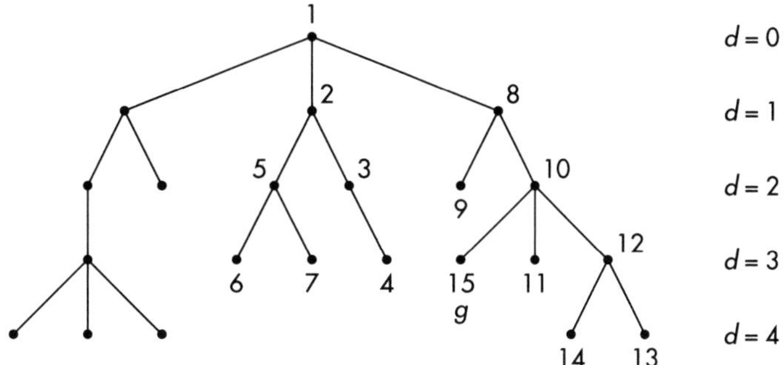

FIGURE 2.6 Another depth-first search

In a similar way, deciding to search a tree in breadth-first fashion still allows us to choose among the unexplored nodes at any particular depth level.

What about the general properties of the two search methods? We will examine these questions in greater detail in the next chapter, but let us consider at this point the question of how much memory is needed by each of the two methods.

In depth-first search, we must keep in memory all unexplored siblings of any node on the path from the current node back to the root of the tree, since each of these siblings will need to be examined as the search backs up and explores other portions of the space. As an example, Figure 2.7 shows the nodes that need to be retained in memory when examining the node n during depth-first search, where we have assumed that the children of each node are considered from left to right.

Now consider breadth-first search. Before examining *any* node at depth d, we will need to examine (and store in memory) *all* the nodes at depth $d - 1$; Figure 2.8 shows the nodes that need to be stored in memory just before we examine the first node at depth d of a search.

At least from the point of view of memory requirements, depth-first search is far more efficient than its breadth-first counterpart.

There are other ways in which we could have reached the same conclusion. As an example, consider a single iteration of the loop in the basic search procedure. How is the size of L changed during this iteration?

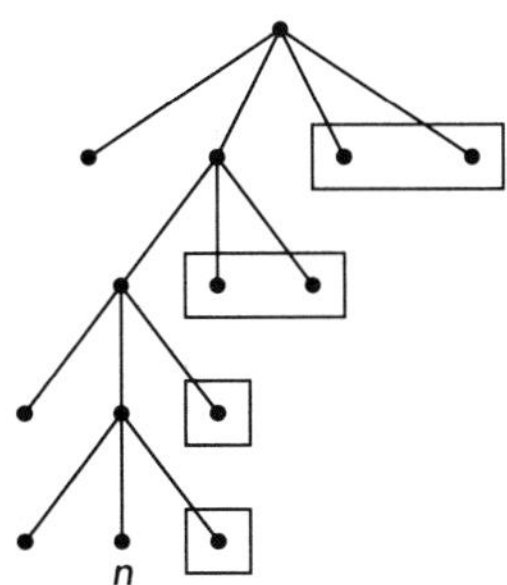

FIGURE 2.7 Space needed by depth-first search

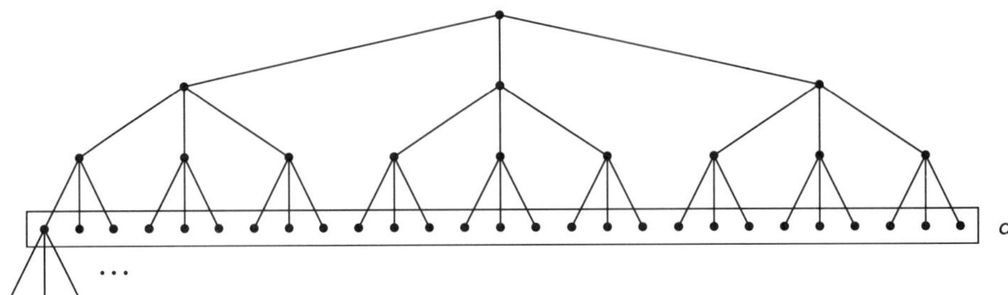

FIGURE 2.8 Space needed by breadth-first search

It is clear that the size of L drops by 1 when the node n is removed; it then increases by either b (the branching factor of the search space being explored) if n has children, or by 0 if n is a terminal node. So the change in the size of L is either $b - 1$ if n is nonterminal, or -1 if n is terminal. It follows from this that a search that encounters terminal nodes early will need less space than one that does not; since depth-first search will tend to reach the fringe of the search tree quickly, we can conclude that this search method needs less memory than its breadth-first counterpart.

What about the crossword-puzzle problem? Here, it is clear that depth-first search is the method of choice, since we know that all of the goal nodes are at a fixed depth (4, for the search space in Figure 2.2) and there is no reason to expand the entire search space at depth 3 in order to find a single solution at depth 4.

Here is another way to think about the same question. Since both depth-first and breadth-first search are blind search techniques, they will each explore the nodes at any fixed depth in a similar and fairly random order. What will make one method more efficient than the other is therefore the speed with which the two methods arrive at this depth—and since depth-first gets to the nodes at depth d much more quickly than breadth-first does, it can be expected to solve this particular problem more efficiently.

It might seem that there is no reason to ever search a space using breadth-first search, but this is not the case. Suppose, for example, that we change the goal in the crossword-puzzle problem from filling the entire frame to legally putting the word *tab* somewhere in the puzzle.

There is a solution at depth 1 in this problem, but depth-first search is quite unlikely to find it. Instead, the depth-first search approach is likely to end up solving a problem even more difficult than the original crossword problem, as it struggles to depth 4, only to find that the crossword so constructed isn't a solution to the new goal! There are so many three-letter words in English that the depth-first approach is unlikely to stumble onto any solution to the problem in question without first exploring a large portion of the search space. We will see quantitative versions of this argument in the next chapter.

2.2.2 Heuristic Search

In the example we have been considering, neither depth-first nor breadth-first search explores the tree in anything resembling an optimal order. What we would *like* to do is to examine the nodes in the order shown in Figure 2.9. By expanding the nodes in this optimal order, we minimize the amount of time needed to solve the problem.

Heuristic search is an attempt to search a tree in an order that is more nearly optimal than either breadth-first or depth-first. Roughly speaking, when we pick a node from the list L in step 2 of the search procedure, what we would like to do is to move steadily from the root node toward the goal by always selecting a node that is as close to the goal as possible. In some domains, it is possible to estimate the distance to the goal and to use this information to guide the search. Although we are unlikely to search the tree in an optimal order such as that appearing in Figure 2.9, we can often approximate this ordering.

As an example, consider the crossword-puzzle problem once again. Since all of the nodes at depth d are goal nodes, it follows that at any given point in time, nodes deeper in the tree are likely to be closer to a goal node than nodes shallower in the tree. So here is another explanation for our observation that depth-first search is the technique of choice in this problem—the depth-first procedure implements a very coarse heuristic for this domain.

Since many of the depth $d - 1$ nodes in the crossword-puzzle problem do not expand into complete solutions, this simple heuristic is far too weak to solve this problem in and of itself. In general, a more accurate estimate of the distance to the goal is needed. How are we to decide which unexpanded node is close to a goal node?

Recall that our basic intention is to select from L a node that is as near as possible to a goal node; one way to do this would be to expand the entire tree below each node on L and to use this information to determine exactly how far each such node was from the goal. Needless to say, this would not be an effective approach to solving a search problem—we would be spend-

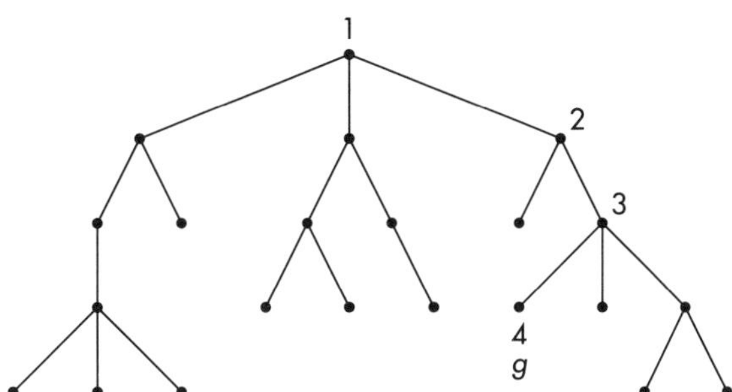

FIGURE 2.9 An optimal search

ing too much time trying to decide what node to expand next. In this simple example, we'd actually be spending more time than we would need to solve the entire problem.

This particular heuristic (expand the entire tree in order to decide what node to expand next) overstates the point, but there is an important issue lurking here:

> *The time spent evaluating the heuristic function in order to select a node for expansion must be recovered by a corresponding reduction in the size of the search space explored.*

What we are seeing here is an instance of a still more general issue: There is a trade-off in problem solving between spending time actually solving the problem and spending time deciding *how* to solve the problem. People in AI typically refer to the effort expended in actually trying to solve the problem as *base-level* activity; the work spent deciding what to do is called *metalevel* activity. Since time spent on one can't be spent on the other, and since the system has no real interest in the metalevel effort other than in helping it decide how to solve the base-level problem, the general form of the above observation is as follows:

> *In efficient problem solving, time spent at the metalevel is recovered by corresponding reductions in the amount of time required to solve the problem at the base level.*

We will refer to this as the *base-level/metalevel trade-off.*

In blind search, no time is spent at the metalevel. There are no heuristic functions that need be evaluated in order to decide what to do next; one simply picks a node at random. If we choose to view depth-first search as heuristic search where the heuristic function is given simply by the depth of the node, we see the reason that this heuristic is so often valuable—it is very cheap to evaluate! In fact, the reason depth-first search is thought of as a blind search technique is that evaluation of the heuristic function takes essentially no time at all.

Other useful heuristics for solving search problems share this property of being cheap to evaluate. We will see examples of this in Chapter 4; one that comes to mind now is that when solving the crossword-puzzle problem, it is probably sensible to work on partially completed crosswords that make use of common letters. After all, why fill a particular six-letter slot with *pizazz* when *assert* would do? The letters in the first choice are much more likely to cause difficulty later; this heuristic is likely to be useful because deciding which words contain rare letters and which contain common ones is computationally inexpensive.

2.2.3 Other Issues

Before turning to knowledge representation, there are two other issues that arise in search that bear discussion.

The first of these is *backtracking*. In the crossword-puzzle problem, suppose that we have filled in a variety of words, and then find that there are no legal choices for a particular word slot, say the one marked in Figure 2.10. What node should we expand next?

Simple depth-first search would have us backtrack to the last word we filled in and try to replace it. But in this example, suppose that this last word is *LAP* in the figure—changing it won't help us with the problem we've discovered.

This problem is even more serious than it appears. Suppose that we do simply backtrack to the last choice point, replacing *LAP* with (say) *MAP* and then noticing that we need to backtrack again. So now we try *TAP* in this slot, and so on. After trying all of the legal three-letter words, we realize that we have made no progress and must back up further.

The problem is that we may *still* fail to address the difficulty; maybe the word we inserted two choices ago was *LAY*. We are in danger of replacing it with some other choice, then going through the *LAP-MAP-TAP-*. . . sequence again, and so on. The amount of effort we will eventually waste is exponential in the number of words we have inserted since the problem actually occurred.

This backtracking technique—returning to the most recent choice point—is known as *chronological backtracking*. What we have seen is that in situations where it is possible to make a "fatal" choice (perhaps the insertion of the word *TOAST* in Figure 2.10), it is important that we backtrack to that mistake without expanding the entire subtree under it.

There are two known solutions to this difficulty. We will delay discussing one of them, known as *iterative broadening*, until the next chapter; the other is known as *dependency-directed backtracking*.

In dependency-directed backtracking, we do not simply backtrack to the last choice point when a dead end is encountered. Instead, we try to

FIGURE 2.10
A dead end

determine the *reason* for the problem, and backtrack to that. In the figure, this would enable us to backtrack directly to the word *TOAST*.

The problem is that things aren't that simple; perhaps when we inserted *TOAST* we were looking for a five-letter word that began with a *T* and ended in *ST*. It may well be that every such five-letter word has an *A* in the third position, so that the problem reappears.

If this happens, the difficulty isn't really with *TOAST*, but is instead with one of the words that preceded it. And now we are faced with the same problem as before—how are we to know to backtrack to this earlier decision?

In true dependency-directed backtracking, we would analyze the situation in some detail and actually determine that *TONAL* was the source of the difficulty. But here is the base-level/metalevel trade-off again—the dependency computation is an expensive one, and the cost will often not be recovered in base-level savings.[4]

The other issue that we will discuss here is that of forward versus backward search.

In many problems, the description of the goal nodes is only implicit. The crossword-puzzle problem is typical; we have no listing of the solution crosswords and only know that any legal node at a certain depth will be a solution.

In other cases, however, we know the initial and goal states of the search and are looking for a path between them. It is now interesting to consider the question of whether we should move from the initial state to the goal or vice versa.

Consider a simple planning problem; imagine that I am trying to mount a light fixture outside my front door. Working "backward," I note that in order to put up the light, I'll need to be outside my front door with the light and with tools to install it; in order to achieve this, I may decide that I have to go to the hardware store to buy some wire and a screwdriver. My search efforts in solving the problem have been focused by the fact that I've been working backwards from my intended goal.

Now suppose that I tried to solve the same problem by working "forward." How many possible actions could I take from my initial situation? Many—I could watch television, kiss my wife, cook dinner, call my mother in New Jersey, cook breakfast, call the president, drive to the hardware store, . . .

The reason that backward search is so much more efficient in this case is that the backward branching factor (the number of situations from which

4 The bottom line, of course, is that blind search problems are hard in a fairly fundamental way, since the size of the search space is growing exponentially with the depth. It follows that there is no *general* way to allocate metalevel effort and guarantee a substantial reduction in the time needed to find a solution to any particular search problem.

I can achieve my goal) is much smaller than the forward branching factor (the number of situations I can reach from my current one). Given this, backward search is more effective than forward.

Of course, it might not be this way. Suppose that my life were so constrained that I had no options at all—that I had only one action available in any particular situation. In this case, in order to see if I was able to install the light, I would be wasting time if I tried to actually generate a plan to do so. Far simpler would be to analyze the sequence of actions to which I knew I was committed, and check to see if the light wound up installed or not. Here, the forward branching factor is lower (in fact, it's only 1), so forward search is the most efficient.

In other cases, one should search in both directions. Consider a maze; most maze designers make the forward branching factor from the initial node in a maze 1, in that you have no choices for a while after you start off; the backward branching factor from the goal node is also often 1, in that there is a long path backward from the exit along which there are *also* no choices. This is why people typically solve mazes by working back from the exit to find out what the "real" goal is, and only then working toward that goal from the entry point. This technique is known as *bidirectional* search.

2.2.4 Search: Examples

I argued in the last chapter that no investigation of an AI problem could be complete unless it was applied to an example of some sort. In this section, we examine some of the problems that are typically used to test and compare various search algorithms.

Game Playing

Chess The best-known search problems are those that arise in game playing. In chess, for example, one is given an initial position and expected to search through sequences of moves and responses in order to determine which is best. Since exploring the entire search space is impractical, a player typically explores only a small portion of it, evaluating the resulting positions using some sort of heuristic and then propagating this information back to the original position when deciding what to do.

The best chess-playing programs are surprisingly special-purpose. The heuristic evaluation functions that they use are clearly useful in the chess domain only, but their domain-specificity runs much deeper. They typically use special-purpose hardware to generate the legal moves in any particular situation, and so on.

These special-purpose techniques have been remarkably successful. The best computer chess program is known as DEEP THOUGHT and recently won the Pennsylvania State Open; it was rated 2551 by the United States

Chess Federation in late 1988. This is well into the Senior Master range and ranks the program among the best thirty players in the United States.

There is an additional point to be made regarding chess-playing programs. A human expert playing chess will typically examine on the order of twenty positions that might result from the given one. This is done by using a tremendous amount of domain-specific metalevel information to reduce the size of the search space; most of the available moves for either player are eliminated as unlikely by human antagonists.

Computers play chess very differently, typically examining *millions* of positions in selecting a move. We see again the general difference between human and machine reasoning—humans typically reason effectively at the metalevel in order to make their base-level tasks manageable; machines are incapable of effective metalevel reasoning and therefore have to do their best with more substantial base-level tasks. Chess is a game where the brute speed of the computer (including the special-purpose hardware already mentioned) enables it to overcome its lack of metalevel knowledge and perform at a level comparable with that of strong human players.

I should remark in passing that there have been attempts to produce chess-playing programs that work in more "human" ways, sharply pruning their search space and examining smaller numbers of positions. The performance of these programs has typically been far worse than that of their brute-force counterparts. Unfortunately, there is currently no explanation for why metalevel reasoning seems to be so easy for us and so difficult for machines, and no clear way to close this gap.

Backgammon Many other games (such as checkers and Othello) are similar to chess, with computers being able to exploit their speed in brute-force search and to exhibit expert-level performance. But there are some exceptions. Some games (such as Go and bridge) have thus far not proven amenable to strong computer play, while one—backgammon—has broken the rule that the machine plays in a fundamentally different way than we do.

In backgammon, a human player will typically look ahead only a single move, examining the options and heuristically evaluating the resulting positions; the position with the highest heuristic evaluation is the one selected. The best computer backgammon player (the performance of which is near to that of the human world champion) works identically.

The reason for this is that the branching factor in backgammon is very large—a roll of two dice is involved, leading to an immediate branching factor of 21 (the number of possible results of rolling the dice); there is an additional branching factor of perhaps 20 because of the number of possible ways to play any particular roll. The overall branching factor is therefore on the order of 400.

Interestingly enough, people are now considering the use of brute-force techniques in backgammon. Stuart Russell and Eric Wefald have been looking at the possibility of enhancing the performance of backgammon and other game-playing programs by having them use decision-theoretic techniques to make (metalevel!) decisions about what portions of the search space should be explored.

Finding a Path to a Goal

Other search problems are more like those discussed at the beginning of this section: There are explicit initial and goal nodes, and the object is to find a path connecting them.

Missionaries and cannibals On one bank of a river are three missionaries and three cannibals. There is one rowboat available that can hold up to two people and that they would like to use to cross the river. If the cannibals ever outnumber the missionaries on either of the river's banks (including the occupants of the boat), the missionaries will get eaten. How can the rowboat be used to safely carry all of the missionaries and cannibals across the river?

This is obviously a search problem; it is also a very easy search problem because the branching factor is so small. In fact, if we disallow moves that bring us back to a state we have already seen, the branching factor is very small indeed. In the initial position, the only legal moves are for one cannibal to cross the river (but then he has to row back, so that is disallowed), or for a cannibal and one other person to cross the river and for the cannibal to remain while the other returns with the boat. Thus there are only six nodes at depths 0, 1 and 2; exploring search spaces of this size is obviously quite straightforward. (See Figure 2.11, where we also include information about the location of the boat.)

Nevertheless, this problem has a variety of interesting features. The first is that the forward and backward search spaces are identical, yet the problem *seems* much simpler working in the forward direction. Why is this? No one knows.

It is also the case that there is room for a great deal of metalevel reasoning in this problem. Suppose that instead of saying simply that there

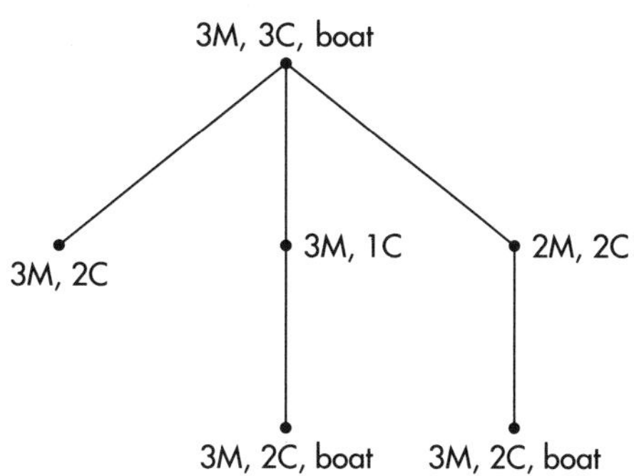

FIGURE 2.11 Occupants of the left bank in the missionaries and cannibals problem

are three missionaries and three cannibals, we name them, calling the missionaries Jimmy, Billy, and Jerry and the cannibals Hughie, Dewey, and Louie.

The apparent branching factor is now much higher—there are fifteen legal initial moves, of which three are eliminated because they must return to the initial state. In three of the other twelve cases, we must decide which of the two cannibals that rowed across is to row back, again making the tree larger.

It's still a small search tree, of course, but the point is that a person working on this problem will realize immediately that the names of the missionaries and cannibals are completely irrelevant to the solution, and will collapse the search space to the original one. Metalevel reasoning again. A computer, faced with the problem in which the individuals are named, may fail to recognize that the search can be simplified.

The towers of Hanoi Consider the initial situation shown in Figure 2.12. There are n disks ($n = 5$ in the figure) arranged on a peg, and there are three pegs. A move in this problem involves taking the top disk off of one peg and putting it on another peg; there is a rule saying that you can never put a big disk on a smaller one. How can you move the entire stack of disks from the leftmost peg to the rightmost one?

The reason that this problem is interesting is that although the branching factor is small (clearly never greater than 9, since there are three pegs from which a disk can be moved and two possible places to move it), the length of the solution is quite large, growing exponentially with the number of disks involved. As a result, the size of the search space grows doubly exponentially with n (the size of the search space grows as b^{2^n}, where b is the branching factor). It follows that some sort of search control is needed if machines are to solve this problem.

A person working on this problem does something very clever—he reduces the n disk towers of Hanoi problem to the $n - 1$ case. To solve the n disk problem, he first uses a hypothetical solution to the $n - 1$ problem to move the top $n - 1$ disks to the center post (realizing that just as names were irrelevant in the missionaries and cannibals problem, the specific target location is irrelevant in this one and he can move the disks to the center post as easily as to the rightmost one). The biggest disk is then moved

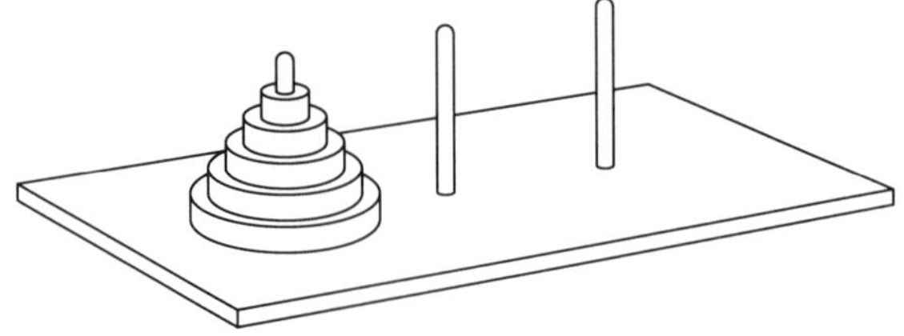

FIGURE 2.12 The towers of Hanoi

FIGURE 2.13 The 8-puzzle

to the rightmost post, and then the $n - 1$ solution is used again to move the remaining stack from the center post to the right. How can we get a machine to duplicate this sort of reasoning?

Sliding tile puzzles Another problem often considered in AI is shown in Figure 2.13. The goal is to slide the tiles around to get from an initial configuration such as the one on the left to the goal configuration on the right. This 3×3 version of the puzzle is called the *8-puzzle* because there are eight tiles to be arranged; larger versions are the 15-puzzle, the 24-puzzle and so on.

One of the reasons that sliding tile puzzles are of interest to AI is that there are good heuristics for estimating the distance an arbitrary node is from the goal node in these problems. The simplest of these involves simply counting the number of misplaced tiles; this heuristic also has the property that it always *underestimates* the distance from an arbitrary configuration to the goal node, since each move is capable of getting at most one tile into its desired location. The distance estimated by this heuristic for the setup in Figure 2.13 is 7.

A more sophisticated heuristic that also has this underestimation property is known as *Manhattan distance*. Here, instead of simply counting the number of misplaced tiles, we add, for each such tile, the number of rows and columns that it needs to move in order to occupy its intended location. The value for the 1 tile in our starting configuration is 4, as shown in Figure 2.14; the total estimated distance to the goal state in this case is

$$4 + 0 + 2 + 3 + 1 + 3 + 1 + 3 = 17$$

FIGURE 2.14 Manhattan distance

Note that the Manhattan distance heuristic[5] continues to underestimate the actual distance to the goal, since each move can decrease the distance for at most one tile, and can decrease this distance by at most one. Note also that the Manhattan distance heuristic, while remaining conservative, always gives a value that is no *less* than the value computed by simply counting the number of misplaced tiles, since every such tile is always at least one square away from its intended destination. We will see in Chapter 4 that this feature of underestimating the distance to the goal is a very important one; heuristics with this property are known as *admissible*. Although the simple counting heuristic and Manhattan distance are both admissible, Manhattan distance is to be preferred because it gives a more accurate estimate of the true distance to the goal state.

There is one more point to be made about the 8-puzzle. Consider the initial position in Figure 2.13; what are the legal moves from this position?

The natural description would have it that the legal moves are to move the 6 down, the 3 to the left, or the 4 up. But if the blank were at the right edge of the figure instead of the left, we would have to select between moving the 8 down, the 3 to the right, or the 1 up. The fact that the children of any particular node are generated in such different ways can make sliding tile puzzles awkward to deal with.

This problem can be avoided if we reformulate the domain. Instead of viewing the legal moves in Figure 2.13 as moving various tiles around, we should view the moves as moving the *blank* to the right, up or down. By doing so, we can generate the legal moves in any specific position by considering only the position of the blank, and not the position of the blank in combination with the labels assigned to the tiles around it. As with other metalevel activities, this sort of reformulation is more likely to be discovered by humans than by machines.

Rubik's cube Rubik's cube is similar to the 8-puzzle; as there are different size sliding tile puzzles, researchers have also considered the $2 \times 2 \times 2$ Rubik's cube, and so on. (Large Rubik's cubes appear to be intractably difficult.) There are no known useful heuristics for Rubik's cube.

Simply Finding a Goal

Finally, there are search problems where the task is not to find a *path* to a goal, but simply to find a goal at all (or perhaps to prove that there isn't one); the goal states are described only implicitly. The crossword-puzzle problem is a typical problem of this sort; here are some others:

5 The name refers to the fact that the distances reflect the distance a taxicab would have to travel in New York City to get from a tile's initial location to its intended destination.

Cryptarithmetic Consider the following problem:

```
  SEND
+ MORE
 -----
 MONEY
```

What distinct integers can we assign to S, E, and so on that will make this a legitimate addition?

This is clearly another search problem. A machine could solve this problem by blind search (with eight letters to be substituted with distinct digits, the size of the search space is $10!/2 = 1.8 \times 10^6$); people take a very different approach. As in chess, we solve cryptarithmetic problems by focusing our search efforts, realizing in this particular example that M has to be 1, therefore that S has to be 8 or 9, and so on.

n-queens The *n-queens problem* involves placing n chess queens on an $n \times n$ chessboard in such a way that none of them attacks another; in other words, no two queens can be on the same row, column, or diagonal of the chessboard.

This, too, is a search problem; it is like the crossword-puzzle problem in that the goal states are described only implicitly, they are all at a fixed depth, and there may be many of them. As a result, the states of the puzzle are most easily thought of as incomplete solutions instead of as intermediate points on some path between an initial and goal state.

Problems such as these are generally referred to as *constraint-satisfaction problems*, or CSPs. In solving a CSP, heuristics are used not to estimate the distance to the goal, but to decide what node to expand next. Which word should be inserted into a crossword? Which queen should be placed next?

The mutilated-checkerboard problem Imagine that you are trying to cover an 8×8 checkerboard with thirty-two 1×2 dominoes. Doing so is easy—you can simply cover each row of the checkerboard with four of the dominoes. But what if we remove two opposite corners of the checkerboard; can we cover what's left with thirty-one dominoes? (See Figure 2.15.)

FIGURE 2.15 The mutilated-checkerboard problem

The branching factor in this problem is obviously quite high, since there are many locations in which dominoes can be placed. Actually solving the problem typically involves metalevel reasoning of the sort that computers find difficult; I'll leave it to you to discover the details.

2.3 KNOWLEDGE REPRESENTATION

In the example with which we began this chapter, we argued that we needed first to capture the knowledge needed to formalize our shopping problem, and then to use search to solve the problem this formalization effort had produced. Roughly speaking, this is the role of knowledge representation in AI generally:

> *The intended role of knowledge representation in artificial intelligence is reduce problems of intelligent action to search problems.*

Why is it that using a formal language to describe the knowledge needed to solve some problem can be expected to transform that problem into one involving search?

To understand this, let us look in a bit more detail at an example we have already mentioned, reconsidering the goal of installing a light that we discussed in Section 2.2.3. Imagine that instead of viewing this as a search problem, we try to *prove* that it is possible for us to get the light installed.

How will such a proof look? Assume that we manage to solve the knowledge representation problem itself, coming up with a list of axioms that describe our domain and that we must now demonstrate that we can install the light.

The demonstration will presumably work by applying "rules of inference" to our database; these rules tell us which conclusions we can legitimately draw from a set of existing knowledge. Suppose that we know that if we can get wire and a screwdriver, we can install the light. If we also know that we can indeed get wire and a screwdriver, then we can derive the fact that we can install the light. In a somewhat schematic way, our reasoning looks like this:

$$\frac{\begin{array}{r}\text{If I can get wire and a screwdriver, I can install the light.}\\ \text{I can get wire and a screwdriver.}\end{array}}{\text{I can install the light.}}$$

The premises are above the line and the conclusion below.

What we have done here is to apply a quite general rule of inference that says that if we know, "If p, then q," and if we also know p, then it is legitimate to conclude q. We could write this as

$$\frac{\begin{array}{r} p \rightarrow q \\ p \end{array}}{q}$$

This particular rule of inference is called *modus ponens*.

Of course, there will typically be many possible ways to apply modus ponens in a particular situation. If the screwdriver is in the garage, we might use a fact saying that if an object o is in a room r and I can walk to that room, then I can get the object o. Since I can walk to the garage and the screwdriver is in the garage, I conclude that I can get the screwdriver.

Of course, I can also walk to the bathroom, or the living room, or my office, or what have you. The aspirin is in the bathroom, the television is in the living room, there are pens, pencils, and paper in the office . . . but none of these potential inferences is going to be of much use in my proving that I can get the light installed.

Because there are typically many ways in which rules of inference can be applied in any particular situation, deduction is a search problem. The initial node is the information with which the system is supplied, and the goal nodes are those in which the desired conclusion has been derived. The operators that generate the successors of a given node are those that draw a new conclusion by applying some rule of inference.

Viewing inference as search suggests that we reexamine some of the observations of the previous section. As an example, the question of forward versus backward search has an obvious analog in an inferential setting—are we to derive a given goal by working forward from the supplied information, or by working backward from the goal itself? As with search generally, which approach is more effective depends on relative branching factors in the forward and backward directions.

Also as with search, there are metalevel decisions to be made in theorem proving; the question of whether to work forward or backward is one of them. And as with search, there appears to be a large qualitative difference between human metalevel abilities and those of our current programs—people are really *good* at deciding things like whether to work forward or backward in an inference problem, while computer programs tend to have tremendous difficulties with such questions. Although we are good at making these decisions ourselves, we have not yet managed to find a way to pass this ability on to our machines. In some cases, the speed of the computer allows it to overcome its metalevel handicap through more effective base-level behavior, but in many other cases, base-level proficiency alone cannot replace the ability to draw useful metalevel conclusions.

In spite of the parallels, there are also differences between the sorts of search problems generated by theorem-proving tasks and those that arise in other areas. In theorem proving, for example, it is generally the case that the result of performing two inference steps is independent of the order in which those inferences are performed; it doesn't matter if we derive *a* first and then *b* or vice versa. A consequence of this is that the associated search space is not a tree, but a densely connected graph, since there are typically a variety of paths to any particular intermediate or terminal node. This is obviously not true of search problems in general. Another difference is a consequence of the fact that the depth of the goal nodes is almost invariably unknown in proof problems.

Finally, inference problems often give rise to conjunctive subgoals, where an attempt to derive a single conclusion leads to a collection of subproblems, all of which must be solved in order for the search to terminate successfully. In the example we have been examining, the single goal of getting the light installed led to the conjunctive goal of getting a screwdriver *and* getting some wire. A search diagram such as that appearing in Figure 2.1 works with the convention that it is sufficient to reach *any* goal node, so many authors display conjunctive goals using a special notation such as that appearing in Figure 2.16. The arc joining the two left-hand nodes at depth 1 indicates that *both* of these subgoals must be solved in order to obtain a solution to the original problem. Since the arc does not involve the third node at depth 1, the problem can also be solved by achieving this subgoal (hire an electrician) in isolation. A graph such as that appearing in the figure is called an AND-OR graph because the subgoals can be combined either disjunctively as in earlier examples or conjunctively using the arc notation just described.

The distinction between AND-OR graphs and those we considered earlier is mostly illusory; although it is sometimes somewhat more convenient to describe problems in these terms, there is no fundamental reason for doing so. As an example, the graph appearing in Figure 2.16 can be rewritten as in Figure 2.17.

2.3.1 Knowledge Representation: Examples

The problems that are used to advance the state of the art in knowledge representation are necessarily more vaguely defined than the search problems described in Section 2.2.4; if they are too sharply defined, they cease to be challenging as knowledge representation problems!

In all of the following examples, a domain is described in which we, as human problem solvers, have no trouble drawing specific conclusions and agreeing on their validity. The challenge to knowledge representation researchers is to find a language in which our knowledge can be encoded, to use the language to capture the knowledge, and then to show that the conclusions generated by the artificial system match the ones generated by common sense.

Inheritance Objects typically inherit the properties of the classes of which they are members. Textbooks, for example, are usually boring, and it is

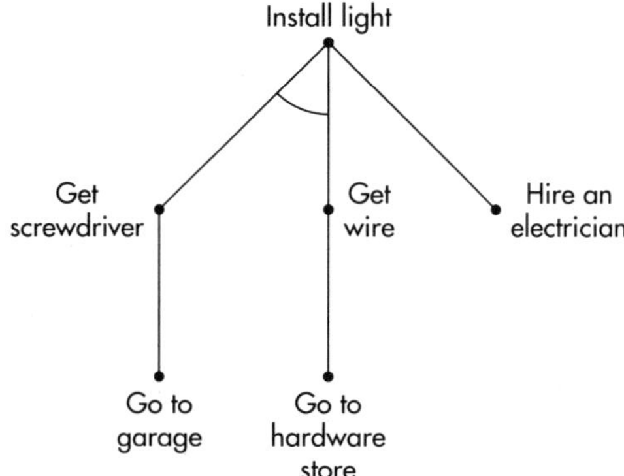

FIGURE 2.16
An AND-OR graph

therefore reasonable to conclude that any particular textbook is going to be boring as well. But there are exceptions; there are some textbooks that aren't boring after all. (Hopefully this is one of them!)

Birds can usually fly. So if Tweety is a bird, we can typically conclude that Tweety can fly. But ostriches are a special type of bird that can't fly; if I tell you that Tweety is an ostrich, you will change your mind and conclude that he can't fly after all. Unless he's from the planet Krypton, of course. How do we know when an object should inherit a property from a class of which it is a member and when it shouldn't? If Fred is an ostrich, then Fred should presumably inherit the inability to fly from the class of ostriches instead of inheriting the ability to fly from the class of birds. Why?

It's tempting here to say that an object should always inherit from the most specific class of which it is a member, but as we will see in Chapter 11, this turns out not to be right. The reason, roughly speaking, is that there may be many "most specific" classes of which an object is a member, and it may not be clear what conclusions should be drawn in these cases.

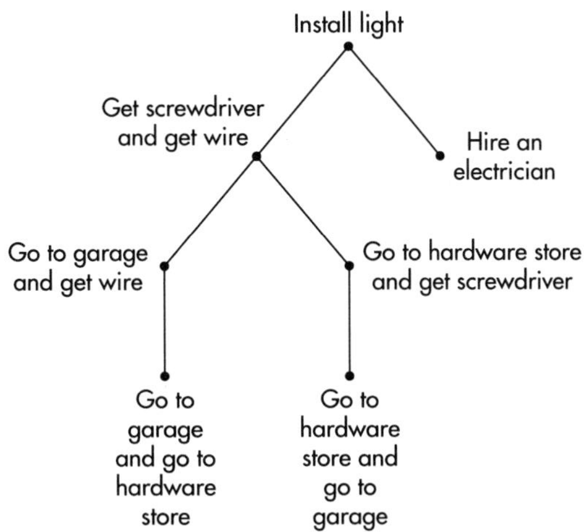

FIGURE 2.17
The graph of Figure 2.16 rewritten

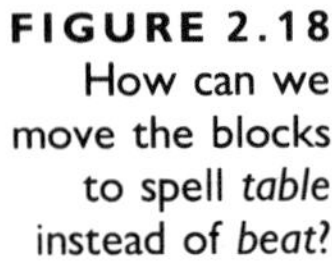
FIGURE 2.18 How can we move the blocks to spell *table* instead of *beat*?

Missionaries and cannibals Let's have a look at the missionaries and cannibals problem once again. Suppose that I ask you to solve it and you simply reply that everyone involved should just walk downstream a few miles and use the bridge. If I disallow that, how about if they use the helicopter parked in a nearby field? What about someone who says that the problem is impossible because the boat has a leak? Somehow, we as humans manage to interpret the original description of the puzzle in a way that disallows all of these unintended solutions; it is not clear what steps need to be taken to get computers to do the same.

The blocks world The final "standard" problem in knowledge representation that I would like to mention involves planning in the *blocks world*. An example is shown in Figure 2.18.

In the figure, the question is how can I rearrange the blocks so that they spell *table* instead of *beat;* what sort of knowledge do I use to construct a plan to do this?

At the very least, I need knowledge about what actions I can take and what their effects are; perhaps I can move a block only after I've moved away all of the blocks on top of it, for example.

But there is more subtle knowledge involved as well. Suppose that I form a plan to spell *table* that begins by moving the *B* onto the *J*, then the *E* onto the table, then the *L* onto the *E*, the *B* onto the *L*, and so on. How is it that I know the *L* will stay on top of the *E* when I move the *B* around?

One possibility, of course, is to say explicitly that everything stays where it is except for the block being moved. But things aren't that simple; what if some of the blocks are connected by strings? It is very difficult to describe actions and their consequences in a way that is robust enough to handle a variety of domains, such as moving blocks, assembling automobiles, organizing a party, or driving to Los Angeles.

As we will see in Chapter 14, planning problems involve substantial amounts of search as well. One of the reasons that AI planning systems have been slow to develop is that planning is difficult from both a knowledge representation *and* a search point of view.

2.4 APPLICATIONS: EXAMPLES

In the search and knowledge representation problems that we have described, the idea is typically to solve the problem using techniques that have wide applicability throughout AI. Even in the construction of a chess-playing program, the ideas used can generally be applied to any game-playing problem.

Problem-solving techniques with wide or universal applicability are referred to as "weak" methods; the reason is that their universality typically makes them less effective than approaches that have been carefully tailored to solve specific problems. Many fielded AI systems use special-purpose algorithms that, although useful in only narrow domains, have had significant practical impact in these domains. We will examine many of these applications and techniques in the last section of this book, and I would like to close this chapter by previewing this material and mentioning a few of these more practical examples.

Expert systems Expert systems are the paradigmatic application of AI techniques to hard problems. The idea is to find a domain in which there are recognized experts, and then to interview those experts to draw out the specialized knowledge that they use when solving problems in their restricted domain. Machines can then (in principle, at least) mimic the reasoning of the experts to derive conclusions similar to theirs using the information with which they have been supplied.

Natural language processing How is it that you make sense of the sentences appearing in this book? The internal language that you use to represent information in your mind is probably not English, so you must have some mechanism that translates information from English into this internal language.

AI faces similar problems: We use natural language so ubiquitously that it is inevitable that our computers must one day come to do the same. Learning how to do this is the focus of this particular subfield of artificial intelligence and of Chapter 17 of this book.

Vision Of course, we don't obtain information only by reading and talking; a great deal of what we know comes from direct observation of the world around us. Once again, effective independent artifacts will need similar abilities. How do we recognize a doorway as we walk down a corridor? What distinguishes the edge of the road when we drive in a car? How do I manage to read a handwritten letter, turning the inaccurate squiggles into a string of characters?

Solutions to any of these problems will have substantial practical import. Robots could deliver messages and packages by reading the labels and identifying the intended recipient. They could process all manner of handwritten documents, from checks to insurance claims. Computer vision is the topic of Chapter 16.

Robotics The final example that we mention is robotics itself. Robots already help manufacture our cars, but they will never deliver packages until they can navigate across a room and hold on to the package while they do so. They will need to interpret the outputs of sensors that are often inaccurate or ambiguous (or both), and to do so in real time.

2.5 FURTHER READING

Dependency-directed backtracking was introduced in Stallman and Sussman [1977a]; a version that appears to be more useful in practice is known as *backjumping* and appears in Gaschnig [1979].

Most of AI's classic problems are described here, but others can be found in introductory texts by other authors such as those cited in the previous chapter (Charniak and McDermott [1985], Rich and Knight [1991], and Winston [1992]).

Computer chess has been described in a variety of places; Levy and Newborn [1987] is a good introduction, although progress in this area is so rapid that this book is already outdated. A more recent technical reference is a special issue of the journal *Artificial Intelligence* [Berliner and Beal 1990]. A program that attempts to duplicate human performance by examining only a few carefully selected positions is described by Wilkins [1980].

A description of BILL, a computer program that is generally considered the best Othello player in the world, can be found in Lee and Mahajan [1990]. Berliner's backgammon program is described in Berliner [1980]; Russell and Wefald's work on deciding what portions of a game tree to examine is reported in Russell and Wefald [1989].

Constraint-satisfaction problems are the topic of Chapter 9, although we present them there in a declarative setting. The crossword-puzzle problem specifically is discussed in Ginsberg *et al.* [1990]; interesting results on the n-queens problem appear in both Minton *et al.* [1990] and Abramson and Yung [1989]. Both of these authors present techniques for solving this problem in time linear in the number of queens involved; Minton's approach appears to be applicable to CSPs generally but is not guaranteed to produce a solution, while Abramson's is a closed-form solution that applies to the n-queens problem but absolutely nothing else.

The example involving birds flying is due to Minsky and has driven a great deal of the work in nonmonotonic and inheritance reasoning; the knowledge representation features of the missionaries and cannibals problem are pointed out by McCarthy [1980]. The blocks worlds was introduced to the AI community by Terry Winograd in his Ph.D. thesis [1972].

References for the applications examples described in this chapter are best found in the associated chapters themselves, but here is one for each of the applications mentioned: Expert systems are discussed in a forthcoming textbook by Stefik [1993]. Natural language processing is the topic of Allen [1987]; vision is discussed by Ballard and Brown [1982] and robotics is covered by Craig [1989], although not from an AI perspective. Because of the differences in methodology between robotics and other areas of AI, robotics has been left untreated in this book.

2.6 EXERCISES

1. How deep are the goal nodes in Figure 2.3? Is there a node shown in the figure below which you would not expect to find any goal nodes?

2. Estimate the *average* branching factor in Figures 2.2 and 2.3. This is the average of the branching factors at all of the nodes in the tree.

3. Draw a search tree of depth 4 and uniform branching factor 3 (that is, the branching factor is 3 at every nonterminal node). How many nodes are there in the space? What is the minimum number of nodes in a space of depth d and uniform branching factor b if the space, instead of a tree, is permitted to be an acyclic graph where no two arcs share the same beginning and ending points?

4. Construct a search tree for which it is possible that depth-first search uses *more* memory than breadth-first search. Is there any tree and distribution of goal nodes for which depth-first search *always* requires more memory than breadth-first?

5. Describe a realistic planning problem that one would solve by bidirectional search.

6. Show that unless all of the disks are on the same peg, the branching factor in the towers of Hanoi problem is exactly 3. What is the branching factor if we disallow the move that returns us to the previous state?

7. (a) How many moves does it take to solve the n disk towers of Hanoi problem?

   (b) It is rumored that a group of Hindu monks is busily working on the sixty-four disk towers of Hanoi problem; when they finish, God's purpose will be fulfilled and the universe will cease to exist. Do we have anything to worry about?

8. The smaller cubes that make up a Rubik's cube are called *cubies*.

   (a) Is the heuristic that estimates the number of misplaced or misoriented cubies in Rubik's cube an admissible one?

(b) How could the above heuristic be transformed into an admissible one?

(c) Why isn't this likely to be of much use in practice?

9. Draw a figure that shows the search space for the missionaries and cannibals problem in its entirety, and show that this space is the same if searched in a forward or backward direction.

10. Is it possible to solve the mutilated-checkerboard problem?

11. We argued in the text that inference could be viewed as search. Provide analogous arguments showing that search can be viewed as theorem proving.

12. Present a proof problem that is best solved using forward reasoning. Present one best approached using backward reasoning.

PART

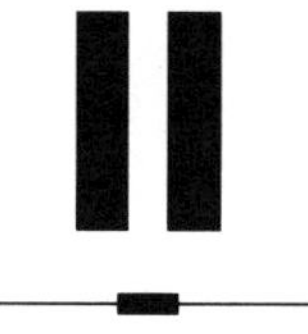

SEARCH

CHAPTER

3

BLIND SEARCH

We argued in the last chapter that intelligent action involves search, and described a variety of specific problems where search is needed for a solution—the 8-puzzle, game playing, crossword-puzzle generation, and reasoning or inference generally. In this chapter and the next two, we examine search in a bit more depth. This chapter discusses blind search, the next discusses heuristic search, and Chapter 5 discusses search procedures that are used in game playing.

We have already presented algorithms for depth-first search and breadth-first search, and we begin this chapter by examining these procedures a bit more closely. Specifically, we consider the question of how much memory and time these algorithms need.

In order to simplify the analysis, we will assume that we are working with a search tree of uniform branching factor b and depth d, and that this tree has a single goal node that is at depth d. A tree of this sort with $b = 4$ and $d = 2$ appears in Figure 3.1. We have denoted the root node by i, the nodes at depth 1 by n_1, n_2, n_3, and n_4, and the children of n_i by n_{i1}, n_{i2}, n_{i3}, and n_{i4}.

Except for the fact that it admits multiple solutions, the crossword-puzzle problem can be thought of in this way: We decide in advance on an order in which to fill the squares, view a completed crossword as a goal node if all of the words are legal and distinct, and view the node as a nongoal node if one of these conditions is violated. Given this interpretation, the branching factor for the crossword-puzzle problem is 26.

3.1 BREADTH-FIRST SEARCH

As discussed in Chapter 2, in breadth-first search we should view the list L of unexpanded nodes as a queue, so that newly generated children are put on the end of this list and expanded only after nodes at shallower depths have been examined. Thus during the first few iterations through the loop in Procedure 2.2.1, L takes the following values:

$$\{i\}$$
$$\{n_1,n_2,n_3,n_4\}$$
$$\{n_2,n_3,n_4,n_{11},n_{12},n_{13},n_{14}\}$$
$$\{n_3,n_4,n_{11},n_{12},n_{13},n_{14},n_{21},n_{22},n_{23},n_{24}\}$$
$$\vdots$$

The complete ordering for the search in Figure 3.1 is shown in Figure 3.2.

Since the total number of nodes at depth k is b^k and we need to store all of these nodes before the first node at depth $k + 1$ is examined, it follows that breadth-first search needs space at least b^{d-1} to explore a tree such as that in Figure 3.1. Note that if the tree continued beyond depth d, even more space would be required as the nodes on the fringe each generated b successors. Just before the goal is found, L would contain the goal node and some fraction of the tree at depth $d + 1$.

How about the amount of time needed by breadth-first search? We will equate the amount of time taken by the algorithm with the number of nodes it examines; remember that a node is checked to see if it is a goal node just before the node is expanded to generate successors, and not when the node itself is added to the list L.

FIGURE 3.1 A uniform search space

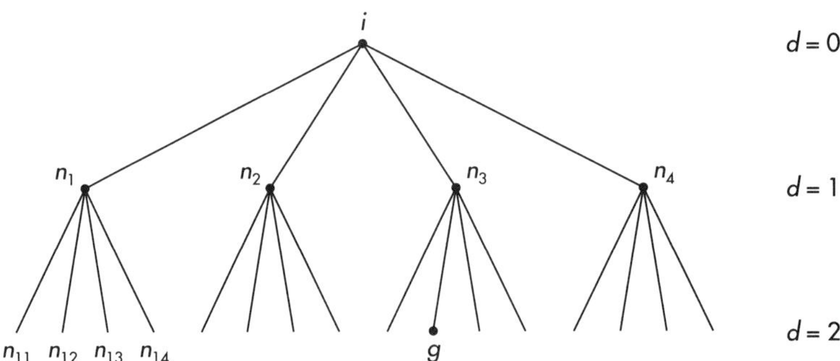

FIGURE 3.2 Breadth-first search

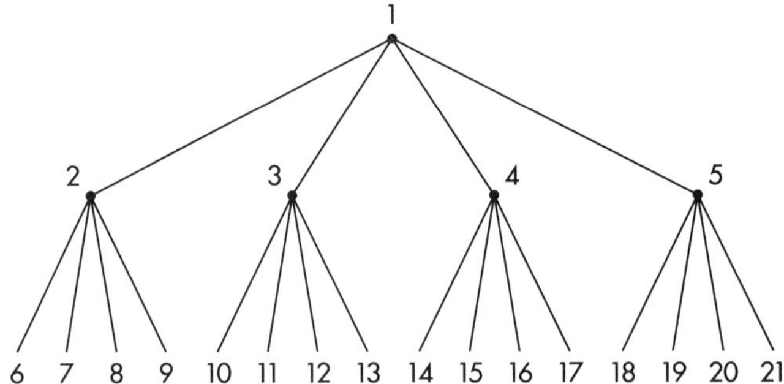

In order to reach the goal at depth d, the *internal* (that is, nonfringe) nodes that must be examined are all of the nodes at depths $0,1,\ldots,d-1$. The number of such nodes is given by

$$1 + b + b^2 + \cdots + b^{d-1} = \frac{b^d - 1}{b - 1} \tag{3.1}$$

What about the fringe nodes? We can't tell exactly how many fringe nodes will be examined, since we don't know where on the fringe the goal node is located. But the best we can do is to examine only one fringe node (the goal); the worst is if we need to examine all b^d of them. The average number of nodes examined on the fringe is therefore

$$\frac{1 + b^d}{2} \tag{3.2}$$

and the average number of total nodes is the sum of (3.1) and (3.2):

$$\begin{aligned}\frac{b^d - 1}{b - 1} + \frac{b^d + 1}{2} &= \frac{2b^d - 2 + b^{d+1} + b - b^d - 1}{2(b-1)} \\ &= \frac{b^{d+1} + b^d + b - 3}{2(b-1)}\end{aligned} \tag{3.3}$$

For large depth, (3.3) reduces to approximately $b^d/2$, which is roughly the same as the amount of time spent at the fringe. This is to be expected—in these cases, most of the time spent searching will be spent at the bottom of the tree. A graphical version of this argument appears in Figure 3.3.

If $b = 2$ on the other hand, then (3.3) simplifies to

$$\frac{3 \cdot 2^d - 1}{2}$$

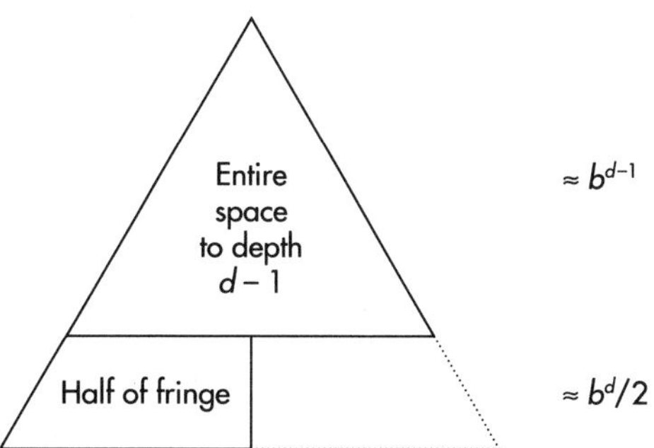

FIGURE 3.3 Time needed by breadth-first search

Once again, we can understand this result directly. The size of the internal tree is

$$1 + 2 + \cdots + 2^{d-1} \approx 2^d$$

and the number of fringe nodes that we need to examine is approximately $2^d/2$. These two values sum to $\frac{3}{2} \cdot 2^d$.

3.2 DEPTH-FIRST SEARCH

If L is thought of as a queue in the breadth-first approach, it is a *stack* in depth-first search. Its first few values as we search the tree in Figure 3.1 are:

$$\begin{gathered}\{i\} \\ \{n_1,n_2,n_3,n_4\} \\ \{n_{11},n_{12},n_{13},n_{14},n_2,n_3,n_4\} \\ \{n_{12},n_{13},n_{14},n_2,n_3,n_4\} \\ \vdots\end{gathered}$$

The complete search is shown in Figure 3.4.

The amount of memory needed by the depth-first approach is easy to compute. The most memory is needed at the first point that the algorithm reaches depth d; in Figure 3.5, the marked nodes need to be saved. In general, we will need to store $b - 1$ nodes at each depth (the siblings of the nodes that have already been expanded), together with one additional node at depth d (since we haven't expanded it yet). Thus the total space needed is given by

$$d(b - 1) + 1$$

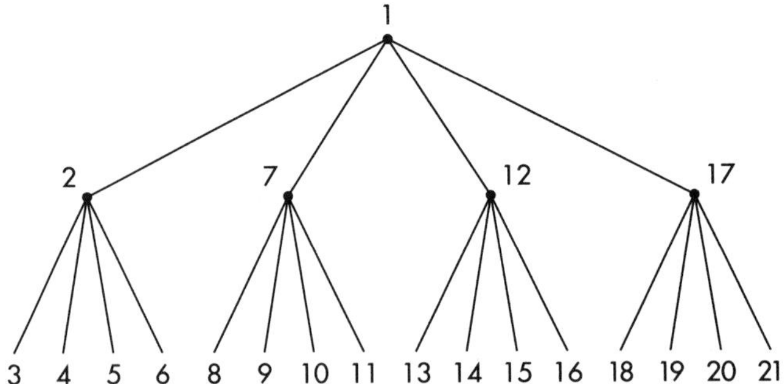

FIGURE 3.4 Depth-first search

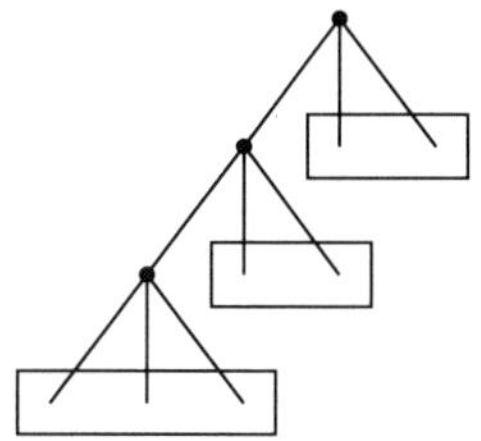

FIGURE 3.5 Memory needed by depth-first search

For fixed b, depth-first search requires an amount of memory that is linear in d, while breadth-first search requires an amount exponential in the depth of the search tree.

The time calculation is more subtle. We begin by noting that if the goal is at the far left of the tree, then depth-first search will proceed directly to it, examining a total of $d + 1$ nodes. If it is to the far right of the tree, the entire space will be examined, a total of

$$1 + \cdots + b^d = \frac{b^{d+1} - 1}{b - 1}$$

nodes in all. If we could average these two expressions, we could conclude that the number of nodes examined in the average case is

$$\frac{b^{d+1} - 1 + bd - d + b - 1}{2(b-1)} = \frac{b^{d+1} + bd + b - d - 2}{2(b-1)} \tag{3.4}$$

But is it legitimate to take the average? It isn't obvious that it is, since the numbers of nodes that might be examined are not distributed uniformly over the integers from $d + 1$ to

$$\frac{b^{d+1} - 1}{b - 1}$$

In Figure 3.4, for example, we might examine three, four, five, or six nodes, but can't examine exactly seven, since the seventh node we examine is n_2, which is at depth 1 and not a fringe node.

To see that we *can* take the average, we will use an argument due to the mathematician Karl Gauss. When Gauss was ten, he was making a nuisance of himself, and the teacher, in order to quiet him, asked him to add the numbers from 1 to 100. Gauss replied almost immediately that the answer was 5050, having reasoned as follows:

> I can pair 1 with 100; they add to 101. If I pair 2 with 99, I get 101 again; similarly for 3 paired with 98 and so on. The last pair is 50 with 51, so the sum of all the numbers is $50 \cdot 101 = 5050$.

Not bad for a 10-year old.[6]

Gauss's argument would apply equally well to showing that the average of all the integers between 1 and 100 was 101/2, and this argument is one that we can apply to our situation. Specifically, if we denote by B the number of nodes examined in the best case and by W the number examined in the worst, then in the tree in Figure 3.4 it is possible to examine a total of B nodes, or $B + 1$, $B + 2$, $B + 3$, $B + 5$ (not $B + 4$) and so on. But on the other side of the picture, we might examine W nodes, or $W - 1$, $W - 2$, $W - 3$, $W - 5$ (not $W - 4$) and so on. As shown for the tree with $b = 3$ in Figure 3.6, the symmetry of the search space guarantees that we can average the best and worst cases, so that the amount of time needed by depth-first search in the average case is indeed given by (3.4).

As in the breadth-first case, we will examine large d and $b = 2$ a bit more closely. For large d, (3.4) is once again

$$\frac{b^d}{2}$$

FIGURE 3.6 Gauss's argument for a tree with $b = 3$ instead of $b = 4$

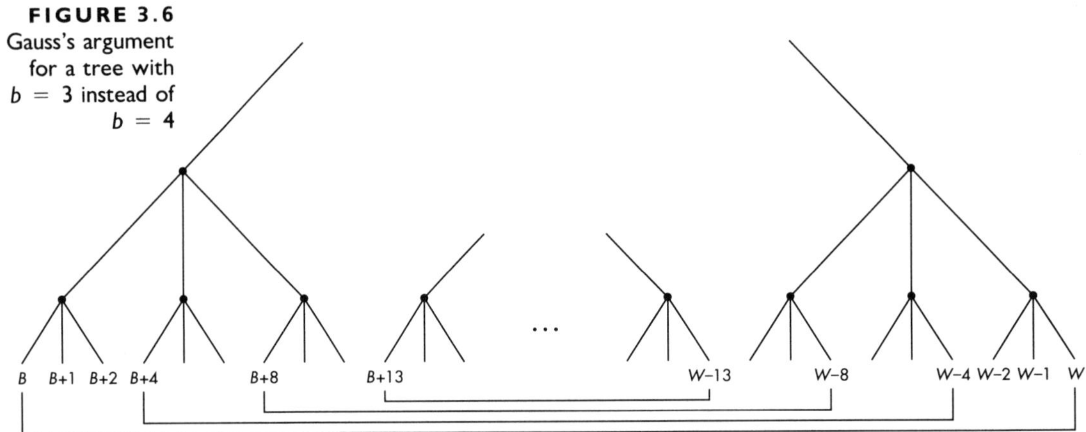

6 Mathematicians have a history of doing things like this. Consider the following famous problem: Two locomotives start 200 miles apart, each traveling toward the other at 50 miles per hour. A bumblebee starts on the front of one train and flies toward the other at 75 miles an hour; when he reaches the second locomotive, he turns around and heads back. Assuming that he continues this behavior, how many miles will he fly before being squashed?

One can solve this problem either by doing a few pages of algebra and summing a fairly complicated series, or simply reason that since the trains are approaching one another at 100 miles an hour, the bumblebee gets to fly for two hours—150 miles—before meeting his demise.

The mathematician von Neumann, given this problem, responded almost immediately and was then told that although physicists typically solved the problem in this way, mathematicians typically summed the series. Von Neumann's reply? "But I did sum the series."

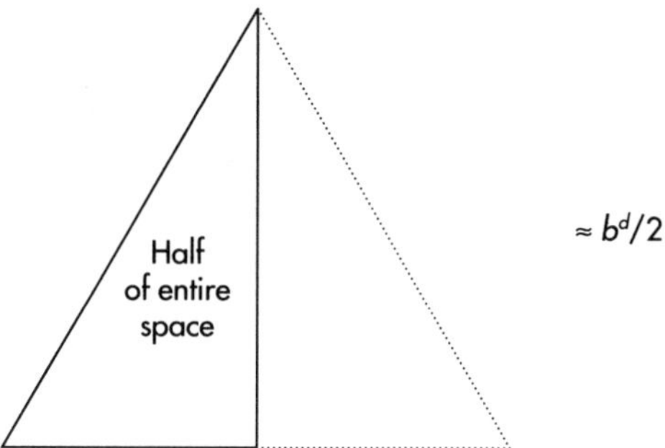

FIGURE 3.7 Time needed by depth-first search

so that the work at the fringe continues to dominate the computation (see Figure 3.7). Note, however, that the term of order $b^{d-1}/2$ that appeared in the breadth-first result (3.3) is missing from (3.4); a slightly more accurate estimate of the time needed by breadth-first search is

$$\frac{b^d}{2}\left(1 + \frac{1}{b}\right)$$

We see from this that breadth-first search is more computationally expensive than depth-first search by a factor of

$$1 + \frac{1}{b} = \frac{b+1}{b}$$

Typical values for this expression appear in Figure 3.8.

For $b = 2$, (3.4) simplifies to

$$\frac{2^{d+1} + 2d + 2 - d - 2}{2} = \frac{2^{d+1} + d}{2} \approx 2^d$$

As in the breadth-first case, we can understand this result directly. The entire search space is of size 2^{d+1}, and depth-first search will, on average, examine about half of it—in other words, 2^d nodes.

Comparing the two approaches, we see that depth-first search is somewhat more efficient in time and vastly more efficient in space than its

FIGURE 3.8 Cost of breadth-first search

b	Ratio
2	1.5
3	1.3
5	1.2
10	1.1
25	1.04
100	1.01

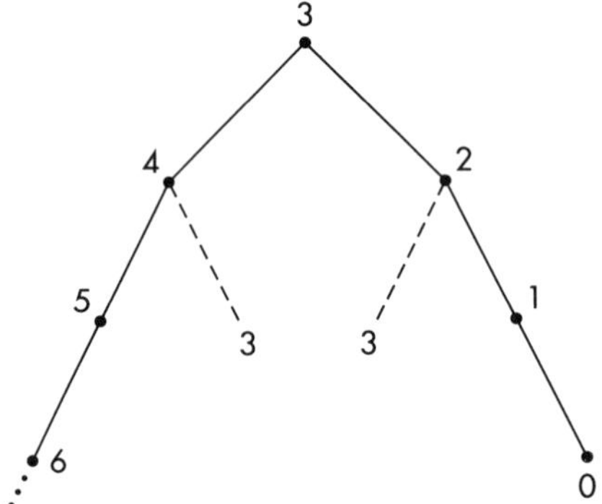

FIGURE 3.9
Is 3 an integer?

breadth-first counterpart. In fact, the amount of space needed by breadth-first methods is typically large enough to be prohibitive.

Depth-first search is not without its difficulties, however. Many problems admit multiple goals with the intention being to find the shallowest one; there is no guarantee that the depth-first approach will do so. Consider using depth-first search to solve a route planning problem, where the goal is to find a path from my house to my neighbor's. If my neighbor lives to the west but I decide to expand nodes to the east first, the route I find may take me all the way around the planet in order to cross the street! At the very least, I will probably make my way to New York before turning around and heading back toward California.

Depth-first search can also have trouble if the depth of the tree is infinite. Consider the problem of proving that 3 is an integer, where we know that 0 is an integer and also that successors and predecessors of integers are integers. The search space for this problem is shown in Figure 3.9, where we have labelled the nodes with the numbers that we are trying to prove are integers, and 0 therefore labels goal nodes. We have simplified the search tree somewhat by pruning any path that takes us from a node back to its predecessor. (Two pruned paths that return us to the root of the tree are shown in Figure 3.9.)

Depth-first search may simply follow the left-hand branch in this problem, trying to prove that 4 is an integer, then that 5 is, then 6, and so on. When searching trees of infinite depth, depth-first search may not find any answer at all. In Exercise 4 at the end of this chapter, we will see that breadth-first search can also outperform depth-first search in finite spaces if the depth of the goal node is smaller than the depth of the tree as a whole.

3.3 ITERATIVE DEEPENING

Is there any way to get the best of both these approaches, using an algorithm that has the space requirements of depth-first search and the performance properties of breadth-first search? The answer is yes; the approach that does this is known as *iterative deepening* and was first thoroughly investigated by Rich Korf.

There are two separate ways to think about iterative deepening. Perhaps the simplest (although it doesn't explain the name) is that it's just the same as breadth-first search, except that instead of storing all of the nodes at intermediate depths, we *regenerate* them when the time comes to expand them.

Why is this a viable approach? It seems as if the amount of time spent regenerating the internal nodes would dwarf the time spent looking for the answer, but this is not the case—recall that in all search problems, the bulk of the computational effort is spent examining the nodes at the fringe.

The other way to think of iterative deepening is the following. In the cases in which depth-first search performs poorly, the depth of the goal node is less than the depth of the tree as a whole—either because the first goal found is at a greater depth than the shallowest solution to the problem, or because the depth of the tree is infinite, and so on. What iterative deepening does is search the tree in a way that guarantees that the goal depth and tree depth match.

The idea is to search the tree initially with an *artificial* depth cutoff of 1, so that any node below depth 1 is not examined. If this approach succeeds in finding a solution at depth 1, the solution is returned. If not, the tree is searched again but with a depth cutoff of 2. Each of these iterative searches proceeds in depth-first fashion.

PROCEDURE 3.3.1

Iterative deepening

1. *Set* c = 1*; this is the current depth cutoff.*
2. *Set* L *to be a list of the initial nodes in the problem.*
3. *Let* n *be the first node on* L*. If* L *is empty, increment* c *and return to step 2.*
4. *If* n *is a goal node, stop and return it and the path from the initial node to* n*.*
5. *Otherwise, remove* n *from* L*. Provided that the depth of* n *is less than* c*, add to the front of* L *all of* n*'s children, labelling each with its path from the initial node. Return to step 3.*

If the shallowest solution is at depth g, the depth-first search to this depth will succeed; it follows from this that iterative deepening will always return the shallowest solution to the problem in question. Since each of the individual searches is performed depth-first, the amount of memory required by the method is the same as for the depth-first approach.

How about the number of nodes examined? The order in which the nodes are expanded in our sample problem is shown in Figure 3.10; the

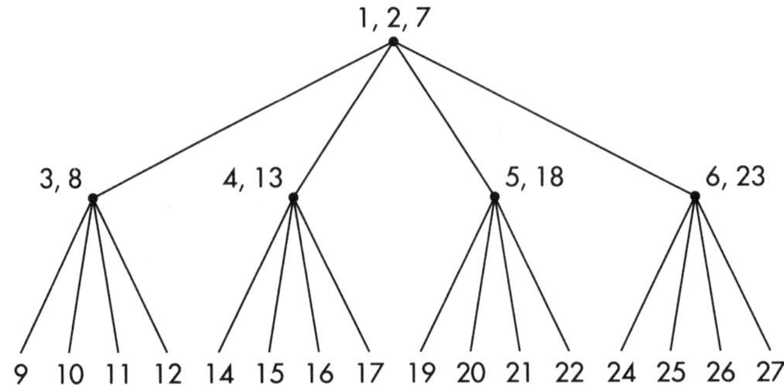

FIGURE 3.10 Node order in iterative deepening

nodes at depth 0 and 1 are labelled with a sequence of numbers since they are examined multiple times.

In general, the number of nodes examined in the final (successful) iteration is given by (3.4). In the previous iterations, the failing searches to depths $1,2,\ldots,d-1$ will need to examine the entire tree at these depths; the size of the tree to depth j is given by

$$1 + b + \cdots + b^j = \frac{b^{j+1} - 1}{b - 1}$$

The total number of nodes examined in the failing searches is therefore

$$\begin{aligned}\sum_{j=0}^{j=d-1} \frac{b^{j+1} - 1}{b - 1} &= \frac{1}{b-1}\left[b\left(\sum_{0}^{d-1} b^j\right) - \sum_{0}^{d-1} 1\right] \\ &= \frac{1}{b-1}\left[b\left(\frac{b^d - 1}{b - 1}\right) - d\right] \\ &= \frac{b^{d+1} - bd - b + d}{(b-1)^2}\end{aligned}$$

Combining this with (3.4) and simplifying the result, the total number of nodes examined in this approach is seen to be

$$\frac{b^{d+2} + b^{d+1} + b^2 d + b^2 - 4bd - 5b + 3d + 2}{2(b-1)^2} \tag{3.5}$$

For large d, this is dominated by

$$\frac{(b+1)b^{d+1}}{2(b-1)^2}$$

Since the time needed by depth-first search is dominated by

$$\frac{b^{d+1}}{2(b-1)}$$

the ratio of the time needed by iterative deepening to that needed by depth-first search is given by

$$\frac{b+1}{b-1} \tag{3.6}$$

Typical values of this expression appear in Figure 3.11. As we can see from the table, the cost of repeating the work at shallow depths is not prohibitive. Since iterative deepening avoids the problems encountered in depth-first search, it is the method of choice in many search problems.

As usual, we examine the case $b = 2$ a bit more closely. In the depth-first case, we need to examine half of the entire tree; since the tree is of size 2^{d+1}, depth-first search needs to examine 2^d nodes. In iterative deepening, the failing searches take time

$$1 + 2 + \cdots + 2^d \approx 2^{d+1}$$

since these are the sizes of the subtrees examined. Since this time is twice the time needed by the successful search to depth d, the overall factor in the $b = 2$ case is 3, in agreement with (3.6) and Figure 3.11.

How good is iterative deepening? In a very real sense, it is an *optimal* blind search procedure. The reason is that for a fixed branching factor, it takes space $o(d)$ and time $o(b^d)$; as we are about to see, it is impossible to improve on this behavior.[7] It is clear, for example, that if the program is

FIGURE 3.11 Cost of iterative deepening

b	Ratio
2	3
3	2
5	1.5
10	1.2
25	1.08
100	1.02

7 By $o(d)$ here, I mean that for large depth the amount of space needed is dominated by a term of the form kd for some constant k. In a similar way, the amount of time needed is dominated by a term of the form $k'b^d$.

expected to return the path to a goal node at depth d, at least space d is required.

What about time? Since the goal node is distributed randomly along the fringe and the search technique is blind, it follows that we will, on average, need to examine at least half of this fringe. Since the fringe is of size b^d, we can therefore expect any blind search procedure to take time $o(b^d)$.

Given this, we can strengthen our remarks with regard to the space needed by the following argument: Consider *any* algorithm that takes time $o(b^d)$ to run; how much space does it need in order to distinguish its own internal states?

If all of the internal states of the algorithm are to remain distinct, it clearly needs at least as much space as it would need to count to b^d. But counting to b^d needs $\log_2(b^d)$ bits; since $\log_2(b^d) = d \log_2(b)$ is $o(d)$ for fixed b, we see that any blind search algorithm needs space $o(d)$ whether it is expected to return a path to the answer or not.

3.4 ITERATIVE BROADENING

Although iterative deepening is optimal in the sense that $o(b^d)$ is the best one can do in general, there is one other blind search technique that can often improve on this result in practice—not by reducing the complexity of the problem, but by making it likely that a smaller portion of the fringe is examined if multiple goal nodes exist. This technique is known as *iterative broadening*.

As we noted in the previous chapter, it is important where possible to recognize bad choices early in the search so that we need not expand the entire search tree under these choices before finding a goal node. But how are we to do this if the search is blind?

The answer lies in realizing that in most practical problems, the goal nodes are not randomly distributed because it is possible to make "fatal" mistakes early in the search. In Figure 3.12, for example, it might well be

FIGURE 3.12
Backtracking

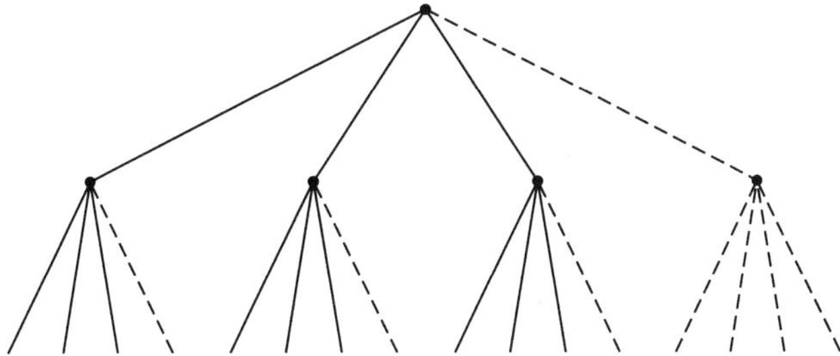

FIGURE 3.13 Search with a breadth cutoff

that the insertion of the word *TONAL* basically doomed us. Although we could fill in a variety of additional words, we would eventually have to insert *TOAST* as described earlier and would then be unable to fill the marked word in the figure. What iterative broadening does is to take continuing failure to find a goal below a node high in the search tree as evidence that such a fatal mistake has been made.

Just as iterative deepening imposes artificial depth limits on the search and gradually increases those limits until a solution is found, iterative broadening imposes artificial *breadth* limits, increasing *them* until a solution is found.

PROCEDURE 3.4.1

Iterative broadening

1. *Set* c = 2; *this is the current breadth cutoff.*
2. *Set* L *to be the set of initial nodes in the problem.*
3. *Let* n *be the first node on* L. *If* L *is empty, increment* c *and return to step 2.*
4. *If* n *is a goal node, stop and return it and the path from the initial node to* n.
5. *Otherwise, remove* n *from* L. *Add to the front of* L *the first* c *of* n's *children, labelling each with its path from the initial node. Return to step 3.*

We initially search the tree with a breadth cutoff of 2, then of 3, and so on. A breadth cutoff of c means that a maximum of c children of any given node can be examined before the node is abandoned as a failure. In Figure 3.13, we show a tree with branching factor 4 but a breadth cutoff of 3. The node ordering given by iterative broadening in our usual example is shown in Figure 3.14.

As with iterative deepening, iterative broadening is a viable search technique because there are at most b searches and the breadth searches with cutoff c take time $o(c^d)$, which will be small relative to b^d if $c < b$. The maximum amount of time spent by the approach is approximately

$$1 + 2^d + \cdots + b^d$$

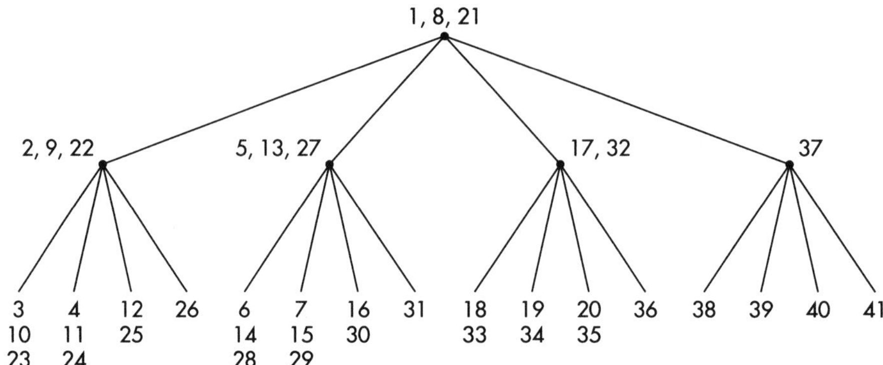

FIGURE 3.14 Iterative broadening

which is approximately b^{d+1}/d for large b (a factor of b/d worse than depth-first search) and is approximately b^d (virtually no cost at all) for large d.

Iterative broadening can lead to large savings in the amount of time needed to solve search problems if multiple goal nodes exist and if it is possible to make fatal errors early in the search. In the large depth limit, the method is likely to find a solution more quickly than simple depth-first search whenever the number of goal nodes exceeds three.

Nonsystematic search Iterative broadening is a useful search technique because it keeps us from concentrating too much of our effort in a region of the search space that contains no goal nodes. This lesson is so important that a variety of authors have suggested recently that when you fail to find a goal in solving a search problem, you should jump to a distant portion of the search space that might be better.

The problem with doing this is that it is difficult to keep track of which nodes you've examined and which you haven't; you can't store all of the examined nodes without using an exponential amount of memory. So what these new approaches suggest is that you simply not worry about this, possibly searching some portions of the search space many times and other portions not at all. Because of the scatter-shot nature of the resulting search, these methods are called *nonsystematic*. There is no guarantee that a nonsystematic search will find a goal node every time that the search space contains one.

In spite of this, the observed performance of nonsystematic methods on large search problems is often comparable to (and in some cases better than) the performance of systematic approaches. Roughly speaking, the search spaces in these examples are so large that the nonsystematic methods are unlikely to examine some area of the space over and over again, and the spaces are also so large that a complete examination in the search for a solution (where the systematic methods could be expected to shine) is simply impractical. This work is all very new, but the next few years should shed substantial light on the general question of whether systematic or nonsystematic methods should be preferred when solving hard problems.

3.5 SEARCHING GRAPHS

Throughout this chapter, we have assumed that the search space being examined is a tree and not a graph, so that it is impossible to reach the same node using each of several paths from the root node.

This assumption is clearly wrong; in sliding tile puzzles, for example, there may be many ways to arrive at a particular configuration of the tiles. The tower of Hanoi is similar, as is the crossword-puzzle problem. In Figure 3.15, we have redrawn Figure 2.11 to show explicitly that the search space in the missionaries and cannibals problem is a graph and not a tree.

We can, of course, search a graph by pretending that it is a tree, as in Figure 2.11 itself. The problem with doing this is that the search may become less efficient as a result. There are two separate ways in which graph search can be simplified.

3.5.1 Open and Closed Lists

The first way is to simply avoid adding a node to L if it already appears there. After all, there is never any reason to commit to searching the same node twice. More efficient still is to keep track of those nodes that have been examined and removed from L; since these nodes have already been considered, we have no need to consider them again should they be regenerated for some reason.

The basic search procedure, Procedure 2.2.1, does not keep track of the nodes that have been examined and removed from L; if we want to do this, we need to maintain a list of these nodes. This list is often referred to as the list of *closed* nodes; the list L of nodes still to be examined is called the list of *open* nodes.

Of course, finding any particular node in the open or closed list takes both time and space, and these resources need to be justified via an effective reduction in the size of the graph being searched. By using hash tables, the time to find (or fail to find) a particular node in the open or closed list can be reduced to a constant; the space requirements are a bit more difficult to deal with.

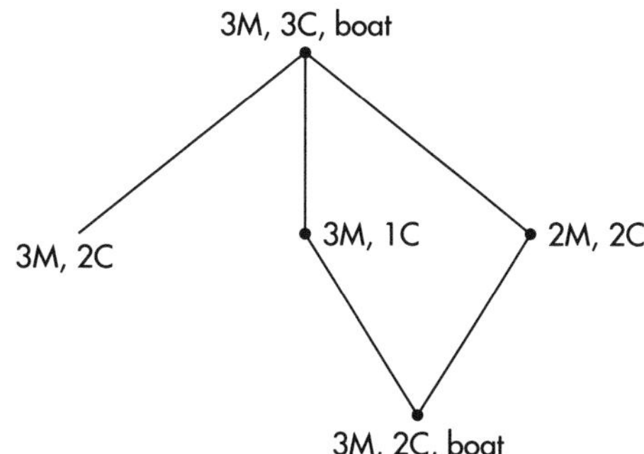

FIGURE 3.15 Missionaries and cannibals again

One possibility here is to store the closed nodes using a hash table of some fixed size, and to simply overwrite an entry in this table whenever a new node is given the same value by the hashing function as an earlier one. The hope here is that nodes that appear multiple times in the search space will tend to remain in the hash table and thereby serve to keep repeated nodes off the open list.

3.5.2 Dynamic Backtracking

The second technique used to exploit the fact that a search space is a graph instead of a tree is known as *dynamic backtracking*.

Suppose that we are searching a graph and that we have just examined the portion of the space below a particular node n. Unfortunately, no goal node was found, and we must therefore back up from n to a node elsewhere in the space.

In most search procedures (depth-first search is typical), the node we consider next will be one of n's ancestors. And in many cases, this ancestor may be much shallower in the tree than n is, and retreating to it may involve abandoning a substantial amount of the work involved in constructing n in the first place. We saw an example of this in Figure 3.12, where we backtracked from the marked word in the puzzle to the earlier choice *TONAL*.

The trick in dynamic backtracking is to backtrack from n not along the path used to generate the node, but along one of the *other* paths that may exist connecting n to the root of the search space. In the crossword-puzzle problem of Figure 3.12, for example, we would like to "erase" the words *TOAST* and *TONAL* directly, leaving words like *LAY* and *LAP* intact. We can do this because we could just as easily have reached the puzzle state in the figure by filling in *LAY* and *LAP* before *TOAST* and *TONAL*.

One must be careful to avoid wandering somewhat aimlessly through the search space; dynamic backtracking is intended to be a systematic as opposed to nonsystematic search method. If we backtrack from n along a path other than that originally used to generate it, how are we to keep our search methodical? It turns out that the nature of the backtrack often allows this problem to be addressed by keeping careful track of the nodes that have been considered thus far; the space requirements are $o(bd^2)$ and the time requirements are minimal.

3.6 FURTHER READING

Probably the best reference on search generally is by Pearl [1984]. This book is encyclopedic in its coverage of the techniques that we discuss in this chapter and the next two.

The story about Gauss is reported by Bell [1937, p. 221]; I know of no specific reference for the story about von Neumann and hope that it is other than urban legend.

Korf's work on iterative deepening is reported in Korf [1985a]. Korf indicates there that the first appearance of the algorithm in the literature is in Northwestern's program CHESS4.5 from the 1970s [Slate and Atkin 1977]. The idea is discussed concurrently by Stickel and Tyson [1985]. Our argument that any procedure taking time $o(b^d)$ takes space at least $o(d)$ appears in Hopcroft and Ullman [1979].

Iterative broadening is introduced and discussed in greater depth in Ginsberg and Harvey [1990]. Three nonsystematic methods are *min-conflicts* [Minton *et al.* 1990], GSAT [Selman *et al.* 1992], and *iterative sampling* [Langley 1992].

Dynamic backtracking is the newest of all the ideas you will find in this book; the description here is probably the first that has appeared anywhere.

3.7 EXERCISES

1. Figure 3.16 contains an instance of the 3-puzzle, where the initial and goal states are as shown.
   (a) Assuming that we prefer to move the blank first right, then left, then up, and then down, draw the search space for this problem. What are the results of depth-first search and breadth-first search?
   (b) How does the answer to part (a) of this exercise change if we disallow the move that returns us to the previous state?
2. Write a computer program that solves the missionaries and cannibals problem using either breadth-first or depth-first search.
3. A farmer is trying to cross a river with a fox, a chicken, and a bag of grain. He has a rowboat that he can use to carry any single item across the river, but he cannot afford to leave either the fox unattended with the chicken or the chicken unattended with the grain. Write a computer program that finds the quickest way for the farmer and his possessions to get across the river.

FIGURE 3.16 The 3-puzzle

4. Suppose that we are searching a tree with uniform branching factor b and depth d, and that the tree contains a single goal node at depth g. Compute the average number of nodes examined and the storage needed by breadth-first search, depth-first search, and iterative deepening. Comment on the results.

5. Suppose that we say that an ordering of the nodes in a search space is *depth-first legal* if expanding the nodes in that order corresponds to depth-first search. How many depth-first legal orderings are there of a search space with uniform branching factor b and depth d? How many breadth-first legal orderings are there?

6. Why isn't iterative deepening a good idea in the crossword-puzzle problem? Would you expect iterative broadening to be any better?

7. Suppose that we are searching a finite tree, and that this tree contains no goal nodes. How does iterative deepening perform in this case? Can you suggest a solution to this problem?

8. This problem considers search in a space with $b = 1$.
   (a) How much time is needed by the depth-first search, breadth-first search, and iterative deepening in a search of this type? Why aren't equations (3.3), (3.4), and (3.5) valid in this case?
   (b) How much worse is iterative deepening than depth-first search?
   (c) Give an example of a search problem where although b is not uniformly 1, there are many nodes with only one child.
   (d) How could you reformulate the search space in a situation such as part (c) of this exercise so as to improve the relative performance of iterative deepening?

9. Why doesn't iterative broadening help in situations where there is only a single goal node?

10. The computational savings provided by iterative broadening grow as the depth of search increases. Explain why this happens.

11. *Island-driven search* is a technique where instead of finding a path directly to the goal, one first identifies an "island" that is a node halfway between the initial node and the goal node. We first attempt to find a path to the goal that passes through this node; if none exists, we simply solve the original search problem while ignoring the hypothetical island.
   (a) Assume that the time needed to search a tree of branching factor b and depth d is of order b^d, that the cost of identifying the island is c, and that the probability that the island actually lies on a path to the goal is p. Find conditions on c and p such that the island-

driven approach will be more effective than the usual one. Comment on the result.

(b) Give an example of a search problem where this is likely to be a good approach.

12. Provide a modification of Procedure 2.2.1 that uses lists of open and closed nodes and is suitable for graph search.

CHAPTER

4

HEURISTIC SEARCH

We argued in the last chapter that any technique used to search blindly through a space of depth d and branching factor b would of necessity take time $o(b^d)$ to find a single goal node on the fringe of the search tree. In practice, this is unacceptable. As an example, if the time needed to generate a plan grows exponentially with the length of the plan, a planner will be unable to produce plans of interesting length.

In exploring a large search space, the trick is to use additional information about the problem being considered to avoid examining most of the nodes that might conceivably lead to solutions. Instead of selecting the node to expand next in a domain-independent way as in the previous chapter, we need to use domain-*specific* information for the same purpose.

Of course, the problem of finding the best node to expand next is generally no easier than the search problem that we are trying to solve. So what we typically do is apply some sort of *heuristic*, or "rule of thumb," to decide what to do.[8] Given a list of nodes to be expanded, we might simply guess how far each is from a goal node and expand the one we thought to be closest.

As an example, consider the instance of the 8-puzzle shown in Figure 4.1, and suppose that our goal is to arrange the tiles from 1 to 8 clockwise around the edge of the puzzle. If we estimate the distance to the goal by

FIGURE 4.1 An instance of the 8-puzzle

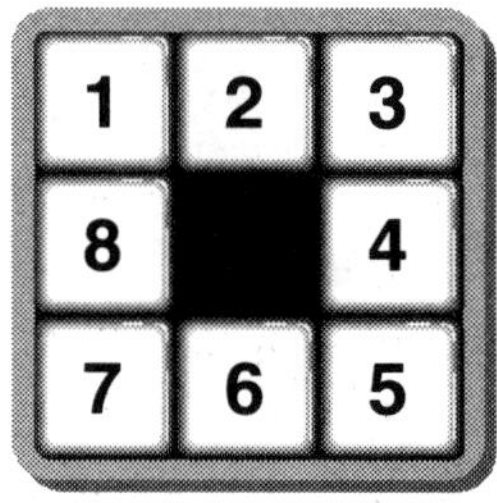

8 The description of a heuristic as a rule of thumb is Feigenbaum's.

simply counting the number of misplaced tiles, then we will expect it to take three moves to solve the problem in Figure 4.1, since three tiles are misplaced there. (The 6, 7, and 8 are all misplaced.) If we move the 6 to the right, then only two tiles are misplaced. Moving the 8 down leaves the heuristic estimate of the distance to the goal unchanged, while moving the 5 to the left actually *increases* the expected distance. We summarize this below.

Blank Moves	Distance
left	2
right	4
up	3

We see from this that if our search heuristic is to move as quickly toward the goal as possible, we will select the move of moving the blank to the left in Figure 4.1. Extending this analysis will lead us to move the blank up next and then to the right, arriving at the goal configuration after three moves. This technique always expands next the child of the current node that seems closest to the goal.

Of course, things may not always work out so easily because our heuristic function estimating the distance to the goal may make mistakes in some cases. After moving the blank up in Figure 4.1, we still estimate the distance to the goal as being only three moves, although it is not too hard to see that four are actually required.

Another problem is that we need to limit the amount of time spent computing the heuristic values used in selecting a node for expansion. We have already discussed this in Chapter 2, where we discussed the inevitable trade-off between base-level and metalevel activity.

There is no real "solution" to these problems of inaccurate or computationally expensive heuristics; the bottom line is that search problems sometimes *will* take an exponential amount of time to solve, and there is simply no way around this. But there is a third problem with our approach that is more tractable.

This problem can best be understood by considering an example. Suppose that we are looking for the solution to a maze, where our estimate of the value of a node is simply the Manhattan distance between our current position and the exit from the maze. Thus at any given point we do our best to move closer to the exit.

Now consider the maze shown in Figure 4.2, where we enter the maze on the left and exit on the right. As shown, there are two solutions—a simple one that begins with a step downward and a much more complex one that begins with a step directly toward the exit but is then deflected in other directions. The algorithm we have described will find the longer

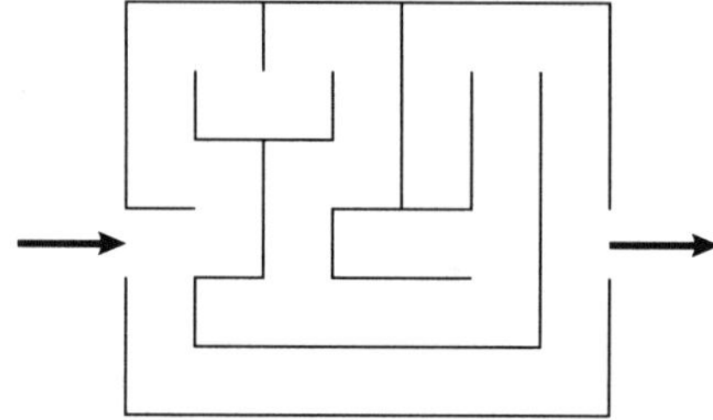

FIGURE 4.2
A maze with two solutions

of these two paths, since it will begin by moving toward the goal and then be committed to this choice.

If we want to find the shortest path to the goal in a problem such as this, a method that avoids this difficulty is a search algorithm known as A*, and we will discuss it later in this chapter. Before doing so, however, let me present heuristic search from a rather different perspective, drawing an analogy between these problems and the conventional problem of maximizing a function of several variables.

4.1 SEARCH AS FUNCTION MAXIMIZATION

Suppose that we have designed a robot whose purpose is to explore the surface of Mars. After being released from a landing craft of some sort, the robot is expected to wander around the surface of the planet to the most interesting location it can find, and then to take a variety of surface measurements at that point.

What makes a surface location interesting is a function of a variety of factors—apparent surface makeup, geological features, alien footprints, what have you. The robot has no difficulty evaluating the interest of the point at which it finds itself, but cannot predict the interest of any other point without actually visiting it. How is it to find the most interesting point on the planet's surface?

From a formal point of view, this is a simple function maximization problem; we have a function $f(p)$ that measures the interestingness of a point p on the surface, and need to find that value of p for which the function's value is maximal.

4.1.1 Hill Climbing

What is the functional analog to the search procedure described earlier? Informally, we always move in the direction of apparently largest f; the functional analog is to attempt to find the global maximum of a function of many variables by always moving in the direction in which the rate of change is greatest.

This technique is known as *hill climbing* or *steepest ascent* for the obvious reason; it is as if one attempted to find the highest point in a landscape by simply walking as much uphill as possible. Here is the search version.

PROCEDURE 4.1.1

Hill climbing

1. *Set* L *to be a list of the initial nodes in the problem, sorted by their expected distance to the goal. Nodes expected to be close to the goal should precede those that are farther from it.*
2. *Let* n *be the first node on* L. *If* L *is empty, fail.*
3. *If* n *is a goal node, stop and return it and the path from the initial node to* n.
4. *Otherwise, remove* n *from* L. *Sort* n*'s children by their expected distance to the goal, label each child with its path from the initial node, and add the children to the front of* L. *Return to step 2.*

In this version of the algorithm, we always take a step from a child of the previously expanded node when possible; this gives hill climbing a "depth-first" flavor. If we drop this restriction, we get an algorithm known as *best-first search.*

PROCEDURE 4.1.2

Best-first search

1. *Set* L *to be a list of the initial nodes in the problem.*
2. *Let* n *be the node on* L *that is expected to be closest to the goal. If* L *is empty, fail.*
3. *If* n *is a goal node, stop and return it and the path from the initial node to* n.
4. *Otherwise, remove* n *from* L *and add to* L *all of* n*'s children, labelling each with its path from the initial node. Return to step 2.*

There are three obvious problems with hill climbing, and these are depicted in Figure 4.3. The first, and most important, involves the problem of local maxima. It is all too easy to construct situations in which the rate of change is negative in all directions even though the global maximum

FIGURE 4.3 Difficulties encountered in hill climbing

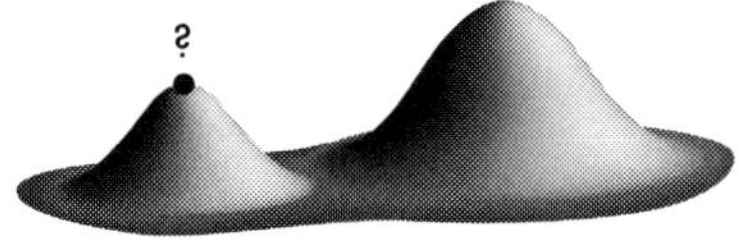

(a)

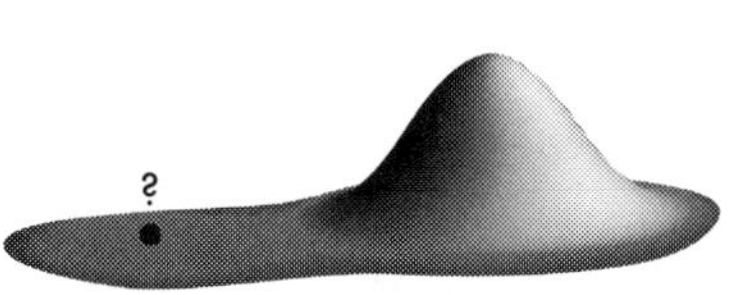

(b)

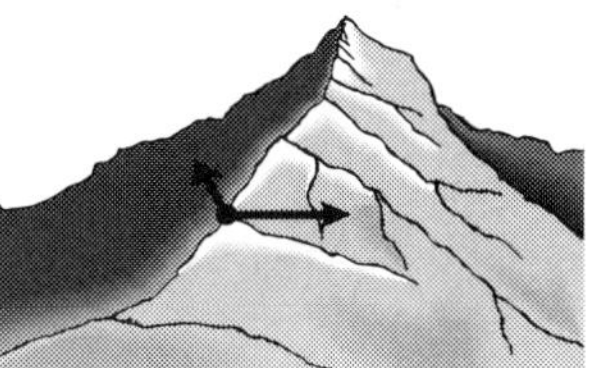

(c)

has not yet been found. In a maze where we are measuring progress by our distance to the exit, it may be necessary to move away from the exit in order to find a solution. Solving the 8-puzzle typically requires that we dislodge correctly placed tiles in order to reposition others satisfactorily. This is known as the *foothill problem* because we have to avoid finding ourselves trapped on a foothill while trying to climb a mountain.

The second problem with hill climbing is that it is difficult to deal with plateaus, or situations where all of the local steps are indistinguishable. In the 8-puzzle, perhaps none of the immediately available moves influences the count of misplaced tiles. In a maze, perhaps one's only choices are to move parallel to the exit because the walls block any other alternative.

The two problems that we have discussed also appear in the crossword-puzzle problem, where the function we are trying to maximize is the number of words that have been successfully entered into the crossword frame. A local maximum occurs when we need to retract words that were inserted earlier in order to address a problem that was not previously recognized. We saw an example of this in Figure 2.10, which we repeat in Figure 4.4. The problem, as we discussed in Section 2.2.3, is that we may backtrack only part way to the real difficulty and then simply return to where we started. In functional terms, a large local maximum can be difficult to avoid simply because there is no incentive to move the distance required to escape it.

A crossword-puzzle plateau is shown in Figure 4.5. Here, most of the words that can be inserted into the marked slot will cause an insurmountable difficulty of some kind (either no legal crossword at the first letter or none at the third). But this may not be apparent when we fill the slot indicated in the figure.

The final problem with hill climbing (which has no analog in the crossword-puzzle problem of which I am aware) involves *ridges*. As shown in Figure 4.3, a ridge involves a situation where although there is a direction in which we would *like* to move, none of the allowed steps (indicated by arrows in the figure) actually takes us in that direction.

FIGURE 4.4
A local maximum

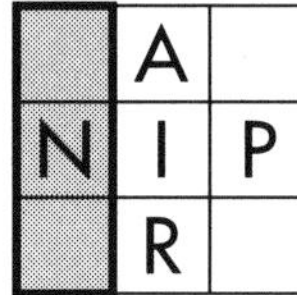

FIGURE 4.5
A plateau

When encountering a problem such as this, we need to do something similar to what is shown in Figure 4.6, taking two steps (one in each direction) in order to move along the ridge. It's like tacking in sailing—if our intention is to move directly upwind, we can do it only by sailing partially upwind in one direction and then partially upwind in another.

More complex examples may require that we take more than two steps in order to move along the ridge. Consider Rubik's cube; if the path to the solution involves interchanging two of the small component cubes, or cubies, we will typically use a multimove sequence in order to interchange the given cubies without affecting the work completed thus far.[9]

These sequences of moves that achieve specific subgoals in the Rubik's cube problem are generally referred to as *macro operators* and have uses far outside the ridge problem. As an example, one way to think about macro operators is as specific, large "steps" that we can use in our function-maximization efforts. They can therefore help to address the problem of local maxima as well.

Another way to think of macro operators is in terms of the islands used in island-driven search (see Exercise 11 in Chapter 3). The macro operators allow us to identify islands that we know we will be able to reach from our current position in the search space. We will return to this idea in Chapter 14 when we discuss hierarchical problem solving.

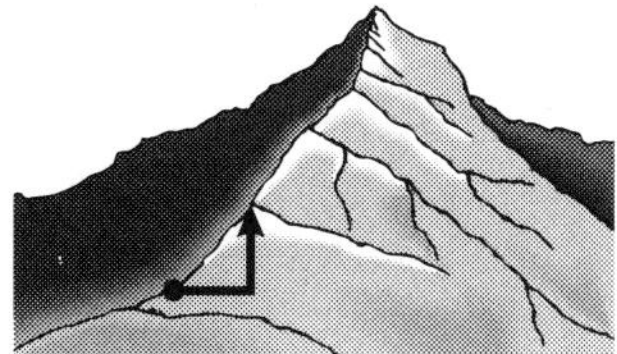

FIGURE 4.6
Moving along a ridge

9 When I was in Oxford (my astrophysicist days), I did some research with Rubik's cousin. This was before Rubik's cubes had appeared throughout the West; to make a long story short, I own the third Rubik's cube to have made its way out of Hungary. The mechanism used in the early cubes was very different from that used in more recent versions—they were very stiff, needed to be aligned precisely before each move, and exuded a very fine black dust when turned. As the cubes were used, more and more dust would come out and they would get progressively looser. Eventually, they would just collapse into a pile of dust and oddly shaped pieces. Not that this has anything to do with AI, of course.

There is no free lunch, of course. The difficulty with solving search problems using macro operators is that these operators need to be discovered in the first place. This is *itself* a search problem—the space of macro operators in the 8-puzzle, for example, is of size approximately 3^l where l is the length of the operator. This space, too, grows exponentially with the difficulty of the problem. It is also not obvious what criteria should be used to select one element of this large space over another as a useful macro operator.

4.1.2 Simulated Annealing

There is another function-maximization technique that appears to have a search analog. This is the idea of *simulated annealing* that was developed in the early 1980s.

The purpose of simulated annealing is to avoid the problem of local maxima that is the most important difficulty encountered in hill climbing. What we do is to solve a problem using conventional hill climbing techniques, but occasionally take a step in a direction other than that in which the rate of change is maximal. As time passes, the probability that a downhill step is taken is gradually reduced.

As shown in Figure 4.7, the idea behind simulated annealing is the following: The undirected steps that are taken clearly will not in general *reduce* the ability of the procedure to find a global maximum of the function in question, although these steps can be expected to increase the running time of the algorithm. But it is possible that these undirected steps dislodge the problem solver from a foothill that has been encountered by accident. The large size of the early steps is intended to avoid local maxima that extend over a wide area of the search space; subsequent undirected steps are smaller in the expectation that it is only more restricted local maxima that need to be avoided.

The name of the procedure is the result of an analogy with metal-casting techniques. When molten metal is poured into a mold, it gradually cools into a solid that will retain its overall shape. In order to make the final solid as nonbrittle as possible, the temperature should be reduced gradually; when this is done and the metal has solidified, it is said to have *annealed*. In simulated annealing, when the probability of the undirected step (related to the "temperature" of the procedure) becomes small enough that it can no longer move the problem solver's attention off of the maxi-

FIGURE 4.7
A non-uphill step avoids a local maximum

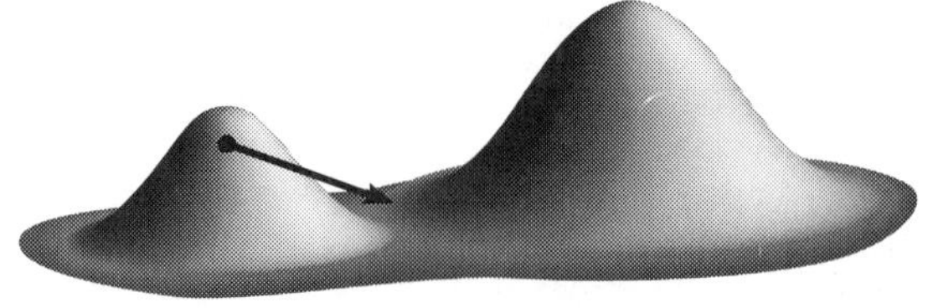

mum with which it is currently dealing, the algorithm's result can be said to have annealed in a similar way.

There are two remarkable things about simulated annealing. The first is that it took so long for it to be discovered—the problem of maximizing functions of multiple variables is an old one, and for an idea of this generality to have gone unnoticed until the past few years is remarkable.

More remarkable than simulated annealing's recency is its effectiveness. As a start, it is possible to prove that if the "temperature" of the algorithm is reduced only very slowly, a global maximum will always be found. The argument, roughly speaking, is the following: Suppose that the function's value at the global maximum is m and that the value at the best *local* maximum is $l < m$.

There will be some temperature t that is large enough to cause an undirected step off of the local maximum l but not off of the global maximum. Since the temperature is being reduced only slowly, the algorithm will spend enough time working with the temperature t that it will eventually stumble onto the global maximum and remain there.

Simulated annealing's practical effectiveness is no less impressive; this simple idea improves the performance of conventional function-maximization techniques tremendously. As an example, consider the problem of sequencing various sections of an automobile through the construction process. These parts need to be fabricated, finished, painted, and so on using a variety of tools that need to work on each part for differing amounts of time. Since the aim is to maximize the output of any particular factory, the problem can be viewed as one of function maximization. An engineer at General Motors recently applied simulated annealing to this problem; the result was so effective that the cost of manufacture of every automobile GM makes fell by about $20, a savings of millions of dollars annually.

Does simulated annealing have a search analog? It does. What this idea suggests is that when attempting to solve a search problem, one should occasionally examine a node that appears substantially worse than the best node to be found on L. In the crossword-puzzle problem, for example, we should occasionally erase some of the most recently inserted words and proceed afresh. Although this idea has received very little attention by the search community *per se*, experimentation on the crossword-puzzle problem shows that it does indeed improve performance in this restricted domain.

4.2 A*

Let us now return to the problem shown in Figure 4.2, where we saw that when hill climbing does manage to solve some search problem, it may well not find the *best* solution.

We have remarked from time to time that in many cases the quality of the solution is measured by its depth in the search tree, the intent being

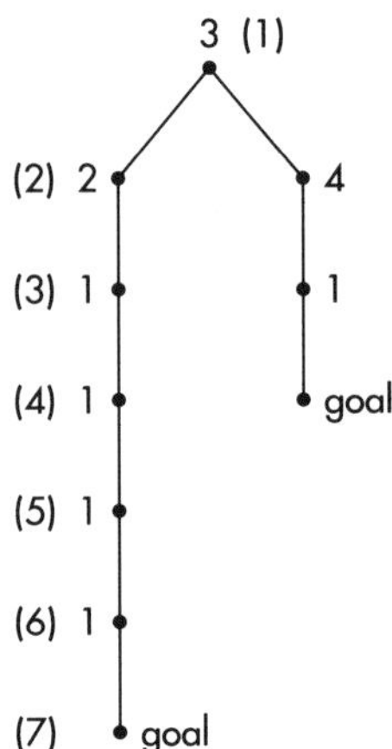

FIGURE 4.8 Finding a suboptimal solution

to find a solution at as shallow a depth as possible. When solving a maze, we look for the shortest path from the entrance to the exit; when solving the 8-puzzle, we look for the solution that slides as few tiles as possible.

We have already seen an example where hill-climbing fails to find an optimal solution in Figure 4.2; a simpler example where both hill climbing and best-first search find a suboptimal solution is shown in Figure 4.8. The number next to each node in the figure is the heuristic value assigned to that node, so that the label of 3 assigned to the root node means that we expect (correctly, in this case) this node to be three steps away from the goal. The heuristic becomes inaccurate for the nodes at depth 1, however; the left-hand node is labelled with a 2 even though the goal is five steps away along this path and the right-hand node is labelled with a 4 even though the goal could be reached in only two steps.

The parenthetical numbers in the figure show the order in which the nodes are expanded. The root node is expanded first, after which we expand its left-hand child because that child is believed to be closer to the goal than the right-hand one. Since each subsequent node on the left side of the tree is also expected to be closer to the goal than the right-hand node at depth 1, the left side of the tree is explored in its entirety and the goal at depth 6 is found instead of the goal at depth 3.

We should not be surprised that best-first search fails to find the best solution in cases such as this. After all, the idea in best-first search is to find *some* solution as quickly as possible by finding any node that is at distance 0 from a goal node; nowhere is any attempt made to find the goal node that is at minimal depth in the search tree. If we want to do this, we need to modify our search algorithm to reflect our interest in finding a goal at as shallow a depth as possible. The order in which we expand the nodes needs to take into account the fact that we want to expand shallow nodes in preference to deep ones.

Slightly more precisely, since the aim in best-first search is to find a goal as quickly as possible, it leads us to expand the node thought to be closest to a goal node. Since our modified aim is to find the *shallowest* goal as quickly as possible, we should expand instead the node that appears to be closest to a *shallow* goal. Instead of ordering the nodes in terms of distance to the goal, we should order them in terms of the quality (that is, expected depth) of the nearest goal to them.

So suppose that we have a node n at depth d in the search tree, and that we judge this node to be a distance $h'(n)$ from the nearest goal to it.[10] This goal is therefore judged to be at depth $d + h'(n)$ in the search space; it follows that instead of choosing for expansion the node with smallest $h'(n)$ as in best-first search (*since* $h'(n)$ is the expected distance to the goal), we should choose for expansion the node with smallest $d + h'(n)$. The depth of the node being considered is also a function of the node, and is typically denoted $g(n)$ and referred to as the "cost" of reaching the node n from the root node. Since our intention is to find a goal of minimal cost, we expand the nodes in order of increasing

$$f(n) = g(n) + h'(n) \tag{4.1}$$

This algorithm is known as the *A* algorithm*, and we apply it to the search problem of Figure 4.8 in Figure 4.9. Instead of labelling each node with the expected distance to the goal, we label it with two numbers, the depth of the node (0 for the root node, 1 for its children, 2 for their children and so on) *and* the expected distance to the goal. We then choose for expansion that node for which this sum is smallest.

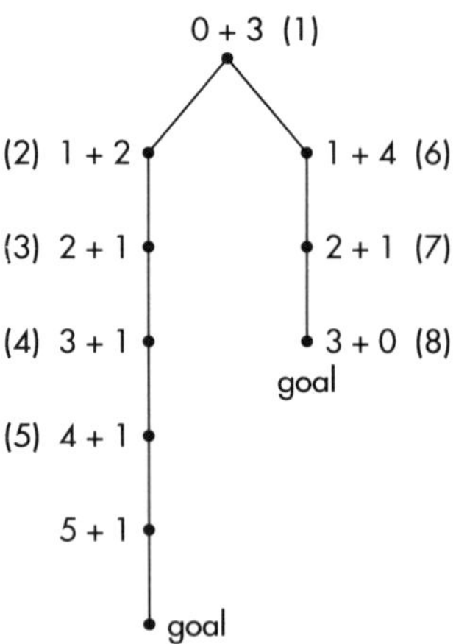

FIGURE 4.9 Finding an optimal solution. The first figure in the sum is the distance from the initial node and the second is the estimated distance to a goal.

10 We will assume throughout that h' is nonnegative, so that $h'(n) \geq 0$ for any node n.

PROCEDURE 4.2.1 **A***

1. *Set L to be a list of the initial nodes in the problem.*
2. *Let* n *be the node on* L *for which* f(n) = g(n) + h′(n) *is minimal. If* L *is empty, fail.*
3. *If* n *is a goal node, stop and return it and the path from the initial node to* n.
4. *Otherwise, remove* n *from* L *and add to* L *all of* n*'s children, labelling each with its path from the initial node. Return to step 2.*

As before, the optimistic value assigned to the left-hand node at depth 1 convinces us to expand this path before the other, since we expect to find a goal node at depth 3 below this node and expect the goal node below the other child to be at depth 5. However, when we actually *reach* depth 5 along the left-hand path and still have not reached the goal, we come to believe that the other path is the better one and examine it instead. The better of the two goal nodes is now found first.

There are two things to note here. The first is that there was no real difference between the nodes labelled (5) and (6) in Figure 4.9; both were expected to lead to goals at depth 5. We chose to expand (5) first because it was thought to be closer to the goal node, but the A* algorithm itself does not require us to make this choice.

The more important thing to note is that there is still no guarantee that A* finds the best solution to any particular search problem. In Figure 4.9, for example, if the node labelled (5) (that is, the one expanded fifth) were a goal node, it would be found before the optimal goal node on the right-hand path. Why is this?

4.2.1 Admissibility

The reason that we avoided expanding the right-hand path in this example is that we have pessimistically labelled the right-hand node at depth 1 with a 4, indicating that we do not expect to find a goal at any depth less than 5 along this path. Given this, we are led to examine the node at depth 4 along the left-hand path before finding the goal at depth 3 on the right-hand side. If the function estimating the distance to the goal had been *optimistic*, this would not have happened.

To formalize this, suppose that we denote by $h(n)$ (without the ′) the *actual* distance from the node n to a goal node. Now the heuristic estimating function h' will be optimistic just in case we always have $h' \leq h$ and in this case we have:

THEOREM 4.2.2 *If* $h'(n) \leq h(n)$ *for every node* n, *the A* algorithm will never return a suboptimal goal node.*

PROOF Suppose that the procedure eventually returns the node x when there was a better goal node s. If the path from the root node to s is

$$\langle n_0, n_1, \ldots, n_k \rangle$$

where $n_k = s$, we will derive a contradiction by showing that if the A* algorithm expands some portion of this path

$$\langle n_0, \ldots, n_i \rangle$$

then it also expands the next node along this path, n_{i+1}. Since the root node n_o is always expanded, it will follow by induction that the node $s = n_k$ is expanded as well, and therefore that s would have been returned instead of x.

Since we have expanded n_i, the parent of n_{i+1}, it is clear that n_{i+1} will be expanded if it appears to be a better node than x is. In other words, if we could show that

$$g(n_{i+1}) + h'(n_{i+1}) < g(x) + h'(x)$$

the inductive step would follow and the proof would be complete. But since h' is optimistic, we must have

$$\begin{aligned} g(n_{i+1}) + h'(n_{i+1}) &\leq g(n_{i+1}) + h(n_{i+1}) \\ &= g(s) \\ &< g(x) \\ &\leq g(x) + h'(x) \end{aligned}$$

The first equality holds because the sum of the costs of getting to n_{i+1} and then from n_{i+1} to the goal node s is just the cost of getting to s directly. The second equality holds because $h(x) = 0$ and $0 \leq h'(x) \leq h(x)$. ■

An optimistic heuristic function h' is called *admissible.*

4.2.2 Examples

As an example, we revisit the search space in Figure 4.9 after modifying the heuristic value assigned to the right-hand node at depth 1 so that the heuristic function is admissible; the result is shown in Figure 4.10. The optimal goal node is indeed found in this case.

There are other examples of interest as well. The "heuristic" function $h'(n) = 0$ is clearly an admissible one, and leads to expanding the nodes simply in order of increasing $g(n)$. Since $g(n)$ is the cost of reaching node n, the A* algorithm reproduces breadth-first search in this case. Since

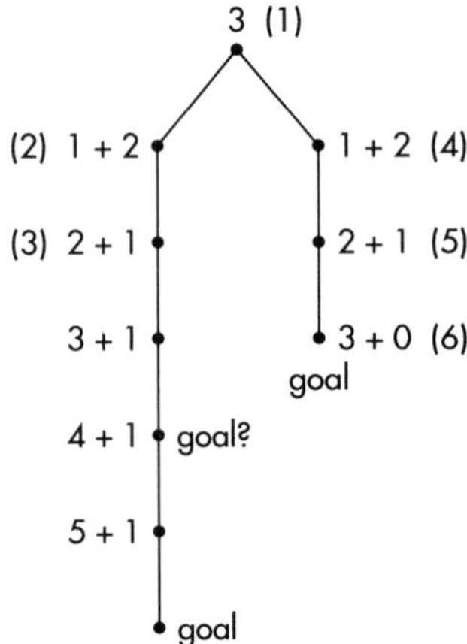

FIGURE 4.10 An admissible heuristic function

depth-first search often fails to find the best solution to a problem, it is clear that there is no admissible heuristic that mimics depth-first search in a similar way.

The perfect heuristic $h' = h$ is also always admissible, and is the topic of Exercise 6 at the end of this chapter.

In specific problems, there are often other admissible heuristics; the 8-puzzle provides a variety of examples. In this puzzle, the simple heuristic of counting the number of misplaced tiles is clearly admissible, since each move can reduce this value by at most one. The Manhattan distance heuristic is also admissible in this domain, since each move relocates only one tile and moves it in such a way that its contribution to the overall heuristic estimate drops by at most one.

Given that both heuristics are admissible, how are we to decide which one to use? Suppose that we denote the Manhattan distance heuristic by h'_M and the heuristic obtained by simply counting tiles by h'_C. Since

$$h'_C \le h'_M \le h$$

we see that h'_M is a better estimate of the true distance to the goal than is h'_C. In general, this means that we should prefer h'_M to h'_C; see also Exercise 12 at the end of this chapter.

Finally, we note that for finite graphs, it is always possible to construct an admissible heuristic function from a potentially inadmissible one by dividing the original heuristic by some large positive number. Of course, we want to choose the constant to be as near to 1 as possible, so that the eventual admissible heuristic is near to the true value h. Thus although counting the number of misplaced or misaligned cubies in Rubik's cube is not an admissible heuristic, this heuristic is admissible after being divided by 8, since each move affects eight cubies. (Unfortunately, the division by 8 tends to make this heuristic too small to be of much use.) The general problem of constructing admissible heuristics from inadmissible ones is open.

4.3 EXTENSIONS AND IDA*

We conclude this chapter by discussing a few extensions to the A* algorithm.

The first situation we consider is that in which the "cost" of a node is not simply its depth in the search space, but is instead evaluated in some other fashion. We will continue to assume that the cost of getting to a node n is the sum of the costs of the individual arcs along the path from the root to n; we simply no longer assume that every arc is of unit cost.

It is now not hard to see that as long as we continue to use $g(n)$ for the cost of reaching the node n, the use of the A* algorithm using the usual evaluation function given by (4.1) continues to find lowest-cost solutions. If we take $h'(n) = 0$ in this case, we get the search procedure known as *branch and bound.*

Next, suppose that we use A* to search a graph instead of a simple tree, as shown in Figure 4.11. Provided that we take $g(n)$ to be the cost of the cheapest path found to the node n thus far and maintain a list of open nodes only, the algorithm remains principally unchanged.

PROCEDURE 4.3.1 **A* on graphs**

1. *Set* L *to be a list of the initial nodes in the problem.*
2. *Let* n *be the node on* L *for which* $f(n) = g(n) + h'(n)$ *is minimal. If* L *is empty, fail.*

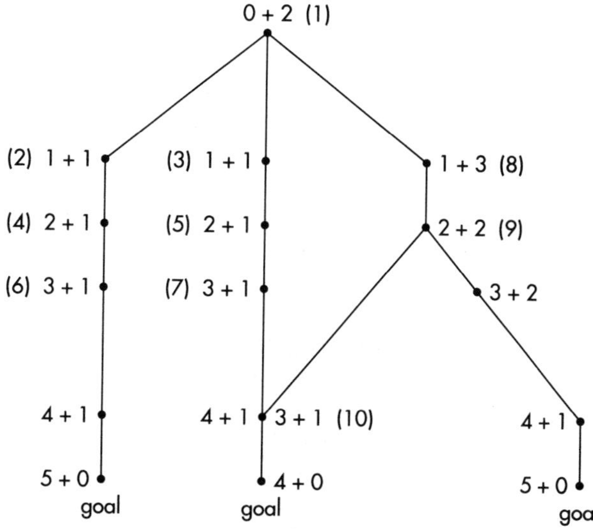

FIGURE 4.11 A* used to search a graph

3. *If* n *is a goal node, stop and return it and the path from the initial node to* n.
4. *Otherwise, remove* n *from* L *and add to* L *all of* n*'s children, labelling each with its path from the initial node. If any child* c *is already on* L, *do not make a separate copy but instead relabel* c *with the shortest path connecting it to the initial node. Return to step* 2.

In the figure, the node that is expanded tenth is initially believed to be at depth 4 but is actually determined to be at depth 3 before it is expanded.

Finally, memory is a problem for the A* algorithm. Since it reduces to breadth-first search if $h' = 0$, we see that A* will potentially use an amount of memory that is exponential in the depth of the optimal goal node.

As in the case of blind search, this problem can be solved using iterative deepening. But now, instead of artificially pruning nodes that lie at a depth below some increasing cutoff, we prune nodes for which the nearest goal node can be shown to lie below the cutoff depth. As in iterative deepening, the cutoff depth is gradually increased until an answer is found.

PROCEDURE 4.3.2 **IDA***

1. *Set* c = 1; *this is the current depth cutoff.*
2. *Set* L *to be a list of the initial nodes in the problem. Set* c′ = ∞; *this will be the cutoff on the next iteration.*
3. *Let* n *be the first node on* L. *If* L *is empty and* c′ = ∞, *fail. If* L *is empty and* c′ ≠ ∞, *set* c = c′ *and return to step* 2.
4. *If* n *is a goal node, stop and return it and the path from the initial node to* n.
5. *Otherwise, remove* n *from* L. *For each child* n′ *of* n, *if* f(n′) ≤ c, *add* n′ *to the front of* L. *Otherwise, set* c′ = min(c′, f(n′)). *Return to step* 3.

It is important to realize that the individual iterations of this algorithm are performed using conventional depth-first search and not using A*; the heuristic function is used to prune nodes but not to determine the order in which they should be expanded. After all, if the original iterations were to be expanded using the A* algorithm, an exponential amount of memory would still be needed! The algorithm is essentially the same as iterative deepening, with the heuristic being used to *anticipate* the nodes that will eventually be pruned because of the depth cutoff.

An example of Procedure 4.3.2 in use appears in Figure 4.12. For $c = 1$ we examine the root node only; for $c = 2$ we examine two nodes and so on. The individual searches are conducted in depth-first fashion, which is why node 12 is expanded before node 14 in the figure even though the

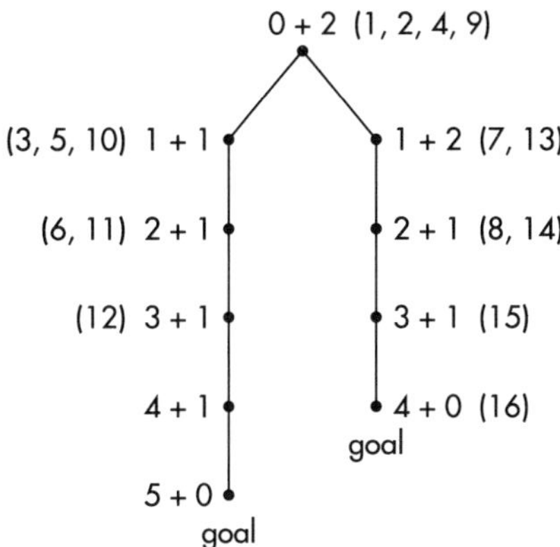

FIGURE 4.12 IDA*

heuristic estimates indicate that node 14 is likely to be the closest to a shallow goal.

Procedure 4.3.2 is known as *iterative-deepening* A^*, or simply IDA*. It is not too hard to show that it uses an amount of memory linear in the depth of the goal node, that it expands only the nodes expanded by A* itself, and that it continues to find optimal solutions when using an admissible heuristic.

4.4 FURTHER READING

Macro operators are discussed by Korf in [1985b]. Simulated annealing was introduced by Kirkpatrick *et al.* [1983]. I am afraid that I can give you no reference for the General Motors application; the work was reported to me personally by the engineer involved. The algorithm itself involves a variety of details that are omitted from the description in the text: An initial temperature needs to be chosen and a protocol needs to be selected by which the temperature is gradually reduced as the search proceeds.

The A* algorithm was developed by Hart, Nilsson, and Raphael [1968]. Although the problem of finding admissible heuristics in arbitrary search domains is open, it has been touched on by a variety of authors; one reasonable reference is Gaschnig [1979]. IDA* is discussed by Korf [1985a].

4.5 EXERCISES

1. Give an example of a search problem where hill climbing and best-first search behave differently.

2. In the text, we stated that the number of macro operators of length l in the 8-puzzle could be approximated by 3^l. Justify this. Can you improve on the estimate in the text?

3. We have defined a *heuristic* search technique to be one that uses domain-specific information; a heuristic function-maximization technique is one that uses information about the function's current value in deciding where to look next. Why is simulated annealing included in this chapter as opposed to the previous one?

4. Describe the similarity between simulated annealing (viewed as a search procedure) and iterative broadening.

5. Suppose that h'_1 and h'_2 are two admissible heuristics in a search problem. Show that $\max(h'_1, h'_2)$ is also admissible. Give an example of a search problem and two admissible heuristic functions, neither of which is always less than the other.

6. What is the behavior of the A* algorithm if $h' = h$? Prove your claim.

7. Write a computer program that implements A* and uses it to find solutions to mazes. Use the program to solve the maze in Figure 4.2.

8. (a) Prove the following generalization of Theorem 4.2.2:

PROPOSITION 4.5.1 *In searching a tree, suppose that* $g(n)$ *is a cost function that increases along the paths from the root node, so that whenever a node* n_1 *is a child of a node* n_2*, then* $g(n_1) \geq g(n_2)$*. Then if* $h'(n) \leq h(n)$ *for every node* n*, any value returned by the A* algorithm will be a goal node for which* g *is minimal.*

   (b) Why did we need to add to the proposition the condition that the A* algorithm return an answer?

9. Prove the following generalization of Theorem 4.2.2:

PROPOSITION 4.5.2 *Suppose that although the distance-estimating function* h' *is not admissible, it is nearly admissible in the sense that there is some small constant* ϵ *such that*

$$h'(n) \leq h(n) + \epsilon$$

for every node n*. The value returned by the A* algorithm will be a goal node for which* g *is within* ϵ *of minimal.*

10. (a) Prove that Procedure 4.3.1 continues to find optimal solutions to search problems.

    (b) How should the procedure be modified if we want to maintain a list of closed nodes as well as a list of open ones?

11. In Exercise 5 in Chapter 3, we defined a search ordering to be depth-first legal if it corresponded to depth-first search. Similarly, for a fixed choice of heuristic function h' we will define a search ordering to be

A legal* if and only if it matches the A* algorithm for this choice of heuristic function. We will say that depth-first search and A* search are *equivalent* if and only if every depth-first legal search ordering is A* legal and vice versa.

Prove that in a domain where every arc is of unit cost, there is a nonnegative heuristic function h' such that depth-first search and A* search are equivalent if the domain being considered has no paths of infinite length and no single node that can be reached by two paths of different lengths. (Note that we do not require the heuristic to be admissible.)

12. This exercise examines the choice between two admissible heuristic functions, one of which is always less than the other.

    Suppose that h_1' and h_2' are two admissible heuristic functions for some domain, and that $h_1'(n) \le h_2'(n)$ for every node n.

    (a) Let S be a search ordering that is A* legal using the heuristic h_1', and suppose that exploring the search space using this ordering involves expanding a set N of nodes. Show that there is some search ordering that is A* legal using the heuristic h_2' that examines a subset of N in solving the problem in question. This shows that it is always *possible* that h_2' leads to a smaller search space than h_1' does.

    (b) Find a search problem and two admissible heuristics h_1' and h_2' with $h_1' \le h_2'$ such that although it is possible that h_2' examines fewer nodes that h_1' does, it is far more likely that h_1' leads to the more efficient search.

13. In what order does IDA* examine the search space associated with the maze appearing in Figure 4.2?

14. Suppose that we modify IDA* as follows:

PROCEDURE 4.5.3

1. Set c = 1; *this is the current depth cutoff.*
2. *Set* L *to be a list of the initial nodes in the problem.*
3. *Let* n *be the first node on* L. *If* L *is empty, increment* c *and return to step 2.*
4. *If* n *is a goal node, stop and return it and the path from the initial node to* n.
5. *Otherwise, remove* n *from* L. *Add to the front of* L *every child* n′ *of* n *for which* f(n′) ≤ c. *Return to step 3.*

Why is the original Procedure 4.3.2 to be preferred?

CHAPTER

5

ADVERSARY SEARCH

This chapter concludes our discussion of search by examining the specific search issues that arise when analyzing game trees.

5.1 ASSUMPTIONS

AI research on game playing typically considers only games that have two specific properties: They are two-person games in which the players alternate moves, and they are games of perfect information, where the knowledge available to each player is the same. There are exceptions to each of these constraints, but most of the work does indeed make these assumptions.

Typical two-person games investigated by AI researchers are tic-tac-toe, checkers, chess, Go, Othello, and backgammon. Other than perhaps Go and Othello, these are probably familiar to you.

Go is played on a 19×19 board with stones of two colors; the object is to place your stones so that they surround those of your opponent. From an AI point of view, it is remarkable for two reasons:

1. The difference between two Go players can be measured quite precisely. A Go player who beats another by a certain margin in one game is very likely to beat him by a nearly identical margin in subsequent games.
2. Computer Go players are currently quite weak. The branching factor is large; perhaps more importantly, Go is a very "positional" game. The best move is (it seems) selected more on the basis of how the position "looks" than on intricate tactical analysis. In those cases where tactical analysis is required, the line that is analyzed is typically of very low branching factor (perhaps $b = 1$) and high depth (ten or more moves by each player).

Othello is played on a checkerboard. The pieces used are black on one

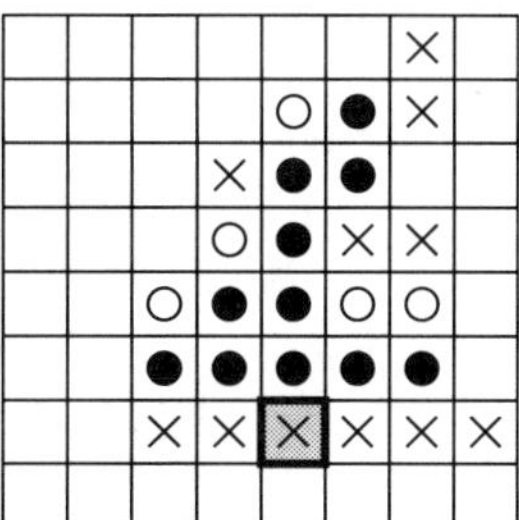
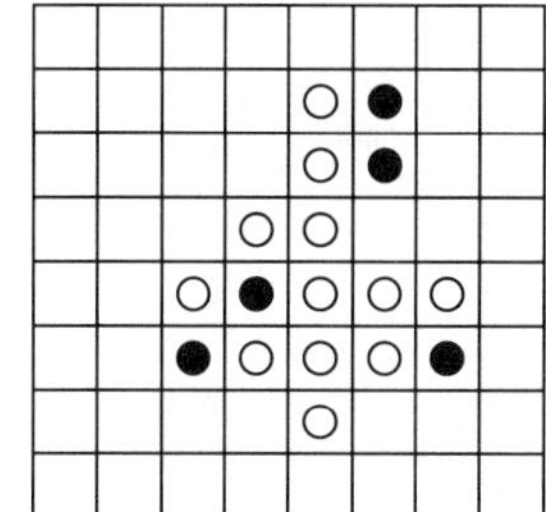

FIGURE 5.1 An Othello position

side and white on the other; a move for White is to place a piece so that a white piece is on each end of some line of Black's pieces. All such black pieces are then flipped and become White's; the object is to end the game with as many pieces of your color as possible. A typical Othello position is shown in Figure 5.1; White's legal moves are denoted by X's. The result if White moves to the square shown in boldface is depicted in the second part of the figure.

Computers are very good at Othello; it is a game that rewards the ability to conduct a brute-force search through one's alternatives and also a game for which it seems to be impossible to recognize a good position at a glance. In fact, computers are significantly better at Othello than people are.

The second assumption made in game search is that the game being considered is one of perfect information. This means that the information available to each of the two players is identical—there is nothing one player knows that the other player could not in principal also know.

Chess is a typical game of perfect information; the differences in beliefs between the two players reflect differing analyses of the position in which they find themselves—not a difference in their raw knowledge about where the pieces are located. Two chess players who disagree about the merits of some particular move will resolve the difference by analyzing the resulting position and not by revealing secrets to one another.

Poker is a classic example of a game of *imperfect* information. Here, one settles a dispute by revealing the contents of one's hand—information that is presumably not available to one's opponent.

Stratego is another game of imperfect information. Each player in this game has an army of pieces of various ranks that attack one another; in each individual battle, the piece of higher rank wins. Although both players know the *locations* of each other's pieces, only blue (for example) knows which blue pieces are of what rank.

In a game such as this, it is often sensible to attack a piece of unknown strength with a weak one; this is not because you expect to win the battle but because you can learn the strength of the opposing piece in this way. This is a typical feature of games of imperfect information—one can expend one's limited resources in order to improve the quality of the information available.

(This sort of activity occurs all the time, not just when playing games. When you stop to buy a paper to find out where some movie is playing, you are expending limited resources—time and money—to improve your knowledge about the behavior of the local theaters. And occasionally—just occasionally—stopping to get the paper will mean that you don't have time to get to the movie; time really is a limited resource that you are expending in order to extend your knowledge in some way.)

Computers make quite good poker players, incidentally. Poker appears to be mostly a matter of working out the probabilities and bluffing with a straight face.

Bridge is another game of imperfect information that has attracted some interest in the AI community. Although there is substantial commercial motivation for developing a competent automated bridge player, the results so far have been disappointing. The reason, it seems, is that bridge is somewhat like Go in that correct bidding and play often hinge (at least initially) upon the sort of pattern recognition that computers find difficult.

The last game of imperfect information that I will mention is called Diplomacy. This is a game where the object is to take over the world by first negotiating treaties with one's fellow players and then breaking them at a suitable moment. Interestingly enough, computers make excellent Diplomacy players once a suitable negotiation language has been developed.

5.2 MINIMAX

Let us return our attention to two-person games of perfect information. We have drawn such a game in Figure 5.2, where we have depicted the game as a tree where the root node is the starting position and the terminal nodes are the ending positions. These terminal nodes are labelled with either 1 or -1 depending on which of the players wins the game.

In a game such as this, one of the players will be trying to get to a node labelled -1, and the other will be trying to get to a node labelled 1. We will call the player trying to achieve an outcome of -1 the *minimizer*, and the other player the *maximizer*. We will assume that it is the maximizer's turn to move in the starting position of Figure 5.2, which corresponds to the root node a.

What is the value of the node o in this position? It's the maximizer's turn, and whatever move he makes will end the game. He can move to either p or r and lose, or he can move to q and win. Assuming that he is playing sensibly, he will obviously choose q. This means that the node o is in fact a win for the maximizer, and can be labelled with 1.

What about node k? Whatever the minimizer does, the maximizer will win—either immediately if the minimizer moves to node n, or in one move if he moves to o. So we can label k with a 1 as well. The node i is different,

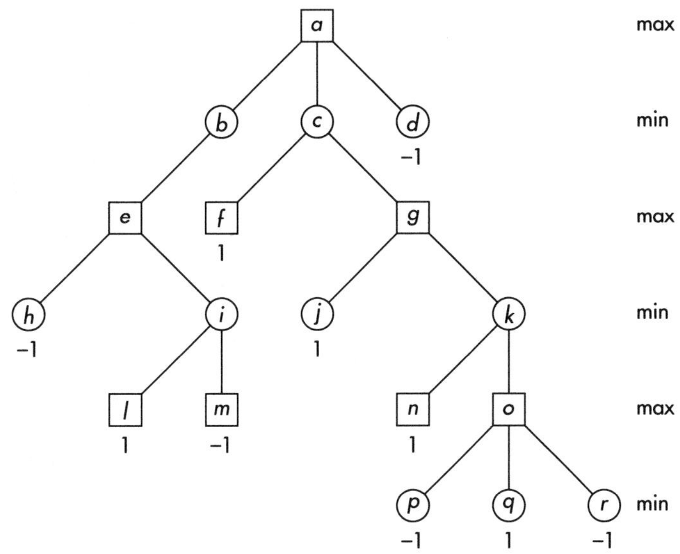

FIGURE 5.2 A simple game tree. Nodes with the maximizer to move are squares; nodes with the minimizer to move are circles.

since here the minimizer has a winning option available (m). So this node should be labelled with a -1.

The algorithm for backing the values up the trees is now apparent. A node with the maximizer to move should be labelled with the *maximum* value that labels any of its children; a node with the minimizer to move should be labelled with the minimum of its children's labels. We have done this in Figure 5.3, and we see from the fact that the starting position is

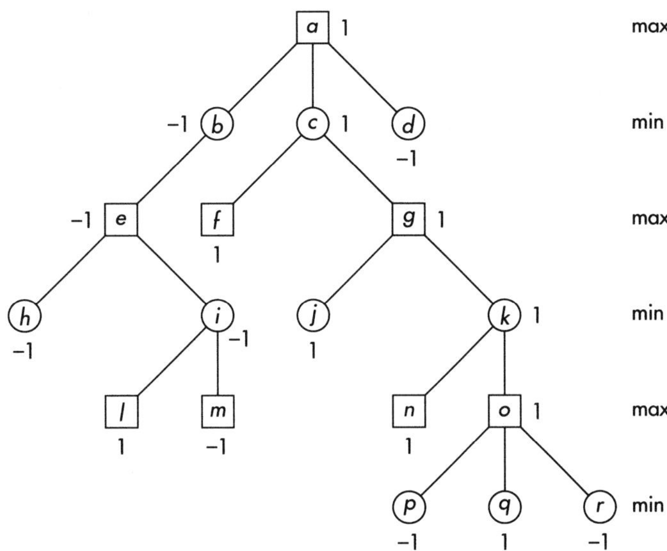

FIGURE 5.3 The maximizer wins

labelled with a 1 that perfect play will win this game for the maximizer. This technique is known as *minimax*.

Before proceeding, suppose that we had continued to back up from the node *k*, determining that g and then *c* had the values 1. We can now stop our analysis and conclude immediately that the value to be assigned to *a* is also 1! The reason is that we know that the maximizer can win from node *a* by moving to node *c*; there is no reason to look for another alternative to this winning line. "Real" games behave similarly; once we find a winning move in a chess game, we typically make that move without examining the alternatives.

Ignoring this possible enhancement, however, here is the basic algorithm for determining the values to be assigned to internal nodes in a game tree.

PROCEDURE 5.2.1

Minimax *To evaluate a node* n *in a game tree:*

1. *Expand the entire tree below* n.
2. *Evaluate the terminal nodes as wins for the minimizer or maximizer.*
3. *Select an unlabelled node all of whose children have been assigned values. If there is no such node, return the value assigned to the node* n.
4. *If the selected node is one at which the minimizer moves, assign it a value that is the minimum of the values of its children. If it is a maximizing node, assign it a value that is the maximum of the children's values. Return to step 3.*

If our game could end in a draw, this would correspond to terminal positions labelled 0 instead of 1 or -1. Draws now fit neatly into the minimax formalism, since each player will pick a winning move if possible and search for a draw if no win exists.

As a matter of terminology, by a *move* in a game tree we will mean a pair of individual actions, one for each player; this is at odds with common usage. An action by only one player is typically called a half-move or a *ply*. Thus the depth of the tree in Figure 5.3 is three moves, or 6 ply.

How much memory and time are needed by the minimax algorithm in Procedure 5.2.1? Since the entire tree needs to be expanded, we can expect this procedure to need an exponential amount of space, as the whole fringe apparently needs to be stored before the values are backed up. A moment's thought reveals, however, that the space needed can be reduced to an amount linear in the depth by searching in a depth-first instead of a breadth-first fashion. Thus in Figure 5.3, we would back the value -1 up to node *b* before expanding the children of node *c*, and so on. This produces the following result, where we update the values assigned to internal nodes as values are assigned to their children:

PROCEDURE 5.2.2

Minimax *To evaluate a node* n *in a game tree:*

1. *Set* $L = \{n\}$, *the unexpanded nodes in the tree.*
2. *Let* x *be the first node on* L. *If* $x = n$ *and there is a value assigned to it, return this value.*
3. *If* x *has been assigned a value* v_x, *let* p *be the parent of* x *and* v_p *the value currently assigned to* p. *If* p *is a minimizing node, set* $v_p = \min(v_p, v_x)$. *If* p *is a maximizing node, set* $v_p = \max(v_p, v_x)$. *Remove* x *from* L *and return to step 2.*
4. *If* x *has not been assigned a value and is a terminal node, assign it the value 1 or* -1 *depending on whether it is a win for the maximizer or minimizer respectively. Assign* x *the value 0 if the position is a draw. Leave* x *on* L *(we still have to deal with its parent) and return to step 2.*
5. *If* x *has not been assigned a value and is a nonterminal node, set* v_x *to be* $-\infty$ *if* x *is a maximizing node and* $+\infty$ *if* x *is a minimizing node. (This is to make sure that the first minimization or maximization in step 3 is meaningful.) Add the children of* x *to the front of* L *and return to step 2.*

Unfortunately, Procedure 5.2.2 continues to use an exponential amount of *time* to determine the value that is assigned to the node *n*. In general, it is simply impractical to expand the whole tree; as an example, we have already remarked in Chapter 1 that the chess tree contains some 10^{160} nodes.[11]

How do people manage to play a game like chess? We don't analyze it all the way to the end; we just look far enough ahead so that we can estimate who's likely to win in some nonterminal position and then back up the values from the nonterminal positions we have found. Minimax still applies; we just apply it to internal nodes in the tree.

In order to do this, we need a way to assign a value to these internal nodes, so that given a node *n* we can label it with some estimated value $e(n)$. If $e(n) = 1$, then we believe absolutely that the node is a win for the maximizer; if $e(n) = -1$, the node is believed to be a win for the minimizer. Intermediate values reflect lower levels of certainty; presumably $e(n) = 0$ is used to label a position in which neither side is perceived to have an advantage, just as $e(n) = 0$ is used to label a *terminal* node that is a draw (that is, a terminal node in which neither player has an advantage).

Crude evaluation functions are often easy to describe. In chess, for example, one can simply add up the values of the pieces each player has (where a pawn counts as 1, a knight 3, a rook 5, and so on according to

11 The *graph* of chess positions is somewhat smaller because many positions can be reached in a variety of ways. It's still intractably large, though.

conventional chess wisdom) and then normalize the result so that a value between -1 and 1 is returned. If the total value of white's pieces is w and the value of blacks is b, we might use

$$\frac{w-b}{w+b} \tag{5.1}$$

as the value to be assigned to the overall position.

There are, however, other features that can be included. In chess, a plan of attack for one player often involves targeting the opponent's pawns. The most natural way to defend a pawn is by using another pawn as shown in Figure 5.4; the white pawn on square a4 defends the one on b5.

In some cases, however, it is impossible to use one pawn to defend another. The white pawn on square d3 in the figure cannot be defended by another pawn, since there are no white pawns on either of the two neighboring files (labelled with c and e in the figure). A pawn with no pawns on adjacent files is called *isolated*, and is a positional flaw whose value has been estimated at $-1/3$ of a pawn.

Positional features abound in chess. How well protected is your king? How much room do you have in which to maneuver? Do you control the center of the board? And so on.

One interesting thing about these positional features is that evaluating them invariably involves more than simply locating a single one of your pieces on the board. Finding your bishops is a matter of simply that—finding them. But finding your isolated pawns involves finding your pawns and then analyzing their positions relative to your other pawns. As a result, including these positional features in the evaluation function makes $e(n)$ more expensive to evaluate, and time spent computing $e(n)$ for the various nodes in the tree is time that cannot be spent searching the tree itself. Here is the base-level/metalevel trade-off again.

FIGURE 5.4 A pawn defending another

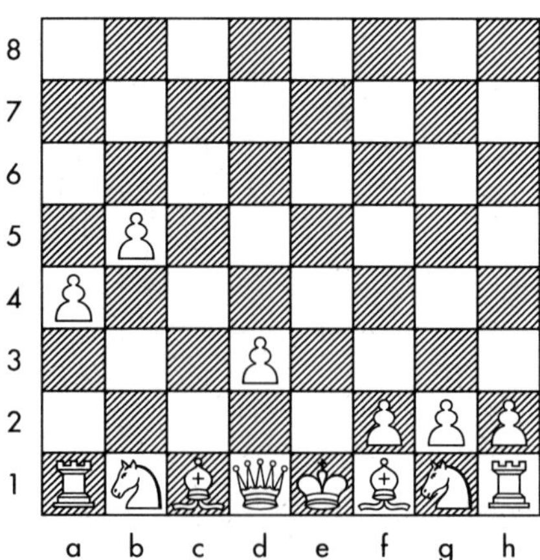

Suppose, however, that we have selected some evaluation function $e(n)$. The modified version of Procedure 5.2.2 is now:

PROCEDURE 5.2.3 **Minimax** *To evaluate a node n in a game tree:*

1. *Set* $L = \{n\}$.
2. *Let* x *be the first node on* L. *If* $x = n$ *and there is a value assigned to it, return this value.*
3. *If* x *has been assigned a value* v_x, *let* p *be the parent of* x *and* v_p *the value currently assigned to* p. *If* p *is a minimizing node, set* $v_p = \min(v_p, v_x)$. *If* p *is a maximizing node, set* $v_p = \max(v_p, v_x)$. *Remove* x *from* L *and return to step 2.*
4. *If* x *has not been assigned a value and* **either** x **is a terminal node or we have decided not to expand the tree further**, *compute its value using the evaluation function. Return to step 2.*
5. *Otherwise, set* v_x *to be* $-\infty$ *if* x *is a maximizing node and* $+\infty$ *if* x *is a minimizing node. Add the children of* x *to the front of* L *and return to step 2.*

The interesting new question is one that is implicit in step 4 of this procedure—how do we select the portion of the search tree to expand? Note that this is an issue only because we expect our evaluation function to be imperfect—we cannot typically look at a chess position and decide who will win without doing some amount of analysis. If our evaluation function *were* somehow perfect, we could simply evaluate the children of the root node and decide from that what to do!

The easiest approach to our computational difficulties is to expand the search to a constant depth, say p ply. The advantage of this is that it's simple—once again, any metalevel effort devoted to intricate decisions about which nodes to expand must be recovered in terms of more effective base-level search. The constant-depth approach is computationally very efficient, but there are several serious problems with it.

5.2.1 Quiescence and Singular Extensions

The first problem is that some portions of a game tree may well be "hotter" than others. A move that leads to tactical considerations involving lengthy exchanges of pieces should probably be investigated in more depth than one that leads to quieter positions. The obvious solution here is to search the tactical portions of the tree to greater depth than the quiet ones, but how are we to recognize these tactical portions automatically?

Tactical portions of the search space are characterized by rapidly changing values of the heuristic evaluation function $e(n)$. In some sense, this is what it *means* for a position to be tactical—single moves by each player drastically affect the apparent value of the position.

This also makes it clear why these portions of the space should be searched to greater depth. Since $e(n)$ is changing rapidly from one ply to the next, the value of $e(n)$ at any particular point is likely to be fairly unreliable; if the tree can be searched to a depth at which $e(n)$ is changing only slowly from ply to ply, this value is more likely to be accurate. The technical term *quiescence* is often used to describe the attempt to search to a depth at which the game becomes fairly quiet.

A related idea that has been implemented to address this concern is that of a *singular extension*. Here, the assumption is made that a particular node should be evaluated to greater depth if one of the opponent's moves leads to a result vastly preferable to him than all other options. The idea is that since this move is "forced" in some sense, the effective branching factor is small, and an extra ply or so of search will be computationally practical. Experimentation has shown that this idea can substantially improve the performance of chess-playing programs.

5.2.2 The Horizon Effect

The second general difficulty with searching a game tree to a fixed depth is known as the *horizon effect*, and is best illustrated by an example.

Suppose that we are searching a chess tree to a depth of 7 ply, and that our opponent has a threat that manifests itself at exactly this depth. We would expect that if we do not respond to the threat, our 7-ply search will reveal the problem and we will therefore be led to a move that addresses it.

But suppose that in the middle of the 7-ply combination, we have some useless move that serves no real purpose other than demanding a response from our opponent. Perhaps we throw in a "nuisance" check, forcing a king move before the rest of the combination can be executed.

The nuisance move hasn't really helped us in any way; in general, such maneuvers tend to make our position worse rather than better. But what the nuisance move *has* done is to make the length of our opponent's combination 9 ply instead of 7. As a result, our 7-ply search will fail to detect the threat when examining the line with the nuisance move in it, and will therefore conclude that the move defeats our opponent's threat! What we have done is to push the culmination of the threat over the search horizon, and mistakenly confused this with the presumably more effective (and necessary) option that deals with the threat instead.

This is a very subtle problem, since it isn't clear how we can distinguish between a move that really *does* neutralize the threat and one that only appears to do so by pushing the threat past the search horizon. The difference is that in the second case, the threat reappears two ply later; in the first case, it doesn't. But determining this involves a search to depth 9, not 7.

(People, of course, deal with this problem by realizing what's going on and determining whether the threat has been addressed or not. But people know what they are doing when they play games; computers are just searching through partial position trees.)

There have been two solutions proposed to the horizon problem; neither is really satisfactory, but we will discuss them both.

Secondary search One proposed solution is to examine the search space beneath the apparently best move to see if something has in fact been pushed just beyond the horizon so that an alternate move should be chosen.

Unfortunately, although this technique can be used to detect the horizon effect, it doesn't really tell us what to do about it. Consider the chess situation again. The move that actually addresses the threat may well appear to be a fairly weak one, since responding to our opponent's threat means that we won't be able to pursue our own intentions.

As a result, if we manage to use this sort of a secondary search to determine that the horizon effect invalidates the apparently best move at a depth of 7 ply, the second-best move is likely to fall prey to the same problem. The move that actually addresses the difficulty is not likely to be expanded until quite late in the search, and there will not be sufficient time to perform secondary searches beneath *all* of these other moves.

The killer heuristic The second idea that can help with the horizon problem is known as the *killer heuristic*. What this suggests is that if you find a move that is good for your opponent, you look at this move early when considering your opponent's options.

This can be combined with the ideas of the previous paragraph as follows: When the apparently best move is found, a secondary search is performed to check it for possible flaws. Let's say that such a flaw is found; our opponent can defeat our 7-ply plan with a particular move at ply 8. We can now do *partial* secondary searches beneath our other alternatives to determine whether or not these alternatives suffer from the same difficulty. By constraining the size of all of the secondary searches except one, some instances of the horizon problem can be avoided.

5.3 α-β SEARCH

The real problem with adversary search, however, is the one that we referred to in our parenthetical remark in the previous section: Computers, playing games, are simply searching through large trees looking for nodes with certain mathematical properties. As a result, most of the nodes examined in the search for a move have no bearing on the course of the game—they are at best pointless and at worst suicidal. Chess-playing programs consider irrelevant pawn moves and meaningless piece sacrifices with the same care that they consider winning combinations or careful positional

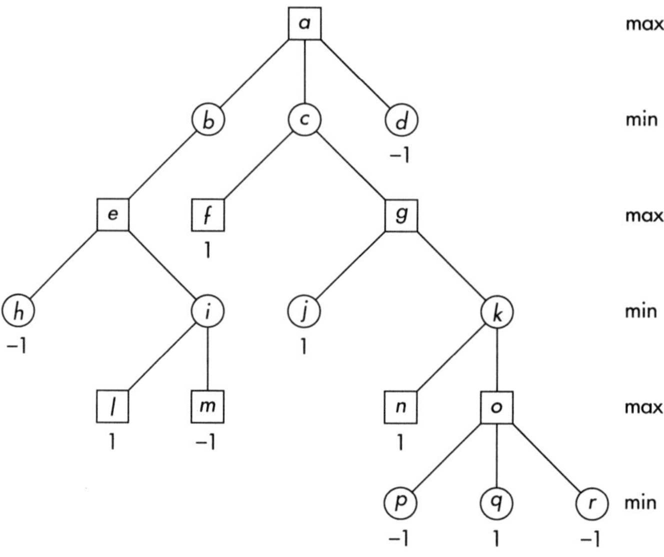

FIGURE 5.5 α-β search: Prune the nodes below *b*

improvements. If we want to improve the performance of these programs, we need a way to reduce the size of the search space.

The most powerful technique known for doing this is called *α-β search*. We've already seen an example of it in Figure 5.3, which we repeat here as Figure 5.5.

What we noticed about the search in Figure 5.5 is that once we realize that the maximizer can win by moving to *c*, we no longer need to analyze any of his other options from *a*. Specifically, the values assigned to all of the nodes under the node *b* are guaranteed not to affect the overall value assigned to the position *a*.

Another example appears in Figure 5.6. Here, we are considering our option *c* of attacking our opponent's queen and are assuming as usual that we are the maximizing player.

If we do attack our opponent's queen, we can be mated at the next move, thereby ending the game and achieving an outcome of -1 (that is, we lose). Clearly, there is no need to consider any of *c*'s other children—we've already seen enough to realize that we should not play *c*!

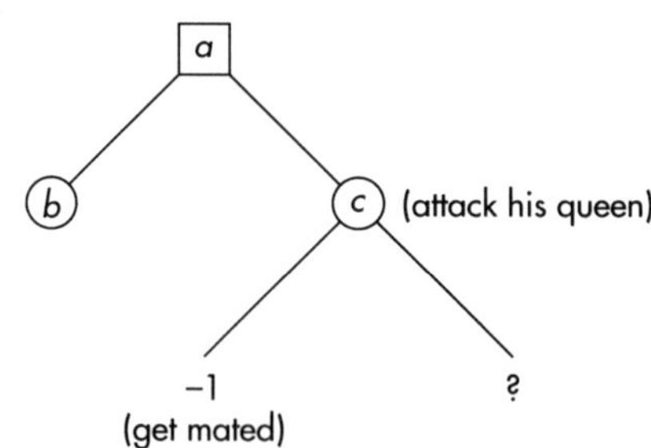

FIGURE 5.6 Another example of α-β search

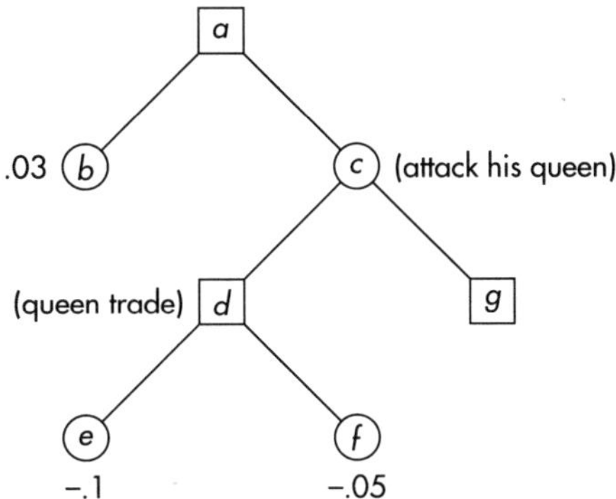

FIGURE 5.7 Another example of α-β search

A slightly more complicated example appears in Figure 5.7. Here, suppose that we are analyzing the tree in a depth-first manner and have determined that the value to be assigned to node *b* is .03, slightly favorable to us. We continue by examining our other option *c*, attacking our opponent's queen with our own.

The first response we consider is *d*, involving an exchange of queens. Further examination of *d*'s children *e* and *f* show that *f* is the better of the two moves, and leads to a backed-up value of $-.05$ for the node *d*.

Before examining node g, suppose that we stop to take stock. Is *c* ever going to be our final selection? If we move to *c*, the *best* result we can expect to obtain is $-.05$, since that's how well we'll do if our opponent replies with *d*. If g is better for our opponent than *d* is, the value to be assigned to *c* will be even *lower* than $-.05$. Why should we accept such a value when we can obtain the outcome of .03 by moving to node *b*?

What we have shown, in effect, is that the node *c* is never on the *main line*, which is the course the game would take if both players played optimally. Since *b* is better for the maximizer than *c* is and the maximizer can select between them, *c* is guaranteed to be avoided. The values assigned to g and the nodes under it can never impact the final value assigned to the node *a*, and the subtree under g can be pruned.

We can reach the same conclusion algebraically. If we denote by g the backed-up value assigned to the node g, then the value assigned to the node *c* will be

$$c = \min(-.05, g)$$

since it is the minimizer who will choose between the alternatives *d* and g.

Continuing, the value assigned to the root node *a* is

$$a = \max[.03, \min(-.05, g)] = .03 \tag{5.2}$$

where the second equality holds because $\min(-.05, g) \leq -.05 < .03$. Since

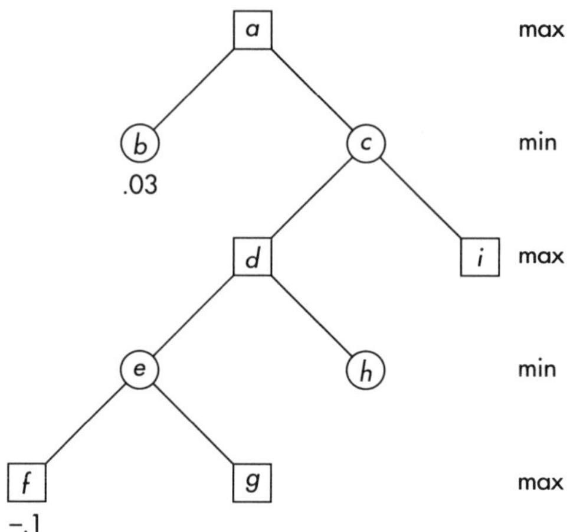

FIGURE 5.8 A deep α-β cutoff

the value assigned to the node *a* is independent of the value g, we see that the nodes below g can be pruned.

A still more complicated example appears in Figure 5.8. Here, the values assigned to *b* and to *f* are .03 and $-.1$ respectively. What can we say about the children of the node g? Can it be shown that g is not on the main line?

Well, if g is going to be on the main line, then its ancestors will need to be as well, so that e will be on the main line. But from e the minimizer has the opportunity to move to node *f* and obtain a payoff of $-.1$. Since this is worse than the payoff of .03 that the maximizer can obtain by moving to *b*, it follows that g cannot be on the main line. Note that it is still possible that *h* is on the main line, or that *i* is—all we can say for sure is that g is *not*. A situation such as this, where the pruned node is more than one ply below the reason for the pruning, is typically referred to as *deep* α-β pruning.

What about the general case? Suppose that *n* is some node in a game tree at which the maximizer gets to move (like the node g in Figure 5.8), and that s is a sibling of *n* with backed-up value v_s (s would be the node *f* in the above figure, so that $v_s = -.1$). Suppose also that $\langle p_0, p_1, \ldots, p_k \rangle$ is the path from the root node down to *n*, with p_0 the root node and $p_k = n$. Now note that the nodes with odd indexes (p_1, p_3, and so on) are minimizing nodes; if any of these nodes has a sibling with backed-up value greater than v_s, then the node *n* can be pruned. (In the figure, $p_1 = c$ has the sibling *b* with backed-up value $.03 > v_s$.) Here is another way to put it.

PROCEDURE 5.3.1 **α-β search** *To evaluate a node* n *in a game tree:*

1. *Set* $L = \{n\}$.
2. *Let* x *be the first node on* L. *If* $x = n$ *and there is a value assigned to it, return this value.*

3. *If x has been assigned a value v_x, let p be the parent of x; if x has not been assigned a value, go to step 5. We first determine whether or not p and its children can be pruned from the tree: If p is a minimizing node, let α be the maximum of all the current values assigned to siblings of p and of the minimizing nodes that are ancestors of p. (If there are no such values, set $\alpha = -\infty$.) If $v_x \leq \alpha$, remove p and all of its descendants from L. If p is a maximizing node, treat it similarly.*

4. *If p cannot be pruned, let v_p be the value currently assigned to p. If p is a minimizing node, set $v_p = \min(v_p, v_x)$. If p is a maximizing node, set $v_p = \max(v_p, v_x)$. Remove x from L and return to step 2.*

5. *If x has not been assigned a value and is either a terminal node or we have decided not to expand the tree further, compute its value using the evaluation function. Return to step 2.*

6. *Otherwise, set v_x to be $-\infty$ if x is a maximizing node and $+\infty$ if x is a minimizing node. Add all of the children of x to the front of L and return to step 2.*

The value corresponding to α but computed by considering p's maximizing ancestors is called β; the two values lead to α and β cutoffs respectively. Because of this, this method of reducing the size of the search tree is called *α-β pruning*. It's a pretty dumb name.

All of this is well and good, but what does it buy us? Although we have seen that α-β pruning can reduce the size of the search space associated with a game tree, we haven't discussed by how *much* the search space is reduced.

It is clear, for example, that in the worst case it is possible that α-β pruning fails to reduce the size of the search space at all. If we perversely order the children of every node so that the worst options are evaluated first, then the nodes examined later will always be the "main line" and will therefore never be pruned.

What about the best case? What if we somehow manage to order the nodes so that the best moves are examined first? We will still need to search the space to confirm that these actually *are* the best moves, but now α-β pruning can save us a great deal of work.

How much is saved? Suppose that we consider a response for the minimizer that is off the main line. In order to prune it, we need to examine just enough of the search space to demonstrate that it is a mistake for the minimizer—in other words, we have to examine the "refutation" of this move that shows how the maximizer can exploit it. In order to do this, we have to examine only one response on the maximizer's part—the best one. Then we have to examine all of the minimizer's options, the maximizer's best response to each, and so on. So although the branching factor for the minimizer is unchanged, the branching factor for the maximizer is reduced to just 1.

If the maximizer deviates, the analysis is similar, but with the roles of the two players reversed. It follows that the *total* number of nodes that we need to examine to depth d is approximately

$$b^{d/2} + b^{d/2} \tag{5.3}$$

where b is the branching factor in the game. The two terms correspond to analysis of the situations where the maximizer and minimizer deviate respectively. In each case, the search to depth d involves $d/2$ nodes with b children and $d/2$ nodes with only one child. Thus the size of the associated search space is $b^{d/2}$ and the expression (5.3) follows.

Instead of searching a space of size b^d, we need to search one of size $2b^{d/2}$; this is potentially a tremendous savings. It is frequently described in terms of an "effective" branching factor, the branching factor b' such that b'^d is the size of the space searched. In this case, we have

$$b'^d = 2b^{d/2}$$

leading to

$$b' = 2^{1/d}\sqrt{b} \approx \sqrt{b}$$

so that the effective branching factor is approximately the square root of the actual branching factor. Yet another way to look at this is to realize that in this best case, α-β pruning allows us effectively to double the depth to which we can search in a fixed amount of time.

These observations mean that it is very important when using α-β search to do a good job of ordering the children of any particular node. A variety of methods exist for this—the evaluation function can be applied to the internal nodes to order them heuristically, the killer heuristic discussed in Section 5.2.2 can be used to move nodes that work well elsewhere to the front of the list of children, and so on.

In practice, this turns out to be an effective way to approximately order the internal nodes when searching a game tree using α-β pruning. Sophisticated chess programs, for example, typically investigate only 1½ times the theoretically minimal number of nodes using this method. We can come quite close to the theoretical limits described above.

5.4 FURTHER READING

The world's best Othello player is a computer program called BILL [Lee and Mahajan, 1990]. The Diplomacy player mentioned in the text is described in Kraus and Lehmann [1988].

Games that violate the typical AI assumptions by involving more than two players, simultaneous action, or including imperfect information are typically the focus of game theorists or economists and not computer scientists; a good introduction to game theory is Luce and Raiffa [1957]. Recently, some authors interested in *distributed* AI (the study of how our putatively intelligent artifacts will interact with one another) have observed that many game-theoretic results can be applied if these independent agents are viewed as players in a formal multiagent game. The work of Genesereth *et al.* [1986] and Rosenschein and Genesereth [1985], reprinted in Bond and Gasser [1988], is typical of this approach.

Singular extensions are introduced by Anantharaman *et al.* [1990] and are believed by many researchers to be the main reason that the chess program DEEP THOUGHT outperforms its predecessor, HITECH.

We remarked in the text that the techniques used to order the search in existing game-playing programs result in their behavior approximating that of the best-case analysis we have presented. As we have explained, this best case doubles the effective search depth; the worst case multiplies it by 1 (that is, leaves it unchanged). It is shown in Pearl [1982] that if the children of a node are randomly ordered, the effective search depth is multiplied by a factor of approximately 4/3.

5.5 EXERCISES

1. The work on game search assumes that deeper searches are more accurate than shallow ones, so that a search algorithm can improve its performance by searching to greater depth. Either prove this to be true or find a game and evaluation function for which it fails, in the sense that the result returned becomes uniformly less accurate as the search deepens. (Search to terminal nodes doesn't count, of course, since it always evaluates correctly.)
2. Consider the chess evaluation function given by (5.1).
   (a) Under what circumstances will this evaluation function take the values $+1$, -1, or 0?
   (b) What material value should be assigned to a king if this evaluation function is used?
   (c) The conventional wisdom in chess is that if you are a pawn ahead, you should try to exchange other pieces so that your extra pawn has a more substantial effect. Does (5.1) support this idea?
3. What might be a sensible heuristic evaluation function for checkers? Consider only the number of men and kings each side has.
4. What modifications should be made to Procedure 5.2.3 to take advantage of the fact that the space being searched may be a graph instead

of a tree? The hash table used to store the closed nodes in this case is usually called a *transposition table* because it is intended to deal with the fact that transposing moves often leads to identical positions in game search.

5. Suppose that generating the children of a node in a game tree takes time g, and that we are considering using one of two evaluation criteria, $e_1(n)$ or $e_2(n)$, that take times t_1 and t_2 to evaluate, respectively. If the branching factor of the tree is b and $t_1 < t_2$, under what conditions will the time needed to search to depth d using e_1 be the same as the time needed to search to depth $d - 1$ using e_2? How about for α-β search, where both heuristics are nearly good enough to order the moves optimally? For which of these two approaches is it more important that the heuristic evaluation function be quick to evaluate?

6. Write a computer program that uses minimax to play a perfect game of tic-tac-toe. Modify your program to use α-β pruning as well.

7. Use Procedure 5.3.1 to show explicitly that the following nodes and their children can be pruned from the search space:
   (a) Node c in Figure 5.6.
   (b) Node c in Figure 5.7.
   (c) Node e in Figure 5.8.

8. Give an algebraic proof that the node g in Figure 5.8 can be pruned, similar to the derivation involving equation (5.2).

9. Use mathematical induction to prove that Procedure 5.3.1 never prunes a node that is needed to compute the value of the root node.

10. Give a "real" example of a deep α-β prune in a game such as chess.

11. Construct a search tree in which the size of the search space can be reduced by applying α-β pruning to both the maximizer and the minimizer.

12. Describe explicitly the way in which p should be treated in step 3 of Procedure 5.3.1 if it is a maximizing node.

13. Suppose that we are using α-β pruning to determine the value of a move in a game tree, and that we have decided that a particular node n and its children can be pruned. If the game tree is in fact a graph and there is another path to the node n, are we still justified in pruning this node? Either prove that we are or construct an example that shows that we cannot.

14. Suppose that instead of labelling a node with a single value, we label it with a *pair* of values $(a, -a)$ that sum to 0. The first value is the

"payoff" to the first player, and the second is the payoff to the second player.

(a) How should minimax be modified to deal with the new labels?

(b) How can these labels be extended to deal with three-player games where the order in which the players move is fixed?

(c) Is there an analog to shallow α-β pruning in three-player games? How about deep α-β pruning?

15. Describe a search technique that might be called *iterative deepening α-β search*. Why might you expect this technique to expand fewer nodes than conventional α-β search?

PART

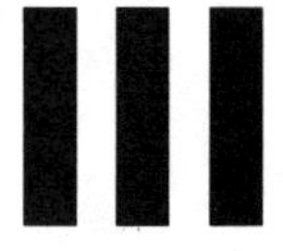

KNOWLEDGE REPRESENTATION: LOGIC

CHAPTER

6

INTRODUCTION TO KNOWLEDGE REPRESENTATION AND LOGIC

6.1 A PROGRAMMING ANALOGY

In Chapter 2, I said, "The intended role of knowledge representation in artificial intelligence is to reduce problems of intelligent action to search problems." Suppose that we look at this claim in a bit more detail.

In order to do so, I would like to draw an analogy between AI problems and more conventional computer programming tasks. When you write a program to solve some problem, you do four things:

1. Devise an algorithm to solve the problem.
2. Select a programming language in which that algorithm can be encoded.
3. Capture the algorithm in a program.
4. Run the program.

Getting a computer to solve a problem of intelligence (like the Christmas-shopping example discussed earlier) involves four quite similar steps:

1. Identify the knowledge needed to solve the problem.
2. Select a language in which that knowledge can be represented.
3. Write down the knowledge in that language.
4. Use the consequences of the knowledge to solve the problem.

It is the final step here that typically involves search—as we will see in Chapter 9 and elsewhere, determining the consequences of our knowledge involves search. The first three steps are what we previously combined into the claim that knowledge representation is used to reduce problems requiring *intelligence* to problems requiring *search*.

Interestingly enough, this analogy can be pushed further, as shown in the following examples.

The first and third steps are harder than the other two The differences between programming languages are fairly well understood; this is a consequence of the fact that the languages themselves have a well-defined syntax and agreed-upon meaning. Beyond this, however, programming is something of a black art: There is all too little fundamental knowledge about how to select an algorithm to solve a problem or how to encode this algorithm in any particular programming language.

Knowledge representation is similar. The existing languages used for knowledge representation all have a well-defined syntax, and sentences in these languages have agreed-upon meanings. But there is no general understanding of exactly what knowledge we bring to bear to solve specific problems, and there is little known about how any particular bit of knowledge is to be encoded in any particular language.

The upshot of this is that in the material that follows, we focus our discussion on the nature of knowledge representation languages themselves—their syntax and the meaning of statements expressed in such languages. We discuss their strengths and weaknesses and present examples of their use, but can present little guidance on the more general questions of how to decide what knowledge to use in solving a problem and how that knowledge is to be encoded.

The variable names don't matter Consider the following two BASIC programs:

```
10  LET A = 100
20  PRINT A
30  END

10  LET XDFSJAJE001 = 100
20  PRINT XDFSJAJE001
30  END
```

Is there any difference between them? Of course not; the fact that we have called the variable A in one program and XDFSJAJE001 in the other is irrelevant to their functioning.

In a similar way, the names of symbols appearing in sentences in a knowledge representation language are also irrelevant. Suppose that we have somehow managed to assign a meaning to the sentence

$$\texttt{my-friend}(x) \rightarrow \texttt{send-birthday-card}(x) \qquad (6.1)$$

We might interpret this as saying that if some object x is a friend, then we should send x a birthday card. The point is that there is no difference in principle between (6.1) and

$$\texttt{p001(x)} \rightarrow \texttt{p002(x)} \qquad (6.2)$$

because the language in which we are working presumably doesn't recognize the difference between `my-friend` and `p001`.

Just as (6.1) is no different from (6.2), it is also no different from

$$\texttt{my-enemy(x)} \rightarrow \texttt{send-birthday-card(x)}$$

What makes `my-friend` different from `my-enemy` is not the characters used, but *other* information about friends and enemies that appears in the database of knowledge. What makes a variable in one program different from a variable in another is the collection of all references to the two variables in the two programs; knowledge representation is similar.

The variables mean something When you write a computer program, the variables appearing in the code typically refer to specific objects within the algorithm. A loop might have a counter indicating how many times the code has been executed; what you aren't likely to find is a variable that is (for example) the bitwise disjunction of every value taken by the program counter when a division occurs.

This idea, too, has an analog in AI—the objects appearing in our sentences should have identifiable referents in the real world. When the phrase `my-friend` is used in (6.1), an implicit claim is made that there is some identifiable feature of our environment that we would like to call "my friend." Even in (6.2), the term `p001` is expected to refer to a specific property of objects in our environment.

We have already seen this notion in Chapter 1, where we described it as the *declarativist* assumption. We also remarked there that although the declarativist idea underlies virtually all work on knowledge representation, it doesn't underlie all of the work in AI as a whole. Neural networks, for example, are not declarative because the signals they propagate need not refer to identifiable properties of the domain being analyzed.

But let us return to the easy two steps of the programming process: Selecting a language to use and understanding the notion of entailment that language includes. The structure of the sentences in our language is referred to as the *syntax* of that language, while the meaning is called its *semantics*. In this chapter, we describe the syntax and semantics of a specific language that can be used to represent facts about our world (or about a game such as chess, or a wide variety of other things). This is the language of first-order logic; we will see in Part IV that many other languages can be used as well.

6.2 SYNTAX

As we have remarked, sentences in logic are intended to tell us things about the world. As such, they need to *mention* things in the world. These things can be either objects or properties of objects. Thus if I tell you that Wendy is tall, I am referring to an *object* (Wendy) and a *property* (tall).

How about if I tell you that Jimmy Durante has a big nose? Well, bigness is a property, just like tallness. And "Durante's nose" is an object in my universe, just like Wendy. But when I say "Durante's nose," you interpret it not in terms of a specific object, but in a functional way—there is this function (let's call it `nose-of`) that you apply to Durante to construct the object "Durante's nose" from the object "Durante."

There are all sorts of functions like this; you can construct Durante's mother-in-law, or his house, or the president's favorite shoes, or what have you. By applying "properties" to these objects, it is possible to make all sorts of statements about the world in which we live. The properties are actually called *relations* or *predicates*, and we will typically write them in a functional way. Thus to say that Wendy is tall we would write

`tall(Wendy)`

To say that Durante's nose is big, we would write

`big(nose-of(Durante))` (6.3)

The notational convention we are using here is that functions end in `-of`, while predicates do not. This allows us to distinguish the *function* `nose-of` from the *predicate* `big` in (6.3). Functions and predicates are alike in that they must both be applied to objects in our domain, and not to complete sentences in our language.

Of course, predicates can take more than just one argument. We might denote the fact that Ginsberg loves his dog as

`loves(Ginsberg, dog-of(Ginsberg))` (6.4)

These, then, are the fundamental components of sentences in first-order logic: Object constants such as `Ginsberg`, function constants like `dog-of`, and relation constants like `loves`. Object constants name things in our domain of discourse (such as Ginsberg). Function constants map objects in this domain (for example, Ginsberg) into other objects (for example, Ginsberg's dog). Relation constants can be used to describe facts about these objects. The arguments to a function constant must be objects in our domain; the function returns another object of this domain. A relation constant accepts objects as arguments and returns either true or false.

Sentences like the one appearing in (6.4) are the basic building blocks of first-order logic. "Basic" sentences such as this one are called *atoms*.

DEFINITION 6.2.1 *An* atom *is the expression formed by applying a relation constant to a set of objects in our domain.*

Most of logic involves combining atoms into more complex sentences. Thus, for example, we might say that Ginsberg *doesn't* love his dog. (Except that would be wrong!) We would write that as

```
¬loves(Ginsberg,dog-of(Ginsberg))
```

where the operator ¬ serves to negate the sentence (6.4) in just the desired way.

Or we might combine two sentences conjunctively, saying that Ginsberg loves both his dog and his country. We would write this as

```
loves(Ginsberg,dog-of(Ginsberg))
   ∧loves(Ginsberg, country-of(Ginsberg))          (6.5)
```

Note that we do *not* write

```
loves(Ginsberg, dog-of(Ginsberg)∧country-of(Ginsberg))
```

where we have passed the conjunction operator ∧ into the second argument of `loves`.

The reason is that we are only allowed to conjoin *sentences*. When we write the subexpression

```
dog-of(Ginsberg)∧country-of(Ginsberg)
```

we are trying to conjoin two *objects*, not two sentences. (`dog-of (Ginsberg)` is an object because it refers to a thing instead of making a claim of some sort. (6.4) is a sentence and not an object.) The rules of logic say that we are allowed to operate only on *sentences* with operators like ¬ and ∧.

We can also combine sentences disjunctively; perhaps Ginsberg loves either his country or his dog:

```
loves(Ginsberg, dog-of(Ginsberg))
   ∨loves(Ginsberg, country-of(Ginsberg))          (6.6)
```

Note, incidentally, that the sense of the disjunction in (6.6) does not preclude my loving both my country *and* my dog. As a result, (6.6) is strictly weaker than (6.5), in the sense that any time (6.5) holds, (6.6) will as well. (6.6) is similarly weaker than (6.4).

The other logical operator that we will introduce is that of *implication*. Suppose that Ginsberg's dog is the national mascot of the United States, so that if Ginsberg loves his country, then he'll love his dog as well. We will write $\rightarrow$ for the connective describing this if-then relationship, so we get:

$$\begin{array}{l}\texttt{loves(Ginsberg, country-of(Ginsberg))} \\ \quad \rightarrow \texttt{loves(Ginsberg, dog-of(Ginsberg))}\end{array} \qquad (6.7)$$

There are a couple of things to note here. The first is that the connective $\rightarrow$ is not commutative; if p and q are two sentences, then $p \rightarrow q$ means something much different than $q \rightarrow p$ (think about the dog example). This is unlike the connectives $\wedge$ and $\vee$.

The second thing to note is that the meaning that we will assign to $\rightarrow$ is not the same as the typical "conversational" meaning people assign to implication. If the premise (or antecedent) of (6.7) is true (so that Ginsberg really does love his country), then the meaning we will assign to (6.7) is indeed the usual one: The compound sentence is true if and only if the consequent (that Ginsberg loves his dog) is also true. But if the antecedent is false (so that Ginsberg doesn't love his country after all), we will say that the compound sentence is true *independent of the truth or falsity of the truth of the conclusion*. Thus, the sentence, "If pigs can fly, Ginsberg loves his dog," is true simply because pigs can't fly. The sentence, "If pigs can fly, Ginsberg doesn't love his dog," is *also* true.[12]

From a commonsense point of view, this is bizarre. Normally, when people make a statement of the form $p \rightarrow q$ for two sentences p and q, they are implying that there is a causal connection between p and q. Our definition of $\rightarrow$ seems to be designed almost intentionally to be *independent* of the relationship between p and q.

In fact, this is exactly the case. As we will see in the next section, first-order logic is designed so that the following rule is valid:

> *The truth or falsity of a compound sentence* s *can be determined from the truth or falsity of the component sentences of* s.

In other words, to determine if $p \rightarrow q$ is true or not, all you need to know is whether p is true or not, and whether q is true or not. You do *not* need to know about the relationship between the two sentences. Put yet another way, the meanings of the connectives are "truth-functional" in that they can be described as functions on the truth values of their arguments.

12 One of mathematics' urban legends involves a philosopher—rumored to be Russell—attempting to explain this idea to a colleague who refused to accept it. The colleague said, "So falsehood implies anything? Fine. $2 = 1$. Prove that John over there is the pope." Russell replied—without missing a beat—"John and the pope are two, therefore John and the pope are one." It's the without missing a beat that strikes me as so impressive.

The language that we have described thus far, consisting of atoms and the four connectives $\neg$, $\vee$, $\wedge$, $\rightarrow$, is typically called *predicate* logic. To extend it to *first-order* logic, we need to add quantifiers.

The purpose of quantification is to allow us to say things about *sets* of constants. If we want to say that Ginsberg loves everything, we don't want to make "everything" an object constant—that would be like conjoining the individual objects that appear in our universe of discourse. Instead, we introduce a variable (say x), and say that for any value of that variable, Ginsberg loves it:[13]

$$\forall x.\texttt{loves}(\texttt{Ginsberg}, x) \tag{6.8}$$

The symbol $\forall$ appearing in (6.8) is called a *quantifier* and indicates that the given sentence has to remain true as we allow the variable x to range over all of the objects in our language. The period following the quantifier doesn't really mean much of anything (and you might well not see it in a more formal text), but we'll use it on occasion to separate the variable being quantified from the sentence in which that variable appears.

Quantifiers can accept multiple arguments if we want to quantify over several variables at once. So instead of

$$\forall x.\forall y.\texttt{loves}(x,y)$$

we might write simply

$$\forall xy.\texttt{loves}(x,y)$$

Just as our other connectives applied only to sentences, so do quantifiers. Thus if we wanted to say that Ginsberg loves all fuzzy things, we would write that for any object f, if f is fuzzy then Ginsberg loves it:

$$\forall f.[\texttt{fuzzy}(f) \rightarrow \texttt{loves}(\texttt{Ginsberg}, f)] \tag{6.9}$$

The result of applying the quantifier is a sentence and not an object, so we cannot reexpress (6.9) as

$$\texttt{loves}(\texttt{Ginsberg},\forall f.\texttt{fuzzy}(f))$$

The second argument to `loves` has to be an object, not a sentence.

13 Our notation is that variables are denoted by lower-case italic letters and object constants are denoted by sequences (usually capitalized) in typewriter font. Thus x is a variable while `Ginsberg` is an object constant. Functions and relations (which are always constant in the language of first-order logic) may be capitalized or not; functions end in the characters `-of`.

How reasonable is it to think of quantifiers as big conjunctions? Pretty reasonable, since if the only objects in our universe are (say) "Democrat" and "Republican," then the quantified sentence

$$\forall x.\texttt{political-party}(x)$$

really is equivalent to the sentence

$$\texttt{political-party(Republican)} \wedge \texttt{political-party(Democrat)} \tag{6.10}$$

Other examples might not be so simple, however. If our universe contains infinitely many objects (the integers, for example), there isn't any way to translate a sentence such as

$$\forall i\ [\texttt{odd}(i) \vee \texttt{even}(i)] \tag{6.11}$$

into a finite conjunction or disjunction such as (6.10). As usual, the disjunction in (6.11) is between two sentences (albeit sentences containing variables) and not between two objects.

The other quantifier used in first-order logic is an *existential* quantifier denoted by ∃. (The quantifier ∀ is called a *universal* quantifier.) If we only want to say that Ginsberg loves *something*, we would write

$$\exists x.\texttt{loves(Ginsberg, x)}$$

There is one final thing to be said about quantifiers before turning to other matters. If you look at the examples, the quantified variable is always ranging over *object* constants; in other words, the quantification is always over the objects in our domain and never over functions (such as `dog-of` or `country-of`) or relations (such as `loves`). This restriction is important; relaxing it produces sentences of what is known as *second*-order logic.

6.3 SEMANTICS

This is all well and good, but there isn't much value to saying what sentences belong to a language unless we also say what those sentences *mean*. Whether or not a particular sentence p is well-formed as a sentence of first-order logic is a matter of *syntax*; it's something that you can tell by examining the sentence itself. But what that sentence means is a matter of *semantics*; to understand this, we have to consider things a bit more carefully.

Suppose that our first-order language had no logical connectives at all, just object, function, and relation constants. In that case, the sentences in our language would simply be what we called *atoms* in Section 6.2, and there wouldn't really be any relation between them because we wouldn't be able to express these relations. Thus, for example, the sentences rich(Tom) and poor(Tom) would be consistent with one another because we would be unable to state the restriction

$$\forall x.\texttt{poor}(x) \rightarrow \neg\texttt{rich}(x)$$

or more specifically

$$\texttt{poor(Tom)} \rightarrow \neg\texttt{rich(Tom)}$$

In fact, if we denote by A the set of all atoms in our impoverished language, it's pretty obvious that any subset of A will be consistent, since we can't have any information that would allow us to conclude otherwise. Such a subset of A is called a *model*.

DEFINITION 6.3.1 *A* model *is a subset of the set of atoms in our language.*

A lot of people think that first-order logic is somehow confusing or difficult. Well, Definition 6.3.1 is probably the hardest thing about first-order logic, so perhaps it's not as worrisome as you might believe.

What does a *model* mean? Since we've never really said what *any* sentence in first-order logic "means," we can define a model to mean whatever we want. Here's the definition that we will use.

By a model $M \subset A$, *we will mean the state of affairs in which all of the atoms in* M *are true and all of the atoms not in* M *are false.*

As an example, suppose that Tom is our only object constant, and that we have two relation constants, rich and poor. Now

$$A = \{\texttt{rich(Tom)}, \texttt{poor(Tom)}\}$$

is the set of atoms in our language, and there are four models. In $M = \emptyset$, Tom is neither rich nor poor. In $M = \{\texttt{rich(Tom)}\}$, he's rich and not poor; in $M = \{\texttt{poor(Tom)}\}$, it's the other way around. The last model has $M = A$ and corresponds to the situation in which Tom is both rich and poor. This doesn't make sense from an intuitive point of view, but we really haven't said anything to disallow it.

Note that models are always completely committed regarding the truth or falsity of any atom in our language—if the atom is in the model, it's true. If it isn't in the model, it's false. As we will see in Exercise 7 at the end of this chapter, this remark applies to compound sentences as well.

Given a model M, it is obviously straightforward to decide whether or not some particular atom a is true in M: it's true if $a \in M$ and false if $a \notin M$.

What makes first-order logic so powerful, however, is that we can also determine whether or not *compound* sentences (sentences that are not atoms) are true or false in M.

As an example, suppose that we have the sentence $a_1 \wedge a_2$ for two atoms a_1 and a_2. Since this sentence is true if and only if the two component sentences are, we will say that $a_1 \wedge a_2$ is true in a model M if a_1 is true in M and a_2 is also true in M. In all other cases, $a_1 \wedge a_2$ is false in M. Of course, there is no real reason to restrict the component sentences to be atoms; they could be anything. So we'll say that a conjunction $p \wedge q$ is true in a model M if and only if p and q are true in M individually.

Other connectives are similar. The sentence $\neg p$ is true in M if and only if p itself is *not* true in M (that is, $\neg p$ is true if and only if p is false). The disjunction $p \vee q$ is true if and only if at least one of p or q is true. Finally, $p \rightarrow q$ is true just in case either p is false (since falsehood implies anything) or q is true.

As an example, consider the sentence

$$\texttt{poor(Tom)} \rightarrow \neg\texttt{rich(Tom)} \tag{6.12}$$

In which models is this true?

In the model in which Tom is neither rich nor poor, the antecedent of (6.12) fails and the sentence itself therefore holds; the same thing can be said of the model in which Tom is rich and not poor.

In the model in which he is poor and not rich, since `rich(Tom)` is false, ¬`rich(Tom)` is true and the conclusion of (6.12) is valid, so once again (6.12) holds. But in the final model in which Tom is both rich and poor, the antecedent of (6.12) holds but the conclusion doesn't, so (6.12) fails in this case (and this case alone).

PROPOSITION 6.3.2 *For any two sentences* p *and* q, *the two sentences* $\mathrm{p} \rightarrow \mathrm{q}$ *and* $\neg\mathrm{p} \vee \mathrm{q}$ *are equivalent in the sense that they hold in exactly the same models.*

PROOF Let M be a model in which $\neg p \vee q$ holds. In this model, we must have either $\neg p$ being true or q being true. If the former, $p \rightarrow q$ holds because the antecedent is false; if the latter, $p \rightarrow q$ holds because the consequent is true. The converse is similar. ■

Here is a similar result:

PROPOSITION 6.3.3 *For any two sentences* p *and* q, *the two sentences* $\mathrm{p} \rightarrow \mathrm{q}$ *and* $\neg\mathrm{q} \rightarrow \neg\mathrm{p}$ *are equivalent.*

If

$$\texttt{dog(Fido)} \rightarrow \texttt{mammal(Fido)} \tag{6.13}$$

so that we can conclude that Fido is a mammal from the fact that Fido is a dog, we can also conclude

$$\neg\texttt{mammal(Fido)} \rightarrow \neg\texttt{dog(Fido)} \tag{6.14}$$

so that Fido is not a dog if he *isn't* a mammal. This transformation of $p \rightarrow q$ into $\neg q \rightarrow \neg p$ is known as *contraposition*, so that (6.14) is the contraposed version of (6.13).

What about quantifiers? Recalling that $\forall$ and $\exists$ are just the infinitary versions of $\wedge$ and $\vee$ respectively, we will say that a sentence

$$\forall x.p(x)$$

holds in a model M if and only if $p(Z)$ holds for every object Z in our domain of discourse; we simply check that p holds for every substitution of an object Z for the variable x. Similarly

$$\exists x.p(x)$$

holds in a model if and only if there is *some* object Z for which p is valid.

In our running example, if Tom is the only object, then (6.12) and

$$\forall x.\texttt{poor}(x) \rightarrow \neg\texttt{rich}(x) \tag{6.15}$$

are equivalent. If there were other objects, then there would be more atoms in our language and the set of models would be correspondingly larger. There would be models in which (6.12) held but (6.15) didn't, although there clearly could never be models in which (6.15) held without (6.12) holding, since (6.12) is an instance of (6.15).

This is an important observation—we have found two sentences, (6.15) and (6.12) respectively, such that every model in which the first holds is also a model in which the second holds. When this happens, we will say that the first sentence *entails* the second:

DEFINITION 6.3.4 *Given two sentences* p *and* q, *we will say that* p entails q, *writing* $p \models q$, *if* q *holds in every model in which* p *holds.*

As an example, consider the following:

$$p \wedge (p \rightarrow q) \models q \tag{6.16}$$

For any sentences p and q, any model M in which $p \wedge (p \rightarrow q)$ holds is a model in which p holds and also a model in which $p \rightarrow q$ holds. But since p holds in M, if $p \rightarrow q$ holds in M, it must be the case that q holds in M as well. By Definition 6.3.4 of entailment, (6.16) follows.

The rule given by (6.16) tells us that if we know that an implication such as (6.12) holds and also that the antecedent of the implication holds, we are justified in concluding that the conclusion of the implication holds as well.

The relevance of first-order logic to AI depends primarily on the entailment relation $\models$. This is a consequence of the fact that if some agent has an initial state of knowledge consisting of the sentences $p_1, \ldots, p_n$, then it can be argued that the agent will be justified in concluding some new sentence q if (and perhaps only if)

$$p_1 \wedge \cdots \wedge p_n \models q$$

The conclusion q here can be taken from a wide range of possibilities. It might involve beliefs about the actions that the agent should take, ideas about other agents with which the given agent is involved, and so on. We have already seen a simple example of this in our ability to conclude that Tom was not rich given that he was poor, from which some putative intelligent agent might conclude that Tom is not a reasonable source of venture capital for its newly invented widget. Many other examples will appear in subsequent chapters; at this point, we will continue to focus on the entailment relation itself.

This, then, is the last step in the process described in Section 6.1, the AI equivalent of running the program: Given two sentences p and q, does $p \models q$ or not?

6.4 SOUNDNESS AND COMPLETENESS

Of course, one way to answer this would be to list all the models involved, to eliminate those in which p failed to hold, and to check that q held in all the rest. But this is unlikely to be viable from a computational point of view—even if there are only finitely many models (and in the presence of functions, there won't be), there are likely to be far too many for this to be a viable means of answering the question.

Instead, we appeal to *rules of inference*. These rules involve thinking of p as a "logical database" from which we are trying to derive q. The rules tell us that if p includes sentences of some specific form, it is legitimate to add sentences of some other form. An example of this is the rule known as *modus ponens*, which we've already seen. It says that if p contains sentences of the form x and $x \rightarrow y$, it is all right to add y to it. We will write this as:

$$\frac{\begin{array}{c} x \rightarrow y \\ x \end{array}}{y}$$

where the sentences above the line need to be in the database before the modification and those below the line are sentences that are added.

To start this process, we can either begin with p itself as our logical database or, if p is a conjunction $p_1 \wedge \ldots \wedge p_n$, we can take our database to be the set of all of the p_i's individually. We stop the process when we have managed to add q to our database.

By using a "procedure" such as this, we aren't necessarily determining whether $p \models q$. The procedure might be completely arbitrary, perhaps saying that if p contains a statistical fact about some object constant c, then it is legitimate to add any other fact about c. (Saying that you really *can* prove anything from statistics!) Now we will probably find ourselves concluding all sorts of things that aren't actually sanctioned by the "official" definition of entailment 6.3.4.

Since our derivation procedure might be computing something different from $\models$, we need another name for it. We'll write $p \vdash q$ to indicate that it is possible to derive q from p, without really committing ourselves on the question of whether or not this derivation is a valid one.

We are hoping, of course, that the derivations produced by our procedure *are* valid; we would like to have $p \vdash q$ if and only if $p \models q$. Modus ponens, for example, is supported by our earlier observation (6.16). But modus ponens isn't the *same* as this earlier observation—modus ponens is a rule of inference and (6.16) gives us information about the entailment relation $\models$.

In fact, there are two ways in which the derivations corresponding to $\vdash$ might differ from the derivations that are sanctioned by $\models$. One we've already seen; $\vdash$ might sanction inferences and conclusions that are not really allowed according to the meaning of $\models$. When this happens, we will say that $\vdash$ is *unsound*. Put the other way (contraposition!), we have:

DEFINITION 6.4.1 *An inference procedure $\vdash$ will be called* sound *if whenever* $p \vdash q$, *it is also the case that* $p \models q$.

In other words, an inference procedure is sound if it is conservative about the conclusions it draws. As we've seen, modus ponens is sound because the conclusions it draws are always sanctioned by the notion of entailment based on models.

The other way $\vdash$ might differ from $\models$ is that it might be *too* conservative. What if we didn't have any rules of inference at all? That would certainly be sound, but it wouldn't be very useful. So we also make the following definition:

DEFINITION 6.4.2 *An inference procedure $\vdash$ will be called* complete *if whenever* $p \models q$, *it is also the case that* $p \vdash q$.

In other words, an inference procedure is complete if it is capable of finding every valid consequence of an initial database p. We will see in Chapter 7 that although modus ponens is sound, it isn't complete.

The most interesting inference procedures are both sound *and* complete. The problem is that these inference procedures tend to be the most expensive to work with. Before considering this point in greater detail, however, we should point out that ideas similar to $\models$ and $\vdash$ appear throughout the study of knowledge representation. One typically has some language L (which may or may not have the same syntax as first-order logic) to which one has assigned a semantics in some way. The associated "theoretical" notion of entailment $\models$ may or may not differ from the procedural entailment $\vdash$ that supposedly implements it.

6.5 HOW HARD IS THEOREM PROVING?

Why is it that determining whether or not $p \models q$ is so computationally difficult?

Did you take a high school geometry class? If you did, you often found yourself working from a set of postulates and trying to prove some theorem. It was often hard deciding what postulate to apply next in your attempt to prove rigorously that (for example) the angles in a triangle always sum to 180°.

This is a general phenomenon; if we are trying to determine whether or not q follows from p, there will typically be many available rules of inference such as modus ponens, and we need to decide which one to use. Here is the reduction of a problem in theorem proving to a problem in search. Provided that $\vdash$ is complete, applying the rules of inference to sentences derived as early as possible is a rough analog to breadth-first search. It is therefore guaranteed to be complete as well: If q is a consequence of the material in the database, this approach will eventually find it. Of course, since search problems are exponentially difficult, we may not find a proof of q quickly using this idea.

What if q is *not* a consequence of what's in the database? Now we might just go merrily along, applying rules of inference to conclude more and more things, but never either stopping or actually concluding q. So what we have is a procedure that is guaranteed to eventually stop successfully if q is derivable, but might not terminate otherwise. If this is the best that we can do, it would mean that the entailment problem is *semidecidable*.[14]

To see that entailment is semidecidable, we will use the fact that first-order logic is *universal*: Roughly speaking, any form of inference or com-

14 A problem is *decidable* if there is a procedure that is guaranteed to terminate with an answer whether that answer is "yes" or "no"; a problem is *semidecidable* if you can guarantee termination in one of these cases but not in both.

putation that can be described formally can be described using first-order logic. Specifically, Turing machines can be described in this way. (If you don't know about Turing machines, skip the rest of this paragraph, take the claim that first-order logic is semidecidable on faith, and don't worry about it.) It is fairly clear that the behavior of a universal Turing machine can be described using the axioms of first-order logic, so that the associated question of whether or not a particular Turing machine M halts can be described in terms of whether a sentence such as `halts`(M) follows from this set of axioms. Since the halting problem is known to be semidecidable (there's no way in general to tell whether or not a Turing machine halts other than by running it and hoping for the best), first-order logic is semidecidable as well.

There are two consequences of this semidecidability. The first is that it makes a lot of problems not decidable at all—these are problems that depend on the *failure* of an attempt to prove some sentence q.

Imagine that I'm trying to figure out what to cook for dinner, and I decide that I'm going to make myself a steak. Have I proved that this plan will work?

Probably not; there are many things that could go wrong and prevent my preparing dinner in this way. I might not have any steak in the refrigerator. I might get hit on the head by a meteor. The president might stop by and ask me to dinner.

Since I can't prove that my plan will work, the best I can do is to "check" this plan to make sure that there isn't anything catastrophically wrong with it. If the power is out and my stove is electric, it's reasonable to expect me to figure this out and have tuna instead of steak. But checking to see that there is nothing wrong with a plan is really the same as being unable to prove that the plan will fail; in this case, it's a matter of being incapable of proving that I *can't* cook my steak for some reason. It's not clear how we manage to limit the amount of computational resources spent on this sort of a check. So here is yet another metalevel decision that people are good at but computers so far are not: How much time do we spend trying to make sure that our intended actions are reasonable before we actually execute them?

There are two things to be noticed here. The first is that planning problems are typically not even semidecidable. The second is that when attacking a nondecidable problem, we need some way to decide how much of our computational resources should be allocated to solving it—at what point do we simply give up and work with the best answer found so far?

The second consequence of the basic semidecidability result is that people spend a lot of time trying to figure out how to get away from it. They look for subsets of first-order logic that restrict the language in some way that makes it decidable. Even in fragments of first-order logic where entailment is decidable, it may still be exponentially difficult, so people continue to work, finding still smaller fragments of the language in which the difficulty of any particular entailment question is low-order polynomial.

What's not clear is what relevance all of this has to AI. After all, people probably know on the order of 10^9 facts; that assumes that you acquire about one new fact a second and live for about 2×10^9 seconds. If you can manage to restrict your language so that inference is of order b^2 (where b is the number of facts in your database), you are still talking about searching a space of size 10^{18} in order to determine whether or not a particular query is a consequence of what you know!

I don't mean to deprecate the place of this work in AI; it's important to understand the theoretical limitations, strengths, and weaknesses of any formal language. But from a practical point of view, it seems likely that getting machines to reason effectively—just like getting them to search effectively—depends more on substantial progress in metalevel reasoning than it does on complexity results.

6.6 FURTHER READING

The description of first-order logic that appears in the text is a compromise; this is not a text about first-order logic. My view is that I would have done you a disservice if I had tried to summarize in a chapter all of the mathematics appearing in a good introductory text on logical methods, such as Enderton [1972]. My aim instead has been to tell you just enough about these ideas for you to understand their relationship to AI as a whole. One particular consequence of this compromise appears in Definition 6.3.1, which properly speaking is correct only if our universe contains an infinite number of objects.

A good book on the role played by logic in AI is Genesereth and Nilsson [1987]. In this book, Genesereth and Nilsson point out the need for not only selecting a knowledge representation language but also deciding what to say in that language:

> The formalization of knowledge in declarative form begins with a *conceptualization*. This includes the objects presumed or hypothesized to exist in the world and their interrelationships. [Genesereth and Nilsson 1987, p. 9]

It is unfortunate that no more can currently be said about how to *produce* a conceptualization of any particular domain.

The role of logic in AI is also discussed in Nilsson [1991]; Birnbaum [1991] is a rebuttal of Nilsson's paper.

Soundness, completeness, and decidability are the topic of a great deal of research on first-order logic and other knowledge representation schemes; let me point out here only a single result: Gödel's theorem. Very roughly speaking, this theorem says that sufficiently powerful extensions of our description of first-order logic (including equality and the axioms of arithmetic, for example) are *necessarily* incomplete in that for any particular procedural scheme $\vdash$, there will always be sentences that are entailed in the sense of $\models$ but not derivable using $\vdash$. An excellent popular introduction to this topic is Hofstadter [1979]; Gödel's original paper is Gödel [1931].

6.7 EXERCISES

1. When we expressed, "Ginsberg loves his dog," as in (6.4), we were implicitly assuming that Ginsberg has only one dog. Why? How could we reexpress this if we wanted to say that Ginsberg loves *all* his dogs? Would this be true if Ginsberg didn't even have any dogs? What could we say about (6.4) if Ginsberg didn't have any dogs?

2. Translate the following sentences into first-order logic:
   (a) Tom is shorter than Karen.
   (b) Karen is taller than Tom.
   (c) There is no one taller than Wilt.
   (d) Both Karen and Harry are taller than Tom.
   (e) For any x and y, if x is taller than y, then y is shorter than x.
   (f) "Shorter than" is transitive.

3. Translate the following sentences into first-order logic:
   (a) You can fool some of the people all of the time, and all of the people some of the time, but you can't fool all of the people all of the time.
   (b) An apple a day keeps the doctor away.

4. Translate the following sentences from first-order logic into English:
   (a) $\exists x.\mathtt{hit}(\mathtt{Tom}, x) \wedge \mathtt{had}(x, \mathtt{Hammer})$
   (b) $\exists x.\mathtt{hit}(\mathtt{Tom}, x) \wedge \mathtt{used}(\mathtt{Tom}, \mathtt{Hammer})$
   (c) Is it possible to translate these two sentences into the *same* English sentence? Justify your answer.

5. Prove that for any sentence p and object a, $\forall x.p(x) \models p(a)$. Under what circumstances is it the case that $p(a) \models \forall x.p(x)$?

6. (a) Suppose that p is some sentence in which the variable x does not appear (such as $p = \mathtt{tall}(\mathtt{Sam})$). What does it mean to replace the variable x with some constant value in p?
   (b) Let p be a sentence in which the variable x does not appear. Show that any of the following sentences entails the other two: $\forall x.p$, $\exists x.p$, and p itself.

7. Let M be a model, and p be any sentence in first-order logic. Show that either p holds in M, or $\neg p$ holds in M.

8. (a) Prove that $p \models q$ is equivalent to $\models p \rightarrow q$.
   (b) Prove that $\models (p \rightarrow q) \vee (\neg p \rightarrow q)$. Does this mean that it is always the case that either $p \models q$ or $\neg p \models q$?

9. Let F be a sentence that doesn't hold in any models at all.
   (a) Show that $F \models p$ for any sentence p whatsoever.
   (b) Give an example of a sentence F with this property.

10. Suppose that we have some collection $\{p_i\}$ of n sentences in first-order logic, where i ranges from 1 to n. Now we can consider $\bigwedge_{i=1}^{n} p_i$. What should this expression mean if $n = 1$? How about if $n = 0$? How about if we used disjunction instead of conjunction?

11. Complete the proof of Proposition 6.3.2.

12. Prove Proposition 6.3.3.

13. (a) For any two sentences p and q, prove that $\neg(p \wedge q)$ and $\neg p \vee \neg q$ are equivalent, in that each entails the other.
    (b) Prove that $\neg\exists x.p(x)$ and $\forall x.\neg p(x)$ are equivalent.

    These equivalences are known as *de Morgan's laws*.

14. Why are there an infinite number of models in a language with function constants?

15. Suppose that we always began our investigation of $p \models q$ by starting with a database containing the single sentence p. What rule or rules of inference would allow us to add the individual conjuncts if p is a conjunction $p_1 \wedge \cdots \wedge p_n$?

16. Let us define a "planning system" to be a system that attempts to determine what sequence of actions would achieve a goal, given background information about the effects and preconditions of each of these actions.
    (a) What would it mean for a planning system to be sound? To be complete?
    (b) Are human beings sound and complete in this sense?
    (c) Given a planning problem, we can arguably reduce it to the proving problem of showing that a plan exists that will achieve the goal. Show that the planning problem is not decidable by showing that an inverse mapping also exists—one that reduces proving problems to planning ones.

17. Prove that entailment is decidable in finite languages without function constants.

18. What is wrong with the following argument? To see if $p \models q$, interleave attempts to prove q with attempts to prove $\neg q$. If the attempt to prove q succeeds, q follows from p. If the attempt to prove $\neg q$ succeeds, then q does not follow from p. Therefore entailment is decidable.

CHAPTER

7

PREDICATE LOGIC

In the last chapter, we gave a broad theoretical overview of first-order logic. We discussed its syntax, and its semantics in terms of $\models$. In this chapter, we begin to discuss the details. In terms of the analogy of Section 6.1, we describe how to "execute" a logical database to decide whether or not it sanctions some particular conclusion. Here, we examine databases that do not involve variables; Chapter 8 extends the discussion to include them. A sentence of first-order logic that does not involve a variable or a quantifier is called a *ground* sentence, or simply *ground*.

In order to drive our discussion, we will focus on a single example throughout. Here it is in English.

1. John is a lawyer.
2. Lawyers are rich.
3. Rich people have big houses.
4. Big houses are a lot of work to maintain.

The conclusion that we wish to draw is that John's house is a lot of work to maintain.

We begin by translating the above four axioms into first-order logic. The first two are pretty easy; we introduce the predicates lawyer and rich, where lawyer(p) means that p is a lawyer and rich(p) means that p is rich. We immediately get:

$$\texttt{lawyer(John)}$$

as the translation of the first axiom, and

$$\forall p.\texttt{lawyer}(p) \rightarrow \texttt{rich}(p) \tag{7.1}$$

as the translation of the second. For the time being, however, we'll assume that John is the only p, so that (7.1) becomes

$$\texttt{lawyer(John)} \rightarrow \texttt{rich(John)}$$

What about the third axiom? In this axiom, we talk about a person's house; if we are to formalize this, we need to decide whether house is to be a function, so that house–of(p) is p's house, or a relation, so that house(h,p) holds just in case h is p's house. Suppose we try the second approach. Now we can write the third axiom as

$$\forall ph.\texttt{house}(h,p) \wedge \texttt{rich}(p) \rightarrow \texttt{big}(h) \tag{7.2}$$

How are we to write the fourth axiom in this framework? It doesn't talk about the house belonging to some particular individual, it talks about houses generally. So we write it as

$$\forall h.[\texttt{big}(h) \wedge \exists p.\texttt{house}(h,p) \rightarrow \texttt{work}(h)] \tag{7.3}$$

where house is the house predicate and work(h) means that h is a lot of work to maintain. If h is big and is *somebody's* house, h is a lot of work to maintain. As in (7.1), we'll remove the quantifiers from (7.2) and (7.3) shortly.

Are (7.2) and (7.3) enough as they stand? It turns out that they aren't because we have no way to conclude that John has a house! So we need the house–of function after all:

$$\forall p.\texttt{house}(\texttt{house-of}(p),p)$$

This axiom says that the result of applying the function house–of to p is indeed p's house.

In sum, here is the axiomatization of our example:

$$\texttt{lawyer(John)} \tag{7.4}$$

$$\forall p.\texttt{lawyer}(p) \rightarrow \texttt{rich}(p) \tag{7.5}$$

$$\forall p.\texttt{house}(\texttt{house-of}(p),p) \tag{7.6}$$

$$\forall ph.\texttt{house}(h,p) \wedge \texttt{rich}(p) \rightarrow \texttt{big}(h) \tag{7.7}$$

$$\forall h.\texttt{big}(h) \wedge \exists p.\texttt{house}(h,p) \rightarrow \texttt{work}(h) \tag{7.8}$$

Given these axioms, it is now possible to conclude

$$\texttt{work(house-of(John))}$$

In this chapter, however, we will draw this conclusion only after restricting our attention in (7.4)–(7.8) to John:

$$\texttt{lawyer(John)} \tag{7.9}$$

$$\texttt{lawyer(John)} \rightarrow \texttt{rich(John)} \tag{7.10}$$

$$\texttt{house(house-of(John), John)} \tag{7.11}$$

$$\texttt{house(house-of(John), John)} \wedge \texttt{rich(John)} \rightarrow \texttt{big(house-of(John))} \tag{7.12}$$

$$\texttt{big(house-of(John))} \wedge \texttt{house(house-of(John), John)} \rightarrow \texttt{work(house-of(John))} \tag{7.13}$$

Once again, `work(house-of(John))` is a consequence of the above axioms.

7.1 INFERENCE USING MODUS PONENS

Given the above database, how exactly are we to conclude that John's house is a lot of work to maintain? From a commonsense point of view, it's straightforward: Since John is a lawyer, he's rich. Since he's rich, he has a big house. And big houses are a lot of work to maintain.

Let's begin with the first of these conclusions. Our database contains the fact

$$\texttt{lawyer(John)}$$

together with the implication

$$\texttt{lawyer(John)} \rightarrow \texttt{rich(John)}$$

and we are justified in concluding from these that `rich(John)`.

This is an instance of modus ponens. Whenever our database contains an implication of the form $a \rightarrow b$ and a fact a, we are justified in concluding b. As in the previous chapter, we write this rule as:

$$\frac{\begin{array}{c} a \rightarrow b \\ a \end{array}}{b}$$

How about the next conclusion, that `big(house-of(John))`? Here, our database contains the implication

$$\texttt{house(house-of(John), John)} \wedge \texttt{rich(John)} \rightarrow \texttt{big(house-of(John))}$$

together with the pair of facts `house(house-of(John),John)` and `rich(John)`. We can handle this by extending the modus ponens rule to read:

$$\frac{\begin{array}{c} a_1 \wedge \cdots \wedge a_m \to b \\ a_1 \\ \vdots \\ a_m \end{array}}{b}$$

In fact, however, we will use a slightly different extension. Here it is:

$$\frac{\begin{array}{c} a_1 \wedge \cdots \wedge a_m \to b \\ a_i \end{array}}{a_1 \wedge \cdots \wedge a_{i-1} \wedge a_{i+1} \wedge \cdots \wedge a_m \to b}$$

What this rule says is that if b depends on the assumptions $a_1, \ldots, a_m$ and we know a_i, we can think of b as depending on only the a's *other than* a_i. This allows us to remove the assumptions one at a time until we can apply the original version of modus ponens.

In fact, we do not need to appeal to the "original version" of modus ponens but can instead apply the above rule again. If $m = 1$, so that there is only one assumption, and that assumption appears in the database, then the conclusion of the rule says that b is a consequence of a conjunction of no entries. We have seen in Exercise 10 in Chapter 6, however, that the conjunction of no items is always true and the conclusion of the rule therefore becomes

$$T \to b$$

This is clearly equivalent to b itself.

We will use the fact that d and $T \to d$ are equivalent for any d to rewrite our inference rule as follows. If $d = a_i$,

$$\frac{\begin{array}{r} a_1 \wedge \cdots \wedge a_m \to b \\ T \to d \end{array}}{a_1 \wedge \cdots \wedge \hat{a}_i \wedge \cdots \wedge a_m \to b}$$

We have included a caret over the term a_i to indicate that it has been dropped from the implication that is the conclusion of the rule.

Before proceeding, there is one useful modification that we can make to the above rule. What if d, instead of appearing explicitly in our database, itself depends on antecedents $c_1, \ldots, c_n$? In that case, in order to conclude b from the a's excepting a_i, we will need to derive a_i, which means that we will need to know all of the c's as well.

DEFINITION 7.1.1 Modus ponens *is the following rule of inference, where* $d = a_i$:

$$\frac{\begin{array}{r} a_1 \wedge \cdots \wedge a_m \rightarrow b \\ c_1 \wedge \cdots \wedge c_n \rightarrow d \end{array}}{a_1 \wedge \cdots \wedge \hat{a}_i \wedge \cdots \wedge a_m \wedge c_1 \wedge \cdots \wedge c_n \rightarrow b}$$

PROPOSITION 7.1.2 *Modus ponens is sound.*

PROOF Consider any model in which the premises of the modus ponens rule hold but the conclusion does not. Since the conclusion fails, it must be the case that

$$a_1 \wedge \cdots \wedge \hat{a}_i \wedge \cdots \wedge a_m \wedge c_1 \wedge \cdots \wedge c_n$$

holds but b does not. But since the second premise of the modus ponens rule is assumed to hold in the model, we also know that a_i holds in the model. It therefore follows from the first modus ponens premise that b holds in the model, a contradiction. We have seen that every model in which the premises of modus ponens hold is also a model in which the conclusion holds, so modus ponens is sound. ∎

We can use modus ponens to complete our derivation that John's house is a lot of work. From

`house(house-of(John), John)` $\wedge$ `rich(John)` $\rightarrow$ `big(house-of(John))`

and `rich(John)`, we can conclude

`house(house-of(John), John)` $\rightarrow$ `big(house-of(John))`

In other words, if `house-of(John)` is John's house, `house-of(John)` is big. Since we know

`house(house-of(John), John)`

we can conclude `big(house-of(John))`. Now we can apply (7.13) in a similar way to conclude

`work(house-of(John))`

7.2 HORN DATABASES

In the examples of the previous section, we dealt exclusively with implications of the form

$$a_1 \wedge \cdots \wedge a_m \rightarrow b \tag{7.14}$$

What if, instead of the implication

$$\texttt{lawyer(John)} \rightarrow \texttt{rich(John)} \tag{7.15}$$

our database contained the fact

$$\neg\texttt{lawyer(John)} \vee \texttt{rich(John)} \tag{7.16}$$

Since (7.15) and (7.16) are equivalent, we should be able to draw the same set of conclusions whichever version we use.

But what if we weren't sure of John's profession? Perhaps we only know that he is a lawyer or a waiter:

$$\texttt{lawyer(John)} \vee \texttt{waiter(John)} \tag{7.17}$$

Can we express this in the form (7.14)?

In a trivial sense, of course we can. Here is one possibility.

$$T \rightarrow [\texttt{lawyer(John)} \vee \texttt{waiter(John)}] \tag{7.18}$$

We have taken $m = 0$ and $b =$ lawyer(John) $\vee$ waiter(John). Here is another description.

$$\neg\texttt{lawyer(John)} \rightarrow \texttt{waiter(John)} \tag{7.19}$$

In this case, $a_1 = \neg$lawyer(John) and $b =$ waiter(John).

These examples differ from those of Section 7.1, however. In our earlier examples, both the a_i's and b were atoms. In (7.18), b is a compound expression; in (7.19), a_1 is a negated atom instead of simply an atom. To exclude this, we make the following definition:

DEFINITION 7.2.1 *A database will be called* Horn *if it is equivalent to a set of sentences of the form (7.14), where* b *and each* a_i *are atoms.*

THEOREM 7.2.2 *Modus ponens is complete for Horn databases.*

I'm leaving the proof as an exercise. (It's a one-liner.)

Horn databases and the modus ponens rule are important for two reasons. First, disjunctions such as that appearing in (7.17) are rare; most of the knowledge that we have about the world can be described in Horn form.

Second, Horn databases have attractive computational properties. Consider the following procedure for computing the entire set of consequences of a Horn database:

PROCEDURE 7.2.3 *Repeat until no new sentences can be added to the database:*

1. *For each sentence* $\mathrm{T} \rightarrow \mathrm{c}$ *in the database:*
2. *If there is another sentence* $\mathrm{p}_1 \wedge \cdots \wedge \mathrm{p}_n \rightarrow \mathrm{c}'$ *in the database such that* $\mathrm{p}_1 = \mathrm{c}$, *add to the database the sentence* $\mathrm{p}_2 \wedge \cdots \wedge \mathrm{p}_n \rightarrow \mathrm{c}'$ *if it is not already present.*

LEMMA 7.2.4 *If an atom* q *is a consequence of a declarative database in which every sentence is of the form (7.14), it is either in the database at the outset or will eventually be added by Procedure 7.2.3.*

PROOF I'm only going to give a sketch of the proof here; the details don't add much.

Since there are no disjunctions in our database, we never have to prove the atom q by case analysis (where we show that q holds if either a holds or b does and then try to prove the disjunction $a \vee b$). It follows that if q holds, there must be *some* sentence

$$p_1 \wedge \cdots \wedge p_n \rightarrow q \tag{7.20}$$

such that all the p_i hold. Furthermore, all of the p_i have to hold without using q in their derivations, so we can drop from the database all of the sentences that mention q. Now we're trying to solve the same problem but with a smaller database, so the lemma follows by induction on the size of the database itself. ∎

How many steps might it take to execute Procedure 7.2.3? Well, if we denote by n the maximum number of premises that appear in any of our database facts, then the maximum size of the final database is obviously bounded by $n + 1$ times the size of the initial database; this is because we are requiring that we remove the premises of the implications sequentially so that an initial sentence of the form (7.20) can generate at most the sequence

$$\begin{aligned} p_1 \wedge p_2 \wedge \cdots \wedge p_n &\rightarrow q \\ p_2 \wedge \cdots \wedge p_n &\rightarrow q \\ &\vdots \\ p_n &\rightarrow q \\ & q \end{aligned}$$

Since the database includes the first of these to begin with, we conclude:

PROPOSITION 7.2.5 *In a database without function constants and where every sentence is of the restricted form (7.14), the time needed to determine whether or* *not a particular atom follows is of order* nd, *where* n *is the maximum number of premises in any implication and* d *is the size of the database.*

Because of the simplicity of working with Horn databases, much of the AI work on reasoning restricts itself to this case. As an example, the programming language PROLOG, which is in many ways a theorem prover for first-order logic, restricts its language to Horn clauses. (Function symbols are allowed, however.)

Another focus on Horn databases is due to Hector Levesque. Imagine that you are at a cocktail party, talking to an attractive member of the opposite sex, and that he or she has a martini in one hand.

Which hand is the martini in? Although I didn't tell you, Levesque noticed that your mental image of this situation is likely to have put the martini in one hand or the other. What I told you explicitly was a disjunction (the martini is in the right hand or the left hand); you, as the listener, selected one of these two disjuncts in constructing your mental model. It can be argued that the *reason* you have done this is because you are establishing a situation in which you will be able to reason quickly about my proposed scenario—in other words, a situation in which you will be able to exploit the computational simplicity of Horn databases. Levesque describes a database that doesn't include any disjunctions as *vivid*; we will encounter vivid databases in a variety of places in the remainder of this book.

7.3 THE RESOLUTION RULE

Unfortunately, not all databases are Horn; recall (7.17). And for databases containing disjunctions, modus ponens is not complete. Here's a specific example.

Suppose that all classes at some university meet either on Monday, Wednesday, and Friday, or on Tuesday and Thursday. Introductory AI meets at 2:30 in the afternoon, and Janet has volleyball practice Thursdays and Fridays at that time. Can Janet take Intro AI?

The answer is clearly no. But let's see what happens when we axiomatize things. We'll write TTh(c,t) to mean that the class c meets on Tuesdays and Thursdays at time t, and similarly for MWF(c,t). We'll write busy(d,t) to mean that Janet is busy at time t on the day d. Our axioms are:

$$\begin{aligned}
T &\rightarrow \texttt{TTh(AI, 2:30)} \vee \texttt{MWF(AI, 2:30)} \\
\texttt{TTh(AI, 2:30)} \wedge \texttt{busy(Thursday, 2:30)} &\rightarrow \texttt{conflict(AI)} \\
\texttt{MWF(AI, 2:30)} \wedge \texttt{busy(Friday, 2:30)} &\rightarrow \texttt{conflict(AI)} \\
T &\rightarrow \texttt{busy(Thursday, 2:30)} \\
T &\rightarrow \texttt{busy(Friday, 2:30)}
\end{aligned} \tag{7.21}$$

AI meets either TTh or MWF at 2:30. If a course meets on TTh at a time when Janet is busy on Thursdays, she has a conflict with that course; similarly for MWF classes and her Friday commitments. Janet is busy on Thursdays and Fridays at 2:30.

The only possible applications of modus ponens remove the conjuncts busy(Thursday,t) and busy(Friday,t) from the premises in the above implications, and we get:

$$\begin{aligned} T &\rightarrow \texttt{TTh(AI, 2:30)} \vee \texttt{MWF(AI, 2:30)} \\ \texttt{TTh(AI, 2:30)} &\rightarrow \texttt{conflict(AI)} \\ \texttt{MWF(AI, 2:30)} &\rightarrow \texttt{conflict(AI)} \end{aligned}$$

It's obvious that conflict(AI) follows from these axioms; either AI meets TTh or it meets on MWF and there's a conflict either way. But modus ponens simply can't be used to derive this conclusion.

The reason that modus ponens isn't helping us here is that we need to reason by cases, considering separately the situation where AI meets on TTh (and Janet's conflict is on Thursday) and where it meets MWF (and the conflict is on Friday). Since there is a conflict either way, we can conclude that Janet's conflict with AI is inevitable—but this is not a conclusion that we can draw using modus ponens alone. This sort of reasoning is known as *case analysis*.

If we want to handle examples such as this, we need to modify modus ponens so that it can cope with the appearance of disjunctions in the conclusions of implications. Here is the basic modus ponens rule again:

$$\frac{\begin{array}{r} a_1 \wedge \cdots \wedge a_m \rightarrow b \\ c_1 \wedge \cdots \wedge c_n \rightarrow d \end{array}}{a_1 \wedge \cdots \wedge \hat{a}_i \wedge \cdots \wedge a_m \wedge c_1 \wedge \cdots \wedge c_n \rightarrow b}$$

Nowhere in our analysis have we used the fact that b is an atom, so let us suppose that b is a disjunction instead.

If $d = a_i$, then

$$\frac{\begin{array}{r} a_1 \wedge \cdots \wedge a_m \rightarrow b_1 \vee \cdots \vee b_k \\ c_1 \wedge \cdots \wedge c_n \rightarrow d \end{array}}{a_1 \wedge \cdots \wedge \hat{a}_i \wedge \cdots \wedge a_m \wedge c_1 \wedge \cdots \wedge c_n \rightarrow b_1 \vee \cdots \vee b_k} \tag{7.22}$$

Instead of requiring the first implication used by the rule to be Horn, we have allowed it to be of the more general form

$$a_1 \wedge \cdots \wedge a_m \rightarrow b_1 \vee \cdots \vee b_k \tag{7.23}$$

What this means is that if all of the a_i's hold, then so does at least *one* of the b_j's. We don't know which one, of course, only that at least one does.

Including disjunctions in the right hand side of (7.23) extends the descriptive power of (7.14) substantially. If $k = 1$, we just get (7.14) back again, so nothing is *lost* by including the disjunction on the right hand side. If $m = 0$, the antecedent of the rule is trivial and we get

$$T \rightarrow b_1 \vee \cdots \vee b_k$$

or simply

$$b_1 \vee \cdots \vee b_k$$

This is the form we need to express (7.17) or the first axiom in (7.21).

What about $k = 0$? Now there are no disjunctions in the conclusion of the rule, but we know from Exercise 10 in Chapter 6 that the disjunction of no terms is F, the sentence that is universally false (that is, it holds in no models). What does

$$a_1 \wedge \cdots \wedge a_m \rightarrow F \tag{7.24}$$

mean?

In order for (7.24) to be true in a model, the antecedent of (7.24) must be false in that model. After all, the antecedent is guaranteed to be either true or false in every model; if it were true, then since the conclusion of F is known to be false in the model, we would have a contradiction. Furthermore, if the premise of (7.24) is false in some model, then (7.24) itself is true, by the definition of $\rightarrow$. So we see that the models in which (7.24) is true are exactly the models in which the premise

$$a_1 \wedge \cdots \wedge a_m$$

is false, and the sentence (7.24) is therefore equivalent to

$$\neg(a_1 \wedge \cdots \wedge a_m)$$

If we want, we can use de Morgan's laws (see Exercise 13 in Chapter 6) to rewrite this as

$$\neg a_1 \vee \cdots \vee \neg a_m$$

If $m = 1$, this just becomes $\neg a_1$. Thus if we want to say that John is not a doctor, ¬`doctor(John)`, we could write it in the form (7.23) as

$$\texttt{doctor(John)} \rightarrow F$$

Finally, if $m = 0$ as well as $n = 0$, (7.24) becomes

$$T \rightarrow F$$

so it is also possible to express an explicit contradiction in the form (7.23).

DEFINITION 7.3.1 *A database will be said to be in* normal form *if every sentence is of the form (7.23), where each* a_i *or* b_j *is an atom.*

Now let's have a look at the rule of inference (7.22) itself. The left-hand side of the conclusion is just the union of the left-hand sides of the two "input" facts, with the repeated clause a_i deleted. The right-hand side is the union of the right-hand sides of the two original implications, with the repeated clause d deleted. So it looks as if the general rule is likely to be

DEFINITION 7.3.2 Resolution *is the following rule of inference, where* $d_j = a_i$*:*

$$\frac{\begin{array}{c} a_1 \wedge \cdots \wedge a_m \rightarrow b_1 \vee \cdots \vee b_k \\ c_1 \wedge \cdots \wedge c_n \rightarrow d_1 \vee \cdots \vee d_l \end{array}}{a_1 \wedge \cdots \wedge \hat{a}_i \wedge \cdots a_m \wedge c_1 \wedge \cdots \wedge c_n \rightarrow b_1 \vee \cdots \vee b_k \vee d_1 \vee \cdots \vee \hat{d}_j \vee \cdots \vee d_l}$$

LEMMA 7.3.3 *The resolution rule is sound.*

PROOF I'd like to argue this two separate ways.

First, suppose that the above rule of inference fails; we want to show this to be impossible. In order for the rule to fail, it must be the case that the premise holds but the conclusion doesn't—in other words, all of the c's hold and all of the a's hold (except possibly a_i), but the disjunct that is the conclusion of the rule *doesn't* hold. Thus all of the b's fail, and all of the d's fail as well (except perhaps d_j).

Since all of the c's hold, one of the d's must hold by virtue of the second axiom appearing in the rule. We know it isn't any of the d's except for d_j, so d_j must hold. Since $d_j = a_i$, that means that a_i holds. All the other a's are already known to hold, so all the a's hold and therefore at least one of the b's must hold. But this is a contradiction—if the rule of inference is to fail, all of the b's have to fail as well.

We can also prove the lemma directly, arguing from the antecedent of the rule's conclusion to its consequent. Suppose that all of the a's hold (except perhaps a_i), and that all of the c's hold as well. Since the c's hold, at least one of the d's must hold. If it isn't d_j, then the disjunction

$$b_1 \vee \cdots \vee b_k \vee d_1 \vee \cdots \vee \hat{d}_j \vee \cdots \vee d_l \tag{7.25}$$

obviously holds, since one of the other d's must hold. If the d that holds is d_j (here's the case analysis), then since $d_j = a_i$, all of the a's hold and therefore one of the b's holds. But that means that (7.25) holds, and the proof is complete. ■

Armed with resolution, let us return to Janet and her volleyball/AI conflict. Here's the database again:

$$T \rightarrow \texttt{TTh(AI, 2:30)} \vee \texttt{MWF(AI, 2:30)} \tag{7.26}$$

$$\texttt{TTh(AI, 2:30)} \rightarrow \texttt{conflict(AI)} \tag{7.27}$$

$$\texttt{MWF(AI,2:30)} \rightarrow \texttt{conflict(AI)} \tag{7.28}$$

Resolving (7.27) with (7.26) (that is, using the resolution rule on these two expressions) gives us

$$T \rightarrow \texttt{MWF(AI, 2:30)} \vee \texttt{conflict(AI)} \tag{7.29}$$

In other words, either the AI class meets on MWF or Janet has a conflict with it; this is the result of the resolution that considers the possible Thursday conflict.

Resolving (7.29) with (7.28) now gives us

$$T \rightarrow \texttt{conflict(AI)} \vee \texttt{conflict(AI)}$$

In other words, either Janet has a conflict with the AI class or Janet has a conflict with the AI class. Realizing that these two conclusions are identical allows us to conclude that Janet does indeed have a conflict with the AI class.[15]

7.4 BACKWARD CHAINING USING RESOLUTION

Now suppose that we have some logical database D and some query q, and we want to determine whether or not q is a consequence of D. How are we to do this?

In order to have our theorem prover function in a uniform way, instead of trying to derive q using resolution, we add $\neg q$ to our database and then try to derive a contradiction (see Exercise 3 at the end of this chapter). As

15 The final operation here—where we collapse identical atoms after applying the resolution rule—is known as *factoring*. We are not discussing factoring in any depth because it tends not to play much of a role in practical applications of resolution.

in Section 7.3, we denote this contradiction as

$$T \rightarrow F$$

where T is the empty conjunction and F is the empty disjunction.

In our usual example, the query is work(house–of(John)); we cannot simply negate this to obtain

$$T \rightarrow \neg\texttt{work(house–of(John))} \qquad (7.30)$$

because the right hand side of this expression is not an atom. Instead, we write this as

$$\texttt{work(house–of(John))} \rightarrow F \qquad (7.31)$$

as in Section 7.3. This is the contrapositive of (7.30) and is equivalent to it.

Here is our database again.

$$\texttt{lawyer(John)} \qquad (7.32)$$

$$\texttt{lawyer(John)} \rightarrow \texttt{rich(John)} \qquad (7.33)$$

$$\texttt{house(house–of(John), John)} \qquad (7.34)$$

$$\texttt{house(house–of(John), John)} \wedge \texttt{rich(John)} \rightarrow \texttt{big(house–of(John))} \qquad (7.35)$$

$$\texttt{big(house–of(John))} \wedge \texttt{house(house–of(John), John)} \rightarrow \texttt{work(house–of(John))} \qquad (7.36)$$

Assuming (7.31), we can now derive a contradiction as follows. We have abbreviated house–of(John) to Jhouse:

	Sentence	Source
1	work(Jhouse) → F	negated query
2	big(Jhouse) ∧ house(Jhouse, John) → work(Jhouse)	(7.36)
3	big(Jhouse) ∧ house(Jhouse, John) → F	resolve 1,2
4	T → house(Jhouse,John)	(7.34)
5	big(Jhouse) → F	resolve 3,4
6	house(Jhouse, John) ∧ rich(John) → big(Jhouse)	(7.35)
7	house(Jhouse, John) ∧ rich(John) → F	resolve 5,6
8	rich(John) → F	resolve 7,4
9	lawyer(John) → rich(John)	(7.33)
10	lawyer(John) → F	resolve 8,9
11	T → lawyer(John)	(7.32)
12	T → F	resolve 10,11

In the future, we will abbreviate this somewhat to:

	Sentence	Source
1	work(house-of(John)) $\rightarrow F$	negated query
2	big(house-of(John)) $\wedge$ house(house-of(John), John) $\rightarrow F$	resolve 1,(7.36)
3	big(house-of(John)) $\rightarrow F$	resolve 2,(7.34)
4	house(house-of(John), John) $\wedge$ rich(John) $\rightarrow F$	resolve 3,(7.35)
5	rich(John) $\rightarrow F$	resolve 4,(7.34)
6	lawyer(John) $\rightarrow F$	resolve 5,(7.33)
7	$T \rightarrow$ F	resolve 6,(7.32)

Note how the reasoning proceeds here: In step 1, we are trying to show work(house-of(John)); this is the negation of the first sentence above. In step 3, we have used the fact that big houses are a lot of work to reduce our goal to big(house-of(John)). We use the fact that rich people have big houses to reduce our goal to rich(John) and finally use the fact that lawyers are rich to reduce it to lawyer(John), which appears in our database.

THEOREM 7.4.1 *Resolution is complete.*

PROOF What we will show is that if D is some database that is contradictory, then repeated applications of the resolution rule will allow us to derive $T \rightarrow F$ from D.

We are assuming that every sentence in D is of the form

$$a_1 \wedge \cdots \wedge a_m \rightarrow b_1 \vee \cdots \vee b_n \tag{7.37}$$

for some m and n. Given a clause of the form (7.37), we will say that the number of *excess atoms* in the clause is $m + n - 1$. The number of excess atoms is the number of atoms that have to be "resolved away" to derive an atom or the negation of an atom from the given complex clause; if there are no excess atoms, then the database sentence is already either an atom or the negation of an atom. This might be because $n = 1$ and $m = 0$, in which case the sentence is

$$T \rightarrow b_1$$

and is equivalent to b_1, or it might be because $m = 1$ and $n = 0$, in which case the sentence is

$$a_1 \rightarrow F$$

and is equivalent to $\neg a_1$. We will say that the number of excess atoms in the entire database D is the sum of the numbers of excess atoms in each sentence in D.

The proof now proceeds by induction on the number of excess atoms in D, which we denote by $n(D)$. If D has no excess atoms so that $n(D) = 0$, then either D contains $T \rightarrow F$ itself (the only sentence with a negative number of excess atoms), or every sentence in D has no excess atoms and is therefore an atom or its negation. It is clear that the only way for a database of this form to imply a contradiction is if it contains some atom a and its negation $\neg a$, or $T \rightarrow a$ and $a \rightarrow F$. Resolving these two clauses allows us to derive $T \rightarrow F$, so the base case of the induction is complete.

Suppose, then, that the theorem is true for any database with $n(D) < k$ for some k; we need to show that it is true if $n(D) = k$ as well. Since $k > 0$, it follows that there is some sentence in D that includes excess atoms; let us suppose that it is of the form

$$T \rightarrow b_1 \vee b_2 \tag{7.38}$$

(The cases where there is more than one excess atom or the excess atom is in the antecedent of the sentence are similar.)

Now consider the database D' that is obtained by removing (7.38) from D and replacing it with

$$T \rightarrow b_1 \tag{7.39}$$

D' is still contradictory, since (7.39) is stronger than (7.38)—knowing b_1 for sure is stronger than knowing either b_1 or b_2. But since D' has one less excess atom than D, it follows that resolution is capable of deriving the contradiction $T \rightarrow F$ from D'. Say that it does so, producing a sequences of sentences $s_1, \ldots, s_k$, where $s_k = T \rightarrow F$ is the final contradiction.

Now suppose that at every point in this derivation where we resolve with (7.39), we had resolved with (7.38) instead. The result would simply have been to introduce an additional b_2 term into the right hand side of the associated s_i. It follows that the modified resolution sequence would have produced as its final result not $T \rightarrow F$, but

$$T \rightarrow b_2 \vee \cdots \vee b_2 \tag{7.40}$$

We can now use factoring to ensure that b_2 appears only once on the right-hand side of (7.40), obtaining $T \rightarrow b_2$.

But now we repeat the argument, noticing that if we replace (7.38) with

$$T \rightarrow b_2 \tag{7.41}$$

instead of (7.39) (note the change in subscript), we can still derive a contradiction. But (7.41) and (7.40) are equivalent, so the proof is complete. ■

Unfortunately, no attractive analog to Proposition 7.2.5 holds for resolution—there is no known polynomial method for determining the consequences of a general normal-form database. Consider once again the basic example of case analysis:

$$T \rightarrow a \vee b$$

$$a \rightarrow q$$

$$b \rightarrow q$$

It is clear that q follows from these axioms because we know that either a holds or b does, and q follows from either. But more complicated examples can involve many more cases; instead of $T \rightarrow a \vee b$ we might have had $c \wedge d \rightarrow a \vee b$ where both c and d depend on case analysis for their proofs, and so on. The number of cases can grow exponentially with the number of axioms in our database, and it is not clear that there is any more effective way to decide the validity of q than to examine each of these cases individually.

7.5 NORMAL FORM

Theorem 7.2.2 reads

Modus ponens is complete for Horn databases.

Theorem 7.4.1, on the other hand, reads simply

Resolution is complete.

Why didn't we need to restrict it to databases that were in normal form?

The reason is that (7.23) is a completely general form for a sentence in predicate logic. Although it is possible for a declarative database to contain information that is not Horn, there is no way for such a database to contain information that cannot be rewritten in normal form.

THEOREM 7.5.1 *Let S be a set of sentences of predicate logic. Then there exists a set S′ of sentences in normal form such that S and S′ are equivalent.*

PROOF The rest of this chapter will be devoted to a proof of Theorem 7.5.1. We begin by noting that it suffices to show that for any individual sentence p, we can always find a set S' that is equivalent to p. The general case can then be handled by taking the union of all the sets corresponding to the individual sentences in S.

Before we get into the details, however, I would like to make a few remarks about why this result itself is important, and why it is important that the proof be constructive. We want to describe the set S' in detail, not just prove that such a set exists.

The reason for this is that our overall goal is to find a sound and complete inference procedure $\vdash$ for computing the consequences of a logical database. We know that both modus ponens and resolution are sound, but modus ponens isn't complete because it can't deal with disjunction. Since we know that resolution *is* complete, our basic plan for deciding whether a logical database D entails a query q will be:

1. Translate D into normal form.
2. Try to derive q using resolution.

To implement this idea (and prove the theorem), all we need is a procedure for translating an arbitrary logical database into normal form.

ALGORITHM 7.5.2 *To translate a sentence* p *into normal form:*

1. *Eliminate* $\rightarrow$ *using the fact that* $(p \rightarrow q)$ *is equivalent to* $(\neg p \vee q)$.
2. *Use de Morgan's laws so that negation applies to atoms only.*
3. *Distribute* $\vee$ *and* $\wedge$ *to write the result as a conjunction of disjunctions.*
4. *Split the conjunction.*
5. *Combine the negated terms.*
6. *Reintroduce* $\rightarrow$ *to get expressions of the form* (7.23).

These steps will be made clearer by considering an example. Here it is:

If John's house is big, then it is a lot of work to maintain, unless it comes with a housecleaner Chuck and doesn't have a garden.

We abbreviate this to:

$$\texttt{big}(H) \wedge \texttt{house}(H,J) \rightarrow \texttt{work}(H) \vee [\texttt{cleans}(C,H) \wedge \neg\texttt{garden}(G,H)] \tag{7.42}$$

In other words, if H is a big house, then either it is a lot of work or C is the cleaner of H and G is not its garden.

1. **Eliminate → using the fact that ($p \rightarrow q$) is equivalent to ($\neg p \vee q$).** We have already seen in Proposition 6.3.2 that for any two sentences p and q, the expressions $p \rightarrow q$ and $\neg p \vee q$ are equivalent. In our example, (7.42) becomes

$$\neg[\mathtt{big}(H) \wedge \mathtt{house}(H,J)] \vee \mathtt{work}(H) \vee [\mathtt{cleans}(C,H) \wedge \neg\mathtt{garden}(G,H)] \quad (7.43)$$

Either it is not the case that H is a big house, or H is a lot of work to maintain, or C is the cleaner and G is not the garden.

2. **Move negation in.** Now we use the fact that $\neg\neg p$ is equivalent to p and that $\neg(p \wedge q)$ is equivalent to $\neg p \vee \neg q$ to make sure that negation is applied to atoms only.[16] Thus (7.43) becomes

$$\neg\mathtt{big}(H) \vee \neg\mathtt{house}(H,J) \vee \mathtt{work}(H) \vee [\mathtt{cleans}(C,H) \wedge \neg\mathtt{garden}(G,H)] \quad (7.44)$$

   Either H is not big, or it is not a house, or it is a lot of work to maintain, or C is the cleaner and G is not the garden.

3. **Distribute ∧ and ∨.** The idea here is to write our overall expression (7.44) as a conjunction of disjunctions. (7.44) becomes

$$[\neg\mathtt{big}(H) \vee \neg\mathtt{house}(H,J) \vee \mathtt{work}(H) \vee \mathtt{cleans}(C,H)] \wedge [\neg\mathtt{big}(H) \vee \neg\mathtt{house}(H,J) \vee \mathtt{work}(H) \vee \neg\mathtt{garden}(G,H)] \quad (7.45)$$

   Either H is not big, or not a house, or a lot of work to maintain, or C is the cleaner; similarly for G not being the garden. Since the only exception to the rule about H involves both C being the cleaner and G not being the garden, it is legitimate to rewrite (7.42) in this way.

4. **Split the conjunction.** We write (7.45) as the pair of sentences:

$$\neg\mathtt{big}(H) \vee \neg\mathtt{house}(H,J) \vee \mathtt{work}(H) \vee \mathtt{cleans}(C,H) \quad (7.46)$$

$$\neg\mathtt{big}(H) \vee \neg\mathtt{house}(H,J) \vee \mathtt{work}(H) \vee \neg\mathtt{garden}(G,H) \quad (7.47)$$

   The reason we can do this is that Theorem 7.5.1 does not require us to reexpress p as a *single* normal-form sentence, only that we find a set S' of such sentences that are collectively equivalent to p.

16 That $\neg\neg p$ is equivalent to p has an obvious linguistic analog; by, "It is not the case that I don't want ice cream," I mean the same thing as "I want ice cream." A linguist once remarked on this use of a double negative as an affirmative, saying that there were no analogous examples where a double affirmative served as a negative. The anonymous reply from the back of the audience? "Yeah, yeah."

5. **Combine any negated terms using de Morgan's laws.** There are two negated terms in (7.46), and three in (7.47). We get:

$$\neg[\texttt{big}(H) \wedge \texttt{house}(H,J)] \vee \texttt{work}(H) \vee \texttt{cleans}(C,H) \quad (7.48)$$
$$\neg[\texttt{big}(H) \wedge \texttt{house}(H,J) \wedge \texttt{garden}(G,H)] \vee \texttt{work}(H) \quad (7.49)$$

   The first sentence now says that either H is not a big house, or it's a lot of work, or C is the cleaner. The second sentence is somewhat more intricate; both will be more palatable after the next step:

6. **Reintroduce implication.** We use the equivalence between $\neg p \vee q$ and $p \rightarrow q$ to rewrite (7.48) and (7.49) as:

$$[\texttt{big}(H) \wedge \texttt{house}(H,J)] \rightarrow [\texttt{work}(H) \vee \texttt{cleans}(C,H)]$$
$$[\texttt{big}(H) \wedge \texttt{house}(H,J) \wedge \texttt{garden}(G,H)] \rightarrow \texttt{work}(H)$$

   The first sentence says that if H is big and a house, then either H is a lot of work or C is the cleaner. If H is a big house and G is its garden, then H is a lot of work for sure. Both of the above sentences are in normal form, and they are collectively equivalent to the original (7.42).

   This completes the proof of Theorem 7.5.1 (and in some sense, the proof of Theorem 7.4.1 as well!). ■

7.6 FURTHER READING

Resolution was introduced and proved complete in Robinson [1965]. Since then, there have been many papers and books on automated theorem proving and deduction; any references I give you are likely to be out of date almost immediately. Ongoing progress is reported in the *Journal of Logic Programming* and the proceedings of the annual conference on automated deduction (typically known as CADE).

Most descriptions of resolution work with a normal form that omits the final two steps of Algorithm 7.5.2, so that the sentences are left as disjunctions of literals. This saves some time in the translation of a declarative database into normal form, but I find the resulting axioms such as (7.46) difficult to understand. The description we have given is a straightforward generalization of the Horn clauses that are the elements of PROLOG programs; two excellent introductions to PROLOG itself are by Clocksin and Mellish [1987] and Sterling and Shapiro [1986]. Our description also bears vague resemblance to the sequent calculus of Gentzen [1969], TABLOG [Malachi *et al.*, 1986], and Robinson's later work reported by Robinson [1979].

Vividness is introduced by Levesque [1986]. Although I find the idea an attractive one, there are many others who would disagree. A coherent argument *against* vividness can be found in Davis [1990].

7.7 EXERCISES

1. Suppose that we had left axiom (7.11) out of our initial description of our lawyer domain. Show that our intended conclusion `work(house-of(John))` would not follow from the remaining axioms by constructing a model in which all of (7.9)–(7.13) except (7.11) hold but the conclusion `work(house-of(John))` fails to hold.

2. The axiom (7.6) says that everyone has a house. Is this really true?
   (a) Which of the four statements at the beginning of the chapter is the one that tells us that John has a house?
   (b) Provide a better formalization of this statement that allows us to derive the fact that John has a house. Do you still need the function `house-of`? What does this axiom mean for people who don't have houses?
   (c) Translate your formalization into normal form and use modus ponens to prove that John's house is a lot of work to maintain.

3. If f is a false sentence (such as the negation of a tautology), prove that $D \models q$ is equivalent to $D \cup \{\neg q\} \models f$.

4. Prove that modus ponens is complete for Horn databases.

5. Instead of using resolution to prove by contradiction that John's house is a lot of work, use it to derive the conclusion

   `work(house-of(John))`

   directly from the axioms (7.32)–(7.36).

6. For Christmas, I have decided to get a friend of mine either a pair of slippers or some ski gloves. Both are available at Macy's. The slippers cost $19.95, and the gloves cost $18.75.
   (a) Use resolution to show that I can buy the gift at Macy's.
   (b) Use resolution to show that I will spend at least $15 on my friend's gift. What additional facts did you have to add to the database to do this?

7. Let x be an arbitrary atom.
   (a) Use resolution to derive $x \wedge x$ from $x \vee x$.
   (b) Can resolution derive the above conclusion without factoring?

8. Translate the following sentence into normal form:

   If John does not have a big house, John is not rich.

   How does this compare with (7.12)? Comment on this.

9. Translate the following sentence into normal form:

   John is a trial lawyer if and only if he is either a district attorney or a defense attorney.

   (By p if and only if q, we mean p if q and p only if q, or $q \rightarrow p$ and $\neg q \rightarrow \neg p$.)

CHAPTER

8

FIRST-ORDER LOGIC

Our aim in this chapter is simple: to extend the results of Chapter 7 so that they can deal with sentences that include quantifiers. After all, when we were trying to prove that John's house was a lot of work to maintain, we showed tremendous foresight in rewriting

$$\forall p.\mathtt{lawyer}(p) \rightarrow \mathtt{rich}(p)$$

as

$$\mathtt{lawyer(John)} \rightarrow \mathtt{rich(John)}$$

How did we know that $p = \mathtt{John}$ was the case of interest?

In order to extend our earlier results, we need to discuss three separate topics:

1. The construction of databases that include quantifiers.
2. The extension of modus ponens and the resolution rule to handle quantifiers.
3. The inclusion of quantifiers in normal form sentences.

8.1 DATABASES WITH QUANTIFIERS

We dealt with some aspects of this in the previous chapter. Here is the description of our usual problem again.

$$\mathtt{lawyer(John)} \tag{8.1}$$

$$\forall p.\mathtt{lawyer}(p) \rightarrow \mathtt{rich}(p) \tag{8.2}$$

$$\forall p.\mathtt{house}(\mathtt{house\text{-}of}(p),p) \tag{8.3}$$

$$\forall hp.\mathtt{house}(h,p) \wedge \mathtt{rich}(p) \rightarrow \mathtt{big}(h) \tag{8.4}$$

$$\forall h.[\mathtt{big}(h) \wedge \exists p.\mathtt{house}(h,p) \rightarrow \mathtt{work}(h)] \tag{8.5}$$

What if we try to drop the function house–of from this description? After all, (8.3) is really telling us only that John has a house:

$$\exists h.\mathrm{house}(h, \mathrm{John}) \tag{8.6}$$

But now how do we write the conclusion of our logical exercise, that John's house is a lot of work? All we can do is say that there is some object h that is both a lot of work and a house belonging to John:

$$\exists h.\mathrm{work}(h) \wedge \mathrm{house}(h, \mathrm{John})$$

This seems a bit awkward; it would be easier if we could refer directly to the object whose existence is guaranteed by (8.6).

We can do this by giving this object an explicit name. To do so, we need to invent a new object constant and add it to our declarative language; we can't use an existing object constant (such as John himself) because that might involve saying something unintended if the name we used appeared in other axioms. Let's call our new object constant Sk–1 (don't worry about why for now), so that we can rewrite (8.6) as

$$\mathrm{house}(\mathrm{Sk{-}1}, \mathrm{John}) \tag{8.7}$$

There are a couple of things to note here. The first is that (8.7) and (8.6) really do say the same thing; recall our observation at the beginning of Chapter 6 that the variable names don't matter. Each of (8.7) and (8.6) is, for example, consistent with John having many houses. This is because neither axiom says that the object being discussed is John's *only* house.

Each description is also consistent with John's house being an object that we already know about but refer to by another name. Thus if John is the president, we know that

$$\mathrm{house}(\mathrm{White{-}House}, \mathrm{John}) \tag{8.8}$$

Since we haven't said that Sk–1 and White–House are distinct objects, it might be the case that the house referred to in (8.7) or in (8.6) is the same as the house in (8.8), or it might not be.

This is actually quite a subtle point, because people typically assume that objects with different names, like Sk–1 and White–House, refer to different things. This assumption is known as the *unique names hypothesis*; what we have just observed is that the unique names hypothesis and the naming process that we have just introduced cannot both be used in a single application.

The other thing to note about our naming process is that it can be applied in a much wider setting than to simple existential statements such as (8.6). Suppose that instead of saying that John has a house, we want to say that *everyone* does:

$$\forall p \exists h.\text{house}(h,p) \tag{8.9}$$

To remove the existential quantifier from (8.9), we need to name "the house belonging to *p*"; the thing to realize is that this isn't a single house for all people, but is instead a *function* of *p*. Thus we can replace (8.9) with

$$\forall p.\text{house}(\text{Sk–2}(p),p) \tag{8.10}$$

where we have introduced the function Sk–2(*p*) for "the house belonging to *p*."[17]

What if, instead of (8.9), we had wanted to remove the quantifier from the sentence

$$\exists h \forall p.\text{house}(h,p) \tag{8.11}$$

This sentence says that there is a *single* house *h* that belongs to everyone, so we can use an object instead of a function constant, writing

$$\forall p.\text{house}(\text{Sk–3},p)$$

Looking at (8.7), (8.10), (8.11) and their quantified equivalents, the following principle emerges:

DEFINITION 8.1.1 *Let* p *be a quantified sentence of the form*

$$\forall v_1 \ldots v_n \exists x.q(v_i,x) \tag{8.12}$$

where the variables v_i *are universally quantified, the variable* x *is existentially quantified, and these variables appear in the component sentence* q. *The* Skolemization *of (8.12) is the sentence*

$$\forall v_1 \ldots v_n.q(v_i, \text{Sk–n}(v_1,\ldots,v_n))$$

where x *has been replaced with* $\text{Sk–n}(v_1,\ldots,v_n))$ *in the subexpression* q. Sk–n *is a new function constant that does not appear elsewhere in the database.*

The term *Skolemization* is derived from the name of the mathematician Thoralf Skolem, and the new constants that appear in Definition 8.1.1 are

17 We are extending our notational conventions here, taking functions to be symbols that either end with -of or begin with Sk–.

often called *Skolem constants*. (This is why we have denoted these new constants using names beginning with Sk.) We now have the following:

PROPOSITION 8.1.2 *Let D be a logical database and* Sk(D) *its Skolemization. Then D and* Sk(D) *are equivalent in the sense that if q is any query that does not contain Skolem constants,* $D \models q$ *if and only if* $\text{Sk}(D) \models q$.

Here is the Skolemized version of our usual logical database:

$$\texttt{lawyer(John)} \tag{8.13}$$

$$\forall p.\texttt{lawyer}(p) \rightarrow \texttt{rich}(p) \tag{8.14}$$

$$\forall p.\texttt{house}(\texttt{Sk-2}(p),p) \tag{8.15}$$

$$\forall hp.[\texttt{house}(h,p) \wedge \texttt{rich}(p) \rightarrow \texttt{big}(h)] \tag{8.16}$$

$$\forall h.[\texttt{big}(h) \wedge \exists p.\texttt{house}(h,p) \rightarrow \texttt{work}(h)] \tag{8.17}$$

We've left the existential quantifier in (8.17) for the time being. Note that we *cannot* use Proposition 8.1.2 to remove this quantifier, since the proposition can be applied only if the existential is at the front of the subexpression q, and not embedded within it as in (8.17).

This new axiomatization is the same as our old one! The Skolemization idea led us to automatically introduce the function house-of; we just happened to call it Sk-2 instead.

Before proceeding, let's have one last look at (8.17); can we somehow remove the existential quantifier that appears in it? What that sentence is telling us is that for any h, if h is big and there is some person p such that h is p's house, then h is a lot of work to maintain. But this is just the same as saying that for any h and p, if h is big and p's house, then h is a lot of work to maintain. (Think about this for a minute if it isn't clear.) So we can rewrite (8.17) as

$$\forall hp.[\texttt{big}(h) \wedge \texttt{house}(h,p) \rightarrow \texttt{work}(h)]$$

Given this, our logical database looks like this:

$$\texttt{lawyer(John)}$$

$$\forall p.\texttt{lawyer}(p) \rightarrow \texttt{rich}(p)$$

$$\forall p.\texttt{house}(\texttt{Sk-2}(p),p)$$

$$\forall hp.[\texttt{house}(h,p) \wedge \texttt{rich}(p) \rightarrow \texttt{big}(h)]$$

$$\forall hp.[\texttt{big}(h) \wedge \texttt{house}(h,p) \rightarrow \texttt{work}(h)]$$

Interestingly enough, all of the variables in these sentences are universally quantified; we've replaced the existential quantifiers with Skolem constants. Since universal quantifiers appear so often in logical databases, it is common simply to omit them, using the convention that any variable not associated with a quantifier is implicitly universally quantified. We will also anticipate some of the needs of subsequent sections and use distinct variables in all of the axioms:

$$\texttt{lawyer(John)} \tag{8.18}$$

$$\texttt{lawyer}(p_2) \rightarrow \texttt{rich}(p_2) \tag{8.19}$$

$$\texttt{house(Sk-2}(p_3),p_3) \tag{8.20}$$

$$\texttt{house}(h_4,p_4) \wedge \texttt{rich}(p_4) \rightarrow \texttt{big}(h_4) \tag{8.21}$$

$$\texttt{big}(h_5) \wedge \texttt{house}(h_5,p_5) \rightarrow \texttt{work}(h_5) \tag{8.22}$$

8.2 UNIFICATION

Suppose that we now try to use the above axioms to conclude that John's house is a lot of work. How can we possibly do this when work(house−of(John)) is not the conclusion of any of the rules in our database?

The answer, of course, is that although work(house−of(John)) isn't the right-hand side of a rule that appears in our database, it is an *instance* of the right-hand side of such a rule, namely (8.22). By taking h_5 to be house−of(John), this rule becomes

$$\texttt{big(house-of(John))} \wedge \texttt{house(house-of(John)},p_5) \rightarrow \texttt{work(house-of(John))} \tag{8.23}$$

and now the right-hand side is of the necessary form.

What we have done is to assign a value, house−of(John), to the variable h_5 that appears in (8.22). This process of modifying a universally quantified sentence by assigning values to some or all of the variables it contains is known as *instantiation*. In general, we will make the following definition:

DEFINITION 8.2.1 *A* binding list *is a set of entries of the form* v = e *where* v *is a variable and* e *is an object in our domain. We will say that the* binding list binds *the variable* v *to the value* e.

In the example above, the binding list is given by

$$\{h_5 = \texttt{house-of(John)}\}$$

and (8.23) is the result of applying this binding list to (8.22). Given an expression p and a binding list σ, we will write $p|_\sigma$ for the result of instantiating p using the bindings in σ. Thus

$$\mathtt{work}(h_5)|_{\{h5=\mathtt{house-of(John)}\}} = \mathtt{work(house-of(John))}$$

Of course, binding lists need not bind only a single variable to a value. Thus the empty binding list $\sigma = \{\ \}$ binds no variables and has the property that $p|_\sigma = p$ for all expressions p. If we apply the binding list

$$\{h_5 = \mathtt{house} - \mathtt{of(John)},\ p_5 = \mathtt{John}\} \tag{8.24}$$

to the implication (8.22), we get

$$\mathtt{big(house-of(John))} \wedge \mathtt{house(house-of(John),\ John)} \rightarrow \\ \mathtt{work(house-of(John))}$$

which is the instance of (8.22) that we need to derive

$$\mathtt{work(house-of(John))}$$

Note also that a binding list can bind variables that do not actually appear in the expression being bound. Thus we can apply the binding list in (8.24) to the expression $\mathtt{work(h_5)}$ to obtain $\mathtt{work(house-of(John))}$ as usual.

Let us now apply these techniques to answer a rather simpler question from our database—who is a lawyer?

We don't know who the lawyer is, so we look for a sentence in our database that is an instance of

$$\mathtt{lawyer}(p)$$

Since

$$\mathtt{lawyer(John)} = \mathtt{lawyer}(p)|_{\{p=\mathtt{John}\}} \tag{8.25}$$

we conclude that we can indeed find a lawyer; John is one.

There are a couple of things to note here. The first is that our query was existentially quantified; we wanted to show that there was *some* lawyer. So our query was really $\exists p.\mathtt{lawyer}(p)$. Why does it seem natural to drop the existential quantifier here, when we typically drop *universal* quantifiers from our database? We will return to this issue presently.

The second thing to note about (8.25) is that the binding list gives us more than an affirmative answer to our existential query—it actually tells us who the lawyer is. This is a typical feature of the approach we are taking;

if a "constructive" proof for an existential query exists (one that succeeds by actually displaying the object in question), then it will appear as a term in the binding list we generate. And note that many proofs *are* constructive—when, for example, we ask, "Can I get to the airport by 5:00?" we are typically asking for a constructive response. Showing that a job is possible usually involves constructing a plan to get the job done.

Here's another example. My dog, Coco, likes everything:

$$\texttt{likes(Coco,}\ x\texttt{)} \tag{8.26}$$

Is there someone who likes brussels sprouts?

Continuing to handle the existential quantification implicitly, the query becomes

$$\texttt{likes(}x\texttt{, Brussels-sprouts)} \tag{8.27}$$

We therefore need to find a fact in the database that is an instance of (8.27).

The fact (8.26) is an obvious choice, except for the fact that `likes(Coco, Brussels-sprouts)` is actually only an *instance* of (8.26). So we see that we really need to find an *instance* of a fact in the database that is itself an instance of our query.

There is one other point to note here. The same variable x appears in both (8.26) and (8.27), and there is no single binding for x that can make these two sentences instances of one another. This is the reason that we used unique variables in (8.18)–(8.22)—we have no reason to assume that multiple occurrences of a single variable should refer to identical objects. With this in mind, we rewrite our query as

$$\texttt{likes(}y\texttt{, Brussels-sprouts)} \tag{8.28}$$

If we now take σ to be

$$\sigma = \{x = \texttt{Brussels-sprouts},\ y = \texttt{Coco}\}$$

then we have

$$\begin{aligned} \texttt{likes(Coco,}\ x\texttt{)}|_\sigma &= \texttt{likes(Coco, Brussels-sprouts)} \\ &= \texttt{likes(}y\texttt{, Brussels-sprouts)}|_\sigma \end{aligned} \tag{8.29}$$

so that the query succeeds by binding y to Coco. Yes, there is someone who likes brussels sprouts—the indiscriminate Coco. Once again, the binding list includes information about the value of the existentially quantified variable that appeared in the query.

In the next two sections, there are two issues that we will address. The first is that of quantification—why is it that existentially quantified variables are handled implicitly in queries, while it is the universally quantified ones that are implicit in the database? The second is the general issue underlying (8.29); given two sentences or expressions p and q, is there a binding list σ such that $p|_\sigma = q|_\sigma$?

DEFINITION 8.2.2 *Given two expressions* p *and* q, *a* unifier *of* p *and* q *is any binding list* σ *such that* $p|_\sigma = q|_\sigma$.

One unifier is called more general than another if it either binds fewer variables or binds them to less specific expressions:

DEFINITION 8.2.3 *Let* σ_1 *and* σ_2 *be two binding lists.* σ_1 *is* more general *than* σ_2 *if, for every expression* p, $p|_{\sigma_2}$ *is an instance of* $p|_{\sigma_1}$.

In general, we want to find not only *some* unifier of p and q, but the most general one. To see why, suppose that our last query, instead of requiring that we find someone who likes brussels sprouts, had been to find someone who likes something:

```
likes(y,z)
```

We can still return the answer binding y to Coco and z to brussels sprouts, but this binding list

```
{y = Coco, z = Brussels-sprouts}
```

is less general than the one

```
{y = Coco}
```

that doesn't bind z at all. Since we may need to bind z later, it is imprudent to bind it prematurely. Perhaps our original query was something like, Find a y and a z such that y likes z and z is not a vegetable:

```
likes(y,z) ∧ ¬vegetable(z)
```

and we simply chose to work on the first conjunct before the second. If we have bound z to brussels sprouts, the second conjunct will become

```
¬vegetable(Brussels-sprouts)
```

and will not have any solutions; if z is unbound after the first conjunct is solved we will presumably not have this problem.

8.3 SKOLEMIZING QUERIES

Before we consider the question of constructing the most general unifier of two expressions, let us consider quantification again. As we have already seen, it is *existential* quantifiers that are implicit in queries; this is at odds with the fact that universal quantifiers are handled implicitly in our declarative database.

Not only are existential quantifiers implicit in queries, but universally quantified variables are Skolemized! To see this, consider the query

$$\forall x.\texttt{lawyer}(x) \tag{8.30}$$

Can we show that everyone is a lawyer?

Clearly the query lawyer(x) is inappropriate for this purpose; we have already seen that this query succeeds by binding x to John. But consider instead the Skolemized query

$$\texttt{lawyer(Sk–4)} \tag{8.31}$$

What can we say about this?

There are two possibilities. Let us suppose that the query succeeds, so that we are somehow able to derive lawyer(Sk–4) from what's in our database. But now if lawyer(John) is some other instance of our quantified query (8.30), the proof that showed Sk–4 to be a lawyer can doubtless be applied to John as well. This is because the Skolem constant Sk–4 is guaranteed not to appear elsewhere in our database—and so anything true of Sk–4 must be true of John as well. Since we are able to prove lawyer(x) for all x, it follows that we can show ∀x.lawyer(x), and the quantified query (8.30) should succeed in this case.

What if lawyer(Sk–4) fails, so that we are not able to prove that Sk–4 is a lawyer? (This doesn't mean we can prove that Sk–4 *isn't* a lawyer; we may not be able to prove anything one way or another.) Now we are clearly also unable to prove (8.30), since lawyer(Sk–4) is an instance of (8.30) and therefore a consequence of it. Since we have no proof of lawyer(Sk–4), we mustn't have a proof of (8.30) either, and the quantified query should fail.

What we have seen is that the universally quantified query (8.30) succeeds in exactly those cases that its Skolemized version does, so that we can drop the quantifier by Skolemizing the variable. Why is this? How could we handle more subtly quantified queries?

In order to understand what's going on here, we should take advantage of the fact that we have a solid understanding of quantification in database sentences; that's what Proposition 8.1.2 is all about. What we don't have is an equally clear understanding of quantification in queries—is there some way that we can somehow get one from the other?

There is. We have already remarked in Chapter 7 that when responding to a query q, we proceed by adding $\neg q$ to our database and then trying to derive a contradiction. If we succeed in doing so, then adding $\neg q$ to our original database was inconsistent, so that q was a consequence of the database and the original query should have succeeded. If we fail in our attempt to derive a contradiction, then since $\neg q$ is consistent with our original database, we know that any attempt to derive q will also fail.

This process has eliminated the quantifiers from our query, since the contradiction $T \rightarrow F$ does not involve quantifiers; the quantifiers in q are interpreted by adding $\neg q$ to the database. And this explains exactly the behavior we have observed.

Proving ∃x.lawyer(x) involves adding

$$\neg\exists \texttt{x.lawyer(x)} \tag{8.32}$$

to our database. But this is equivalent to

$$\forall \texttt{x.}\neg\texttt{lawyer(x)}$$

or simply ¬lawyer(x)—the existentially quantified variable in the query is implicitly quantified in this example.

The universally quantified sentence ∀x.lawyer(x) corresponds to the database addition

$$\neg\forall \texttt{x.lawyer(x)}$$

or

$$\exists \texttt{x.}\neg\texttt{lawyer(x)}$$

When we drop the quantifier, this becomes

$$\neg\texttt{lawyer(Sk-4)}$$

as in (8.31).

In both cases, the Skolemization is "backward" because negating the query and adding it to the database inverts the sense of the leading quantifier. More complex examples can obviously be handled similarly; in Section 8.6 we discuss the general problem of removing quantifiers from sentences as we translate them into normal form.

8.4 FINDING THE MOST GENERAL UNIFIER

Given two expressions p and q, we now return to the problem of finding their most general unifier, or mgu. The following procedure suffices:

ALGORITHM 8.4.1 *To compute the mgu of two expressions* p *and* q:

1. *If either* p *or* q *is either an object constant or a variable, then:*
   (a) *If* p = q, p *and* q *already unify and we can return* { }.
   (b) *If either* p *or* q *is a variable, return the result binding that variable to the other expression.*
   (c) *If* p ≠ q *and neither is a variable,* p *and* q *do not unify. Return failure.*
2. *If neither* p *nor* q *is an object constant or variable, then they must both be compound expressions of some sort—conjunctions such as* $p_1 \wedge \cdots \wedge p_n$, *disjunctions, relational expressions like* $r(p_1, \ldots, p_n)$ *or functional expressions such as* $f(p_1, \ldots, p_n)$. *In this case, both the type of the expression and any function/relation constant must match for* p *and* q *to have a chance of unifying at all. In other words, a relational expression can never match a conjunction. Two functional expressions can never match unless they begin with the same function constant, and so on.*
   If the types and any function/relation constant are not equal for the two expressions, return failure. Otherwise, the lists of arguments $p_1, \ldots, p_n$ *and* $q_1, \ldots, q_m$ *must be of the same length* (m = n); *if* m ≠ n, *return failure. If* m = n, *do the following:*
   (a) *Set* σ = { } *and* k = 0. σ *is the unifier constructed thus far by unifying successive subexpressions of* p *and* q; k *indicates how many of these embedded subexpressions have been unified successfully.*
   (b) *If* k = n, *stop and return* σ *as the mgu of* p *and* q.
   (c) *Otherwise, increment* k *and invoke the algorithm recursively to find the mgu of* $p_k|_\sigma$ *and* $q_k|_\sigma$. *Add any new bindings into the result being computed by appending this new mgu to* σ *and return to step 2. If* $p_k|_\sigma$ *and* $g_k|_\sigma$ *fail to unify, then* p *and* q *do not unify and return failure.*

Here are some examples of this algorithm in use.

Example 1 To unify *p* = x and *q* = `John`, we note that since *p* is a variable, we need simply bind it to *q* and return the binding list {x = `John`}.

Example 2 To unify *p* = x and *q* = `house-of(John)`, we once again note that *p* is a variable and therefore return

{x = `house-of(John)`}

Example 3 Here is an example from earlier in this chapter. *p* is `lawyer(x)` and *q* is `lawyer(John)`. Since both of these expressions are relational, we need for their relation symbols to match (they do, since the relation symbol is `lawyer` in both cases) and now work our way through the loop in Algorithm 8.4.1. With the relation `lawyer` accepting only a single argument, we need only unify x and `John` as in Example 1 to be able to return

$$\{x = \texttt{John}\}$$

Example 4 Another example from earlier in this chapter unified

$$\texttt{likes}(\texttt{Coco}, x)$$

and

$$\texttt{likes}(y, \texttt{Brussels-sprouts})$$

As before, the relation symbols and number of arguments match. Considering the first argument leads us to unify `Coco` with y to get $\sigma = \{y = \texttt{Coco}\}$. Using this to bind the second arguments doesn't modify them, since neither involves y; we therefore need to unify x and `Brussels-sprouts`.

Doing this gives us $\{x = \texttt{Brussels-sprouts}\}$; appending this to σ gives us as our overall unifier

$$\{x = \texttt{Brussels-sprouts}, y = \texttt{Coco}\}$$

Example 5 What if we hadn't used distinct variables in the preceding example? Now we would be trying to unify the expressions `likes(Coco, x)` and `likes(x, Brussels-sprouts)`.

As before, we unify the first arguments to get $\{x = \texttt{Coco}\}$. But now when we use this binding list on the second arguments of x and `Brussels-sprouts`, these second arguments become `Coco` and `Brussels-sprouts`—and these two different object constants do not unify. Thus the original expressions in this example do not unify either.

On an intuitive level, there is no single binding for x that can make the expressions

$$\texttt{likes}(\texttt{Coco}, x) \tag{8.33}$$

and

$$\texttt{likes}(x, \texttt{Brussels-sprouts}) \tag{8.34}$$

identical; we need $x = \texttt{Coco}$ for the first terms to match and x = Brussels-sprouts for the second. This is the reason that the two expressions (8.33) and (8.34) fail to unify.[18]

Example 6 If we unify $f(x,y)$ with $f(y,a)$, we begin by unifying x with y to get $\sigma = \{x = y\}$. We next unify y with a to get a complete answer of

$$\{x = y,\ y = a\}$$

In practice, it is useful to rewrite this as

$$\{x = a,\ y = a\}$$

Note that we change the binding for x from y to a. Since y is itself bound to a, this change has no real effect on the meaning of the unifier; from a computational point of view, however, it will make it far easier to compute $p|_\sigma$ for various p.

Example 7 Suppose we know that everyone likes his house, which we write as

$$\texttt{likes}(x, \texttt{house-of}(x)) \tag{8.35}$$

Suppose that we also say that anyone who likes himself is conceited:

$$\texttt{likes}(y, y) \rightarrow \texttt{conceited}(y) \tag{8.36}$$

What can we now say about the goal conceited(z); is there someone known to be conceited?

The given goal generates the subgoal of finding a z such that likes(z,z); any such z will be conceited by virtue of (8.36). We therefore need to unify likes(z,z) with (8.35).

As usual, the relation symbols and argument counts match. Unifying x with z gives us $\sigma = \{x = z\}$; applying this binding list to the second arguments house-of(x) and z means that we need to unify house-of(z) with z. Since z is a variable, we can return the overall result

$$\{x = z,\ z = \texttt{house-of}(z)\} \tag{8.37}$$

18 By taking x = Coco we could make both (8.33) and (8.34) *true*, but that is not what unification is about. The purpose of unification is to make the expressions *identical*, not just equivalent to one another against the background of our declarative database.

But what does this actually mean? It didn't *seem* that our simple database was enough to conclude that anyone was conceited.

Consider the binding list in (8.37) a bit more closely. What it is telling us is that if x = z and z = `house-of(z)`, then x is conceited. But in this case, we would have x = `house-of(x)`. In other words, x is conceited if x is equal to x's house!

This doesn't really make sense; the problem is that we are attempting to bind x to an expression in which x itself appears. This should not be allowed, and we need to modify step 1 of the unification algorithm to read:

> If either p or q is a variable *that does not appear in the other*, return the result binding that variable to the other expression.

This modification to the unification algorithm is known as the *occurs check*. It comes up only rarely, and is extremely awkward from a computational point of view.

To see why the occurs check is so awkward, consider the computational requirements involved in constructing the unifier of two expressions. The length of the intermediate expressions constructed when we apply σ to the subexpressions appearing in Algorithm 8.4.1 can grow exponentially with the length of the original expressions, but, by avoiding the instantiation and simply setting each variable to its intended value, it is not hard to see that a linear-time algorithm can be developed. If we need to do the occurs check, however, it seems that the results of applying σ to the intermediate expressions will need to be computed, and that computing most general unifiers is a potentially exponential process.

In fact, it turns out that the problem of constructing the mgu of two expressions really is linear in the lengths of the expressions, although the linear algorithms that include the occurs check are far more complex than those that do not. As a result, although the worst-case performance of these algorithms is linear, their performance on simple examples is typically far worse than that of a procedure such as 8.4.1. Since unification is central to the use of declarative databases, it is impractical to use linear unification algorithms that include an occurs check, and two options remain:

1. The occurs check can simply be ignored. This is the approach taken by PROLOG, for example. The result is that expressions are occasionally thought to unify when they do not, and incorrect answers can occasionally be returned to declarative queries.

2. A nearly linear algorithm can be used that includes the occurs check but is as effective as Algorithm 8.4.1 on the usual sorts of examples. Such an algorithm is described in Escalada-Imaz and Ghallab [1988], for example.

8.5 MODUS PONENS AND HORN DATABASES

Armed with unification techniques, we can work with (8.18)–(8.22) instead of (7.9)–(7.13). As an example, given the facts

$$\texttt{lawyer(John)}$$

and

$$\texttt{lawyer}(p_2) \rightarrow \texttt{rich}(p_2) \tag{8.38}$$

we can bind p_2 to John and then apply modus ponens to conclude rich(John).

Here is the original statement of the modus ponens rule: When $d = a_i$, the following conclusion is valid:

$$\frac{\begin{array}{r} a_1 \wedge \cdots \wedge a_m \rightarrow b \\ c_1 \wedge \cdots \wedge c_n \rightarrow d \end{array}}{a_1 \wedge \cdots \wedge \hat{a}_i \wedge \cdots \wedge a_m \wedge c_1 \wedge \cdots \wedge c_n \rightarrow b}$$

What we see now is that we do not need d and a_i to be equal, but only for them to unify. This produces the following:

DEFINITION 8.5.1 Modus ponens *is the following rule of inference, where* d *and* a_i *unify with mgu* σ*:*

$$\frac{\begin{array}{r} a_1 \wedge \cdots \wedge a_m \rightarrow b \\ c_1 \wedge \cdots \wedge c_n \rightarrow d \end{array}}{[a_1 \wedge \cdots \wedge \hat{a}_i \wedge \cdots \wedge a_m \wedge c_1 \wedge \cdots \wedge c_n \rightarrow b]|_\sigma}$$

PROPOSITION 8.5.2 *Modus ponens is sound.*

PROOF If $d|_\sigma = a_i|_\sigma$, we can apply the binding list σ to the two premises of the rule to get

$$\begin{array}{r} [a_1 \wedge \cdots \wedge a_m]|_\sigma \rightarrow b|_\sigma \\ [c_1 \wedge \cdots \wedge c_n]|_\sigma \rightarrow d|_\sigma \end{array}$$

Since $[a_1 \wedge \cdots \wedge a_m]|_\sigma = a_1|_\sigma \wedge \cdots \wedge a_m|_\sigma$, we can now apply Proposition 7.1.2 to conclude

$$[a_1 \wedge \cdots \wedge \hat{a}_i \wedge \cdots \wedge a_m \wedge c_1 \wedge \cdots \wedge c_n]|_\sigma \rightarrow b|_\sigma$$

This is equivalent to the conclusion of the modus ponens rule. ∎

The above result generalizes Proposition 7.1.2, saying that modus ponens remains sound in a setting that includes quantification. Theorem 7.2.2 also generalizes, allowing us to conclude that modus ponens is complete for Horn databases.

What about Proposition 7.2.5, which bounded the time needed to compute the consequences of a Horn database? Here is the old result.

PROPOSITION 7.2.5 *In a Horn database without function constants, the time needed to determine whether or not a particular atom follows is of order* nd*, where* n *is the maximum number of premises in any implication and* d *is the size of the database.*

If there are no function constants in our language, we can generalize this result by realizing that the number of possible bindings for the variables in our language is strictly limited—there aren't any functions around that we can use to create new objects. This means that we can replace our universally quantified sentences with their ground versions by making a copy of each sentence for each possible variable instantiation. As an example, if our universe of object constants consists of the three objects Hughie, Dewey, and Louie, the single quantified sentence

$$\text{duck}(x) \rightarrow \text{likes}(x,y)$$

(saying that ducks like everything) would become the nine ground sentences:

$$\begin{aligned}
\text{duck(Hughie)} &\rightarrow \text{likes(Hughie, Hughie)} \\
\text{duck(Hughie)} &\rightarrow \text{likes(Hughie, Dewey)} \\
\text{duck(Hughie)} &\rightarrow \text{likes(Hughie, Louie)} \\
\text{duck(Dewey)} &\rightarrow \text{likes(Dewey, Hughie)} \\
\text{duck(Dewey)} &\rightarrow \text{likes(Dewey, Dewey)} \\
\text{duck(Dewey)} &\rightarrow \text{likes(Dewey, Louie)} \\
\text{duck(Louie)} &\rightarrow \text{likes(Louie, Hughie)} \\
\text{duck(Louie)} &\rightarrow \text{likes(Louie, Dewey)} \\
\text{duck(Louie)} &\rightarrow \text{likes(Louie, Louie)}
\end{aligned}$$

LEMMA 8.5.3 *Suppose that there are* d *sentences and* o *object constants in our database. Then if the maximum number of variables appearing in any database sentence is* v*, the size of the equivalent quantifier-free database is at most* $o^v d$*.*

PROOF A single database sentence has at most v variables, so the number of ground instances of each sentence is limited to o^v. There are d sentences, so the entire database is of size $o^v d$. ■

PROPOSITION 8.5.4 *In a Horn database without function constants, the time needed to determine whether or not a particular atom follows is of order* $no^v d$, *where* n *is the maximum number of premises in any implication and* o, v, *and* d *are as in Lemma 8.5.3.*

PROOF This is a straightforward combination of Lemma 8.5.3 and our earlier Proposition 7.2.5. ■

Unfortunately, the appearance of the o^v term in the above result makes it much less attractive than its predecessor in the last chapter. As we remarked in Section 6.5, the number of objects in a realistic database is likely to be large, and the number of variables in the most complex rule is likely to result in $o^v d$ being many orders of magnitude too big to provide a useful bound in practice.

8.6 RESOLUTION AND NORMAL FORM

Generalizing the resolution rule to our wider setting is no harder than generalizing modus ponens. Here is the result.

DEFINITION 8.6.1 Resolution *is the following rule of inference, where* d_j *and* a_i *unify with mgu* σ:

$$\frac{\begin{array}{c} a_1 \wedge \cdots \wedge a_m \rightarrow b_1 \vee \cdots \vee b_k \\ c_1 \wedge \cdots \wedge c_n \rightarrow d_1 \vee \cdots \vee d_l \end{array}}{[a_1 \wedge \cdots \wedge \hat{a}_i \wedge \cdots \wedge a_m \wedge c_1 \wedge \cdots \wedge c_n \rightarrow b_1 \vee \cdots \vee b_k \vee d_1 \vee \cdots \vee \hat{d}_j \vee \cdots \vee d_l]|_\sigma}$$

In our usual example, our intention is to find something that is a lot of work to maintain, so the query is work(x). Here is a suitable modification of the derivation of the last chapter:

	Sentence	Source	Bindings
1	$\texttt{work}(x) \rightarrow F$	negated query	
2	$\texttt{big}(h_5) \wedge \texttt{house}(h_5,p_5) \rightarrow F$	resolve 1,(8.22)	$x = h_5$
3	$\texttt{big}(\texttt{house-of}(p_3)) \rightarrow F$	resolve 2,(8.20)	$h_5 = \texttt{house-of}(p_3), p_5 = p_3$
4	$\texttt{house}(\texttt{house-of}(p_3),p_4) \wedge \texttt{rich}(p_4) \rightarrow F$	resolve 3,(8.21)	$h_4 = \texttt{house-of}(p_3)$
5	$\texttt{rich}(p_3) \rightarrow F$	resolve 4,(8.20)	$p_4 = p_3$
6	$\texttt{lawyer}(p_3) \rightarrow F$	resolve 5,(8.19)	$p_2 = p_3$
7	$T \rightarrow F$	resolve 6,(8.18)	$p_3 = \texttt{John}$

(8.39)

The object that has been proven to be a lot of work can be identified by finding the binding for x in the above derivation. In step 2, we bind x to h_5 (the house mentioned in (8.22)); in step 3, we bind it to house-of(p_3). The variable p_3 is bound to John in step 6, so we can conclude that x itself is bound to house-of(John). John's house is a lot of work to maintain.

As in the previous chapter, resolution as described in Definition 8.6.1 is sound and complete, provided that we can extend our discussion of normal form to include variables. The description of normal-form sentences themselves is unchanged, except that the sentences appearing in Definition 8.6.1 are now permitted to include variables. The key result is the following:

THEOREM 8.6.2 *Let S be a set of sentences of first-order logic. Then there exists a set S′ of sentences in normal form such that S and S′ are equivalent.*

PROOF Here is the algorithm, where differences from Algorithm 7.5.2 appear in boldface:

ALGORITHM 8.6.3 *To translate a sentence* p *into normal form:*

1. *Eliminate* →, *using the fact that* (a → b) *is equivalent to* (¬a ∨ b).
2. *Move negation in.*
3. ***Standardize variables apart.***
4. ***Eliminate existentials using Skolemization.***
5. ***Move the quantifiers to the left.***
6. ***Drop the prefix.***
7. *Distribute* ∨ *and* ∧ *to write as conjunction of disjunctions.*
8. *Split conjunction.*
9. *Combine negated terms.*
10. *Reintroduce implication.*
11. ***Standardize variables apart again.***

As usual, we explain the steps via an example:

$$\forall h.\mathtt{big}(h) \wedge \mathtt{house}(h) \rightarrow \mathtt{work}(h) \vee [\exists m.\mathtt{cleans}(m,h) \wedge \neg\exists\, g.\mathtt{garden}(g,h)] \tag{8.40}$$

Big houses are a lot of work to maintain unless they have a house cleaner and no garden.

1. **Eliminate →.** This produces

$$\forall h.\neg[\mathtt{big}(h) \wedge \mathtt{house}(h)] \vee \mathtt{work}(h) \vee [\exists m.\mathtt{cleans}(m,h) \wedge \neg\exists g.\mathtt{garden}(g,h)] \tag{8.41}$$

2. **Move negation in.** In addition to the equivalence that we used in the

nonquantified case, we need to use the fact that $\neg\exists x.p(x)$ is equivalent to $\forall x.\neg p(x)$. Now (8.41) becomes

$$\forall h.\neg\texttt{big}(h) \vee \neg\texttt{house}(h) \vee \texttt{work}(h) \vee [\exists m.\texttt{cleans}(m,h) \wedge \forall g.\neg\texttt{garden}(g,h)] \quad (8.42)$$

3. **Standardize variables apart.** It may be the case that the same variable appears in multiple places in the expression with which we are working; this step requires that we replace any multiple occurrences of a single variable with distinct variables. Thus, our original expression (8.40) might have used the same letter for the house cleaner and the garden:

$$\forall h.\texttt{big}(h) \wedge \texttt{house}(h) \rightarrow \texttt{work}(h) \vee [\exists x.\texttt{cleans}(x,h) \wedge \neg\exists x.\texttt{garden}(x,h)]$$

   In this case, (8.42) would have been

$$\forall h.\neg\texttt{big}(h) \vee \neg\texttt{house}(h) \vee \texttt{work}(h) \vee [\exists x.\texttt{cleans}(x,h) \wedge \forall x.\neg\texttt{garden}(x,h)] \quad (8.43)$$

   Standardizing apart the variables appearing in (8.43) would force us to replace at least one of the appearances of x here with a different choice, reproducing (8.42) again.

   The reason that the x in $\exists x.\texttt{cleans}(x,h)$ needs to be a different variable than the x in $\neg\exists x.\texttt{garden}(x,h)$ is that the two variables appear under the scope of distinct quantifiers. The various appearances of h in (8.43) are all under the scope of a single universal quantifier, so there is no need to replace these h's with different variables. In fact, doing so would change the meaning of the sentence being manipulated.

4. **Eliminate existentials using Skolemization.** We've already discussed this at some length; since the only existential in (8.42) appears inside a universal quantifier involving h, we introduce the Skolem function `Sk-cleans` to get

$$\forall h.\neg\texttt{big}(h) \vee \neg\texttt{house}(h) \vee \texttt{work}(h) \vee [\texttt{cleans}(\texttt{Sk-cleans}(h),h) \wedge \forall g.\neg\texttt{garden}(g,h)] \quad (8.44)$$

   For any h, either h is not big, or not a house, or a lot of work to maintain, or both `Sk-cleans`(h) cleans h and h has no garden.

5. **Move the quantifiers to the left.** Since the variables have been standardized apart, we know that the variable g doesn't appear in the above

expression other than inside the scope of the last quantifier. Given this, it is legitimate to move the quantification over g to the front of (8.44):

$$\forall gh.\neg\texttt{big}(h) \vee \neg\texttt{house}(h) \vee \texttt{work}(h) \vee [\texttt{cleans}(\texttt{Sk-cleans}(h),h) \wedge \neg\texttt{garden}(g,h)] \quad (8.45)$$

6. **Drop the prefix.** Given the convention that any variables appearing in the final expression are universally quantified, we can drop the leading quantifier in (8.45) to get

$$\neg\texttt{big}(h) \vee \neg\texttt{house}(h) \vee \texttt{work}(h) \vee [\texttt{cleans}(\texttt{Sk-cleans}(h),h) \wedge \neg\texttt{garden}(g,h)]$$

Since no quantifiers remain, we can return to the procedure already introduced for handling ground sentences.

7. **Distribute ∧ and ∨.** This produces

$$[\neg\texttt{big}(h) \vee \neg\texttt{house}(h) \vee \texttt{work}(h) \vee \texttt{cleans}(\texttt{Sk-cleans}(h),h)] \wedge [\neg\texttt{big}(h) \vee \neg\texttt{house}(h) \vee \texttt{work}(h) \vee \neg\texttt{garden}(g,h)]$$

Either h is not big, or not a house, or a lot of work to maintain, or Sk-cleans(h) is its cleaner; similarly for g not being the garden.

8. **Split the conjunction.** We get

$$\neg\texttt{big}(h) \vee \neg\texttt{house}(h) \vee \texttt{work}(h) \vee \texttt{cleans}(\texttt{Sk-cleans}(h),h)$$
$$\neg\texttt{big}(h) \vee \neg\texttt{house}(h) \vee \texttt{work}(h) \vee \neg\texttt{garden}(g,h)$$

9. **Combine any negated terms using de Morgan's laws.** Just like in the ground case. We get

$$\neg[\texttt{big}(h) \wedge \texttt{house}(h)] \vee \texttt{work}(h) \vee \texttt{cleans}(\texttt{Sk-cleans}(h),h)$$
$$\neg[\texttt{big}(h) \wedge \texttt{house}(h) \wedge \texttt{garden}(g,h)] \vee \texttt{work}(h)$$

10. **Reintroduce implication.** And finally, we put the implication back to get

$$[\texttt{big}(h) \wedge \texttt{house}(h)] \rightarrow [\texttt{work}(h) \vee \texttt{cleans}(\texttt{Sk-cleans}(h),h)]$$
$$[\texttt{big}(h) \wedge \texttt{house}(h) \wedge \texttt{garden}(g,h)] \rightarrow \texttt{work}(h)$$

As before, the first sentence says that if h is big and a house, then either h is a lot of work or Sk-cleans(h) is the cleaner. If h is a big house and g is its garden, then h is a lot of work for sure. Both of the above sentences are in normal form.

11. **Standardize the variables apart again.** Because it is often important that distinct database sentences use distinct variables, the last step in the standardization process requires that we take care of this:

$$[\texttt{big}(h) \wedge \texttt{house}(h)] \rightarrow [\texttt{work}(h) \vee \texttt{cleans}(\texttt{Sk-cleans}(h),h)]$$
$$[\texttt{big}(h') \wedge \texttt{house}(h') \wedge \texttt{garden}(g,h')] \rightarrow \texttt{work}(h')$$

8.7 FURTHER READING

What we have called *binding lists* are called *substitution lists* by a variety of authors; these authors also sometimes use special-purpose notation to denote these lists. In Genesereth and Nilsson [1987], for example, the binding list {x = John} is denoted {x/John}.

Our concerns regarding the applicability of worst-case complexity results to AI as a whole are echoed by Doyle and Patil [1991].

Generalizing results such as Theorem 7.4.1 to the setting of first-order logic is somewhat harder than we have indicated here and requires the use of a general-purpose lemma known as the *lifting lemma*. The details of the proof are technical and can be found in Genesereth and Nilsson [1987] (among many other sources).

Rather than determine the binding for a variable in a query by tracing back through the resolution proof as in Section 8.6, it is possible to add a dummy term answer(x) to the query itself, so that instead of trying to derive work(x) we actually try to derive

$$\texttt{work}(x) \wedge \texttt{answer}(x)$$

Instead of stopping when we derive the contradiction $T \rightarrow F$, we stop when we have reduced the problem to an instance of

$$\texttt{answer}(x_1) \wedge \cdots \wedge \texttt{answer}(x_k) \rightarrow F$$

The answer is then known to be one of the x_i's; multiple answers must be considered in case the answer itself is not determined uniquely by the axioms. This idea of an *answer literal* is due to Green [1969] and is described by Rich and Knight [1991] and Genesereth and Nilsson [1987].

8.8 EXERCISES

1. Is it possible to extend Proposition 8.1.2 to say simply that D and Sk(D) are logically equivalent databases? Why or why not?

2. Suppose that we write $\sigma_1 \le \sigma_2$ if σ_1 is less general than σ_2.
   (a) Show that if σ' is a subset of σ, then $\sigma \le \sigma'$.
   (b) Find two binding lists such that one is less general than the other even though neither is a subset of the other.
   (c) Show that $\le$ is transitive and reflexive, in other words, that
      i. If $\sigma_1 \le \sigma_2$ and $\sigma_2 \le \sigma_3$, then $\sigma_1 \le \sigma_3$.
      ii. $\sigma \le \sigma$ for all σ.
   (d) Is $\le$ antisymmetric? In other words, can you show that if $\sigma_1 \le \sigma_2$ and $\sigma_2 \le \sigma_1$, then $\sigma_1 = \sigma_2$?

3. How would Algorithm 8.4.1 need to be modified to compute the mgu of three or more expressions?

4. Compute the mgu of p and q for each of the following cases:
   (a) p = big(x), q = big(house-of(John)).
   (b) p = lawyer(x), q = big(house-of(John)).
   (c) p = big(x), q = big(y).
   (d) p = lawyer(father-of(John)), q = lawyer(father-of(x)).
   (e) p = house-of(x,y), q = house-of(h, John).
   (f) p = house-of(x,y), q = house-of(John, John).
   (g) p = house-of(x,y), q = house-of(h,h).

5. Compute the mgu of p and q in each of the following situations, where letters late in the alphabet are variables and letters early in the alphabet are object constants. Simplify your results (as in Example 6 of the text) in all cases. All of these examples appear in Escalada-Imaz and Ghallab [1988].
   (a) (from Paterson and Wegman [1978]) $p = f(g(v),h(u,v))$ and $q = f(g(w),h(w,j(x,y)))$.
   (b) (compare with 6a) $p = f(g(v),h(u,v))$ and $q = f(g(w),h(w,j(x,u)))$.
   (c) (from Huet [1975]) $p = f(x,f(u,x))$ and $q = f(f(y,a),f(z,f(b,z)))$.
   (d) $p = f(h(x_1,x_2,x_3),h(x_6,x_7,x_8),x_3,x_6)$ and $q = f(h(g(x_4,x_5),x_1,x_2),\ h(x_7,x_8,x_6),g(x_5,a),x_5)$.
   (e) (from Martelli and Montanari [1982]) $p = f(x_1,g(x_2,x_3),x_2,b)$ and $q = f(g(h(a,x_5),x_2),x_1,h(a,x_4),x_4)$.
   (f) (from Robinson [1971]) $p = j(f(x,g(x,y)),h(z,y))$ and $q = j(z,h(f(u,v),\ f(a,b)))$.

6. Implement Algorithm 8.4.1 and use the result to compute the mgus in the previous problem.

7. PROLOG systems typically require that negated subgoals not contain

free variables. This exercise explores some ideas that can be used to lift this restriction. Suppose that we make the following definitions:

DEFINITION 8.8.1 *Let* f *be a functional expression, and* σ *a binding list. We will say that* σ is nontrivial for f *if the set of ground instances of* $f|_\sigma$ *is a proper subset of the set of ground instances of* f.

Essentially, σ is nontrivial for f if it gives a nontrivial binding for some variable or variables that appear in f.

DEFINITION 8.8.2 *Let* f *be a functional expression, and* S *a set of ground instances of* f. *We will say that* S is of measure 0 in f *provided that one of the following conditions holds:*

(a) There is a nontrivial binding σ *for* f *such that every element of* S *is an instance of* $f|_\sigma$, *or*

(b) S *is the finite union of sets of measure 0 in* f.

If S *is a set of ground instances of* f, *we will say that* S is of measure 1 in f *whenever the complement of* S *in the set of instances of* f *is of measure 0 in* f.

The terminology here is borrowed from mathematical analysis. Roughly speaking, if f is a functional expression involving n variables, we can think of the ground instances of f as making up an n-dimensional space; after applying a nontrivial binding to f, the ground instances make up at most an $n-1$-dimensional space. Assuming that the set of possible instantiations for a single variable is infinite, any finite union of $n-1$ or smaller dimensional subsets will be small relative to the n-dimensional space that contains them.

(a) Consider the functional expression g(x). Show that the $S = \{g(A)\}$ consisting of a single ground instance is of measure 0 in the set of all ground instances of g(x).

(b) Assuming that our language contains an infinite number of distinct Skolem constants, show that for any functional expression f, there is no set S that is both of measure 0 and of measure 1 in f.

(c) Let $q(x)$ be a query, f a functional expression, and α a ground instance of f in which all of the variables have been bound to unique Skolem constants. Show that the set of instances of f for which q is a consequence of our database is of measure 1 in f if $q(\alpha)$ is a consequence of the database and is of measure 0 in f otherwise.

8. We know that unifying two expressions of the form $f(x_1, \ldots, x_n)$ and $f(y_1, \ldots, y_n)$ involves unifying the lists of the arguments to f in the two cases. Suppose that we extend our language to include "sequence" variables, where a sequence variable will be denoted something like

x* and can match an arbitrary sequence of objects, not just a single one. Thus $f(x^*)$ now unifies with $f(a,b)$ with binding list

$$\{x^* = \langle a,b \rangle\}$$

(a) In each of the following cases, compute the mgu of p and q:
  i. $p = f(a,x^*)$ and $q = f(a,b)$.
  ii. $p = f(a,x^*)$ and $q = f(a,b,c)$.
  iii. $p = f(a,x^*)$ and $q = f(a)$.
  iv. $p = f(x^*,y^*)$ and $q = f(a,b)$. Is the mgu unique in this case?
  v. $p = f(x^*,y^*)$ and $q = f(y^*,x^*)$.

(b) How can Procedure 8.4.1 be modified to handle sequence variables if they only appear at the end of argument lists?

(c) How can Procedure 8.4.1 be modified to handle sequence variables if only one of the expressions being unified contains a sequence variable and if that sequence variable appears only once in the corresponding expression?

9. Given two binding lists σ_1 and σ_2, we will say that σ_1 and σ_2 are *compatible* if there is a binding list σ that is less general than σ_1 and less general than σ_2 as well. We will denote the most general such σ by $\sigma_1 \cdot \sigma_2$.

(a) In each of the following cases, determine if σ_1 and σ_2 are compatible and compute $\sigma_1 \cdot \sigma_2$ if they are.
  i. $\sigma_1 = \{x = \texttt{Mary}\}$ and $\sigma_2 = \{y = \texttt{John}\}$.
  ii. $\sigma_1 = \{x = \texttt{Mary}\}$ and $\sigma_2 = \{x = \texttt{John}\}$.
  iii. $\sigma_1 = \{x = y\}$ and $\sigma_2 = \{y = \texttt{house-of}(x)\}$.
  iv. $\sigma_1 = \{\ \}$.

(b) Show that σ_1 and σ_2 are compatible if and only if for every expression p, $p|_{\sigma_1}$ and $p|_{\sigma_2}$ can be unified.

(c) Show that the problem of determining whether or not σ_1 and σ_2 are compatible and computing $\sigma_1 \cdot \sigma_2$ if they are can be solved in linear time.

10. Express the following in normal form:

(a) You can fool some of the people all of the time, and all of the people some of the time, but you can't fool all of the people all of the time.

(b) An apple a day keeps the doctor away.

11. Remove the quantifiers from the following queries:

(a) Is it the case that although you can fool all of the people some of the time, and some of the people all of the time, you can't fool all of the people all of the time?

(b) Does an apple a day keep the doctor away?

12. Suppose that we know that if a person p steals an object o, then p is a thief:

$$\texttt{steals}(p,o) \rightarrow \texttt{thief}(p)$$

We also know that Robin Hood steals rich people's things:

`steals(Robin–Hood, rich–folks–stuff)`

and that the Sheriff of Nottingham steals poor people's things:

`steals(Sheriff, poor–folks–stuff)`

(a) Try to use resolution to prove that Robin Hood and the Sheriff are both thieves, so that the goal is

$$\texttt{thief(Sheriff)} \wedge \texttt{thief(Robin–Hood)}$$

(b) What went wrong? Can you suggest a solution to this problem?

13. Consider the following information:

(a) Animals can outrun any animals that they eat.

(b) Carnivores eat other animals.

(c) Outrunning is transitive: If x can outrun y and y can outrun z, then x can outrun z.

(d) Lions eat zebras.

(e) Zebras can outrun dogs.

(f) Dogs are carnivores.

Use resolution to find three animals that lions can outrun.

14. An apple a day keeps the doctor away. But the doctor is here! Assuming that the doctor can't be both here and away, what can we use resolution to conclude?

15. Mozart visited Vienna three times, and he died there. On which of the three visits did he die? Formulate this problem and use resolution to obtain the answer. What additional information do you need to add in order for the desired conclusion to follow from your axioms?

16. Implement a resolution theorem prover and use it to respond to some of the above questions.

17. Consider the following question: Are there irrational numbers x and y such that x^y is rational? Here is a proof that there are such numbers:

Let $z = \sqrt{2}^{\sqrt{2}}$. If z is rational, then we're done. If z is irrational, consider $z^{\sqrt{2}}$. We have

$$z^{\sqrt{2}} = (\sqrt{2}^{\sqrt{2}})^{\sqrt{2}} = \sqrt{2}^{\sqrt{2}\cdot\sqrt{2}} = \sqrt{2}^2 = 2$$

so that $z^{\sqrt{2}} = 2$ is an irrational number raised to an irrational power.

Translate this proof into resolution. Does the result allow you to exhibit irrational x and y such that x^y is rational?

CHAPTER

9

PUTTING LOGIC TO WORK: CONTROL OF REASONING

I remarked earlier that AI systems use knowledge to reduce problems of intelligent action to search. But where is the search in our attempt to find someone whose house is a lot of work to maintain? At any point in the derivation (8.39), we didn't seem to have much choice about which resolution to do next. Here is that proof again.

	Sentence	Source	Bindings
1	$\texttt{work}(x) \rightarrow F$	negated query	
2	$\texttt{big}(h_5) \wedge \texttt{house}(h_5, p_5) \rightarrow F$	resolve 1,(8.22)	$x = h_5$
3	$\texttt{big}(\texttt{house-of}(p_3)) \rightarrow F$	resolve 2,(8.20)	$h_5 = \texttt{house-of}(p_3), p_5 = p_3$
4	$\texttt{house}(\texttt{house-of}(p_3), p_4) \wedge \texttt{rich}(p_4) \rightarrow F$	resolve 3,(8.21)	$h_4 = \texttt{house-of}(p_3)$
5	$\texttt{rich}(p_3) \rightarrow F$	resolve 4,(8.20)	$p_4 = p_3$
6	$\texttt{lawyer}(p_3) \rightarrow F$	resolve 5,(8.19)	$p_2 = p_3$
7	$T \rightarrow F$	resolve 6,(8.18)	$p_3 = \texttt{John}$

(9.1)

The reason there is no search in this example is that our knowledge is perfectly tailored to the problem at hand—we know nothing more or less than we need to in order to conclude that John's house is a lot of work. In this chapter, we look at the question of making effective use of our knowledge when we have more of it to use.

Let's begin by adding some additional information to our knowledge base. Is the stock market going to go up? This is obviously something that is very difficult to predict, but let's say that we have some information about it:

$$\texttt{hard} \rightarrow \texttt{stocks-up} \quad (9.2)$$

The intended meaning of this is that if we can prove hard, then we can conclude that the stock market is going to rise. We will assume that we can spend a lot of time trying to prove `hard` from a variety of sources, and we don't know if this attempted proof will succeed or not. But there are all manner of resolutions we can do in order to decide which way the market is heading—we might have information allowing us to derive `hard` from information about the gross national product, or interest rates, or a variety of other sources. All of these facts will resolve with (9.2), so we have added plenty of potential resolutions to our database.

9.1 RESOLUTION STRATEGIES

Needless to say, none of these resolutions has any impact on our original question of finding something that is a lot of work to maintain; our strategy in (8.39) is that each line is a resolution step that uses the result appearing in some previous line. This is known as the *set of support* strategy, and provides a natural focus to our proving efforts—we begin with the negated query and work from there.

Is the set of support strategy complete? Clearly not; suppose that our initial database D contained of the sentences

$$T \rightarrow \mathrm{p}$$

$$\mathrm{p} \rightarrow F$$

and therefore implied a contradiction. Now if we ask whether or not some sentence q follows from D (it does, since D is contradictory), there are no sentences to resolve with $\neg q$ and we are likely to conclude that q does not follow after all. If our initial database is consistent however, then the set of support strategy *is* complete (see Exercise 2 at the end of this chapter). Here is an algorithmic description:

ALGORITHM 9.1.1

Set of support *To respond to a query* q:

1. *Set* L = {¬q}. *This is a list of all the sentences that have been generated thus far.*
2. *Select an element* p ∈ L. *If* p = T → F, q *has been proven. Return success. Otherwise, if* p *can be resolved with either a database sentence or another element of* L, *do so and add the result to* L. *If there are no sentences to resolve with* p, *remove it from* L.
3. *If* L *is now empty, return failure. Otherwise, go back to step 2.*

Note that we are being deliberately vague about the element of L that is selected in step 2. If we think of L as a stack and pick an element added recently, we will search the proof space in a depth-first fashion. If we treat L as a queue, breadth-first search results.

Have a look at (9.1) again. In line 4, we have reduced the problem to finding some p_4 who is rich, and a p_3 whose house belongs to p_4. We chose to solve the second of these subgoals first, using (8.20) to conclude that $p_3 = p_4$ and then proceeding to find someone rich.

We could just as easily have worked on the goal `rich`(p_4) first, reducing this to `lawyer`(p_4) and then binding p_4 to `John`. The remaining goal would now be `house(house-of(`p_3`),John)` and this could once again be solved using (8.20).

In this example, it doesn't make much difference which of `rich` and `house` we choose to work on first. In general, however, suppose that we are using the following rule to prove that some object h is big:

$$\texttt{house}(h,p) \wedge \texttt{rich}(p) \rightarrow \texttt{big}(h) \tag{9.3}$$

We can either prove that h is big by first finding a rich person and then hoping that h is that person's house, or by first showing that h is a house owned by p, and only then trying to show that p is rich. The second of these approaches is obviously more likely to be effective in practice; a randomly selected rich person is hardly likely to be the owner of h. How are we to ensure that our theorem prover follows the course of (9.1) instead of working on the subgoal `rich`(p_4) first?

One way to do this—we will see others shortly—is to require that in (9.1) we not only resolve with an earlier conclusion, but always resolve with the first clause that conclusion contains. This ensures that in moving from (4) to (5), we resolve with `house` instead of `rich`. This procedure is known as *ordered resolution*.

ALGORITHM 9.1.2 **Ordered resolution** *To respond to a query* q*:*

1. *Set* L = {¬q}. *This is a list of all the sentences that have been generated thus far.*
2. *Select an element* p ∈ L. *If* p = T → F, q *has been proven. Return success. Otherwise,* ***if the first atom in*** p *can be resolved with either a database sentence or another element of* L, *do so and add the result to* L. *If there are no sentences that resolve with* p *in this way, remove* p *from* L.
3. *If* L *is now empty, return failure. Otherwise, go back to step 2.*

As with the set of support strategy, ordered resolution is complete for consistent databases.

The point of the ordering condition is that by stating (9.3) as we have instead of writing

$$\texttt{rich}(p) \wedge \texttt{house}(h,p) \rightarrow \texttt{big}(h) \tag{9.4}$$

we have controlled the search to some extent, guaranteeing that the subgoal `house`(h,p) will be considered before `rich`(p) is.

This is progress; we have used the syntactic difference between (9.3) and (9.4) to help us control the search of our theorem prover. But there are two limitations to this approach:

1. The control information is static. We have decided, once and for all, that the `rich` subgoal should be deferred. We will see shortly that there are situations in which this static choice is inappropriate and something more flexible is needed.
2. The control information is provided by the user. It is the user, not the machine, that determines the exact form of an axiom such as (9.3). It would be better if the machine could derive the control information itself, thereby sparing the user the burden of deciding which subgoals should be preferred to others.

The rest of this chapter will discuss ways around these difficulties. Before doing so, however, I would like to extend our discussion to include search problems generally; lessons learned there will apply to examples such as (9.3) as well.

9.2 COMPILE-TIME AND RUN-TIME CONTROL

Consider the crossword-puzzle problem once again; let's suppose that we have decided to fill in the frame a word at a time using depth-first search. Now consider the following methods of choosing the word to fill next:

1. Alternate between horizontal and vertical words, always filling the leftmost or uppermost word possible (that is, the one with the smallest "number" if you were to find the crossword in the newspaper).
2. Fill the words in an order that ensures that every word filled intersects the previous word filled.
3. Always fill in the word for which there are the fewest number of legal choices remaining (that is, always fill in the most constrained word).

These three choices all appeal to principles that we will be considering in greater depth later, so let's examine the reasons underlying them before returning to more general issues.

The rationale behind the first two orderings is that we would like to avoid a situation like that in Figure 9.1, which we have repeated from Chapter 2. The problem is that there is no legal word that we can put in the marked slot, but the last word filled in was *LAP*. If we simply retract that word and replace it with another one, we won't have made any progress

FIGURE 9.1
How far should we back up?

on the real difficulty. The situation is similar if we retract the last *two* words inserted, *LAP* and *LAY*. Since we don't want to perform an exhaustive search over the possible choices for the last *n* words inserted, we would like to ensure that every word intersects the previous one; that would help to guarantee that when we backed up we would be doing something useful. The first ordering is a cheap and dirty way to achieve this effect; the second ordering above is a more carefully thought out way to do so.

The rationale behind the third ordering (fill in the most constrained word) is rather different. Here, rather than trying to find an ordering that will make backtracking more efficient, we are attempting to find an ordering that reduces the likelihood that we will need to backtrack at all. By recognizing the troublesome words early and filling them in when they are discovered to be difficult, we hope that our program doesn't need to do as much backtracking as it otherwise would.

Before discussing these ideas in greater detail, let us consider the basic question of when control decisions are made. Do we decide what word to fill in or what subgoal to explore:

1. When the database is constructed?
2. When the query appears?
3. As we actually search?

The first choice is generally referred to as *compile-time* control, since the cost involved is not incurred while an answer is being found. The last choice is referred to as *run-time* control, since the cost *is* incurred while we solve the problem. The second of the three choices—deciding on the search ordering after receiving the query but before actually beginning the work—has both compile- and run-time features.

Compiled code runs more efficiently than interpreted code because the expense of translating into machine language has already been paid; for analogous reasons, it is important to make control decisions as early in the search process as possible. Another way to look at this is to realize that the amount of problem-solving time spent on control decisions goes up as we work our way down the above list. Control information obtained when the database is built can be used without delaying the problem-solving process; control information obtained as the problem space is actually searched requires some sacrifice of the computational resources that are being used to find a solution.

Control information available when the database is constructed As we have seen in the discussion surrounding (9.3), explicit control information supplied by the user is typically of this form.

Control information available when the query appears Sometimes there is no single static ordering that is appropriate for all queries; the ordering can depend on the interaction between the query and the statistical properties of the database. Here's an example.

$$\texttt{related}(x,y) \wedge \texttt{loves}(x,y) \rightarrow \texttt{family-oriented}(x) \tag{9.5}$$

If x loves a relative, then x is family oriented. Suppose also that we know about two people, John and Mary. John has a small family and loves at least some of them; Mary has a huge family but loves only her cat.

The two queries `family-oriented(John)` and `family-oriented(Mary)` should now be approached using different orderings for the conjuncts appearing in (9.5). For John, we should begin by enumerating his relatives and then checking to see if he loves any of them; for Mary, we should notice that she loves only her cat and then check that the two of them are unrelated.

The crossword-puzzle domain is another one where the ordering cannot be determined in advance; there are simply too many possible factors that need to be considered either when the frame is first encountered or as we actually insert the words.

Control information available as the search proceeds Suppose that we add the following axiom to (9.5):

$$\texttt{rich}(x) \wedge \texttt{family-oriented}(x) \rightarrow \texttt{happy-kids}(x) \tag{9.6}$$

Rich people who are family oriented have happy kids.

Now suppose that the query is `happy-kids(x)`—who has happy kids? Let's assume that we honor the ordering information in (9.6), responding to this query by first finding someone rich and then trying to prove that person to be family oriented. The point of the example is that we have no way of knowing, at this point, whether the query `family-oriented(x)` will be attempted with x bound to John or to Mary—and that means that we won't be able to order the conjuncts in (9.5) until we have begun to solve the original query `happy-kids(x)`.

We will return to these ideas in Section 9.4, but I would like first to discuss the topic in a more general way. This is something that we have touched on from time to time already in our discussion of the trade-off between deciding how to solve a problem and actually solving it.

9.3 THE ROLE OF METALEVEL REASONING IN AI

There is a single computational principle that determines whether or not it makes sense to spend time trying to decide how to solve a particular problem: If the time spent is recovered via a quicker path to the solution of the original problem, it was time well invested. Otherwise, we would have been better off solving the original problem directly.

Of course, you can't expect to tell in advance whether or not you'll solve a problem more quickly after doing some metalevel analysis, so this principle should really read:

> *Metalevel computation is worthwhile only to the extent that the time spent is expected to be recovered via base-level computational savings.*

It would seem that this principle would be sharp enough to allow us to determine, in any specific situation, whether metalevel reasoning is a good idea or not. Unfortunately, too little is currently known about the expected time needed to solve any particular problem, so it tends to be impossible to make a quantitative determination of whether or not metalevel analysis will be useful.

This has forced AI researchers to examine more general issues in metalevel reasoning. As an example, consider the question of what sort of a protocol one might have for combining metalevel and base-level effort. Two extreme answers come to mind:

1. One might simply ignore the metalevel entirely, taking actions without worrying about their suitability to the situation at hand. This "shoot from the hip" approach is typically taken by the heroes in old Western movies.

2. Alternatively, one might work compulsively at the metalevel, refusing to take *any* action before rigorously proving that it was the right thing to do. This is the approach taken by the people who get shot in the movies.

The problem with these protocols is that it is not hard to generate search problems for which either is arbitrarily worse than the other. In solving a search problem, we might refuse to expand a node until we had actually proven that it was closer to the goal than any other candidate—but generating such a proof will typically require us to solve our original problem! In the crossword-puzzle or sliding-tile puzzles, however, simply selecting words or moves at random is not likely to be an effective search technique.

Put another way, refusing to take any metalevel action means that we will fail to apply cheap and powerful heuristics when they are available. Compulsive metalevel activity, however, will commit us to the use of heuristics whose computational costs far outweigh their value.

Once again, not much is known; there is currently no way to distinguish situations in which metalevel analysis is likely to be useful from those in which it isn't. The only specific proposal in this area is some sort of interleaving: By merging two computational processes, one of which never introspects and the other of which does so compulsively, it is possible to guarantee that the time needed by the resulting system will be no worse than twice the time needed by the better of the above two approaches. In many cases where the results of the metalevel computation are made available to the base-level routine doing the search, this interleaving protocol is within a factor of two of optimal.

Human problem solvers seem to proceed rather differently. Instead of evenly interleaving base-level and metalevel activity, we seem to tackle most problems by simply pounding away at them, expecting them to be easy enough that extensive metalevel effort is unnecessary. But as time passes and we realize that the problem is more difficult than expected, we devote an increasing fraction of our effort to metalevel concerns, "thinking about" the problem as opposed to tackling it directly. As shown in Figure 9.2, the fraction of time spent at the metalevel increases with the total amount of time spent on the problem.

Why is this? No one knows; the protocol in Figure 9.2 undoubtedly reflects complex assumptions about the distribution of problems in terms of difficulty, about the relative value of metalevel effort on hard and easy problems, and so on. Beyond this, however, little is known.

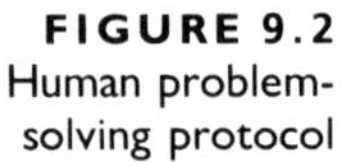

FIGURE 9.2 Human problem-solving protocol

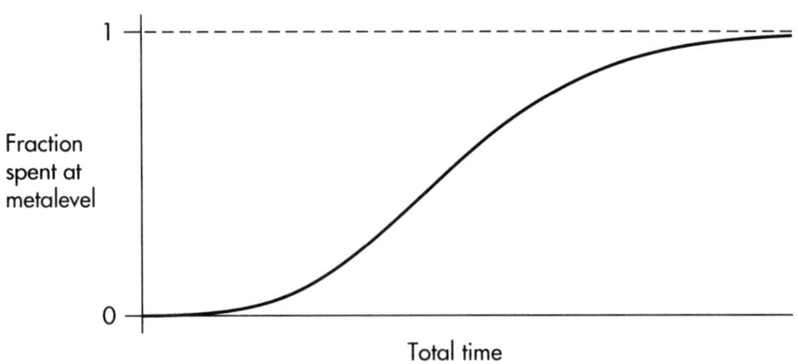

9.4 RUNTIME CONTROL OF SEARCH

Let's suppose, however, that we have somehow decided that we *are* going to try to make an informed decision about what to do next. What sort of information can we use to do so?

As we've seen, there are a variety of techniques that can be used to make the decision before we actually begin working on the problem in question; these techniques typically rely on information provided either implicitly or explicitly by the user, such as the ordering of conjuncts within a particular database sentence or perhaps the ordering of sentences within the database itself. In this section, we will focus on machine-generated control information based on properties of the search space being explored.

9.4.1 Lookahead

Probably the simplest control heuristic can be understood by considering the following axiom:

$$\texttt{mother}(m,c) \wedge \texttt{lives-at}(m,h) \wedge \texttt{married}(c,s) \wedge \\ \texttt{lives-at}(s,h) \rightarrow \mathsf{sad}(s) \tag{9.7}$$

What this axiom says is that people are unhappy if they live with their mothers-in-law: If m is the mother of a child c, and the child is married to a spouse s, and m and s live in the same house h, then s will be sad. Suppose in addition that we have decided to conform to the ordering strategy, so that we resolve with the early conjuncts in (9.7) before considering the later ones.

If our goal is to find someone sad, we begin by finding a mother and a child, and then trying to figure out where the mother lives. But what if the child isn't married? Clearly there is then no point to exploring this portion of the search space; we need to find a different binding for the variable c before proceeding. The general principle is this one:

> *When binding a variable, it is reasonable to check that every remaining term involving that variable continues to have some solution; if there is some term that can easily be shown to be insoluble, there is no point in continuing to explore this possible binding for the variable in question.*

Of course, we need to understand what it is for a term to be "easily shown" to be insoluble—but in many problems, this will not be a difficulty. When filling in a word in a crossword, we can make sure that there are still solutions for every crossing word. These solutions may conflict with one another, but we aren't going to look that far ahead—we just want to make sure there is *some* word at each crossing point. We don't *solve* the subsequent terms; we just check to see that they are likely to have solutions. In the example (9.7), we might know that all of the information in our database about marriages is in the form of explicit entries, so that we can easily check to see if c has a spouse or not.

This technique has typically gone by the name *forward checking* in the literature, but we'll refer to it simply as *lookahead*. It can be extended fairly easily: If we should prune nodes for which the subsequent search space has no solutions, then we should prefer to examine nodes for which this space has as many solutions as possible.

> *When binding a variable* v, *we should prefer to bind it to a value for which the remaining terms involving* v *are likely to have as many solutions as possible.*

There are some details still to be worked out here—what if there are two unsolved terms involving the variable v, and one choice of binding for v leads to three possibilities for the first term and four for the second, while a second binding leads to eight for the first but only one for the second? Which binding is to be preferred?

A reasonable choice here is to order the nodes by the product of the number of solutions for the unsolved terms, since this is an indication of the total size of the search space involving these terms. In the example of the preceding paragraph, there are $3 \cdot 4 = 12$ possible bindings for the remaining variables given the first choice but only $8 \cdot 1 = 8$ given the second. Assuming that each possibility is equally likely to be part of a solution, we should prefer the first binding in this example. The case in which some unsolved node has no solutions is also covered by this heuristic.

A second issue involved in the above principle involves the time spent counting the number of solutions for subsequent terms in the first place—the usual trade-off between base-level and metalevel work means that we need to limit the time spent on this activity. We may not want to examine all possible solutions to the current term, instead choosing the best of the first few on the grounds that subsequent solutions aren't likely to be a great deal better but that examining them may be costly.

9.4.2 The Cheapest-First Heuristic

The second idea that we would like to explore that addresses the conjunct-ordering problem is known as the *cheapest-first heuristic*.

Suppose that as we are solving a problem, we have a group of unsolved terms $t_1, \ldots, t_n$; in the mother-in-law example of the previous section, we might be left with the two terms `married(Chris,s)` and `lives-at(s,house-33)`; the variable c has been bound to `Chris` and h has been bound to `house-33` (the place where Chris's mother lives). The ordering implicit in the statement of the rule (9.7) would have us find Chris's spouse before checking to see if she lives in `house-33`; does this make sense?

It does. Imagine that `house-33` is a busy place, with many occupants. Now if we solve `lives-at(s,house-33)` first, we will have to check each of those occupants to see if he or she is Chris's spouse. If we instead solve `married(Chris,s)` first, we will have to check at most one person to see if they live in `house-33`.

In general, it is a good idea to first solve terms for which there are only a few solutions; this simultaneously reduces the size of the subsequent search space and also tends to reduce the need for backtracking because the "hard" conjuncts are solved before they become completely impossible. This strategy is known as the *cheapest-first heuristic* because the first conjunct we solve is the one for which it is cheapest to enumerate all the solutions (because there are the fewest of them).

Let's have a look at this in a bit more detail. Suppose that we want to find a carpenter whose father is a senator, so our goal is

$$\texttt{carpenter}(x) \wedge \texttt{father}(y,x) \wedge \texttt{senator}(y) \qquad (9.8)$$

Furthermore, to make things as specific as possible, suppose that the numbers of solutions to each of the conjuncts appearing here are expected to be as follows:

Conjunct	**Number of Solutions**
`carpenter(x)`	10^5
`senator(y)`	100
`father(y, x)`	10^8
`father(y, const)`	1
`father(const, x)`	2.3

In other words, our database contains information about 10,000 carpenters, 100 senators, and one hundred million father-son pairs. We also know that once the variable x is bound to a constant, the term `father(y,x)` has exactly one solution—everyone has exactly one father. If it is y that is bound, we expect there to be about 2.3 solutions because people have on average 2.3 children.

Given this information, we can estimate the size of the search space corresponding to the ordering appearing in (9.8). There are 10^5 choices for the x who is a carpenter; for each of these there is one choice of father. This will bind y and the result will either be a senator or not. The total size of the search space using this ordering is therefore 10^5.

Of course, one would not normally find a carpenter whose father is a senator by enumerating all of the carpenters in the country; enumerating the senators is a much more sensible plan. It is also the approach suggested by the cheapest-first heuristic, since senator(y) is the term with the fewest number of solutions.

After binding y to a senator, carpenter(x) continues to have 10^5 solutions; father(const,x) has 2.3 solutions so that is the term we consider next. This will bind x and father(const,const) will now have 0 or 1 solutions depending on whether we've solved the problem or not. The resulting search space is of size $100 \cdot 2.3 = 230$, a substantial reduction. In this case, the cheapest-first heuristic reproduces the "obvious" order in which we should solve the problem.

Note, however, that the cheapest-first heuristic is just that—a heuristic. There are examples where it will actually lead you to do the wrong thing. One involves finding a Southern state and a senator from that state:

$$\texttt{Southern-state}(s) \wedge \texttt{senator}(y) \wedge \texttt{from}(y,s) \tag{9.9}$$

Here is the statistical information as in the previous example.

Conjunct	Number of Solutions
Southern-state(s)	18
senator(y)	100
from(y, s)	10^8
from(y, const)	10^6
from(const, s)	1

Note that from(y,const) has 10^6 solutions because each state has about a million inhabitants listed in our database. If we only had state information for senators, from(y,const) would have two solutions—but we are assuming that we know what state many people are from, not just senators.

The cheapest-first heuristic now would have us find a Southern state, then a senator, and then check to see if the senator is from that state. But this is obviously not as effective as first finding a senator, then determining what state he is from, and only then deciding whether or not that state is in the South.

We will see in the exercises that it is possible to come up with a weaker version of the cheapest-first heuristic that is in fact provably correct. The problem is that this weakened version doesn't tell you exactly what conjunct to work on next, but only restricts your choice somewhat. The cheapest-first heuristic isn't always right, but it does at least specify the choice completely.

9.4.3 Dependency-Directed Backtracking and Backjumping

The final example of run-time control that we would like to discuss relates to the problem in Figure 9.1, where we have reached a dead end in our search and need to decide how far to back up.

The simplest thing to do, and what is done by an approach like depth-first search, is to simply back up to the last choice point; in this example, that will presumably involve backing up to the previous word and replacing it with a different choice. But as we have seen, this is likely to be very inefficient in a situation such as that of the figure, where the problem is the result of a choice made some time ago.

The most general solution to this difficulty is known as *dependency-directed backtracking*. The idea here is to maintain or to develop information about what previous choice has led to the failure and then to back up far enough for the problem to be addressed.

Unfortunately, it may not be obvious exactly what the source of the difficulty is. In Figure 9.1, for example, it appears that the problem is in the use of the word *TOAST*, but perhaps lookahead forced us to make that choice because of a still earlier selection in the search process. Determining the exact causal dependencies among the various nodes in the search space may not be much easier than solving the problem in the first place!

Because dependency-directed backtracking is so expensive to implement, a cheaper alternative known as *backjumping* is typically used in practice. The idea is that instead of backtracking to the point in the search that actually is responsible for some current problem, we backtrack to a point that at least appears to bear on the difficulty. In the crossword example, we would backtrack to *TOAST* and hope for the best. If we are unable to find a value for a variable x, we will backtrack far enough to ensure that a variable affecting x changes its value.

Backjumping is cheap to implement; we can tell from the order in which the terms are solved what the specific backtrack point should be. In Figure 9.1, the method suggests that we back up to the word *TOAST*, since doing so may let us fill the marked word successfully.

Here is a declarative example: Let's say that if you have a child who's married and successful, you're a proud parent:

$$\texttt{parent}(p,c) \wedge \texttt{successful}(c,j) \wedge \texttt{married}(c,s) \rightarrow \texttt{proud}(p) \quad (9.10)$$

If p is c's parent, and c is successful at the job j and married to a spouse s, then p is proud.

In using this axiom to find a proud person, suppose that we have bound p to `John` and c to John's daughter, `Mary`. Mary is a successful surgeon, but our attempt to prove that she is married fails and we therefore need to backtrack.

Either backjumping or dependency-directed backtracking will tell us that there is no point in backtracking to $\texttt{successful}(c,j)$ and trying to find another job at which Mary is successful. The problem is not with our choice of surgeon for the job j, but with our choice of Mary for c. If we want to make progress, we need to backtrack to the first clause in (9.10).

The difference between dependency-directed backtracking and simple backjumping is that dependency-directed backtracking now records the fact that we have failed to find a spouse for Mary. The effect of this is that if we find another solution to parent(p,c) with c bound to Mary (perhaps binding p to Mary's mother instead of her father), dependency-directed backtracking will realize immediately that this binding is doomed to failure and work on something else. Backjumping will repeat the earlier work, proving that Mary is a surgeon and then failing on the next term in (9.10).

Does this mean that dependency-directed backtracking should be preferred to simple backjumping? Not necessarily. The reason is that every time the system backtracks, some new goal has failed. Search systems spend most of the time backtracking, so the number of failed goals stored by dependency-directed backtracking will be proportional to the time spent working—and we already know that this will often be exponential in the size of the problem being considered.

In addition, storing the fact that Mary has no spouse only helps us if Mary appears a *second* time as a solution to parent(p,c). There is really no reason to expect that this will happen; here is another argument that the space requirements of dependency-directed backtracking are unlikely to be justified in practice. The experience of the AI community confirms these ideas: Many implemented systems use backjumping, but there are no large systems that use full dependency-directed methods.

9.5 DECLARATIVE CONTROL OF SEARCH

Given the work we have described, it seems as if search control is a problem just like any other. Perhaps this means that we should provide a declarative system with *declarative* information about how to search. Is this a good idea?

Maybe, but probably not. The first reason is that introducing declarative control information immediately presents us with another problem—how are we to solve the control problem itself? If deciding what to do next involves invoking a theorem prover on our declarative control information, how are we to control *this* theorem prover? Are we to use yet another level of information, and is it to be declarative as well?

The second reason can best be understood by considering an example. Suppose that we are planning to go on a trip, and are trying to arrange an itinerary that will get us to our eventual destination on time. When should we leave our house to go to the airport?

The answer depends on what time our flight leaves, so we need to select a flight before deciding what time to head to the airport. Here is the control rule we're invoking:

When planning a long trip, plan the airplane part first.

Note that this rule really is *control* information—it isn't telling us anything about the domain of travel itineraries, but is only telling us how to solve problems in this domain.

But have a look at the argument we made for this control rule, where we noticed that we had more flexibility in the time we left our house than we had in the time our flight left the airport—after all, airline flights are scheduled in a way that trips to the airport are not. This is the reason *why* we pick a flight first:

Airplane flights are scheduled.

The point here is that once we've noticed that flights are scheduled, we can invoke general principles to conclude that we should plan the flight before the other legs of our journey. Furthermore, it appears that *all* control information is of this form, relying directly on base-level information about the domain itself. When we store the control rule directly, we lose the information about its justification.

This can be important. Imagine that we're trying to get to Los Angeles from San Francisco, and that there are flights leaving every half hour. The San Francisco area traffic, however, has deteriorated to the point that it is impractical to drive to the airport except between 1:00 and 1:30 in the afternoon. In this case, we should plan our trip to the airport before the plane flight—because this is the part of our voyage that is the most tightly constrained. If we simply stored the rule, "Plan the plane flight first," we would be unable to modify our problem-solving behavior to take advantage of the new information we have about the domain.

This appears to be a very general phenomenon. Essentially *all* control rules can be explained as the application of general-purpose control strategies to domain-specific information such as, "Airplane flights are scheduled." By viewing them in this way, we are able to exploit the control ramifications of any new information that we manage to learn about the domain.

An additional advantage of this view is that the problem of multiple levels of control reasoning goes away. Since the control information we use is always independent of the domain being investigated, we can decide once and for all exactly what sort of domain-independent reasoning protocol is appropriate, and then apply it. Provided that we do not learn a new *principle* of reasoning (backjumping, for example), we can continue to use our general protocol as we encounter new domains and problems.

In using base-level information for control purposes, we should modify our response to the original question of whether control information should be declarative. While there appears to be no need for explicitly declarative *control* information, much of the declarative information likely already to be present in our database can be expected to have useful control ramifications.

9.6 FURTHER READING

A variety of resolution strategies are described by Chang and Lee [1973], Loveland [1978], and Wos [1984]; related results also appear in Smith and Genesereth [1985], Smith *et al.* [1986], Smith [1989], Phipps *et al.* [1991], and Ullman [1989]. What we have called *ordered resolution* is a variant of a technique introduced by Genesereth and Nilsson [1987]; they in turn credit Boyer [1971] and Kowalski and Kuehner [1971]. Ordered resolution is also used to control the search of PROLOG systems.

A topic that we have left uncovered in this book is that of backward versus forward reasoning in theorem proving. Roughly speaking, reasoning from the negated goal to a contradiction corresponds to backward reasoning; reasoning directly from the database to the desired conclusion (as in Exercise 5 in Chapter 7) corresponds to forward reasoning. The arguments of Chapter 2 continue to apply; a more detailed investigation that applies to inference only can be found in Treitel and Genesereth [1987].

There has been very little work on protocols for combining base-level and metalevel activity. The specific idea of interleaving a compulsive deliberator and an agent working at the base level only is discussed by Smith [1985]. The observation that this protocol is often within a factor of two of optimal is due to Baker and has not previously appeared in print, although Shekhar and Dutta [1989] is related.

Backjumping was introduced by Gaschnig [1979]; dependency-directed backtracking first appeared in Stallman and Sussman [1977b]. The new technique of *dynamic backtracking* [Ginsberg 1992], which we discussed briefly in Chapter 3, appears to combine the attractive features of both of these earlier approaches. There have also been many papers experimentally comparing these and other search methods; two of the more recent ones are Dechter and Meiri [1989] and Ginsberg *et al.* [1990].

The observation that most control information is obtained by combining domain-dependent control principles with existing base-level information appears in Ginsberg and Geddis [1991].

An important area that we have not considered in this chapter involves applying techniques from decision theory to decide what action a theorem prover (or other AI system) should take next. There is a substantial literature here, but examining it would unfortunately take us rather far afield. Two useful references are Russell and Wefald [1991] and Horvitz *et al.* [1988].

9.7 EXERCISES

1. Find a resolution proof of `work(house-of(John))` from the usual axioms such that although every resolution step is necessary to the proof, the derivation as a whole does not satisfy the set of support strategy.

2. Show that the set of support strategy and ordered resolution are both complete for consistent databases.

3. Suppose that we view the problem of trying to derive q from a database as a search problem, where each node in the space is the result of applying resolution to its parent node and another fact. (In other words, we use the set of support strategy.) Suppose further that our intention is not just to find any proof of q, but to find the shortest such proof. Is the heuristic that labels a node by the number of excess literals it contains admissible?

4. In our usual example, use ordered resolution to find something that is a lot of work to maintain.

5. Suppose that we have a graph, consisting of a group of nodes connected by arcs. A path through the graph that visits every node exactly once is known as a *Hamiltonian path;* the problem of finding a Hamiltonian path through a particular graph is known to be NP-hard.

   (a) Consider the second heuristic in Section 9.2, where we want to fill a crossword using an ordering where each word filled intersects its predecessor. How hard is it to find such an ordering?

   (b) Can you construct a crossword for which there is no such ordering?

6. Give an example of a situation where never thinking about what to do next is computationally ineffective. Describe a situation where *always* thinking about what to do next is ineffective.

7. It is typically assumed that metalevel reasoning is more important on hard problems than easy ones. Explain why this can be expected to be true and how this assumption is reflected in Figure 9.2.

8. Explain how each of the control heuristics described in Section 9.4 can be applied to the crossword-puzzle problem.

9. What is the *worst* ordering in the example involving (9.8)? Prove your claim.

10. Show explicitly that the cheapest-first heuristic behaves as described on the example involving (9.9). Also show that the most efficient ordering of the conjuncts for this example is as described in the text.

11. Consider the following weakening of the cheapest-first heuristic, known as the *adjacency restriction* [Smith and Genesereth 1985]: When solving a conjunctive query, if the optimal ordering of the conjuncts is $c_1, \ldots, c_n$, then after $i - 1$ conjuncts have been solved, c_i will be at least as cheap as c_{i+1}.

    (a) Prove that the adjacency restriction is correct, in the sense that the ordering that leads to the smallest search space satisfies this condition. (Hint: Suppose that the ordering

$$c_1, \ldots, c_i, c_{i+1}, \ldots, c_n$$

violates the adjacency restriction in that c_i is more expensive than c_{i+1} after the first $i - 1$ conjuncts have been solved. Compare the above ordering to

$$c_1, \ldots, c_{i+1}, c_i, \ldots, c_n$$

where the ith and $i + 1$st conjuncts have been swapped.)

(b) Prove that the cheapest-first heuristic is correct if there are only two conjuncts involved.

(c) Show explicitly that the optimal ordering in the example involving (9.9) satisfies the adjacency restriction.

(d) Prove that it is never right to solve the most *expensive* conjunct next when proving a conjunctive query.

12. Given that we are using lookahead to ensure that every unsolved term in a problem has some solution, how is it possible that we ever fail to solve a particular term and therefore need to consider backtracking methods such as chronological backtracking, dependency-directed backtracking, or backjumping?

13. Consider Figure 9.1 once again, and suppose that we have decided to backtrack to *TOAST*, the most recently filled word intersecting the marked one.

    (a) Is there any point to replacing *TOAST* with another word that has an *A* as its third letter? Why or why not?

    (b) How can backjumping be modified to take advantage of this observation?

14. Consider the following control rule: When looking for a job, decide on what you want to do before you start filling in applications. What base-level information does this rule depend on?

PART

IV

KNOWLEDGE REPRESENTATION: OTHER TECHNIQUES

CHAPTER 10

ASSUMPTION-BASED TRUTH MAINTENANCE

With the occasional exception, the material in the first two parts of this book is part of "classical" AI—pick up an introductory book from the early 1980s and you'll find descriptions of search, heuristic search, and first-order logic that are not too different from ours.[19]

The rest of this book is different. As we discuss more current topics, we will find ourselves more often bumping into the fringe of what is known. I've tried hard not to speculate about what will remain important as AI matures, but some speculation of this sort is inevitable. Hopefully, I've gotten it pretty much right—you should find the rest of this book a useful selection of important emerging or recently emerged ideas from across the discipline of AI as a whole. In this chapter, we will discuss one of the most firmly entrenched of all of these ideas—the notion of an *assumption-based truth maintenance system* or ATMS.

10.1 DEFINITION

To understand the ideas behind ATMSs, suppose that we return to our example of the previous few chapters. We have managed to draw the conclusion that John's house is a lot of work, and someone now approaches us and asks *why* this is the case.

Recalling our derivation, the reason that John's house is a lot of work is that it is big. But why is it big? Because John is rich, and rich people have big houses. And how do we know that John is rich? Because he is a lawyer. How do we know that he is a lawyer? Because that fact appears explicitly in our database.

19 For what it's worth, the new things in our presentation are the iterative search techniques, dynamic backtracking, and the discussion of vividness.

In some sense, this is the fundamental reason that we know John's house to be a lot of work: because John is a lawyer. Imagine that a friend comes to us looking for a recommendation for a handyman. We might not know of anyone, but we might suggest that he ask John. If he asks us why, we might reply, "He's a lawyer. He's probably got some big house that needs a lot of maintenance."

What we're doing here is giving our friend the two pieces of information that we suspect he either doesn't already have or isn't using in his search for a handyman recommendation—that John is a lawyer, and that big houses are a lot of work to maintain. Our friend is expected to fill in the missing steps that lawyers are rich and therefore have big houses, and that people whose houses are a lot of work to maintain are likely to know of reliable handymen.

Note, incidentally, that when we give our friend the explanation that John is a lawyer and that big houses are a lot of work to maintain, we don't give him any information about the order in which these inferences are used in drawing the conclusion that John knows a handyman. We are simply telling him some things that he can add to his database and from which we expect him to be able to draw the same conclusions about John that we do. Since whether or not a group of sentences entails a particular conclusion p is independent of the order of the sentences, this is to be expected. Another way to think of this is to realize that we could have applied the rules of inference in a completely different order when deriving the conclusion that John's house is a lot of work. Compare this derivation with the one appearing in the last chapter:

	Sentence	Source
1	work(x) $\rightarrow$ F	negated query
2	$T \rightarrow$ house(house-of(p_3),p_3)	(8.20)
3	rich(p_3) $\rightarrow$ big(house-of(p_3))	resolve 2,(8.21)
4	lawyer(p_3) $\rightarrow$ big(house-of(p_3))	resolve 3,(8.19)
5	$T \rightarrow$ big(house-of(John))	resolve 4,(8.18)
6	house(house-of(John),p_5) $\rightarrow$ work(house-of(John))	resolve 4,(8.22)
7	$T \rightarrow$ work(house-of(John))	resolve 6,2
8	$T \rightarrow F$	resolve 7,1

(10.1)

This derivation doesn't satisfy the set of support condition but is valid nevertheless. Although the order of use of the database facts that John is a lawyer and that big houses are a lot of work to maintain has been reversed, these two facts are still the underlying reason that the proof has succeeded.

There are many reasons why we may be interested in the assumptions underlying the conclusions drawn by our reasoning system. In an example such as the one above, we may not agree with the machine's conclusion that John's house is a lot of work to maintain; in order to debug the program's knowledge, we need to know what database facts underlie this conclusion.

We saw another sort of example in the last chapter. In backjumping, we use information about the *reason* that a particular node has no children to decide how far back we need to go in our search before proceeding. Later in this chapter, we will see other examples from the domains of planning, design, and diagnosis; in all of these cases, we need to know the reason that a particular conclusion has been drawn by the system.

Before considering these examples, however, let's see if we can understand what's going on from a slightly more formal point of view. The usual query in our running example has been

$$\exists h.\mathtt{work}(h) \tag{10.2}$$

From the fact that this query succeeds, we know that our database D entails (10.2); when we explain our conclusion, we are simply reporting the facts that were used in the resolution proof (10.1) of (10.2). In order to do this, we need to modify our resolution algorithm so that it keeps track of which database sentences have been used to derive its conclusions. Here is a suitable modification to the set-of-support algorithm appearing in the last chapter:

ALGORITHM 10.1.1

To respond to a query q:

1. *Set* L = {⟨¬q,Ø⟩}. *This is a list of the sentences that have been generated thus far; each sentence is labelled with the database sentences used in the derivation.*
2. *Select an element* ⟨p,S⟩ ∈ L, *where* p *is a derived sentence and* S *is the reason. If* p = T → F, q *has been proven and we should return* S. *Otherwise, if* p *can be resolved with a database sentence* d *to obtain a result* r, *add* ⟨r,S ∪ {d}⟩ *to* L. *If* L *contains an entry* ⟨p′,S′⟩ *such that* p *and* p′ *can be resolved to obtain* r, *add* ⟨r,S ∪ S′⟩ *to* L. *If there are no sentences to resolve with* p, *remove it from* L.
3. *If* L *is now empty, return failure. Otherwise, go back to step* 2.

After S is returned in step 2, we can also continue the search, looking for additional proofs of the query.

As an example, here is how we can find a subset of our usual database that entails that John's house is big. The query is big(x):

	Sentence	S	Source
1	big(x) → F	Ø	negated query
2	house(h_4,p_4) ∧ rich(p_4) → F	{(8.21)}	resolve 1,(8.21)
3	rich(p_3) → F	{(8.20),(8.21)}	resolve 2,(8.20)
4	lawyer(p_3) → F	{(8.19),(8.20),(8.21)}	resolve 3,(8.19)
5	T → F	{(8.18),(8.19),(8.20),(8.21)}	resolve 4,(8.18)

We used everything in our database except (8.22) (which says that big houses are a lot of work to maintain).

PROPOSITION 10.1.2 *If Algorithm 10.1.1 returns a set S in response to a query q, then S is a subset of our logical database such that* $S \models q$.

PROOF That S is a subset of our logical database is clear. To see that $S \models q$, we will show the equivalent result that

$$S \cup \{\neg q\} \models F$$

by showing that for every entry $\langle p,S \rangle \in L$,

$$S \cup \{\neg q\} \models p \tag{10.3}$$

This is certainly true initially, since the first pair we add to L is $\langle \neg q, \emptyset \rangle$ and $\neg q \models \neg q$. When we add a new element $\langle r,S \rangle$ to L in step 2 of the algorithm, we know that there are pairs $\langle p_1,S_1 \rangle$ and $\langle p_2,S_2 \rangle$ such that p_1 and p_2 can be resolved to obtain r and

$$S_i \cup \{\neg q\} \models p_i \tag{10.4}$$

for $i = 1,2$. This is either because we are resolving with another element of L or because p_i is a database sentence and $S_i = \{p_i\}$. But since r is the result of resolving p_1 and p_2, we know that $\{p_1,p_2\} \models r$; combining this with (10.4) allows us to conclude that

$$S_1 \cup S_2 \cup \neg q \models r$$

A look at the algorithm will make it clear that $S = S_1 \cup S_2$, so that (10.3) continues to hold as we add new elements to L and the proof is therefore complete. ∎

We could, of course, simply return our entire database as the "reason" that we were able to derive some query q, but this would be terribly inefficient, since this database will presumably contain many facts that were not used in the proof. When we explained our earlier reasoning by saying that John was a lawyer and that big houses are a lot of work to maintain, we didn't bother to include the fact that John's wife is named Alicia because that wasn't relevant to the conclusion that we were trying to explain.

But there is something else going on here—when we explained our reasoning, there was actually some information that we didn't bother to report because it seemed natural to assume that the person requesting the information already knew it. In the example where our friend was looking for a handyman, we don't bother to remind him that people whose houses need a lot of maintenance are likely to be able to make good handyman recommendations. It is as if we have split our database D into two sets C and A such that $D = C \cup A$. C is the set of facts that are "common knowledge" and don't need to be repeated, while A is the set of things that our friend might not know (such as that John is a lawyer) and of which we will inform him if they are relevant to the problem at hand.

We can summarize the above two observations in the following definition:

DEFINITION 10.1.3 *Suppose that we have split our database into a set* C *of common knowledge and a set* A *of other information. By an* explanation *for a sentence* p *we will mean a minimal subset* E *of* A *such that*

$$E \cup C \models p$$

In other words, an explanation is a minimal set of facts from A that, together with the common knowledge in C, is sufficient to entail the conclusion p.

There are a couple of points to be made here. The first is that we are assuming that the splitting of D into C and A is given to us; little is known about conditions under which a fact is common knowledge as opposed to otherwise. It is possible to make some educated guesses, however. Here are a couple:

1. Universally quantified sentences (those sentences that contain variables when expressed in normal form) tend to be common knowledge because they often describe general rules about the way the world works. Everyone knows that lawyers are rich; facts about a specific lawyer (such as John) are less likely to be shared knowledge.

2. The above rule should not be applied blindly, however. Even in the example we are considering, the fact that big houses are a lot of work to maintain seems worth reporting when we explain our reasoning. This may be because it is somehow less "certain" a rule than the fact that lawyers are rich. When I picture a big house in my mind, I don't imagine it surrounded by maintenance workers; when I picture a lawyer, I *do* picture someone in a fancy suit and wearing a Rolex.

   This makes sense—if our reasoning depends upon the use of a fact of questionable validity, it is probably worth reporting. Our listener may not be aware of our belief, or may choose to disagree with it.

The other thing to point out about Definition 10.1.3 is that when we say "minimal," we mean minimal in the sense of set inclusion. In other words, if E and E' both have the property that they entail p when combined with C, and $E \subset E'$, then E' can only be an explanation of p if the two sets are actually equal. Put yet another way, no proper superset of an explanation can also be an explanation.

What we do *not* mean by minimal is anything involving counting. In our example, the explanation we have for `knows–handyman(John)` is that John is a lawyer and that big houses are a lot of work to maintain; this explanation e_1 uses two facts from our database. (The other database facts are presumably in the set C of common knowledge.)

Suppose that we also had in our database (in the set A of noncommon knowledge) the fact that John employed a handyman last week, which we know directly for some reason. Now the fact that John just hired a handyman is a *second* explanation for the fact that he's a good person to ask; this new explanation e_2 uses only one fact from A as opposed to the two used by e_1.

In spite of this, e_1 is still an explanation for our conclusion. The only way in which it might fail to be an explanation would be if one of the two sentences it contains were to become irrelevant for some reason.

Armed with Definition 10.1.3, the definition of an ATMS is easy:

DEFINITION 10.1.4 *An* assumption-based truth maintenance system, *or* ATMS, *is any system that takes a database* $D = C \cup A$ *and a query* q *and returns some or all of the explanations for* q.

(What isn't clear is why one would want to call such a system an ATMS; the reason has to do with the historical development of the ideas and isn't worth pursuing here.)

The reason that ATMSs are important is that this single idea—take a sentence and return some of its explanations—has a surprisingly wide range of applications. We turn to these next, but before we do so, we need to extend Definition 10.1.4 to cater to the possibility that the complete set A is inconsistent with the set C. This can't happen if we are using the ATMS for explanation, but we will see that it is a possibility with other applications.

In fact, the modification that we need to make is to Definition 10.1.3. Rather than taking an explanation to be *any* subset of A that is sufficient to entail the desired conclusion, we require it to be a subset *that is consistent with C*:

DEFINITION 10.1.5 *Suppose that we have split our database into a set* C *of common knowledge and a set* A *of other information. By an* explanation *for a sentence* p *we will mean a minimal subset* E *of* A *that is consistent with* C *and such that*

$$E \cup C \models p$$

A subset of A *that is* inconsistent *with* C *is called a* nogood.

10.2 APPLICATIONS

The first application of ATMS techniques is the one that we have already discussed—explaining a logical consequence of our deductive database. In this case, the set C is the set of facts that we believe already to be shared by the recipient of the explanation, and A is the set of facts that may be news to him.

10.2.1 Synthesis Problems: Planning and Design

Another application involves the use of ATMSs to solve what are known as *synthesis problems*. In a synthesis problem, the aim is for the machine to generate a solution to a problem that involves "creating" something—a plan to achieve a goal, a circuit design that will cause the output of the circuit to be a certain function of the inputs, something along those lines.

As an example, suppose that I need to spend a day in each of Boston and Philadelphia next week, but that I'd like to be back home in California by the weekend. A reasonable plan would be for me to fly to Boston on Monday, on to Philadelphia on Wednesday, and back home on Friday. A sensible explanation for the fact that there exists a plan to achieve my goals is exactly this—my itinerary.

Now suppose that instead of taking the set of assumptions A to be my specific itinerary, I had taken it to be all possible airline flights that I *could* take—in some sense, the collection of all possible itineraries. What would constitute an explanation in this case?

The answer is that explanations continue to correspond to plans that achieve my travel goals; the difference is that in this case, rather than validating a specific plan (fly to Boston Monday, Philadelphia Wednesday, home Friday), the ATMS will actually *create* the plan given information about possible itineraries. It does this by developing a suitable set of travel assumptions.

This is a fairly general phenomenon. By taking as our set A of assumptions the set of possible actions that we might take, we can use an ATMS as a planning tool—the "explanation" for the fact that we expect to achieve our goal will in fact consist of a group of planning assumptions that is sufficient to achieve it.

From a practical point of view, there are problems with this approach, as we will see in Chapter 14. From a theoretical point of view, however, an ATMS can serve as a perfectly viable planner when set against the background of first-order logic.

There is one subtlety, however. Suppose that our database of airplane flights includes a flight from California to Boston that arrives at 4:50 in the afternoon and another flight from California to Philadelphia that arrives at the same time. Our ATMS is now in danger of generating the plan that we take both of these flights on the same day, then fly back from Boston and from Philadelphia separately later in the week! After all, this would—at least on the face of it—achieve our goals of spending a day in each of the two cities.

We need here to take advantage of the fact that an ATMS will not return a set E of assumptions that is inconsistent with the basic knowledge in the set C; we need to state explicitly that it is impossible for us to take two flights at the same time in order to keep our ATMS planner from suggesting that we do so. Note that this is something we would not need to do when simply validating a plan, assuming that the plan we were checking already satisfied the constraints of the domain in question. But for synthesis problems, when the set A typically contains conflicting assumptions about the actions we might take, we need to be careful to include enough information to eliminate these potential plans.

Other synthesis problems are similar. A system designed to reason about digital circuits, for example, might contain the following axiom:

$$\texttt{type}(c,\texttt{or-gate}) \wedge \texttt{value}(\texttt{input}(i,c),1) \rightarrow \texttt{value}(\texttt{output}(c),1) \quad (10.5)$$

In other words, if c is an OR gate (that is, a component of type or-gate), and the ith input to c is 1, then the output of c will also be 1. We might also have:

$$\texttt{connected}(i,j) \wedge \texttt{value}(i,v) \rightarrow \texttt{value}(j,v) \quad (10.6)$$

If a signal i is connected to another signal j, they must have the same value.

Now suppose that we want a circuit that functions as an inverting OR gate, so that its output is 0 if any of the inputs is 1, and the output is 1 if all of the inputs are 0. If we call this circuit N (for NOR), we need (10.5), (10.6), and an axiom like (10.5) but describing inverters. Our goal q is:

$$\begin{aligned}&[\texttt{value}(\texttt{input}(i,N),1) \rightarrow \texttt{value}(\texttt{output}(N),0)] \wedge \quad (10.7)\\ &\quad [\texttt{value}(\texttt{input}(1,N),0) \wedge \texttt{value}(\texttt{input}(2,N),0) \rightarrow \texttt{value}(\texttt{output}(N),1)]\end{aligned}$$

This goal is a consequence of the following design assumptions, describing the circuit shown in Figure 10.1:

$$\texttt{type}(I,\texttt{inverter})$$
$$\texttt{type}(O,\texttt{or-gate})$$
$$\texttt{connected}(\texttt{input}(i,N),\texttt{input}(i,O))$$
$$\texttt{connected}(\texttt{output}(O),\texttt{input}(1,I))$$
$$\texttt{connected}(\texttt{output}(I),\texttt{output}(N))$$

FIGURE 10.1
A NOR gate

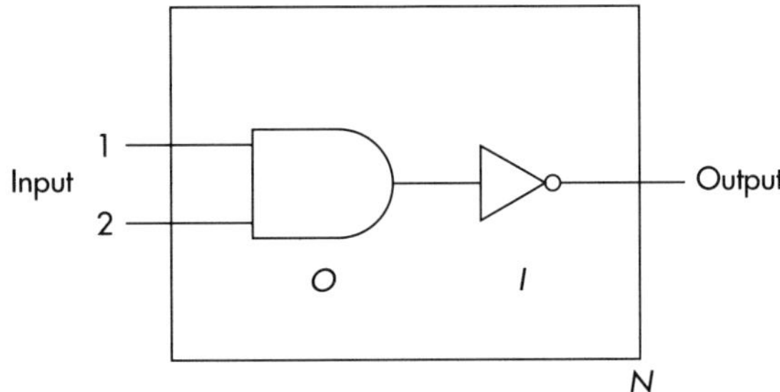

In other words, the inputs of N are connected to the inputs of the OR gate, the output of the OR gate drives the inverter, and the output of the inverter drives the output of N. It should be fairly clear that by allowing our set A to include all possible `type` and `connection` assumptions, we can use the ATMS to design digital circuits of this sort.

10.2.2 Diagnosis

Yet another use of ATMSs involves not the synthesis of devices like digital circuits, but the diagnosis of such circuits when they malfunction. A fairly extended diagnostic example appears as Exercise 12 at the end of this chapter, so I will leave you to puzzle out the details of how ATMSs can be used in this way. But let me make some comments here about the overall nature of this approach to diagnosis.

The most important thing to realize about diagnosis using ATMSs is that it is diagnosis from "first principles." This means that the diagnosis is performed by reasoning from an understanding of how the device is *supposed* to function. Thus the underlying information used in the analysis consists of rules like (10.5) and (10.6), which are essentially of the form

$$\texttt{components-ok} \rightarrow \texttt{behavior-ok} \tag{10.8}$$

We can contrapose this to get

$$\texttt{behavior-bad} \rightarrow \texttt{components-bad} \tag{10.9}$$

where both of these rules are obviously intended to be suggestive as opposed to specific examples.

This seems quite natural, but it's not how diagnosis typically works! As an example, imagine that a friend of yours has a headache and you, ever the optimist, diagnose it as a brain tumor. If this diagnosis were based on a rule like (10.8), you would need an axiom saying that in the absence of a brain tumor (and presumably many other causes), your friend *can't* have a headache:

$$\neg\texttt{brain-tumor} \wedge \neg\texttt{stress} \wedge \neg\texttt{head-cold} \wedge \cdots \rightarrow \neg\texttt{headache} \tag{10.10}$$

Of course, information like this isn't what underlies your suggesting that your friend has a brain tumor; you are probably just using a fact like

$$\texttt{brain-tumor} \rightarrow \texttt{headache} \tag{10.11}$$

Now, when you are told the conclusion of (10.11), you use this as some form of inductive evidence that the premise holds as well, concluding in this general way that your friend has a brain tumor. The rule (10.11) predicts the symptoms from the causes, and is the converse of a rule like (10.9), which allows you to derive the causes from the symptoms.

This is a subtle but important distinction. While an ATMS reasons from symptoms backwards to a fault, conventional diagnosis is often based on knowledge like (10.11), which links faults with the symptoms they cause. The ATMS diagnosis is based on a complete model of the system that is malfunctioning (which is why we are able to write down rules like (10.5) in the first place), while conventional diagnosis is based on expectations like (10.11). The reason that we can't use an axiom like (10.5) to diagnose disease in humans is that we don't know enough biology to write it down. Put a slightly different way, we don't know enough biology to write down a version of (10.10) that is actually correct; we are simply unable to enumerate *all* the potential causes of a headache. We can, on the other hand, fairly easily describe precise conditions under which the output of an electrical circuit will have a specific value.

I should point out in passing that although the rule (10.11) does allow us to diagnose systems about which we have only partial knowledge, the rule itself is flawed—it may be the case that a patient has a brain tumor, but doesn't have a headache for some reason. (Perhaps he's dead, to take a particularly extreme example.) Our knowledge of human biology is so incomplete that we can't write down *any* guaranteed diagnostic rules; the advantage of using a rule of thumb like (10.11) is that it does allow us to draw correct diagnoses most of the time.

In sum, the differences between conventional and ATMS-based diagnosis is that ATMS-based diagnosis is based on a correct and complete description of the artifact exhibiting the fault, while conventional diagnosis uses an incomplete and possibly incorrect description. Hardware is a typical domain in which ATMS-based techniques are often appropriate; medicine is a domain in which conventional techniques are best.

10.2.3 Database Updates

Suppose that we are working with a logical database D, and that we learn some new fact p that we want to add to D. In many cases, p will be consistent with D and there will be no problem. In some cases, however, the new fact that we learn may conflict with our old knowledge in some way.

An example involves reasoning about action. Suppose that the walls in a certain room are initially plaid, and we then paint them white. When we add the fact that the walls are white to our database, this database will become inconsistent (assuming that the walls can't be both plaid and white simultaneously). Assuming that we wish to avoid this contradiction, how are we to identify the conflicting fact or facts so that we can remove them before adding the new fact p? Here is the database we are using:

$$\texttt{color(walls,plaid)}$$

$$\texttt{color(x,plaid)} \rightarrow \neg\texttt{color(x,white)}$$

Since $\neg p = \neg$`color(x,white)` is a consequence of these two facts, we need to modify the database if we are to add p to it.

More generally, if we are to add p to a database D, there can't be any proof of $\neg p$ from the material in D—in other words, there can't be any explanation for $\neg p$. One way to guarantee this is to use an ATMS to find all possible explanations for $\neg p$ from the original database and to then remove from D enough facts so that none of these explanations remains valid. Specifically, what we propose to do is the following:

ALGORITHM 10.2.1 *To make a database* D *consistent with a new fact* p:

1. *Use an* ATMS *to find the explanations for* $\neg$p *in* D; *call these explanations* $e_1, \ldots, e_k$.
2. *Find a minimal set* H *that has the property that* $H \cap e_i \neq \emptyset$ *for every* e_i.
3. *Remove* H *from* D.

The set H constructed in step 2 of the above algorithm is called a *minimal hitting set* because it is a minimal set that "hits" each of the explanations e_i. As usual, we mean minimal in the set-theoretic sense, so that the actual number of elements in H is not considered by this construction. If there are many such sets H, we will somehow need to select one to remove from D before adding p.

What does the split of D into C and A correspond to in this application? Since facts in C will never appear in explanations of $\neg p$, it follows that they will also never appear in the minimal hitting set H and will therefore never be removed from D. We see that the facts in C are "protected" in some sense against removal when p is added; they might correspond to general rules about the domain that we are not prepared to abandon in order to allow p.

Let's add some more information to our earlier example to make it a bit more interesting. Here are the axioms we will use:

$$\texttt{color(walls,plaid)} \tag{10.12}$$

$$\texttt{color(x,plaid)} \rightarrow \neg\texttt{color(x,white)} \tag{10.13}$$

$$\neg\texttt{pretty(room)} \tag{10.14}$$

$$\texttt{color(walls,white)} \rightarrow \texttt{pretty(room)} \tag{10.15}$$

Informally, the walls are currently plaid, walls can only be one color, the room is not pretty, and rooms with white walls are pretty. The fact that we want to add is color(walls,white). What do we have to remove to do this?

We begin by attempting to prove ¬color(walls,white)—how can we prove that the walls *aren't* white? In this example, there are two proofs. One uses the fact that the walls are plaid and rule (10.13); the other uses the fact that the room is ugly and the rule (10.15). Assuming that the rules are all protected elements of C, the unique minimal set that hits both of these explanations is

$$H = \{\texttt{color(walls,plaid)}, \neg\texttt{pretty(room)}\}$$

and these are the two facts that we need to remove if we are to add the fact that the walls are white.

The construction that we have described is fine as it stands. If we want to add a new sentence p to a declarative database D, the ATMS and hitting-set constructions are reasonable ones to use. But when we want to use these techniques to reason about action specifically, a variety of subtle issues emerges.

The most important of these can be seen if we imagine dropping the axiom (10.15) above, which said that white rooms are pretty. Now when we add the fact that the walls are white, we have no reason to drop the fact that the room is ugly—after all, the database gives us no reason to believe that it's ugly *because* of the color of the walls; it could well be because of some other feature.

But what if we also replace (10.14) with the axiom

$$\texttt{color(walls,plaid)} \rightarrow \neg\texttt{pretty(room)}$$

which explicitly says that plaid rooms are ugly? Now when we add the fact that the walls are white, it seems as if we *should* withdraw our belief that the room is ugly, since it has apparently become unfounded. But what information is there that would allow us to do so? How are we to distinguish between the case where the room is ugly because it has plaid walls and that where it is ugly for some other reason? This issue has been discussed by a variety of authors, but the question is still open.

10.3 IMPLEMENTATION

The final topic that we will consider in this chapter is that of implementation—how can we actually design a system to find the explanations an ATMS is supposed to construct?

We have already given a partial solution to this problem in Algorithm 10.1.1, where we showed how to find a subset of our database D that entailed a particular query q. In this section, we modify this algorithm to guarantee that all minimal such subsets are returned.

ALGORITHM 10.3.1 *Let* q *be a sentence. To construct* E, *the set of explanations of* q:

1. *Set* E $= \emptyset$.
2. *Use Algorithm 10.1.1 to find a subset* $U \subset D$ *such that* $U \models q$. *If no such subset can be found, return* E. *Otherwise, set* $V = U \cap A$, *the sentences used in the proof that are in the assumption set* A *instead of the common knowledge set* C.
3. *Unless* V *is either inconsistent or a superset of an element of* E:
   (a) *Remove from* E *all elements that are supersets of* V.
   (b) *Add* V *to* E.
4. *Return to step 2.*

The purpose of step 3 is to ensure that E contains only *minimal* explanations of q.

PROPOSITION 10.3.2 *The result returned by Algorithm 10.3.1 in response to a query* q *will be the set of all explanations for* q.

PROOF The proof rests on the fact that Algorithm 10.1.1 will eventually produce all of the proofs for q, in the sense that if U is any subset of D such that $U \models q$, then Algorithm 10.1.1 will eventually produce some subset of U (perhaps U itself). This can be shown in a way quite similar to the proof in Theorem 7.4.1 that resolution is complete.

Given this result, the proposition is straightforward: Every element added to E by the algorithm is enough to entail q by virtue of Proposition 10.1.2, and E eventually contains only minimal such elements by virtue of step 3a of the algorithm itself. To see that E contains every explanation, let e be such an explanation. We have already seen that a subset of e will eventually be added to E; since e is minimal, it follows that e itself will be added to E at some point. ■

Algorithm 10.3.1 appears to be the most natural way in which to generate ATMS labels, but there are a variety of interesting issues that it raises:

1. In step 1 of the algorithm, we see that we need the theorem prover to be "resumable," in the sense that we can invoke it, find a proof of p, use this proof to modify the set of explanations for p, and then reinvoke the prover to find another proof of p. We did not discuss resumable theorem provers in Part III, but this feature is not difficult to obtain. Since proof problems can be thought of as search problems, we can simply continue searching (for a proof) where we left off upon finding the previous answer. Searching for all proofs of a sentence is not unlike looking for all of the solutions to any other search problem.

2. Step 2 of the algorithm requires that we run the theorem prover to exhaustion, since we need to find *all* proofs of p in order to construct all of the possible explanations. Since first-order logic is only semi-decidable, this process may fail to terminate.

   Unfortunately, there is no theoretical way around this. One method that may work in practice is to realize that in many applications, we don't need all of the explanations for p; one of them may suffice. Synthesis problems often have this property.

   It might seem that we could avoid this problem by terminating the execution of the algorithm early, returning a partial set of explanations E before all proofs of p had been considered. Unfortunately, there is no way to guarantee that the elements of E are *minimal* proofs of p until all such proofs have been examined.

3. Another way to address the above difficulty is to prune the space being searched by the theorem prover. Given that we have no use for a potential explanation that is a superset of an explanation already in E, it is reasonable to check for this as the proofs are being constructed. If we are working on a potential proof that has already used all the assumptions that a completed proof used, that portion of the search space can be pruned. Of course, implementing this idea requires that we interrupt our theorem prover even more frequently, but this poses little difficulty in practice.

4. Finally, we need to address the problem of nogoods; theorem provers typically assume that the underlying database is consistent. It is therefore possible that an inconsistent set of assumptions be returned as a possible explanation, and we check for this at the beginning of step 3

of the algorithm. But this approach may commit us to a great deal of effort completing proofs that we could have eliminated as inconsistent early on. This suggests the following:

(a) We can check U for consistency as the proof is assembled, just as we suggested checking to see if it was a superset of an existing explanation. The problem is that this consistency check is computationally expensive; doing it frequently will have a big effect on the performance of the overall system.

(b) Alternatively, we can use forward-chaining to generate a list of all nogoods before the proposition q is investigated at all; this makes it fairly easy to check U for consistency as it is generated.

In practice, the best solution to this problem appears to be to perform a quick consistency check (like taking two airplane flights at the same time) as the proofs are generated, and then to perform a more complete check when the proof is complete. Maintaining a complete list of nogoods simply seems not to be viable in practice; there are too many of them.[20]

An example may make this clearer. Suppose that you are planning a trip from Boston to a small town in Oregon, and that there are two airports that service the town (let's say Portland and Eugene). Getting to or from each of these airports involves a change of plane in Chicago.

As you plan your itinerary, some mistakes are obvious; you can't leave Chicago before you get there, for example. You will therefore not even consider plans that assume that you arrive in Chicago from Boston at 12: 18 and then leave for Portland at 12:14. This is the sort of mistake that you eliminate as you construct potential itineraries, as in possibility (4a) above.

Other mistakes are more like those in possibility (4b). If you travel a lot, you probably know that changing planes in Chicago is something of a hassle and you're unlikely to be able to make a connection unless you have at least half an hour to do so. Eliminating those partial plans where you arrive in Chicago at 12:18 and leave again at 12:32 involves the use of nogoods that you have constructed before considering the particular travel problem in question.

Finally, there are problems that you consider only after the plan is complete. Perhaps the best itinerary involves flying into Portland, renting a car, and dropping it off and departing from Eugene on your way home. This is the sort of plan that you will likely complete before checking on the details by making sure that there is a single car rental company that

20 It is interesting to note that de Kleer's original description of the ATMS suggested that *all* explanations be computed by forward-chaining. This was found to be impractical in most applications, although there are specific problems for which forward-chaining is to be preferred to backward-chaining.

serves both Oregon airports and from whom you can pick up at one location and drop off at the other.

10.4 FURTHER READING

The idea of an ATMS is due to Johan de Kleer and appears in de Kleer [1986], although many of the ideas appeared earlier in de Kleer [1984]. The work itself builds on a variety of earlier authors' work in this area, including Doyle's original development of a truth maintenance system, or TMS [Doyle 1979], McAllester's RUP system [McAllester 1982], and Shapiro and Martins's work on MBR [Martins and Shapiro 1983].

In many cases, the realization that ATMSs could be used to solve problems such as those described in the text actually predates the description of the general computational mechanism, as different authors developed the same ideas for a variety of purposes. The use of assumption-based techniques to solve synthesis problems is described by Finger [1987]; the recognition that diagnosis is a truth-maintenance problem first appears in Ginsberg [1986]. Other early authors who discuss the relationship between ATMSs and first-principles diagnosis are Reiter [1987b] and de Kleer and Williams [1987]; de Kleer *et al.* [1992] is a more recent extension of this work. The alternative approach to diagnosis, where one uses information like that appearing in (10.11) to reason from symptoms to causes, is described in Poole *et al.* [1985]. This sort of reasoning, where one views the consequence of an implication as evidence in favor of its premises, is known as *abduction* and is the focus of considerable research in its own right [Poole 1973]. A comparison between the two types of diagnosis is the subject of Poole [1989].

Database updates are described using ATMS-like techniques in Fagin *et al.* [1983] and Ginsberg [1986]. These papers have generated a considerable flurry of successors; much of the work is extremely technical and the most useful single pointer I can give you is probably to Gardenförs [1988]. The relationship between database updates and reasoning about action is cited in much of this work as well, and also in Ginsberg and Smith [1988] and Winslett [1988]. The problem discussed in the text (where one cannot tell whether to remove a sentence that has become unsupported but is not outright contradicted by new information) is the focus of Myers and Smith [1988] and is touched on by Ginsberg [1991a] also.

10.5 EXERCISES

1. In Exercise 13 in Chapter 8, we used resolution to find three animals that lions can outrun.

   (a) For each such animal a, what is the explanation for the fact that lions can outrun a? What is the explanation for the fact that there is *some* animal that lions can outrun? Use the convention that quantified sentences are common knowledge and ground sentences are not when constructing your answer.

(b) What would we have to remove from our database if we wanted to add the fact that lions are slower than zebras? To add the fact that lions are slower than dogs? To add the fact that lions are the slowest animals around?

2. How can Algorithm 10.1.1 be modified so that it does not include elements of the common knowledge set C in its explanations?

3. Assuming that either $C = \emptyset$ or the algorithm has been modified as in the previous exercise, either produce a counterexample or prove each of the following claims:

   (a) Every set returned by Algorithm 10.1.1 is an explanation for the query q.

   (b) Every explanation for a query q will eventually be returned by the algorithm.

4. What is a good explanation for the fact that Mozart died on his last visit to Vienna in Exercise 15 in Chapter 8? How did you decide which facts were in C and which were in A in this example?

5. What would Algorithm 10.3.1 return if the query were a tautology? What would be returned if the sentence did not follow from the database at all?

6. Let p be a sentence, and suppose that an ATMS labels p with a set of explanations E. Each explanation e in E is a list of assumptions that entail p and if $e = \{w_1, \ldots, w_n\}$, e can be thought of as the conjunction $w_1 \wedge \cdots \wedge w_n$. Other explanations in E can also be thought of as conjunctions; suppose that we define $s(E)$ to be the disjunction of all of these individual conjunctive sentences.

   (a) Show that if the ATMS label for p is E, then $s(E)$ is consistent with C and $C \cup \{s(E)\} \models p$.

   (b) Let q be any sentence that is the disjunction of conjunctions of elements of A such that q is consistent with C and $C \cup \{q\} \models p$. Prove that $q \models s(E)$.

   (c) Interpret these results.

7. Let s be the sentence-constructing operation in the previous exercise.

   Suppose that we are working with a domain that includes two individuals, Sue and Tom. Suppose further that we are prepared to assume that either of these individuals is honest, so that our assumption set is

$$A = \{\texttt{honest(Sue)}, \texttt{honest(Tom)}\}$$

Now suppose that while investigating some crime, we learn that either Sue or Tom is the culprit. This becomes common knowledge, and we take

$$C = \{\neg \texttt{honest(Sue)} \vee \neg \texttt{honest(Tom)}\}$$

(a) What is the ATMS label for the sentence

$$\texttt{honest(Sue)} \vee \texttt{honest(Tom)}$$

In other words, what are the explanations for the fact that although one of Sue or Tom is a crook, they aren't *both* crooks?

(b) If the label computed above is E, what is the associated sentence $s(E)$?

(c) What is the ATMS label for $\neg s(E)$? Interpret this result.

8. Prove that any superset of a nogood is also a nogood.

9. Formalize the travel-planning example appearing in Section 10.2.1. Be sure to include axioms indicating that you can only take one flight at a time.

10. (a) What axiom or axioms can be used to describe inverters in a fashion similar to the description of OR gates given by (10.5)?

    (b) Complete the derivation of (10.7) using the assumptions given in the text.

11. In the travel-planning example, we needed an axiom indicating that we could only take one flight at a time. What similar axioms are needed in circuit design?

12. This exercise involves diagnostic reasoning. The basic problem involves a car; the common knowledge about the car is the following:

    - If the battery is OK and the headlight bulbs are OK, then the headlights will work.
    - If the battery is OK and the starter is OK, then the engine will start.

    The sort of reasoning we want to capture is the following: If we come up to the car and try to start it, but it doesn't start, then presumably something is wrong with the battery or the starter, but we have no reason to worry about the headlight bulbs. You should begin by formalizing the above knowledge about automobiles as a pair of implications. The possible assumptions we might make are that the battery, headlight bulbs, and starter are OK.

    (a) What are the explanations for the following conclusions:

        i. The engine will start.

ii. The headlights will work.
iii. Either the headlights will work *or* the engine will start.

(b) What are the possible diagnoses for each of the following failures:
i. The engine doesn't start.
ii. The headlights don't work.
iii. The headlights don't work *and* the engine doesn't start.
How can these diagnoses be constructed from the answers to (a)?

(c) In general, suppose that the ATMS set of explanations for any sentence p is $\phi(p)$. Now if we observe a failure f, how can we compute the possible diagnoses for f in terms of the explanations assigned to various sentences related to f?

(d) Suppose that we write $p > q$ to mean, "Upon observing the failure p, conclude q." Now consider the following potential rule of inference:

$$(p > r) \wedge \neg(p > \neg q) \rightarrow (p \wedge q > r) \tag{10.16}$$

This means that if p allows us to conclude r, we can still conclude r if we also learn q, provided that q is not a "surprise" in that p led us to believe $\neg q$. (If q is a surprise, we might still be able to conclude r and might not.)
Is (10.16) valid given the ATMS approach to diagnosis? Prove it or find a counterexample.

13. Why is it important that the hitting set used in Algorithm 10.2.1 be minimal?

14. Implement an ATMS using the algorithm presented in this chapter and use it to respond to some of the above questions.

15. Develop a version of Algorithm 10.3.1 that generates explanations using forward chaining. Can you give an example of a problem for which such an algorithm is well-suited?

CHAPTER

11

NONMONOTONIC REASONING

Let us turn our attention now from ATMSs to another oddly named idea, that of *nonmonotonic reasoning*. (The name makes more sense this time, as we will see shortly.)

Nonmonotonic reasoning was "invented" around 1980; I've put invented in quotes because nonmonotonic reasoning itself has been around for a very long time; what happened in 1980 was that it began to receive attention from the AI community and that a variety of specific formalizations were developed to describe it.

I'm not going to tell you about these specific formalizations; to focus either on them or on the small details that distinguishes one formalization from another would not live up to my promises in the introduction. Instead, I'm going to focus on the ideas underlying work on nonmonotonic reasoning. I'll tell you the names of some of the official versions at the end of the chapter in the interests of completeness.

11.1 EXAMPLES

Before discussing the formalization of nonmonotonic reasoning, though, it would be a good idea if I told you what it was. Here is something between an example and a definition:

Nothing is certain but death and taxes.

What Benjamin Franklin was telling us here is that every conclusion we draw—that our car will start when we turn the key in the ignition, that the sun will come up tomorrow, that the Cubs won't win the World Series, that this book doesn't contain a picture of the Eiffel tower (!), and so on—is subject to reversal. It is, after all, *possible* that the earth will be stopped in its rotation and the sun won't come up tomorrow. It's possible that something is wrong with my car (perhaps there is no gas in the tank, perhaps someone has stuck a potato in my tail pipe). And it is even possible, albeit unlikely, that the Cubs will win the Series some day.

The point is that we typically reason not using the ironclad methods of first-order logic, but in a sort of *defeasible* way—the conclusions we draw can typically be defeated if we obtain new information that contradicts them or that undermines the arguments we used to draw the conclusions in the first place.

11.1.1 Inheritance Hierarchies

These examples are hardly the only ones possible. The "standard" example of nonmonotonic reasoning involves reasoning about the inheritance of properties from one class to another. As an example, suppose that I tell you that birds fly. If I also tell you that Tweety is a bird, should you be able to conclude that Tweety can fly?

One would certainly expect so. In fact, one may well be *required* to expect so—if you hire me to build a cage for Tweety, and I leave off the roof on the grounds that I couldn't decide whether or not Tweety could fly, it would be reasonable for you to refuse to accept my product. It would be much less reasonable for you to refuse to pay if I were to put a roof on the bird cage that you didn't need because Tweety can't fly after all.[21]

But notice what we said in the last paragraph—it is *possible* that Tweety can't fly after all. Perhaps Tweety is an ostrich, or a penguin. Maybe Tweety is dead. Maybe Tweety's feet have been set in concrete, and so on. If we learn any of these things, we will need to retract our earlier conclusion that Tweety could fly.

What we see is that the rule that birds fly isn't really

$$\texttt{bird}(x) \rightarrow \texttt{flies}(x) \tag{11.1}$$

(with the usual implicit quantification), since it is not the case that all birds fly. Instead, (11.1) is something like

$$\texttt{bird}(x) \wedge \texttt{normal}(x) \rightarrow \texttt{flies}(x) \tag{11.2}$$

which says only that all *normal* birds fly. (11.2) is typically written

$$\texttt{bird}(x) \wedge \neg\texttt{ab}(x) \rightarrow \texttt{flies}(x) \tag{11.3}$$

which says that a bird x can fly unless x is abnormal.

Of course, (11.3) doesn't say that all abnormal birds *don't* fly; this isn't true, either! An ostrich with a ticket on United can fly, for example. Unless the flight is cancelled—so even exceptions to exceptions have exceptions.

But let us return to (11.3). Given that we know that Tweety is a bird, what allows us to conclude ¬ab(Tweety) in order to apply (11.3) and derive the fact that Tweety can fly?

21 This example and many others in this chapter are due to John McCarthy.

We can't derive ¬ab(Tweety), of course—what we do is *assume* that Tweety is a normal bird in the absence of information to the contrary. And in the presence of contrary information, we abandon the assumption. So if we know that ostriches are nonflying birds

$$\texttt{ostrich}(x) \rightarrow \texttt{bird}(x) \wedge \neg\texttt{flies}(x) \tag{11.4}$$

we can derive that ostriches are abnormal:

$$\texttt{ostrich}(x) \rightarrow \texttt{ab}(x)$$

Thus if Fred is an ostrich, we are not tempted to assume ¬ab(Fred).

Examples such as the one we have been discussing are often drawn as in Figure 11.1, where arrows indicate default rules such as

$$\texttt{bird}(x) \wedge \neg\texttt{ab}_b(x) \rightarrow \texttt{flies}(x) \tag{11.5}$$

An arrow with a line through it corresponds to a default in which the conclusion has been negated, as in

$$\texttt{ostrich}(x) \wedge \neg\texttt{ab}_o(x) \rightarrow \neg\texttt{flies}(x) \tag{11.6}$$

There are a few things to note about this notation. First, we have introduced subscripts onto the abnormality predicates in (11.5) and (11.6) in order to distinguish x's that are abnormal birds in that they cannot fly from x's that are abnormal ostriches in that they can. Just because an object is abnormal in one sense doesn't necessarily mean that it's abnormal in all other ways as well—a default that birds are typically small will be violated for an eagle, and the default that birds fly should not fail as a result.

Next, note that our diagrammatic notation doesn't distinguish between default rules (which include an abnormality clause as in (11.3)) and nondefaults (as in (11.4)). In some cases the notation in Figure 11.1 needs to be extended to allow one to express nondefault information. We have done this using double arrows in Figure 11.2, which says that ostriches are definitely birds.

FIGURE 11.1 An inheritance diagram

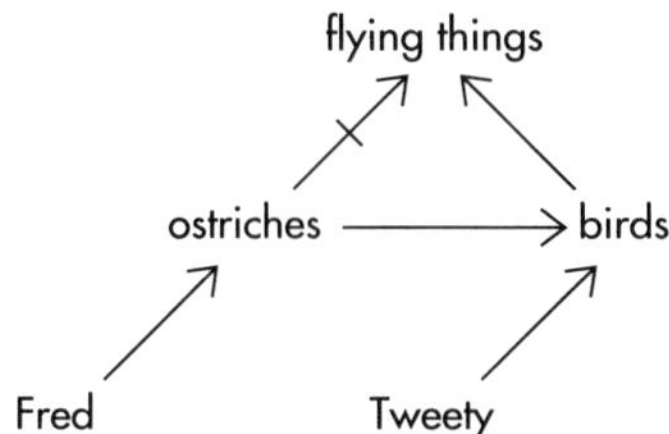

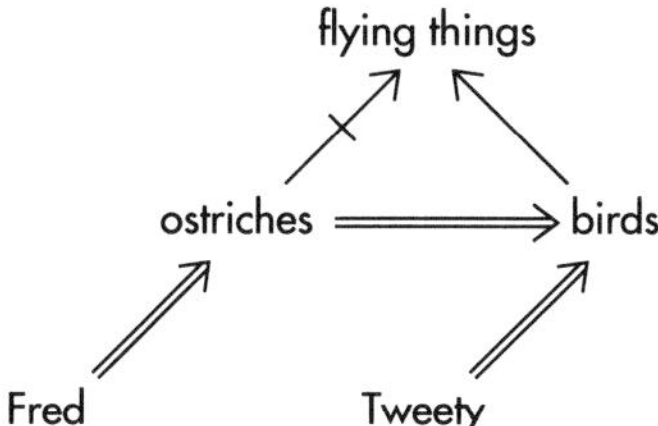

FIGURE 11.2 Ostriches are always birds

Finally, the axiom appearing in these diagrams saying that Tweety is a bird appears somewhat strange:

$$\texttt{Tweety}(x) \rightarrow \texttt{bird}(x) \tag{11.7}$$

In other words, if x satisfies the "Tweety" property, then x will be a bird. But upon further reflection this is quite reasonable; all we've done is change `Tweety` from an object constant to a predicate. If we add the axiom

`Tweety(Tweety)`

to our database, then (11.7) does indeed allow us to recover

`bird(Tweety)`

We will return to examples such as this one from a formal point of view in Section 11.2.1, and discuss more general considerations on inheritance and related topics in Chapter 13.

11.1.2 The Frame Problem

Another application of nonmonotonic reasoning has been to what is known as the *frame* problem, which is the question of how we represent the fact that things tend to stay the same in the absence of information to the contrary.

What color is your best friend's hair? Brown, you say? (Or red, or gray, or whatever.) But how do you know? Why couldn't your best friend have dyed his hair since you last met? Perhaps because he isn't the sort of person who dyes his hair on a whim. But why couldn't *that* have changed since you last met?

The point, of course, is that we typically conclude that things stay pretty much the same in the absence of information to the contrary. People don't change their hair color all the time. My car or bicycle is presumably still where I left it. As I write this chapter of the book, the electronic image of the previous chapter is still on the disk. My mother still lives in New Jersey. My mother-in-law still lives in Seattle. My dog still likes me, and the Eiffel tower is still in France. (And a picture of it is still on page 6.)

Of course, some things *do* change as time passes. If I learn that my wife has borrowed my car, then I will no longer conclude that it's still where I left it. A somewhat simpler example is shown in Figure 11.3.

In this figure, suppose that we move the block A onto the block C. Is C still located at l_2? Presumably it is; it's at l_2 before the move action takes place, and there's no reason to assume that it's anywhere else as a result of the action.

But what about the fact that A is at l_1? Assuming that we know that blocks can be in only one place at a time, it follows from the fact that A is newly located on top of C that it can't be at l_1 any more. Similarly, from the fact that C is only big enough to have one block on top of it, the fact that A is on top of C means that B has to be somewhere else.

As with the inheritance examples, we have no way to *prove* that C will stay where it is when we move A; we simply assume that it does. And also as with these earlier examples, it isn't too troubling if we find out that we're wrong and that moving A actually has managed to displace C somewhat. It's a bit of a surprise, but nothing like the surprise we would feel if we discovered that A were in two places at once.

In fact, our "frame" assumption that things stay the same in the absence of information to the contrary is wrong a *lot*—so much so that we are likely to be surprised if it *isn't* violated, at least in some small way, as time passes. Do you really expect your house or apartment to be *exactly* the same when you leave for class and when you return? Not if you have a roommate, that's for sure. And also not if you have a pet, or leave a window open through which a breeze can come in (which will rearrange the dust in the room if nothing else), or have a package delivered, or have a telephone-answering machine, or set your VCR up to record something, or even if you have a clock! As with inheritance, the list of possible exceptions is endless.

11.1.3 Diagnosis

Like assumption-based truth maintenance, nonmonotonic reasoning can be used in diagnosis from first principles. The basic reason is that when one builds a device of some sort, one assumes that all of the components are working. In the presence of a failure, this conclusion becomes inconsistent with what we already know and we are forced to retract it in a nonmon-

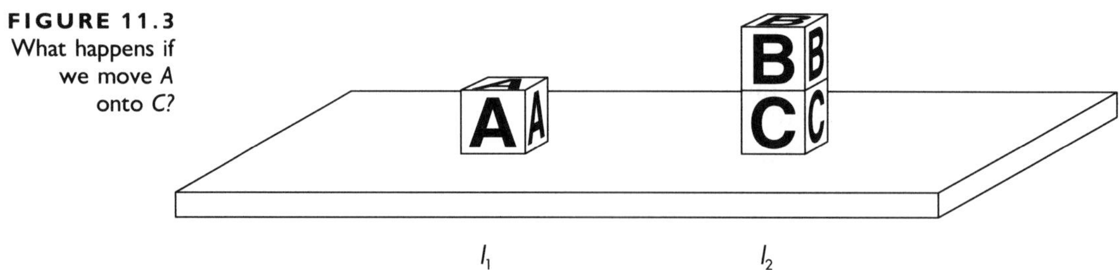

FIGURE 11.3 What happens if we move A onto C?

otonic way. As in ATMS-based diagnosis, the analysis proceeds using a complete description of the object whose behavior is faulty; I'll let you work out the details in Exercise 3 at the end of this chapter.

In fact, the tie between nonmonotonic reasoning and ATMSs is closer than their merely leading to similar sorts of diagnostic reasoning. The frame problem, as discussed in Section 11.1.2, is quite similar in flavor to the database update problem discussed in Section 10.2.3. We will see more about this connection in the exercises at the end of this chapter and in Section 11.3, where we discuss the possibility of using an ATMS to actually compute the consequences of a nonmonotonic database.

11.2 DEFINITION

Before we can compute these consequences, however, we need to actually say what they are! But before doing that, let me spend a paragraph or two explaining why the defeasible reasoning that we're discussing is called *nonmonotonic* reasoning.

In classical inference (that is, first-order logic), suppose that we have some database D that entails a sentence p, $D \models p$. Now if S is some superset of D, S will entail p as well. After all, any inference steps we took (using resolution or some other method) involving the set D will continue to be valid if we are using the superset S instead. Another way to think of this is that the set of legal conclusions grows *monotonically* with the set of facts appearing in our initial database.

Nonmonotonic reasoning is not like this. When I tell you that Tweety is an ostrich, you *retract* the conclusion that Tweety can fly. In fact, that's exactly what *defeasible* means—in some cases, you may learn something new and be forced to retract a conclusion. Since the set of conclusions is not growing uniformly with the set of input assumptions, this sort of reasoning is called *nonmonotonic*. Just calling it "defeasible" reasoning might make more sense, but it's not too terrible a name.

OK. But how do we actually decide what assumptions to make when analyzing a nonmonotonic problem? How is it that we decide to assume that Tweety is a normal bird and can therefore fly?

11.2.1 Extensions

The basic answer is that we have a set of assumptions that we would *like* to make, and we believe as many of these assumptions as possible. (Now you can begin to see why the connection between nonmonotonic reasoning and ATMSs is so strong.) To formalize this, suppose that we take T to be the sentences that we know to be true for sure, and take A to be the set of assumptions that we would like to make. A might, for example, consist of all possible normality assumptions we could make about the objects in our domain. We will call the pair (T,A) a nonmonotonic *theory* and refer to T—the portion of the theory about which we are certain—as the *base theory*.

DEFINITION 11.2.1 *An* extension *of the nonmonotonic theory given by* (T,A) *is any maximal subset of* A *that is consistent with* T.

Loosely speaking, an extension is a possible way that things might be, given what we already know for sure as reflected in the facts in T. As an example, suppose we return to birds, flying, and Tweety. Here are the facts in our base theory T in this case:

$$\begin{gathered} \texttt{bird(x)} \wedge \neg\texttt{ab(x)} \rightarrow \texttt{flies(x)} \\ \texttt{ostrich(x)} \rightarrow \texttt{bird(x)} \wedge \neg\texttt{flies(x)} \\ \texttt{bird(Tweety)} \\ \texttt{ostrich(Fred)} \end{gathered} \tag{11.8}$$

Normal birds fly, ostriches are nonflying birds, Tweety is a bird, and Fred is an ostrich. In the interests of simplicity, we have dropped the normality assumption from (11.8), so that all ostriches are nonflying birds, not just the normal ones.

The assumptions we would like to make are that both Fred and Tweety are normal. Thus A contains the following sentences:

$$\begin{gathered} \neg\texttt{ab(Tweety)} \\ \neg\texttt{ab(Fred)} \end{gathered}$$

But we have that $T \models$ `ab(Fred)`, since Fred is an ostrich and ostriches are known to be abnormal birds. Thus the sentence ¬`ab(Fred)` cannot appear in any extension of this nonmonotonic theory. Since ¬`ab(Tweety)` is consistent with T, there is a unique extension given by

$$E = \{\neg\texttt{ab(Tweety)}\}$$

Note that this extension, together with our base theory T, is sufficient to entail the desired conclusion that Tweety can fly. That's why we said that `flies(Tweety)` is a nonmonotonic consequence of this particular theory.

11.2.2 Multiple Extensions

Nowhere in Definition 11.2.1 does it say that the default theory has to have a *unique* extension; any maximal consistent subset of the assumptions will suffice. (Maximal is to be taken in the set-theoretic sense here, as usual.)

FIGURE 11.4 A theory with multiple extensions

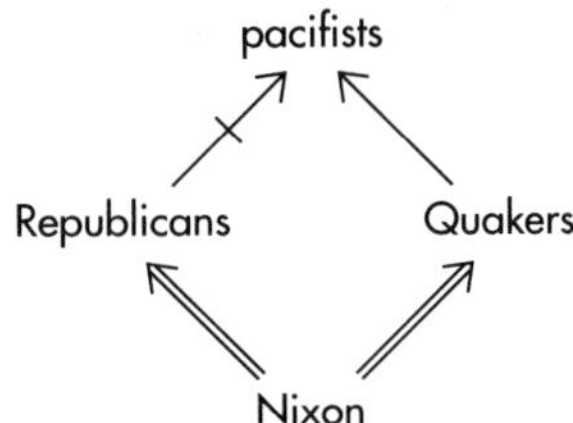

Probably the most famous example of a theory with multiple extensions is shown in Figure 11.4, and is called the *Nixon diamond*.

In this example, we know that Quakers tend to be pacifists and Republicans tend not to be; Nixon is both a Quaker and a Republican. So here is our base theory T:

$$\texttt{Quaker}(x) \wedge \neg \mathrm{ab}_r(x) \rightarrow \texttt{pacifist}(x)$$

$$\texttt{Republican}(x) \wedge \neg \mathrm{ab}_p(x) \rightarrow \neg \texttt{pacifist}(x)$$

$$\texttt{Quaker(Nixon)}$$

$$\texttt{Republican(Nixon)}$$

Note that we have subscripted the abnormality predicates in the above axioms; ab_r says that if a Quaker is not *religiously* abnormal, he will be a pacifist. ab_p says that if a Republican is not *politically* abnormal, he will not be a pacifist.

What we would like to assume is that Nixon is both politically and religiously normal:

$$A = \{\neg \mathrm{ab}_r(\texttt{Nixon}), \neg \mathrm{ab}_p(\texttt{Nixon})\}$$

Unfortunately, our base theory T implies

$$\mathrm{ab}_r(\texttt{Nixon}) \vee \mathrm{ab}_p(\texttt{Nixon})$$

so that Nixon has to be abnormal in one sense or the other. This leads to two extensions, given by

$$E_1 = \{\neg \mathrm{ab}_p(\texttt{Nixon})\}$$

$$E_2 = \{\neg \mathrm{ab}_r(\texttt{Nixon})\}$$

since each of these sets is a maximal subset of A that is consistent with T. In one of the extensions, Nixon is a pacifist; in the other, he isn't. In this particular example, there is no real reason to prefer one extension over the other—given the information that we have, there is no way to tell whether Nixon is a pacifist or not.

Suppose that we were to combine our last two examples, so that T included both the facts about birds and flying and those about Nixon. Now we continue to get two extensions:

$$E_1 = \{\neg ab_p(\texttt{Nixon}), \neg ab(\texttt{Tweety})\}$$

$$E_2 = \{\neg ab_r(\texttt{Nixon}), \neg ab(\texttt{Tweety})\}$$

Since Fred the ostrich is known to be abnormal, ¬ab(Fred) appears in neither extension. And since there is no reason to believe that Tweety is abnormal, the fact that he is normal appears in both extensions.

What are the consequences of the extensions in this case? The query flies(Tweety) holds in both extensions; pacifist(Nixon) holds in only one. This reflects the fact that we have some reason to believe both queries, but also some reason *not* to believe that Nixon is a pacifist. This leads to the following definition:

DEFINITION 11.2.2 *Let* (T,A) *be a default theory. A sentence* p *is called a* cautious consequence *of* (T,A) *if* p *holds in every extension of this theory, so that*

$$T \cup E \models p$$

for every extension E. p *is called a* brave consequence *of the default theory if* $T \cup E \models p$ *for* some *extension* E.

Roughly speaking, cautious consequences are those for which there are arguments in favor but no arguments against. Consequences that are brave but not cautious are those for which there are arguments both for and against.

Another example involving multiple extensions appears in Figure 11.5. Here, we say that Quakers are pacifists and Republicans are hawks; nothing

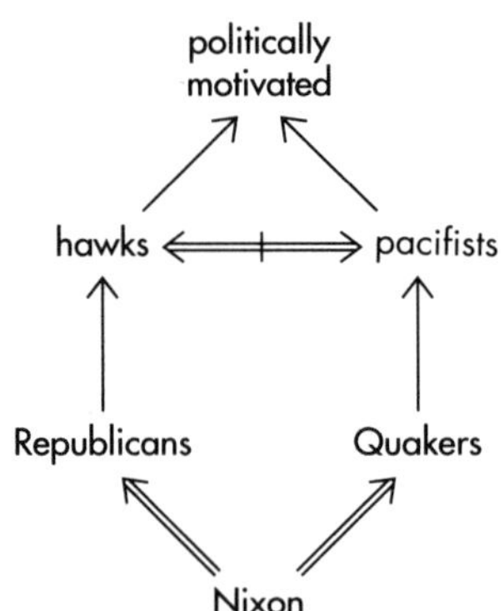

FIGURE 11.5 Is Nixon politically motivated?

can be both a pacifist and a hawk. But given that both pacifists and hawks are politically motivated, Nixon certainly should be as well. Many existing formal approaches to inheritance reasoning cannot deal with this example.

Let us return to the problem of distinguishing among competing extensions. As we saw, there is no reason to prefer one of the extensions to the other in the Nixon diamond, but this is not always the case.

As an example, consider the diagram appearing in Figure 11.6, where we have once again made the fact that ostriches do not fly a default rule. Thus our base theory T, instead of being the one presented earlier, is now:

$$\texttt{bird(x)} \wedge \neg \texttt{ab}_b\texttt{(x)} \rightarrow \texttt{flies(x)} \tag{11.9}$$

$$\texttt{ostrich(x)} \rightarrow \texttt{bird(x)}$$

$$\texttt{ostrich(x)} \wedge \neg \texttt{ab}_o\texttt{(x)} \rightarrow \neg \texttt{flies(x)} \tag{11.10}$$

$$\texttt{ostrich(Fred)}$$

We've added subscripts to the abnormality predicates and dropped the information about Tweety because it isn't relevant to this problem. The assumptions we would like to make are that Fred is in all regards normal:

$$A = \{\neg \texttt{ab}_b\texttt{(Fred)}, \neg \texttt{ab}_o\texttt{(Fred)}\}$$

Unfortunately, since Fred can't both fly and not fly, these normality assumptions are in conflict with one another; as in the Nixon diamond, we are able to derive

$$\texttt{ab}_b\texttt{(Fred)} \vee \texttt{ab}_o\texttt{(Fred)}$$

The similarity to the Nixon diamond is even clearer in Figure 11.7, where we have explicitly included in the diagram the derived conclusion that Fred is a bird.

In this example, we somehow use the fact that ostriches are a subclass of birds to prefer the rule about ostriches, (11.10), to that about birds, (11.9). The only difference between Figures 11.4 and 11.7 is the presence of the horizontal arrow in Figure 11.7, and this somehow allows us to pick one extension over the other. But how might we formalize this?

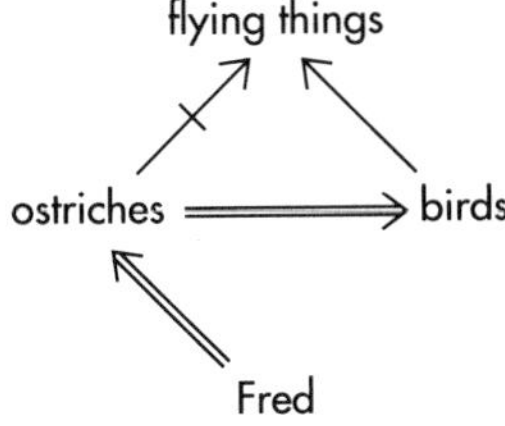

FIGURE 11.6 Does Fred fly or not?

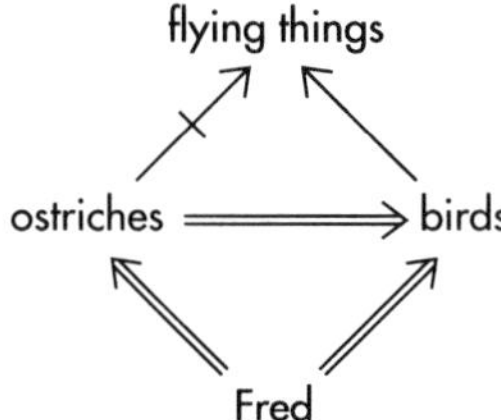

FIGURE 11.7
Fred's diamond

One way would be to rank our assumptions explicitly in some way, and then to say that we should never accept a low-priority assumption if doing so forces us to drop a higher-priority one. Given the fact that ostriches are a special type of bird, we should prefer assumptions about ostriches to competing assumptions about birds.

The problem with this approach is that it sometimes isn't obvious when one assumption should be preferred to another. Put another way, if we say, "Prefer assumptions about ostriches to those about birds," we've lost track of the *reason* for this preference. Maybe the preference itself has exceptions for some reason. Maybe the existence of the preference depends on domain-specific information that is much more subtle than the bald statement that ostriches are a subclass of birds.

We would like the information about which extensions should be preferred over others to be declarative in some way; after all, choosing an extension typically involves an appeal to declarative information similar to that used to reason about the domain generally. Unfortunately, no general way of doing this is known at the time of this writing; work on disambiguating multiple extensions is an active research topic in the nonmonotonic community.

Before turning to other matters, however, let me describe a fairly new approach to this problem that may have some merit. Consider the rule that ostriches don't fly:

$$\texttt{ostrich}(x) \wedge \neg ab_o(x) \rightarrow \neg\texttt{flies}(x) \tag{11.11}$$

Now imagine that this rule *didn't* take precedence over the rule about birds flying. If Fred is an ostrich and therefore a bird, we can combine (11.11) with (11.5) to conclude that Fred is either ab_o or ab_b. If we can't at least occasionally go on to conclude that ab_b is to be preferred here, $\neg ab_o$ will not be true for any ostriches and we will never be able to draw useful conclusions from (11.11). So one way to distinguish between the two extensions in Figure 11.7 is to argue that there is no reason to include (11.11) in our domain description unless the intention is that Fred be a normal ostrich.

This argument would not apply if ostriches were not a subclass of birds, since (11.11) could then affect our conclusions if it were applied only to those ostriches that were not birds. The fact that the above argument relies onthe fact that ostriches are a subclass of birds is encouraging, since this subclass relationship is the intuitive argument we used when solving the particular instance of the multiple extension problem in Figure 11.7.

Will this sort of an approach work in general? It's too early to say, but it's an interesting idea with a flavor somewhat different from a simple declarative approach; it depends instead on some sort of "conversational" principle that if you add a rule to a declarative database, you mean for that rule to have force.

11.3 COMPUTATIONAL PROBLEMS

Setting the multiple-extension problem aside, how are the consequences of a particular nonmonotonic theory (T,A) to be computed?

Before discussing this question in detail, I should confess that the question itself doesn't do justice to the original motivation for introducing nonmonotonic reasoning into AI. When we jump to the conclusion that Tweety can fly because Tweety is a bird, we are doing just that—*jumping* to a conclusion. We draw the conclusion that Tweety can fly quickly, without carefully checking to see that the assumption ¬ab(Tweety) really is consistent with everything else we know. When I conclude that my car is where I left it, I also don't bother with a complete consistency check—in fact, I might "know" that my wife was planning on borrowing the car but simply have forgotten to take this information into account when concluding that it was still where I left it.

There is an implicit promise in the motivation underlying nonmonotonic reasoning that this approach can somehow make our inference go *faster*, but this promise has been lost in the formalization of Definition 11.2.1 and in other approaches that have appeared in the literature. The reason appears to be that people have many uses for conclusions that are drawn quickly but might be in error (if I'm looking for my car and I'm in a hurry, I need to decide *now* where the car is); computers don't yet have such uses. It would be nice if things were otherwise, but there isn't much to report here yet.

Given this disclaimer, let us return to our original question: Suppose that we have some default theory (T,A), and a query q. Does q hold in some extension of the default theory?

There are two ways in which we might answer this question. The first would be to simply begin enumerating the extensions of the default theory, and seeing if q held in any of them. This is unlikely to be productive in practice, however, since we aren't really focusing our search for a specific extension in which q holds and it may be extremely expensive to construct even a single extension in its entirety if the set A is large.

Instead, suppose that we begin to construct the ATMS label for q using Algorithm 10.3.1. As soon as we find *some* proof of q that uses a consistent set S of assumptions, we know that q holds in some extension of (T,A):

PROPOSITION 11.3.1 *Let* (T,A) *be a default theory, and* q *be a query. Then* q *holds in some extension of the default theory if and only if* q *has an explanation using facts in* A.

PROOF Suppose first that q has an explanation using the facts in a subset S of A, so that $T \cup S \models q$ and S is consistent with T. We can now simply add facts from A to S until it becomes a maximal subset S' consistent with T. Since $S \subset S'$ and $T \cup S \models q$, it follows that $T \cup S' \models q$ as well and q therefore holds in the extension given by S'.

For the converse, suppose that q holds in some extension E of the default theory, where $E \subset A$ is consistent with T and has the property that $T \cup E \models q$. By removing facts from E while retaining this property, we retain consistency with T and will eventually produce an ATMS-like explanation of q from A. ∎

Proposition 11.3.1 can be used to construct an algorithm to determine whether or not a particular sentence q is a brave consequence of the default theory (T,A). A similar result that can be used to determine if q is a *cautious* consequence of the default theory is the focus of Exercise 9 at the end of this chapter.

11.4 FINAL REMARKS

There are a few more things to say about nonmonotonic reasoning before we turn our attention to other matters.

The first is that it seems that default rules are trying to solve the same sorts of problems that are often attacked using probability theory; instead of saying, "Birds typically fly," we might say that the probability of a randomly selected bird being able to fly is 0.95.

In fact, it turns out that defaults correspond most closely to infinitesimal probabilities; what we mean by the default, "Birds fly," is that the probability of a random bird flying is $1-\epsilon$ for some arbitrarily small ϵ. The reason is that in the absence of specific information to the contrary, it is possible to chain together long strings of defaults without affecting the strength of our belief in any of the conclusions in the string. This is not true in probability theory; the conclusion of an argument that depends on probabilistic assumptions becomes weaker as the number of assumptions grows. There are other differences as well, but this is probably the most important one.

There is a very general problem here—when trying to reason with uncertain information, are numeric methods (like probabilities) or symbolic methods (like default reasoning) to be preferred? There is no consensus on this within the AI community; any individual scientist will typically argue that one method is the one of choice and that the other is nonsense. This is a point to which we will return in the next chapter, when we examine the probabilistic side of the coin.

Finally, of all of the formal descriptions that have appeared in the literature for describing nonmonotonic reasoning, three are generally recognized as the most important. I have been careful to avoid giving you details of any specific formalization in this chapter, but let me at least give you the names: circumscription [McCarthy 1980], default logic [Reiter 1980], and autoepistemic logic [Moore 1985].

11.5 FURTHER READING

There are two good introductions to nonmonotonic reasoning that go into more depth than what has been presented here. One is the introduction to Ginsberg [1987], which also contains a variety of articles about topics in nonmonotonic reasoning generally. (This collection is out of print, however.) The other survey article is by Reiter [1987a], which is somewhat more technical than the introduction in Ginsberg [1987].

The formal connection between ATMSs and nonmonotonic reasoning systems is the topic of Reiter and de Kleer [1987]; the result itself has been around for quite a while. The Nixon diamond (Figure 11.4) first appears in Reiter and Criscuolo [1981] and has become one of the most-cited examples in the nonmonotonic literature (second only to Tweety, in fact). The solution to the multiple extension problem described at the end of Section 11.2.2 first appears in Geffner [1990].

The suggestion in the text that computers have no use for inaccurate information will probably be outdated fairly soon; a variety of authors are considering issues here. The idea of an "anytime" algorithm, one that is gradually refined as time passes, appears in Dean and Boddy [1988a] and is likely to be fairly central if AI programs are to be used in real-time applications. The work of Russell and Wefald [1989] that we described in Chapter 2 uses information about how likely a conclusion is to be in error in order to decide whether to devote additional computational resources to considering it. Finally, I point out in Ginsberg [1991b] that the fact that metalevel conclusions must be drawn quickly is an indication that nonmonotonic reasoning may have a natural role to play in search control generally; control of reasoning is a domain where it is better to draw inaccurate conclusions quickly than to draw accurate conclusions slowly.

11.6 EXERCISES

1. Why did we use double arrows from `Tweety` into `bird` and from `Fred` into `ostrich` in Figure 11.2?

2. Axiomatize the simple blocks-world example appearing in Figure 11.3. Show that there is a unique extension in this case, and that it involves B moving but C remaining where it is.

3. **Diagnosis** This problem uses the same setting as Exercise 12 in Chapter 10. But instead of using an ATMS, suppose that we have default rules indicating that each of the components is likely to be working.
   (a) What are the possible extensions in each of the following cases?
      i. The headlights work and the engine starts.
      ii. The various failures appearing in part (b) of Exercise 12 in Chapter 10.
   (b) In general, suppose that we add to our nonmonotonic database a fact indicating that the failure f has been observed. How do the possible diagnoses for the failure relate to the extensions of the resulting nonmonotonic theory?
   (c) Consider once again the potential rule of inference

$$(p > r) \wedge \neg(p > \neg q) \rightarrow (p \wedge q > r) \qquad (11.12)$$

   where we have written $p > q$ to mean, "Upon observing the failure p, conclude q." In other words, if p allows us to conclude r, we can still conclude r if we also learn q, provided that q is not a "surprise" in that p led us to believe $\neg q$. (If q is a surprise, we might still be able to conclude r or we might not.) This is known as the rule of *rational monotony*, since it gives weak conditions under which inference might be expected to be monotonic.
   Suppose that we take $p > r$ to mean that if we add p to our base theory T, r is a cautious consequence of the resulting theory. Is (11.12) valid? Prove it or find a counterexample.

4. In which of the two extensions in the Nixon diamond is Nixon a pacifist?

5. Let (T,A) be a default theory. Prove that (T,A) has a single extension if and only if the set of brave consequences of this theory is consistent. Does this result continue to hold even if T itself is inconsistent?

6. Suppose that we augment our birds flying example to include a fact saying that flying things are not acrophobic, as shown in Figure 11.8. Formalize this rule and then answer the following questions:
   (a) Is the fact that Tweety is not acrophobic a consequence of this theory? Brave or cautious?

FIGURE 11.8 Flying things are not afraid of heights

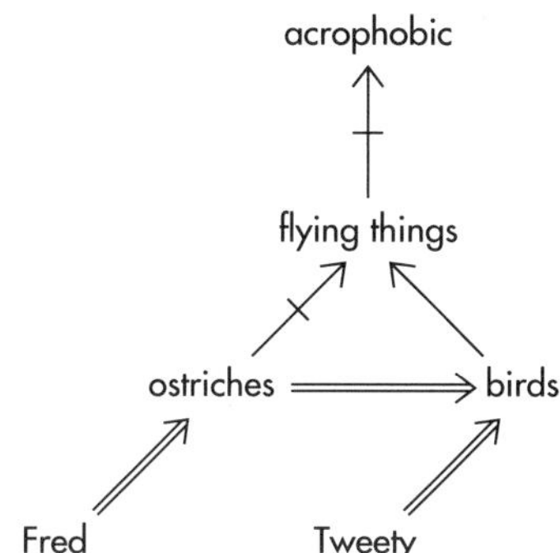

(b) Is the fact that Fred is not acrophobic a consequence of this theory?

(c) Is the fact that Fred *is* acrophobic a consequence of this theory?

(d) Is it really right to say that the brave but not cautious consequences of a default theory are those for which there are arguments both for and against? What would be a more appropriate description?

7. Show that the fact that Nixon is politically motivated is a cautious consequence of the inheritance theory shown in Figure 11.5.

8. An early attempt to formalize the rule that defaults about subclasses should take precedence over defaults about superclasses is known as the *shortest-path heuristic* [Touretzky 1984]. This says that when two paths through an inheritance diagram such as that in Figure 11.6 give conflicting conclusions, the shorter of the two paths should be preferred to the longer.

   (a) Explain why this makes sense in terms of rules about subclasses taking precedence over rules about superclasses.

   (b) Construct an example of an inheritance diagram where the shortest-path heuristic leads to the wrong conclusion.

9. Let (T,A) be a default theory, and q a query. Suppose that the set of explanations for q is E. As in Exercise 6 in Chapter 10, it is possible to associate a sentence $s(E)$ to E; $s(E)$ is a sentence that "describes" the explanations in E. Prove that the following conditions are equivalent:

   (a) q holds in *all* extensions of the default theory.

   (b) q is a cautious consequence of (T,A).

   (c) The ATMS label assigned to $\neg s(E)$ is Ø.

   (d) $\neg s(E)$ holds in no extensions of the default theory.

   Comment on this result.

10. Can you *prove* Franklin's statement that nothing is certain except death and taxes?

CHAPTER 12

PROBABILITY

In this chapter, we will look at one of the other main approaches to reasoning with uncertain information in AI—methods based in one way or another on probability theory. Rather than dive directly into the details of these methods, though, suppose that we begin by considering our usual example of nonmonotonic reasoning: We know that Tweety is a bird and that birds fly but ostriches don't.

Given this information, suppose we conclude that Tweety can fly, and that we add this fact to our declarative database. Only *now* do we learn that Tweety is an ostrich, so that our database consists of the following:

$$\texttt{bird}(x) \wedge \neg \texttt{ab}(x) \rightarrow \texttt{flies}(x)$$

$$\texttt{ostrich}(x) \rightarrow \texttt{bird}(x)$$

$$\texttt{ostrich}(x) \rightarrow \neg \texttt{flies}(x)$$

$$\texttt{bird(Tweety)}$$

$$\texttt{flies(Tweety)} \qquad (12.1)$$

$$\texttt{ostrich(Tweety)} \qquad (12.2)$$

Unfortunately, the simultaneous presence of (12.1) and (12.2) makes this database contradictory! And furthermore, we have no way to tell that what we need to retract is our conclusion that Tweety can fly—why shouldn't we retract the rule that ostriches don't fly? Or the fact that ostriches are birds? How about if we simply refuse to accept the new fact that Tweety is an ostrich?

None of these other actions really makes sense, however; it seems much more natural to simply give up gracefully on our conclusion that Tweety can fly. But if we are to distinguish this conclusion from the other information in the database (so that we know what to abandon when we encounter the contradiction), we need to label the sentence `flies(Tweety)` as explicitly defeasible in some way. We might, for example, give all of the other sentences in our database the label *t* ("true"), while labelling the sentence in question as *dt* ("true by default").

Given this, it becomes clear that we will need other labels as well. The fact that Tweety *can't* fly should presumably be labelled as false by default, or *df*. And the fact that Nixon is a pacifist in the Nixon diamond should probably be labelled as both true *and* false by default, since there are good reasons to believe both. This label—indicating the presence of a default contradiction—is typically denoted *.

ATMSs also work by labelling the sentences that they analyze. But this time, instead of labelling a sentence as having some (potentially default) truth value, they label a sentence with the set of explanations for it. In fact, we saw in Definition 10.1.4 that this is precisely what an ATMS does, nothing more or less.

Probabilities are similar; the difference is that here we don't give sentences *symbolic* labels like *dt* or "true by virtue of either of the following explanations." Instead, probabilistic systems label sentences with numbers—their probabilities.

In all of these schemes, *inference* has a uniform meaning. Given a declarative database that consists of a collection of sentences and labels for those sentences, and given a query *q*, what label are we to assign to *q*? Is it true by default? False by default? What explanations would entail it? Or, in the probabilistic case, what is the probability that *q* is true? Note that first-order logic fits this mold as well; the labels are just restricted to "true," "false" and "unknown" (that is, unlabelled).

In nonmonotonic reasoning, we respond to a query by constructing the extensions of the theory with which we are working (or perhaps by doing something equivalent but computationally cheaper, as discussed in Section 11.3). In the ATMS case, we construct a label by finding the explanations for the sentence in question. And in the probabilistic case, we do some sort of numeric manipulation to produce the labels.

12.1 MYCIN AND CERTAINTY FACTORS

What sort of numeric manipulation we do, of course, is up to us; we could, for example, assign zero probability to any sentence that mentioned ostriches or days in June. Such a system likely wouldn't be of much use in practice, but we could certainly do things that way if we chose to.

We might, on the other hand, use a well-developed formal system like that given by the rules of probability. Or we might do something that seemed likely to be useful but that was a bit more *ad hoc*. We'll have a look at legitimately probabilistic methods in the next section, but I'd like to spend at least some time discussing the best-known of the nonprobabilistic methods first. This is the method used by the diagnostic expert system MYCIN.[22]

In MYCIN, sentences are labelled not with probabilities (which would range from 0 to 1), but with *certainty factors*, which range from -1 to $+1$. A certainty factor of -1 indicates that the sentence in question is known to be false; a certainty factor of $+1$ indicates that it is known to be true. A certainty factor of 0 indicates no belief either way.

When reasoning about a particular query q, MYCIN may decide to use a rule saying that

$$p_1 \wedge \cdots \wedge p_n \rightarrow q$$

In order to do so, however, it needs to assign a certainty factor to the conjunction $p_1 \wedge \cdots \wedge p_n$; the value given by MYCIN to this expression is simply the minimum of the certainty factors assigned to each of the p_i.

The intuitive justification for this is that we can't be more convinced of the conjunction than we are of any of the conjuncts it contains. And we certainly get the right answer in the case where each of the p_i's is true or where one of them is false.

MYCIN also uses a special version of modus ponens that is appropriate for use with certainty factors. If a sentence p has certainty factor c and the implication $p \rightarrow q$ has certainty factor d, then the certainty factor assigned to q is given by the product cd if c is positive, and 0 otherwise. After all, if c is nonpositive, we have no confidence in our ability to use the implication to derive q, and our beliefs should therefore be unaffected.

As an example, suppose that we have assigned a certainty factor of .8 to the sentence, "Tom is asleep," and a certainty factor of .7 to, "If Tom is asleep, he is snoring." These two sentences allow us to assign a certainty factor of .56 to the conclusion that Tom is snoring.

What if there had been another way to conclude that Tom is snoring? Suppose that there are two such arguments, indicating that the certainty factor assigned to some conclusion q should be x and y respectively. Then the overall certainty factor assigned by MYCIN is given by

$$\mathrm{CF}(x,y) = \begin{cases} x + y - xy, & \text{if } x,y > 0; \\ x + y + xy, & \text{if } x,y < 0; \\ \dfrac{x+y}{1 - \min(|x|,|y|)}, & \text{if } x \text{ and } y \text{ are of opposite signs.} \end{cases} \tag{12.3}$$

We see in Exercise 1 at the end of this chapter that this, too, is fairly reasonable.

22 I am being faithful to history here by describing MYCIN as ad hoc; it was eventually shown that there are in fact good probabilistic justifications for MYCIN's methods. (See Section 12.5.)

As an example, suppose that we know that Tom sleeps with his brother Dick, and that if Tom snores, then with certainty .3, Dick will complain about it over breakfast the next morning.

If Dick doesn't complain, this provides us with a argument that Tom wasn't snoring, and a contribution of $-.3$ to the certainty factor that Tom was snoring. We combine this with the earlier value of .56 using (12.3) to get an overall answer of $(.56 - .3)/(1 - .3) = .37$. The fact that Dick hasn't complained weakens somewhat our certainty in the conclusion that Tom was snoring.

The choices made by MYCIN in assigning labels were developed not to be in accord with the laws of probability theory, but because they give reasonable results. In its domain (the diagnosis and treatment of bacterial infections), MYCIN's performance is on a par with that of medical experts. In this sense, it manages to pass a very restricted version of the Turing test—and it certainly appears to be the case that the limits on MYCIN's performance come from limitations in the scope of its declarative knowledge and not from limitations in its numerical algorithms. This is an argument that the full power of probability theory, although useful to AI, may not be *necessary* to it.

In fact, one can say something even stronger. An experiment was done in which MYCIN's set of truth values (the real numbers between -1 and 1) was replaced with a set of just four values: -1 (certainly false), $-.3$ (evidence against), $+.3$ (evidence for) and $+1$ (certainly true). The declarative sentences labelled with certainty factors that fell between these values were simply given the closest label possible.

The interesting thing is that MYCIN's performance did not degrade significantly after this change was made; MYCIN simply doesn't require the fine grain provided by a continuum of numerical truth values. So just as MYCIN's performance is an argument that probability may not be needed to pass the Turing test, the performance of this modified system is an argument that numeric truth values may not be needed, either. We will return to this question at the end of the chapter.

Although numeric truth values may not be needed, it seems that something stronger than first-order logic *is* necessary in many applications. We often have information that doesn't justify writing ironclad facts like "all birds fly" or "the house will always win at roulette." *Most* birds fly. The house *usually* wins at roulette. Nonmonotonic formalisms, probability theory, and other methods give us ways to express this information.

12.2 BAYES' RULE AND THE AXIOMS OF PROBABILITY

The best-developed formal approach to numeric reasoning in AI is probability theory. This is not intended to be a text on probability theory, so my presentation of it will be somewhat abbreviated. What I'd like to do is to start with a few specific axioms, and then to show that most of the typical rules of probability can be derived from these.

In the probabilistic approach, each sentence in our database is labelled with a number from 0 to 1; a label of 0 means that the sentence is surely false and one of 1 means that it is surely true. A label of .5 means that the sentence is equally likely to be true or false.

There is a fairly strong assumption here—that you can assign, even implicitly, some probability to each sentence in the database. It might seem like a small thing to say that the probability that a particular coin comes up heads is .5, but you are really saying quite a bit when you make this statement. You are saying, for example, that the coin is a fair one. What probability could you assign if you didn't know if the coin were fair or not? We will return to this issue, too, at the end of this chapter.

The language of probability is extended to include *conditional* probabilities; in addition to saying that the probability of a sentence p has some value x, $\mathtt{pr}(p) = x$, we can say that the probability of p *conditioned on* q has a value. By $\mathtt{pr}(p|q) = y$ we will mean that in the presence of the information that q holds (but no other information), the probability of p is y.

Note that a conditional probability is not the same as the probability of the corresponding implication; we do *not* in general have

$$\mathtt{pr}(p|q) = \mathtt{pr}(q \rightarrow p)$$

To see this, consider the case where $p = \mathtt{flies}$ and $q = \mathtt{bird}$. The conditional probability $\mathtt{pr}(\mathtt{flies}|\mathtt{bird})$ indicates the likelihood that a randomly selected object can fly, given that it is a bird. Let's say that it's .9.

What about $\mathtt{pr}(\mathtt{bird} \rightarrow \mathtt{flies})$? This is the probability that the sentence $\mathtt{bird} \rightarrow \mathtt{flies}$ holds for an arbitrary x; since $\mathtt{bird} \rightarrow \mathtt{flies}$ holds both for birds that fly *and for nonbirds*, this probability will be greater than the conditional probability $\mathtt{pr}(\mathtt{flies}|\mathtt{bird})$. All nonbirds contribute to the probability of the conditional, while none of them contributes to the conditional probability.

Given the extension of our language to include conditional probabilities, one description of the basic axioms of probability is the following:

1. $\mathtt{pr}(p \wedge q) = \mathtt{pr}(p) \cdot \mathtt{pr}(q|p)$. Since $p \wedge q$ means that p and q are both true, the only way for $p \wedge q$ to hold is for p to hold and then for q to hold given p. We combine the probabilities by multiplying them and require that the result is the same as the probability of the conjunction.

2. $\mathtt{pr}(\neg p) = 1 - \mathtt{pr}(p)$. The probability of a negated sentence is the complement of the probability of p itself. This is a generalization of the fact that p is true if and only if $\neg p$ is false and vice versa.

3. If $p \equiv q$, then $\mathrm{pr}(p) = \mathrm{pr}(q)$. The symbol $\equiv$ denotes logical equivalence; equivalent sentences have the same probability.

These axioms are sufficient to reproduce classical probability. As an example, here is one of the most important consequences of probability theory, known as *Bayes' rule* after the philosopher who discovered it.

THEOREM 12.2.1 *Consider two sentences* H *(the hypothesis) and* E *(the evidence). Then provided that* $\mathrm{pr}(E) \neq 0$,

$$\mathrm{pr}(H|E) = \frac{\mathrm{pr}(E|H)\mathrm{pr}(H)}{\mathrm{pr}(E)}$$

PROOF This follows immediately from the fact that

$$\mathrm{pr}(H)\mathrm{pr}(E|H) = \mathrm{pr}(E \wedge H) = \mathrm{pr}(E)\mathrm{pr}(H|E)$$ ■

Bayes' rule is typically used to compute the probability of some hypothesis after the evidence E has been observed. In order to perform the computation, we need to know the probabilities $\mathrm{pr}(H)$ and $\mathrm{pr}(E)$, which are typically referred to as the *prior* probabilities of H and E, and $\mathrm{pr}(E|H)$, the probability of the evidence given the hypothesis. We will see some specific examples after we have examined some theoretical consequences of Bayes' rule itself.

COROLLARY 12.2.2 *If* $\mathrm{pr}(E|H) = 0$, *then* $\mathrm{pr}(H|E) = 0$.

In other words, if H precludes E, then E precludes H; either way, H and E are mutually inconsistent.

COROLLARY 12.2.3 *Suppose that* $\mathrm{pr}(E|H_1) = \mathrm{pr}(E|H_2)$, *so that the hypotheses* H_1 *and* H_2 *give us the same information about a piece of evidence* E. *Then*

$$\frac{\mathrm{pr}(H_1|E)}{\mathrm{pr}(H_2|E)} = \frac{\mathrm{pr}(H_1)}{\mathrm{pr}(H_2)}$$

In other words, these assumptions imply that the evidence E will not affect the relative probabilities of H_1 and H_2.

As an example of the use of Corollary 12.2.3, suppose that we know that the probability of a particular traffic light being green is 0.45, of its being yellow is 0.1, and of its being red is 0.45. Furthermore, suppose that we know that the police are perfect enforcers of the traffic rules—we will get a ticket if and only if the light is red when we enter the intersection. If we now learn the evidence that we crossed the intersection without getting a ticket, what are the probabilities that the light was green, yellow, or red when we did so?

Since we got no ticket, we know that the light couldn't have been red, so the probability of this event is 0. Furthermore, since we have

$$\mathtt{pr(no\text{-}ticket|green)} = \mathtt{pr(no\text{-}ticket|yellow)}$$

the relative probabilities of the light's being yellow or green are unaffected by the fact that we got no ticket. Initially, the relative probability is .1/.45, so we get

$$\frac{\mathtt{pr(yellow|no\text{-}ticket)}}{\mathtt{pr(green|no\text{-}ticket)}} = \frac{.1}{.45}$$

and

$$\mathtt{pr(yellow|no\text{-}ticket)} + \mathtt{pr(green|no\text{-}ticket)} = 1$$

This gives us

$$\mathtt{pr(yellow|no\text{-}ticket)} = \frac{2}{11}$$

and

$$\mathtt{pr(green|no\text{-}ticket)} = \frac{9}{11}$$

In this particular example, note that we can compute the conditional probabilities without knowing the prior probability that we got a ticket or didn't.

Here is another application of Bayes' rule.

DEFINITION 12.2.4 *For two sentences* H *and* E, *we will say that* H *is* independent *of* E *provided that*

$$\mathrm{pr}(H|E) = \mathrm{pr}(H)$$

We will say that H *is* conditionally independent of E *given* F *if*

$$\mathrm{pr}(H|E \wedge F) = \mathrm{pr}(H|F)$$

COROLLARY 12.2.5 *If* H *is independent of* E, *then* E *is independent of* H.

PROOF From $\mathrm{pr}(H|E) = \mathrm{pr}(H)$ we get

$$\mathrm{pr}(E|H) = \frac{\mathrm{pr}(H|E)\mathrm{pr}(E)}{\mathrm{pr}(H)} = \mathrm{pr}(E)$$

■

Note that independence and conditional independence are purely statistical notions; they are not the same as the commonsense notion of "causal" independence. As an example, suppose that Tom skips out of third grade one day and goes to the local train tracks to watch the trains go by; every time one does, he waves.

Since the probability that Tom is waving changes when a train appears, the fact that he is waving is not independent of the fact that a train is going by. But it is *also* the case that the fact that the train is going by is not independent of the fact that Tom is waving. Although there is no *causal* link from Tom's waving to the train's appearance, there is a statistical link. This link might be of value—if we knew Tom's behavior and were in a position to observe him but not to see the train itself, we could draw useful conclusions about the train by exploiting this statistical information. Causal dependence is an asymmetric notion; conditional dependence is not.

Some other well-known probabilistic results are also a consequence of the axioms we have given. Consider the following:

PROPOSITION 12.2.6 *For any two sentences* p *and* q,

$$\mathrm{pr}(p \vee q) = \mathrm{pr}(p) + \mathrm{pr}(q) - \mathrm{pr}(p \wedge q)$$

A consequence of this is that if p and q are mutually exclusive, then $\mathrm{pr}(p \vee q) = \mathrm{pr}(p) + \mathrm{pr}(q)$.

PROOF Since $p \vee q$ is equivalent to $\neg(\neg p \wedge \neg q)$, we have:

$$\begin{aligned}
\mathrm{pr}(p \vee q) &= 1 - \mathrm{pr}(\neg p \wedge \neg q) \\
&= 1 - \mathrm{pr}(\neg p)\mathrm{pr}(\neg q|\neg p) \\
&= 1 - [1 - \mathrm{pr}(p)\,][1 - \mathrm{pr}(q|\neg p)] \\
&= \mathrm{pr}(p) + \mathrm{pr}(\neg p)\mathrm{pr}(q|\neg p) \\
&= \mathrm{pr}(p) + \mathrm{pr}(\neg p \wedge q) \\
&= \mathrm{pr}(p) + \mathrm{pr}(q)\mathrm{pr}(\neg p|q) \\
&= \mathrm{pr}(p) + \mathrm{pr}(q)\,[1 - \mathrm{pr}(p|q)] \\
&= \mathrm{pr}(p) + \mathrm{pr}(q) - \mathrm{pr}(p \wedge q)
\end{aligned}$$ ■

There is one final result that we would like to describe. Suppose that we have some sentence p, and we would like to know the prior probability of p. Given that we know the relationship between p and other sentences in the database, how can this prior probability be computed?

To make the problem a bit more specific, suppose that we return to our traffic-light example. What is the prior probability that we not get a ticket if we enter the intersection?

The way we answer this question is by realizing that the light has to be red, yellow, or green. If it's red (probability .45), we'll get a ticket. If it's yellow (probability .1) or green (probability .45), we won't get a ticket. Adding these two figures, we see that the overall probability that we won't get a ticket is .55.

In general, we can find the probability of a sentence p by partitioning our world into a set of disjoint possibilities $w_1, \ldots, w_n$ such that we know that exactly one of the w_i's holds, we know the prior probabilities of each of these w_i's, and we know the probability of p given each of the w_i's. In the example p is the sentence, "I won't get a ticket," and the w_i's correspond to the possible colors of the traffic light. Here's the basic result, also known as the *law of total probability*.

THEOREM 12.2.7 *Suppose that we have a set of sentences* w_i *such that*

$$\mathrm{pr}(w_1 \vee \cdots \vee w_n) = 1$$

and

$$\mathrm{pr}(w_i \wedge w_j) = 0$$

if $i \neq j$. *Then for any other sentence* p,

$$\mathrm{pr}(p) = \sum_i \mathrm{pr}(p|w_i)\mathrm{pr}(w_i)$$

It is this theorem that justifies our earlier conclusion that the overall probability of our not getting a ticket is .55.

Among AI systems, probably the most famous use of probabilities and Bayes' rule is in a system known as PROSPECTOR. PROSPECTOR was used to predict the likely locations of mineral deposits based on a variety of survey data about possible sites. The way PROSPECTOR worked was to compute `pr(site-properties|mineral-deposits)` from statistical data about previously explored sites, and then to use Bayes' rule to compute `pr(mineral-deposits|site-properties)`. These probabilities were then used to predict which of a group of sites were likely to have mineral deposits (such as aluminum) based on evidence (such as whether or not there were pine trees in the area).

The reason PROSPECTOR became famous is that it was successful. The system successfully predicted the presence of a large molybdenum deposit in Mt. Tolman, Washington.

12.3 INFLUENCE DIAGRAMS

Let's have another look at our traffic-light example. First, suppose we modify it to reduce the efficiency of the police somewhat, assuming that we have a 25 percent chance of running a red light successfully, but also a 5 percent chance of getting a ticket for running a yellow light.

Additionally, suppose I go on to tell you that if I get a ticket, there is a 90 percent chance that I will subsequently be in a bad mood; if I don't get a ticket, there is only a 5 percent chance. What is the overall probability that I will later be in a bad mood?

It is quite tempting to respond to this using the law of total probability and arguing as follows:

$$\begin{aligned}
\texttt{pr(bad-mood|green)} &= \texttt{pr(bad-mood|green} \wedge \texttt{ticket)} \cdot \texttt{pr(ticket|green)} \qquad (12.4)\\
&\quad + \texttt{pr(bad-mood|green} \wedge \texttt{no-ticket)} \cdot \texttt{pr(no-ticket|green)}\\
&= \texttt{pr(bad-mood|ticket)pr(ticket|green)} \qquad (12.5)\\
&\quad + \texttt{pr(bad-mood|no-ticket)} \cdot \texttt{pr(no-ticket|green)}\\
&= .9 \cdot 0 + .05 \cdot 1 = .05\\
\texttt{pr(bad-mood|yellow)} &= \texttt{pr(bad-mood|ticket)} \cdot \texttt{pr(ticket|yellow)}\\
&\quad + \texttt{pr(bad-mood|no-ticket)} \cdot \texttt{pr(no-ticket|yellow)}\\
&= .9 \cdot .05 + .05 \cdot .95 = .0925\\
\texttt{pr(bad-mood|red)} &= \texttt{pr(bad-mood|ticket)} \cdot \texttt{pr(ticket|red)}\\
&\quad + \texttt{pr(bad-mood|no-ticket)} \cdot \texttt{pr(no-ticket|red)}\\
&= .9 \cdot .75 + .05 \cdot .25 = .6875\\
\texttt{pr(bad-mood)} &= \texttt{pr(bad-mood|green)} \cdot \texttt{pr(green)}\\
&\quad + \texttt{pr(bad-mood|yellow)} \cdot \texttt{pr(yellow)}\\
&\quad + \texttt{pr(bad-mood|red)} \cdot \texttt{pr(red)}\\
&= .05 \cdot .45 + .0925 \cdot .1 + .6875 \cdot .45 = .341125
\end{aligned}$$

Unfortunately, this analysis is not right—we assumed, when moving from (12.4) to (12.5), that the probability of my being a bad mood depended only on whether or not I got a ticket, and was conditionally independent of the color of the light when I went through the intersection. This might well not be the case—it is, after all, much more aggravating to get an undeserved ticket than a justified one.

We see from this that if our aim is to evaluate pr(bad–mood), we need to know not just the probability of my being in a good or bad mood depending on whether I've gotten a ticket or not, but the probability given information about both whether I've gotten a ticket and what color the light was when I entered the intersection.

In general, in order to compute the probability of a query q given probabilities of the sentences $p_1, \ldots, p_n$ that bear on q in some way, we will need to know 2^n conditional probabilities $\texttt{pr}(q|p_1 \wedge \cdots \wedge p_n)$, $\texttt{pr}(q|p_1 \wedge \cdots \wedge \neg p_n)$ and so on. This is far too much information to expect the designer of a probabilistic system to supply!

To make probabilistic methods useful in practice, we need to make conditional independence assumptions like those used in deriving (12.5) above, and to find a compact way of expressing these assumptions. *Influence diagrams* are one way of doing this.[23]

An influence diagram for our traffic example appears in Figure 12.1. The arcs in the figure indicate that whether we get a ticket depends on the color of the light, and our mood is a function of whether or not we got a ticket. We've included a new arrow indicating that we might lose our driving license if we get a traffic ticket.

The point here is that the topology of the influence diagram is intended to contain the conditional independence assumptions that underlie the derivation of (12.5) from (12.4). More specifically, we make the following definition:

DEFINITION 12.3.1 *Given an influence diagram* I, *we will say that a set* E *of nodes* splits *a node* x *from another node* y *if every path from* x *to* y *passes through* $E - \{x,y\}$.

We now interpret a diagram such as that in Figure 12.1 by saying that if a set E splits x from y, then x is conditionally independent of y given E.

In the figure, the only path from the node `color` to `bad-mood` passes through `ticket`, so `bad-mood` is conditionally independent of `color` given `ticket`—exactly as we need to derive (12.5).

In this example, the only probabilistic information we need in order to evaluate the probabilities of the nodes in the diagram are the prior probabilities of the colors for the light, the probabilities of `ticket` conditioned on these colors, and the probabilities of `lose-license` and `bad-mood` conditioned on our receiving a ticket or not. This is a total of ten values—three prior probabilities, and seven conditional ones. In the absence of the independence assumptions, twenty-three probabilities would be needed. (We need to assign probabilities to each of the twenty-four basic possibilities, each of which selects a color for the light and determines whether or not we get a ticket, lose our license, and are in a bad mood. Only twenty-three numbers are needed because the probabilities must sum to 1.)

FIGURE 12.1 Influence diagram for the traffic example

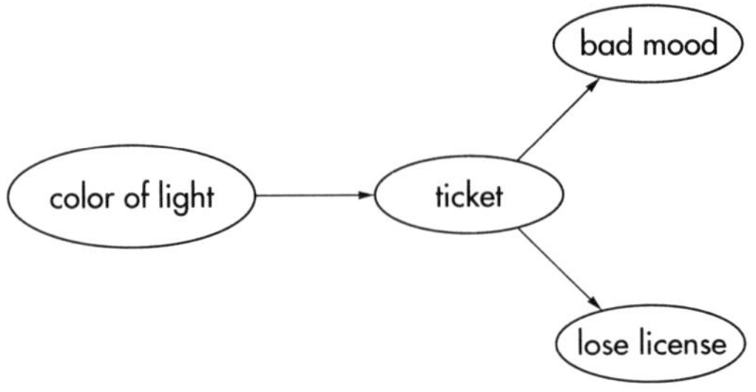

23 Influence diagrams are also often called *Bayesian networks* or *causal nets*.

Suppose now that we modify Figure 12.1 to include information to the effect that in addition to running a red light, we can get a traffic ticket for driving without insurance, obtaining Figure 12.2. Presumably, driving without insurance and running a red light are independent of one another, but they actually become *dependent* once we know that we have gotten a traffic ticket. After all, if we know that we got a ticket and that we *didn't* run a red light, we have substantial reason to believe that we were driving without insurance. How can we modify Definition 12.3.1 to handle this?

Suppose that we have two nodes, x and y, and some path p connecting them. Let n be a node on p (but not x or y); under what conditions does the inclusion of n in this path mean that there is no direct contribution by x to the probability of y?

Clearly, if n is in the evidence set E and has only one ancestor, then y will depend on the node n in E and not on x directly. This is the intuition that underlies our earlier definition and the analysis of Figure 12.1.

If n has multiple ancestors, the situation is like that in Figure 12.2; we actually *need* n to be in the evidence set E if x is to bear on y. In fact, it suffices for a descendent of n to be in E; as an example, driving without insurance and running the red light are conditionally dependent if we know that I was in a bad mood. Knowing that I was in a bad mood raises the probability that I got a ticket, and we can now apply our earlier argument.

The definition we need, therefore, is the following:

DEFINITION 12.3.2 *Given an influence diagram* I, *an evidence set* E, *nodes* x *and* y *and a path* $p = \langle x = n_0, \ldots, n_k = y\rangle$ *between them, we will say that* p *d-connects* x *and* y *if for every interior node* n_i *on* p:

1. *If both* n_{i-1} *and* n_{i+1} *are predecessors of* n_i *in* I, *then* n *or one of its descendents is in* E.
2. *Otherwise,* $n \notin E$.

We will say that E *splits* x *and* y *if there is no path that d-connects them.*

We can now continue to interpret influence diagrams as meaning that

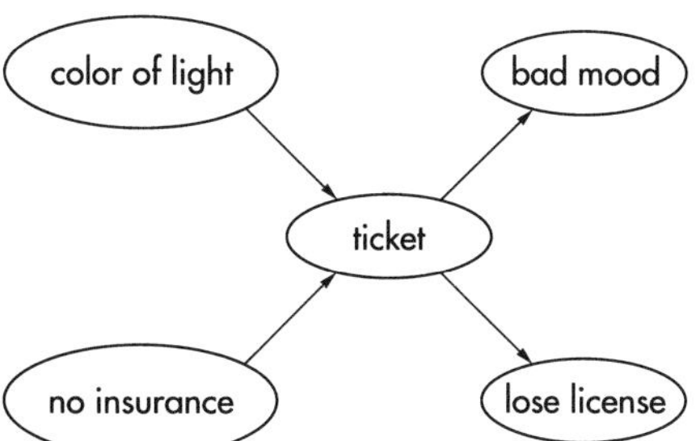

FIGURE 12.2 Multiple causes

if E splits two nodes x and y, then the probabilities to be assigned to these nodes are conditionally independent given E.

Given these definitions, the conditional independence assumptions implicit in influence diagrams seem to be reasonable ones—if the arcs in a diagram like that in Figure 12.1 or Figure 12.2 correspond to the causal connections in our domain, so that the color of the light can only affect our mood via the possibility of our getting a ticket, the conclusion that sanctions the derivation of (12.5) from (12.4) seems a valid one. The reason that influence diagrams are of such interest to the probabilistic community is that they provide a compact, effective, and useful way to represent the wealth of independence assumptions needed by practical probabilistic systems.

There is another way to look at this as well. In order to evaluate all of the probabilities in the traffic example of Figure 12.1, we need to know the probability

$$\mathrm{pr}(c \wedge t \wedge m \wedge l) \tag{12.6}$$

for each choice of color c, ticket possibility t (yes or no; did I get a ticket or not?), mood m (good or bad), and loss of license l (yes or no). As we have already remarked, there are twenty-four of these probabilities, and they are potentially constrained only by the requirement that they sum to 1.

Of course, we know that we can always rewrite (12.6) as

$$\mathrm{pr}(c) \cdot \mathrm{pr}(t|c) \cdot \mathrm{pr}(m|c \wedge t) \cdot \mathrm{pr}(l|c \wedge t \wedge m)$$

The conditional independence assumptions associated with the influence diagram allow us to rewrite this in the simpler form

$$\mathrm{pr}(c) \cdot \mathrm{pr}(t|c) \cdot \mathrm{pr}(m|t) \cdot \mathrm{pr}(l|t) \tag{12.7}$$

Once again, only ten values are needed to evaluate the various instances of (12.7)—one probability for each color, three for the probability of getting a ticket as a function of color, and two each to give my mood and chances of losing my license depending on whether I've gotten a ticket or not.

Either way we think of it, the lesson is the same:

> *Influence diagrams allow us to conveniently represent the conditional independence assumptions used to reduce the amount of information needed by a probabilistic reasoner.*

12.4 ARGUMENTS FOR AND AGAINST PROBABILITY IN AI

My final aim in this chapter is to discuss the philosophical questions underlying the application of probability to AI. After all, the success of PROSPECTOR is not necessarily evidence that probabilities have a fundamental role to play in AI as a whole. What evidence is there that probabilities are a good knowledge representation scheme generally?

The argument that there is rests on a theorem of Cox. Suppose that we return to the arguments with which we began this chapter, viewing the purpose of a knowledge representation scheme as being to label the sentences in our declarative language *L* with values taken from some set *B* of possible labels. Cox's result is the following:

THEOREM 12.4.1

Suppose that we accept the following conditions:

1. *Our language* L *is well defined.*
2. $B \subseteq \mathbb{R}$: *The labels that we assign to sentences of* L *are real numbers.*
3. *The labelling function* $f: L \rightarrow B$ *is defined over all of* L.
4. *The labelling function also assigns labels to conditionals of the form* $p|q$ *for* $p,q \in L$.
5. *Given a conjunction* $p_1 \wedge \cdots \wedge p_n$, *there is some* i *such that* $f(p_1 \wedge \cdots \wedge p_n)$ *(the label assigned to the conjunction) can be computed from* $f(p_i)$ *and*
$$f(p_1 \wedge \cdots \wedge p_{i-1} \wedge p_{i+1} \wedge \cdots \wedge p_n \,|p_i)$$
6. *If* $f(p) < f(q)$, *then* $f(\neg p) > f(\neg q)$. *In other words,* $f(\neg p)$ *goes down as* $f(p)$ *goes up.*
7. *If* $p \equiv q$, *then* $f(p) = f(q)$. *Identical labels are assigned to equivalent statements.*

Then the labelling function f *is essentially equivalent to one obeying all the laws of classical probability.*

By *essentially equivalent,* we mean that there is a conversion function $c: B \rightarrow [0,1]$ such that if we change the labels of every sentence $p \in L$ from $f(p)$ to $c(f(p))$, then the new labels will obey the rules of probability theory. Furthermore, the conversion function is monotonic; if $x \geq y$, then $c(x) \geq c(y)$.

The reason that Theorem 12.4.1 is so important is that it gives us compelling reason to adopt probability theory as our principal method of knowledge representation; indeed, if we accept the apparently reasonable premises of the theorem and profess *not* to have adopted probability theory, we're just kidding ourselves. So let's have a look at these seven axioms.

The first says only that our language is well-defined; we've been assuming that throughout this book and will continue to do so here. As far as the third axiom, this says that every sentence in our language gets *some* label. Satisfying this axiom is in some sense trivial—if there are unlabelled sentences in our language, we can simply extend the set of labels to include a new value "unlabelled" and map all of the unassigned sentences to this new value.

What about the sixth axiom, saying that $f(\neg p)$ goes down as $f(p)$ goes up? Rather than thinking of this simply as a constraint on the values assigned to negated sentences, we can think of it as telling us what negation itself is all about; inverting the sense of the labelling function is the essence of what negation is supposed to do. Note the resemblance, incidentally, between the sixth axiom in Theorem 12.4.1 and the second axiom of probability appearing in Section 12.2.

The fifth axiom (which resembles the first axiom of Section 12.2) is similar; it isn't so much a constraint as a description of conditionalization itself. After all, extending the labelling function to include conditionalization doesn't buy us much if we don't say what the extension is supposed to do!

That's the easy stuff; the remaining axioms bear a bit more thought.

4. The labelling function deals with conditionals This is probably the least controversial of the three axioms that are left. There are good reasons to keep our labels and language simple, but they are principally computational ones; on what theoretical grounds could we object to extending our language to include conditionalization?

7. Identical labels are assigned to equivalent sentences This seems straightforward enough, and was included as an explicit axiom of probability theory in Section 12.2. But let's have a closer look at it.

Suppose that we are trying to color the countries on a map, following the rule that adjacent countries always have to be colored different colors to make sure that they continue to look like two countries instead of just one. Can every map be colored using four colors or fewer?

The map of the United States certainly can; a suitable coloring is shown in Figure 12.3. But can *every* map be similarly colored?

This is one of the most famous problems of mathematics, and is known as the *four-color problem*. It was generally believed to be true, in part because no map was ever found for which a four-coloring did not exist.

Now consider the sentence $p =$ "Every map can be colored in four colors." What label are we to assign to p? After all, either the four-color theorem is true or it isn't. If it's true, then p is equivalent to other sentences that we do know, such as $0 \neq 1$. Since we assign these sentences probability 1, axiom 7 requires us to assign the probability 1 to p as well. If there is a map that *can't* be colored in four colors, p is equivalent to $0 = 1$ and we need to assign it probability 0.

But we don't know! We have no way to guarantee satisfaction of the final axiom in this case; we know that we should have $\mathtt{pr}(p) = 1$ or $\mathtt{pr}(p) = 0$, but we don't know which.

Actually, we do know. It turns out that the four-color theorem is true; every map *can* be colored in four colors or fewer. This result was proved at the University of Illinois at Urbana-Champaign in 1976 by showing that the problem could be reduced to that of showing that maps containing one

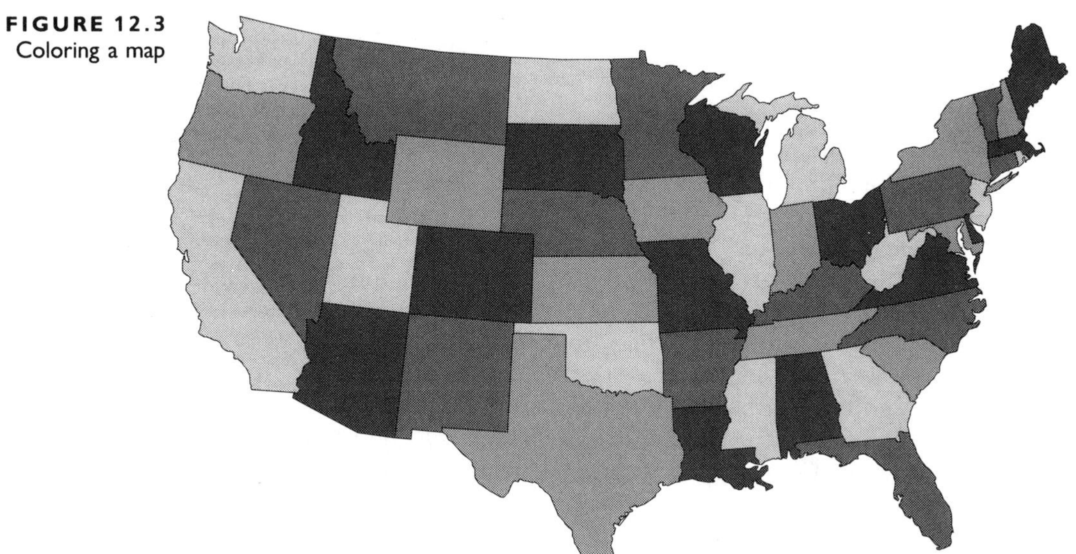

FIGURE 12.3
Coloring a map

of some 1,500 patterns could, if uncolorable in four colors, be replaced with smaller maps that had the same property. A computer was then used to prove this result for each of the 1,500 patterns in question.[24] So important was this solution to a longstanding problem that the Urbana post office temporarily changed its postmark to, "Four colors suffice."

OK. Armed with our new information, we label p as having probability one. But what label were we to assign to p before 1976?

First-order logic is only semidecidable. As a result, we can't always be expected to know whether $p \equiv q$ for arbitrary p and q; it's unfair to require that we label them with the same probabilities if they *are* equivalent.

Since the requirement that $f(p) = f(q)$ for equivalent p and q is the same as a requirement that we are omniscient with regard to logical equivalence, axiom 7 is known as *logical omniscience*. It is an unreasonable requirement of any declarative system.

Unreasonable or not, however, virtually *every* formal system assumes that equivalent sentences have identical labels. A first-order system is expected to label any sentence equivalent to $0 \neq 1$ as true—including the four-color theorem. An ATMS is expected to label logically equivalent sentences as having the same explanations.

Yes, axiom 7 is unreasonable. But we shouldn't reject probability theory on the grounds that it fails to solve a problem that other declarative systems can't solve either!

24 This raises interesting questions in its own right. If no human has ever managed to check the 1,500 proofs involved, is it reasonable to view the theorem as proved? And who should get credit for the proof?

2. The labels are real numbers Of all of Cox's axioms, this seemingly innocuous one is all that remains for us to question. But is it really as simple as it seems? How clear is it that the only labels we will need are single real numbers?

In some cases, a real number does suffice; probability theory is a testament to this. And it is certainly possible that real numbers suffice without their being explicit probabilities—here's an example.

I was on the faculty at Oxford for a while; they have this amazingly anachronistic custom that the faculty members in a particular college, before going to dinner, often get together in one another's room to share some sherry or other before-dinner drink. As faculty, I was often included.

That was the easy part. The hard part was that I had to invite my colleagues back. I went out and bought a couple of bottles of sherry, but had no idea whether or not the sherry I had purchased was of respectable quality—and since I don't drink, I had no way to test the sherry to make sure.

What I did was to go to my neighbor, Harry Judge. Harry was (and still is, I trust!) an absolutely prototypical Englishman, and I was sure that he'd be able to pass sound judgement on my sherry.

And he did. But not by tasting it; when I asked him for help, he simply said, "How much did it cost?" Two pounds fivepence, I told him. "It's fine," he told me. And so it was.

The point here is that Harry's evaluation was indeed based on a single real number. He had no need to pour my sherry into a glass, check its color, aroma, and what have you, and finally to taste it. The price alone was sufficient.

Other examples, however, are not like this. Suppose a friend asks you what you think of this textbook. If you tell him that it's "OK .7," that's probably not going to be the information he's looking for. Is it easy or hard to read? How are the exercises? Are there a lot of typos? Does it seem to be worth the price? And so on. Judgement of a textbook isn't the sort of thing for which a single-number evaluation is typically sufficient, although multiple numbers might be.

If we want to decide on the merits of axiom 2 in general, it turns out that there is basically one theoretical argument in favor of this axiom, and one against it. Let me start out with the argument against.

This argument is a simple one: Where do the probabilities come from? For any sentence p, we must be able to assign a value to $\texttt{pr}(p)$. What, for example, is the probability that there are lions on the surface of Mars? It's small, no doubt, but just how small? Probability theory requires that we be able to assign this sentence a *specific* value, but it is not clear how we can do so.

As another example of this, saying that p has probability 0.5 is not the same as saying that we don't know anything about p. We've already pointed out that when we say that the probability of a particular coin coming up heads is 0.5, we are saying something very strong about the fairness of the coin. Or imagine an engineer who has just designed a nuclear reactor, and is asked what the chances are that the reactor will melt down during its first year of operation. If he says that the chances are 0.5 we should worry for one reason; if he says that he has no idea, we should worry for another.

The advocates of the probabilistic approach have proposed two ways around this problem; one tells us where to get the numbers and the other tells us how to deal with situations where no numbers can be obtained.

To get the numbers, an approach known as *maximum entropy* is often used. This suggests that we distribute the probability "uniformly" among the various possible alternatives. The reason that a coin has a 50 percent chance of coming up heads is that we want to split the likelihood equally between the two alternatives of heads and tails.

Unfortunately, things aren't so simple all the time. Suppose that we are looking for a boat that has become lost in the North Atlantic. It seems reasonable to distribute the probability uniformly based on the surface area of the region in which the boat might be; each square mile of ocean is equally likely to be the place to look.

But what if the boat is a submarine? Now we should probably take the depth into account as well, taking each *cubic* mile of ocean to be equally likely. And if the depth of the ocean varies, these are going to lead to different probabilities.

To see this more specifically, suppose that the boat is somewhere in an area of 100 square miles, but in a volume of 250 cubic miles. If we are considering a particular square mile of ocean that is 2 miles deep, the probability that the boat is somewhere in this area is .01 (if distributed equally by area) or .008 (if distributed equally by volume). Which figure should we use?

There is no way around this difficulty; the results of the maximum entropy assumption are dependent on that attribute of the problem with respect to which the probability is divided.

The other approach to the "where do the numbers come from?" problem is to extend the language slightly to allow us to say, "I don't know," (or something like it) explicitly. This is typically done by labelling sentences not with one number, but with two; when we say that the label assigned to p is $[x,y]$, we mean that the probability of p lies somewhere *between* x and y.

Thus if we want to say that we know nothing about p, we label it with the probability interval [0,1], indicating that the probability could be any legal value. The probability that there are lions on Mars might be somewhere in the region $[0,10^{-5}]$.

The two formal schemes that use intervals of this sort are *probabilistic logic*, developed by Nils Nilsson, and *Dempster-Shafer theory* (developed, not surprisingly, by Dempster and Shafer). Unfortunately, there are problems with both of these approaches. Nilsson's logic is too conservative about drawing new conclusions; sentences tend to end up labelled [0,1] even if there is some information that could be brought to bear on them. As an example, if we have weak reason to believe each of p and q, so that the labels for p and for q are [.5,1], the label assigned to the conjunction $p \wedge q$ will be [0,1] because it's *possible* that p and q are mutually inconsistent even though each has probability at least .5. Dempster-Shafer theory has been beset by its own difficulties, although recent work by Halpern and Fagin has strengthened its formal underpinnings and given the approach some new life. Further details are in Section 12.5.

Of course, both probabilistic logic and Dempster-Shafer theory violate axiom 2 in the first place, since they label sentences with two real numbers instead of just one. Nevertheless, they retain a strong probabilistic flavor and that is why I've chosen to mention them here.

What is the argument in favor of probability theory and axiom 2? It's very simple: Probability theory is formally well grounded and well understood, and has been shown to be applicable to a wide range of problems in the past. And this is a reasonable argument—science generally proceeds most effectively when it builds on its own successes.

Reasonable though it may be, this argument should not be pushed too far. The fact that probability theory has a solid formal foundation and a history of success is reason to *try* to apply it to AI problems, but it is no reason to assume without question that it will turn out to be the method of choice. AI problems are different from the ones that scientists have previously considered. Maybe a probabilistic approach to them will work; maybe not.

It's all a bit like looking for your wallet if you've dropped it on a dark street. Initially, it makes sense to look under the street lights—in the easily visible area illuminated by the corpus of existing work on probability theory. But after a while, if you don't find your wallet, it's a good idea to look somewhere else.

Am I suggesting that we've looked under the probabilistic street light for so long that it's time we looked elsewhere? Not really. But we've looked long enough that we should probably begin to be at least *suspicious* that probability theory alone isn't going to solve all of the problems of knowledge representation, effective though it may be at solving some of them.

12.5 FURTHER READING

As with first-order logic, there are many possible sources of additional information on probability and its role in AI. The best is arguably Pearl's [1988] *Probabilistic Reasoning in Intelligent Systems: Networks of Plausible Inference.* This book is encyclopedic in its coverage of the topics that we have only touched upon here.

The description of MYCIN in the text, although historically accurate, is a bit unfair. It was shown in Heckerman [1986] that the numeric manipulations done by MYCIN are in fact sanctioned by the laws of probability theory, provided that one interprets certainty factors suitably and makes independence assumptions that are somewhat stronger than those appearing in influence diagrams. The assumptions are actually strong enough that it is unlikely that they will ever hold in practice, though; our claim in the text that MYCIN's effectiveness is somewhat independent of its numerical methods is a valid one.

MYCIN itself is described in Shortliffe [1976]; this book also contains descriptions of the experiments demonstrating the performance of the system with both full and restricted values for the certainty factors.

Bayes' original paper [Bayes 1763] is reprinted in Deming [1963]. The PROSPECTOR system is described in Duda *et al.* [1976]; the molybdenum discovery is reported in Campbell *et al.* [1982]. An excellent survey article on influence diagrams is Charniak [1991]; the diagrams themselves probably make their first appearance in Duda *et al.* [1976], although Pearl is responsible for developing the formal understanding of them that has been so useful to the probabilistic community.

Cox's argument in favor of probability theory appears in Cox [1946] and Reichenbach [1949]. An article in support of the use probabilities in AI is Cheeseman [1988]; the issue of *Computational Intelligence* in which Cheeseman's paper appears also contains a variety of replies on both sides of this particular issue. Finally, there has been some very recent work on the development of "qualitative" probability [Wellman 1988] or other nonnumeric methods that retain all of the attractive computational features of probability theory, including the use of conditional independence assumptions and the treatment of influence diagrams [Darwiche and Ginsberg 1992].

The four-color theorem and its solution is discussed in Campbell and Higgins [1984] and Steen [1978].

Nilsson's probabilistic logic is introduced in Nilsson [1986]; Dempster-Shafer theory is discussed in Dempster [1968] and Shafer [1976]. Some examples on which Dempster-Shafer gives counterintuitive results are discussed in Zadeh [1984]; Halpern and Fagin [1992] argue that these examples rest on a misinterpretation of the conditions under which Dempster-Shafer theory should be applied.

Finally, there is one major approach to numerical reasoning that we have not discussed at all: Zadeh's [1975] *fuzzy logic*. Other articles on this topic can be found in the journal *Fuzzy Sets and Systems*.

12.6 EXERCISES

1. (a) All of the numeric methods have the property that the operation that conjoins the labels of independent sentences p and q to get a label for $p \wedge q$ is associative and commutative. Why is this?

(b) Consider the combination function CF appearing in (12.3).
  i. Prove that for any x, CF(x,0) = x.
  ii. Prove that CF is commutative.
  iii. Prove that if x, y and z are all positive,

$$\mathrm{CF}(x,\mathrm{CF}(y,z)) = \mathrm{CF}(\mathrm{CF}(x,y),z)$$

  iv. Prove that if x and y are positive and z is negative,

$$\mathrm{CF}(x,\mathrm{CF}(y,z)) = \mathrm{CF}(\mathrm{CF}(x,y),z)$$

Discuss these results.

2. What certainty factor would MYCIN assign to a conjunction of sentences, each of which had been assigned certainty 0? Does this seem reasonable?

3. Suppose that we agree that MYCIN should assign $\neg p$ the certainty $-c$ whenever c is the value assigned to p. Suppose that we also agree that the label assigned to $p \wedge q$ should be the same as that assigned to $\neg(\neg p \vee \neg q)$, since these sentences are equivalent. What does this say about the label assigned to $p \vee q$ in terms of the labels assigned to p and to q?

4. (a) What certainty factor will MYCIN assign to the sentence $p \vee \neg p$?
   (b) MYCIN's underlying theorem prover uses modus ponens instead of resolution. Given your answer to (a) above, does this seem like a reasonable choice?

5. Consider the example shown in Figure 12.4, where we have written $A \xrightarrow{x} B$ to indicate that the certainty factor assigned to the implication $A \rightarrow B$ is x. What certainty factor would MYCIN assign to the conclusions that Tweety and Fred can fly? That they are afraid of heights?

6. Consider the example shown in Figure 12.5. What certainty factor would MYCIN assign to the conclusion that Bob is happy?

7. Prove rigorously that $\mathrm{pr}(p|q) \leq \mathrm{pr}(q \rightarrow p)$, with equality holding if and only if either $\mathrm{pr}(\neg q) = 0$ or $\mathrm{pr}(q \rightarrow p) = 1$.

8. Prove Corollary 12.2.3.

FIGURE 12.4 Certainty factors and Tweety

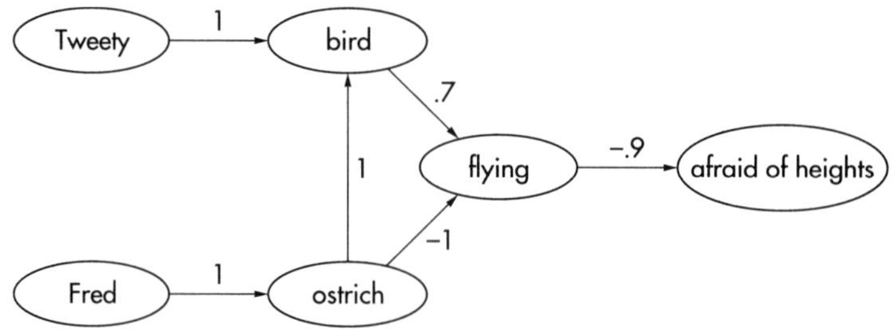

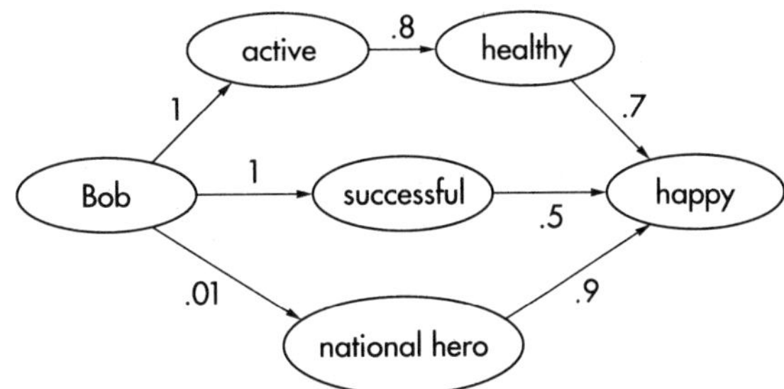

FIGURE 12.5
Be happy!

9. State and prove an analog to Corollary 12.2.5 that deals with conditional independence.

10. Generalize Proposition 12.2.6 to deal with n disjuncts instead of just two.

11. In discussing the amount of probabilistic information needed in Figure 12.1 in the absence of conditional independence assumptions, we made the assertion that all of the conditional probabilities could be computed if we assigned probabilities to each of the 24 basic possibilities, each of which selects a color for the light and determines whether or not we get a ticket, lose our license, and are not in a bad mood. Why is this possible?

12. Consider the influence diagram in Figure 12.6, which consists of a chain of k nodes connected in series. We assume that all of the nodes are binary, so that each corresponds to two possible outcomes. They are like the `bad-mood` node in Figure 12.1, as opposed to the `color` node, which can take one of three values.

    (a) Given the conditional independence assumptions implicit in the diagram, how many probabilities are needed to evaluate all of the probabilities and conditional probabilities in this diagram?

    (b) What would the answer be in the absence of the conditional independence assumptions?

13. How many probabilities are needed to completely specify the influence diagram in Figure 12.2, given the assumptions of conditional independence associated with Definition 12.3.2? How many would be needed without those assumptions?

14. **Diagnosis** Suppose that we return to the diagnostic problem appearing in Exercises 12 in Chapter 10 and 3 in Chapter 11, but approach it

FIGURE 12.6
An influence diagram

using probabilities. Suppose that the prior probabilities that the headlight bulbs fail, that the battery fails, and that the starter fails are p_h, p_b, and p_s, respectively, and that these three events are independent of one another.

(a) There are eight possible situations, depending on whether each of the three components is failing or not. What are the prior probabilities of each of these eight possible situations?

(b) Suppose that the engine doesn't start.
   i. Assuming that either the starter or the battery not working is enough to cause the failure, what is the prior probability of the engine not starting?
   ii. Use Bayes' rule to compute the new probability that the headlight bulbs are broken, that the battery is failing, and that the starter is broken respectively.

(c) Repeat the analysis of (b) for the other two failures in the previous exercises.

(d) Simplify your answers to (b) and (c) given the following assumptions about the probabilities of failure:
   i. All of the probabilities are small and equal to each other: $p_h = p_b = p_s \ll 1$.
   ii. The battery is far more reliable than the other components: $p_b \ll p_h p_s$ and $p_h, p_s \ll 1$.

   In each of these cases, is one diagnosis much more likely than the others?

(e) Once again, consider the rule of inference given by

$$(p > r) \wedge \neg(p > \neg q) \rightarrow (p \wedge q > r) \tag{12.8}$$

   where we continue to write $p > r$ to mean that if p holds, we conclude r. More specifically, we write $p > r$ to mean that $\mathrm{pr}(r|p) \approx 1$. As usual, this rule means that if p allows us to conclude r, we can still conclude r if we add q to our knowledge, unless q is a surprise in that p led us to believe $\neg q$. If q is a surprise, we might still be able to conclude r and might not.
   Does (12.8) hold in the probabilistic case? Hint: Use the identity

$$\mathrm{pr}(r|p) = \mathrm{pr}(r|p \wedge q)\mathrm{pr}(q|p) + \mathrm{pr}(r|p \wedge \neg q)\mathrm{pr}(\neg q|p)$$

(f) Why isn't the example of (b) a counterexample to (12.8) in the probabilistic case? Consider the two approximations of part (d) only.

15. The difference between the analysis of (12.8) in the nonmonotonic case (Exercise 3 in Chapter 11) and the probabilistic one where all of the

probabilities are equal appears to depend on whether or not multiple possible diagnoses arise in the case where both the headlights and engine are not working.

(a) Imagine that you walk up to the car and independently try the lights and the engine; neither works. Do multiple possible diagnoses seem reasonable?

(b) Imagine that you walk up to the car and try to start it; nothing happens. To see if the problem is the starter or the battery, you try the headlights. They don't work either—do multiple possible diagnoses still seem reasonable?

(c) It seems unreasonable that the acceptability of multiple diagnoses depends on your mental condition when the tests are conducted. Discuss this.

16. Which of the axioms in Section 12.4 are true for the certainty factors used by MYCIN?

CHAPTER

13

PUTTING KNOWLEDGE TO WORK: FRAMES AND SEMANTIC NETS

Let's have another look at one of the examples we discussed in Chapter 11. Here it is:

$$\texttt{bird}(x) \wedge \neg ab_b(x) \rightarrow \texttt{flies}(x)$$

$$\texttt{ostrich}(x) \rightarrow \texttt{bird}(x)$$

$$\texttt{ostrich}(x) \wedge \neg ab_o(x) \rightarrow \neg\texttt{flies}(x)$$

$$\texttt{bird}(\texttt{Tweety})$$

$$\texttt{ostrich}(\texttt{Fred})$$

Birds typically fly; ostriches are nonflying birds. Tweety is a bird and Fred is an ostrich. We begin by sprucing our example up a bit:

$$\texttt{bird}(x) \rightarrow \texttt{feathers}(x)$$

$$\texttt{bird}(x) \wedge \neg ab_b(x) \rightarrow \texttt{flies}(x)$$

$$\texttt{ostrich}(x) \rightarrow \texttt{bird}(x)$$

$$\texttt{ostrich}(x) \wedge \neg ab_o(x) \rightarrow \texttt{walks}(x)$$

$$\texttt{mammal}(x) \rightarrow \texttt{hair}(x)$$

$$\texttt{mammal}(x) \wedge \neg ab_m(x) \rightarrow \texttt{walks}(x)$$

$$\texttt{tiger}(x) \rightarrow \texttt{mammal}(x)$$

$$\texttt{whale}(x) \rightarrow \texttt{mammal}(x)$$

$$\texttt{whale}(x) \wedge \neg ab_w(x) \rightarrow \texttt{swims}(x)$$

bird(Tweety)

ostrich(Fred)

tiger(Hobbes)

whale(Moby)

This seems to be getting a bit out of hand; we can simplify it somewhat by thinking of things like birds, tigers, and whales not as predicates, but as objects in our domain. Have a look at the following description:

$$\mathtt{subclass}(x,y) \wedge \mathtt{instance}(a,x) \rightarrow \mathtt{instance}(a,y) \quad (13.1)$$

$$\mathtt{subclass}(x,y) \wedge \mathtt{subclass}(y,z) \rightarrow \mathtt{subclass}(x,z) \quad (13.2)$$

$$\mathtt{instance}(a,x) \wedge \mathtt{certain}(x,p,v) \rightarrow \mathtt{value}(a,p,v) \quad (13.3)$$

$$\mathtt{instance}(a,x) \wedge \mathtt{default}(x,p,v) \wedge \neg \mathtt{ab}(a,x,p) \rightarrow \mathtt{value}(a,p,v) \quad (13.4)$$

What these axioms say is the following:

(13.1) If all x's are y's, and a particular a is an x, then a is a y. Since ostriches are birds and Fred is an ostrich, Fred must be a bird as well.

(13.2) The subclass relation is transitive.

(13.3) If a is an instance of a class x and for every instance of x the property p is certain to have the value v, then a must have this value as well. Since all birds have feathers covering their bodies and Fred is a bird, Fred must be covered with feathers also.

(13.4) If a is an instance of a class x and for instances of x the property p typically has the value v, then a will typically have this value as well. Since ostriches typically move around by walking and Fred is an ostrich, Fred presumably moves around by walking also.
Note the arguments to ab in this axiom: a inherits the value of the property p from the class x unless a is abnormal with respect to both that property and that class. The inclusion of the extra arguments allows us to continue to conclude that Fred is a normal bird in most ways (with regard to having wings, for example) even after we decide that he is abnormal with regard to how he gets around.

We can now describe the objects in our domain as follows:

subclass(ostrich,bird) (13.5)

subclass(tiger,mammal) (13.6)

```
subclass(whale,mammal)
certain(bird,covering,feathers)
certain(mammal,covering,hair)
default(bird,locomotion,flies)                (13.7)
default(ostrich,locomotion,walks)
default(mammal,locomotion,walks)
default(whale,locomotion,swims)
instance(Tweety,bird)
instance(Fred,ostrich)
instance(Hobbes,tiger)                        (13.8)
instance(Moby,whale)                          (13.9)
```

This description isn't really any shorter than the earlier one, but it somehow seems to make more sense; it's telling us more directly what it is that we know about our domain. In order to say that birds fly by default, we say in (13.7) exactly that. Extending our description to include more classes, subclasses, and individual objects will be easier using this description than the previous one.

This technique of changing something like `ostrich` from a predicate symbol into an object constant is known as *reification*. We will see other examples of it in the next chapter.

13.1 INTRODUCTORY EXAMPLES

There are two reasons that people have proposed making the switch to a representation such as the one just presented. The first we have already commented on: The resulting description, although not necessarily more compact, is more intuitive and easier to work with. Related to this is the idea that these more intuitive representations lead to written descriptions that are easier to work with than those of predicate calculus; two specific written descriptions are known as *frames* and *semantic nets*, and we will discuss these in a moment.

The other argument often presented in favor of these restricted descriptions is that they allow more efficient reasoning than first-order logic. After describing frames and semantic nets themselves later in this section, we will examine this point in some detail, considering the expense of drawing various conclusions in each of these formal settings.

FIGURE 13.1 A simple frame system

bird
  covering: feathers
  locomotion: flies
ostrich
  subclass-of: bird
  locomotion: walks
mammal
  covering: hair
  locomotion: walks
tiger
  subclass-of: mammal
whale
  subclass-of: mammal
  locomotion: swims
Tweety
  instance-of: bird
Fred
  instance-of: ostrich
Hobbes
  instance-of: tiger
Moby
  instance-of: whale

13.1.1 Frames

Although the exact details of a frame system are dependent on the system chosen, the overall ideas are the same from one system to another. One way in which (13.5)–(13.9) might be represented using frames appears in Figure 13.1.

DEFINITION 13.1.1 A frame system *consists of a collection of* objects (`bird`, `ostrich`, *and so on), each of which consists of* slots (`covering`, `instance-of`, *and so on) and values for these slots (*`feathers`, *other objects, and so on).*

Suppose that O is some object in the description.[25] Then if O has an `instance-of` slot that is filled with a class C, this corresponds to the first-order sentence

$$\texttt{instance}(O,C) \tag{13.10}$$

25 Throughout this chapter, we use capital letters for constants (for example, specific objects or classes) and lowercase letters for variables.

If O has a `subclass-of` slot filled with a class C, that means that O is a class (like `mammal`) instead of an instance (like `Hobbes`), and the associated first-order sentence is

$$\texttt{subclass}(O,C) \tag{13.11}$$

What about O's other slots? There is no indication in the frame description of whether these slots correspond to certain truths or to defaults; our original example included both.

Early frame systems translated the other slots into certain conclusions; more recent systems translate them into default rules. We will say that the *monotonic* translation of the fact that O has a property slot P filled with a value V is

$$\texttt{certain}(O,P,V) \tag{13.12}$$

and that the *nonmonotonic* translation is

$$\texttt{default}(O,P,V) \tag{13.13}$$

DEFINITION 13.1.2 *The* monotonic translation *of a frame system is the axioms (13.1)–(13.3), and appropriate instances of (13.10), (13.11), and (13.12). The* nonmonotonic translation *is similar, with (13.3) replaced by (13.4) and instances of (13.12) being replaced by instances of (13.13).*

We will say that the frame system $\mathcal{F}$ monotonically entails *a conclusion* p *if* p *is a consequence of the monotonic translation of $\mathcal{F}$, and that $\mathcal{F}$* nonmonotonically entails p *if* p *is a consequence of the nonmonotonic translation of $\mathcal{F}$.*

What we have done here is to give a precise semantics to frame systems such as that in the figure; that we are able to do this should hardly be a surprise, since we remarked in Chapter 6 that first-order logic is universal. Even before we began the description in this section, we knew that there would be *some* way to develop a first-order translation of what frame systems mean.

The example that we have been discussing makes clear one of the reasons that frame systems are so convenient to work with. Because they collect all of the available information about a particular object or class of objects (like mammals) in one place, frame-based descriptions are easy to understand and to modify if new information is obtained.

Before turning to semantic nets, I should point out that some authors refer to frames as "slot-and-filler" architectures. The reason is obvious: Each object in a frame system consists of a collection of slots and values supplied to fill those slots.

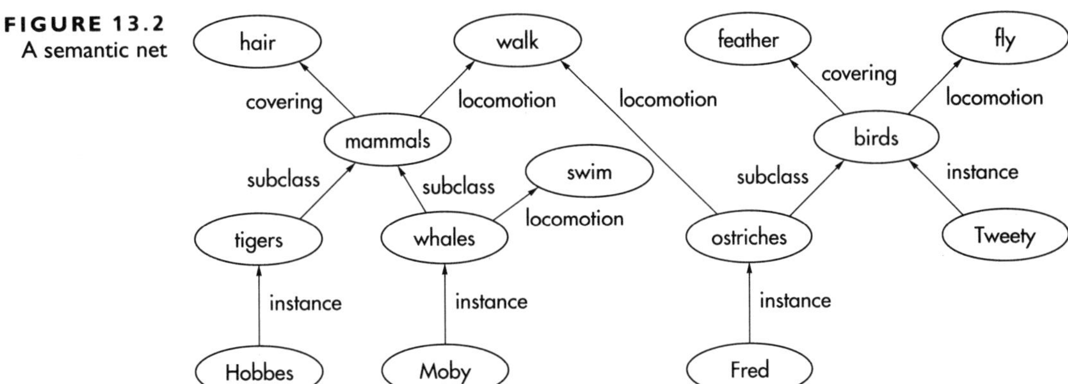

FIGURE 13.2 A semantic net

13.1.2 Semantic Nets

Semantic nets are little more than another way of representing the information in a frame system. As an example, the information appearing in our running example is shown in Figure 13.2.

It should now be clear how we construct a semantic net from a frame system $\mathcal{F}$. Each object in $\mathcal{F}$ is associated with a node in the semantic net, and each slot with an arc. The arc goes from the object to the value that fills the slot in the frame representation.

Translating from semantic nets to frames is no harder. Each node corresponds to an object, and each arc to a slot and filler combination.

As with frames, semantic nets collect all of the available information about any particular object in one place. In fact, semantic nets are even more effective, since *all* of the information about mammals—including the fact that they include tigers as a subtype—is easily obtained from the diagram in Figure 13.2.

13.2 EXTENSIONS

The sample frame system of Section 13.1 is a very simple one. In this section, we look at some more interesting examples.

13.2.1 Multiple Instances

Consider first the semantic net shown in Figure 13.3, which should be reminiscent of an example from Chapter 11 (and as such, is a harbinger of the problems we will need to deal with when we discuss inference in

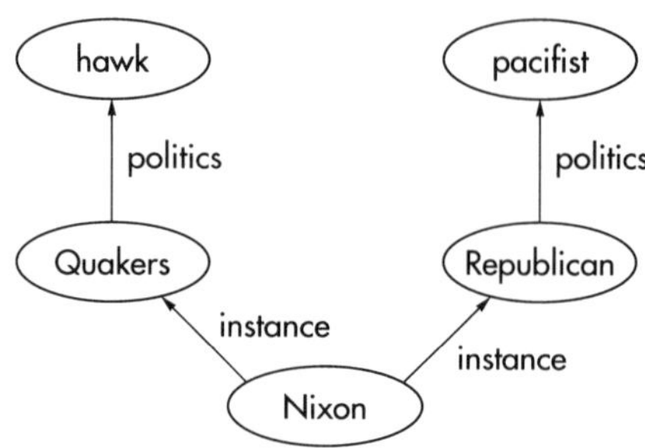

FIGURE 13.3 The Nixon diamond

Section 13.4). Here is the associated frame system:

Republican
  subclass-of: hawks
Quaker
  subclass-of: pacifists
Nixon
  instance-of: Quaker
  instance-of: Republican

Nothing in what we have described so far precludes an object being an instance of multiple classes. Similarly, nothing precludes one class being a subclass of multiple superclasses; as an example, the class of fast cars is often viewed as a subclass of the classes `expensive` and `fun`.

13.2.2 Nonunary Predicates

What if we want to say something a bit more complex in our frame language, perhaps that Hobbes is smaller than Moby. Can we do this without extending our representation?

We can, although there's a trick involved. What we want to say is that

`smaller(Hobbes, Moby)`

is true, so that the pair (`Hobbes, Moby`) is an instance of the predicate `smaller`. To express this in our frame-based system, all we need do is to give this pair a name:

Hobbes-and-Moby
  instance-of: smaller
  smaller: Hobbes
  bigger: Moby

We've cheated a little here, writing `smaller` for the operation that extracts the first element of the Hobbes/Moby pair and `bigger` for the operation that extracts the second. Using these more general names allows us to write things like

Hobbes-and-Moby
  instance-of: smaller
  instance-of: more-ferocious
  first: Hobbes
  second: Moby

This says that Hobbes is both smaller than Moby and more ferocious than he is.

The same example is shown using a semantic net in Figure 13.4. The advantage of the network representation is even clearer here, since it provides easy answers to questions like, "What do we know about Hobbes and Moby relative to one another?"

The conversion to first-order logic remains straightforward as well. We already know that the above frame translates into

$$\texttt{value(Hobbes-and-Moby,first, Hobbes)}$$
$$\texttt{value(Hobbes-and-Moby,second, Moby)}$$
$$\texttt{instance(Hobbes-and-Moby,smaller)}$$

and we need to add the general rule that

$$\texttt{value}(p,\texttt{first},x) \wedge \texttt{value}(p,\texttt{second},y) \wedge \texttt{instance}(p,r) \rightarrow \texttt{holds}(r,x,y) \tag{13.14}$$

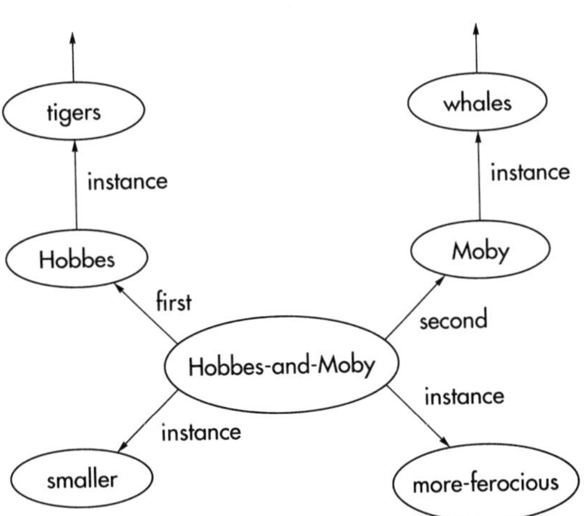

FIGURE 13.4 Nonunary predicates in a semantic net

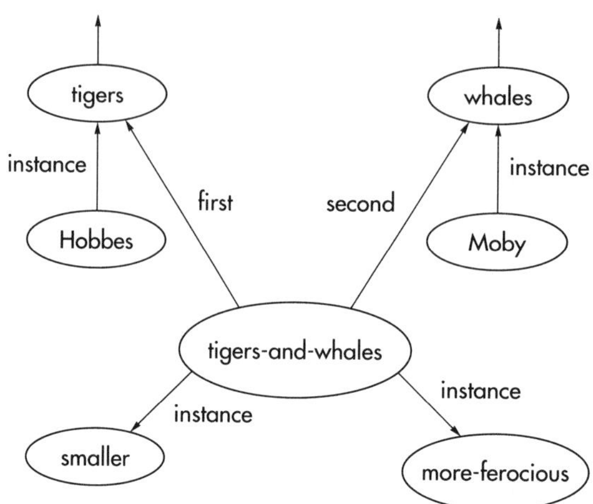

FIGURE 13.5 Tigers are smaller than whales

In other words, if p is the pair (x,y) and p is an instance of the relation r, then r holds for x and y. Note that we have reified the relation into an object in our language.

Finally, we might want to extend our notation further, saying things like, "Tigers are smaller than whales," from which we would want to be able to conclude that Hobbes is smaller than Moby. In order to do this, we need simply add to (13.14) the axiom

$$\texttt{instance}(a,x) \wedge \texttt{instance}(b,y) \wedge \texttt{holds}(r,x,y) \rightarrow \texttt{holds}(r,a,b)$$

saying that if a is an x and b is a y, and the relation r holds for x's and y's, then r holds for a and b as well. The corresponding semantic net is shown in Figure 13.5.

13.3 INFERENCE IN MONOTONIC FRAME SYSTEMS

We saw in the previous sections that frames and semantic nets serve the useful function of collecting all of the information about objects in single locations. The other main advantage claimed for these systems is that they speed the reasoning process; in this section, we will examine this claim under the assumption that we are using a monotonic interpretation of the frame or semantic net in question.

Suppose, then, that we have a frame or semantic net; we'll assume that we're actually working with a semantic net but the problem isn't really any different if we work with frames instead. Given a query of the form `instance`(A,X) for a specific object A and class X, how are we to respond?

This is easy: We start with all of the classes pointed to by `instance` arrows coming out of A, and see if we can then follow `subclass` arrows to eventually arrive at the class X. If we can, A is an instance of X. If we can't, it isn't. An example appears in Figure 13.6, where we have used the path shown to conclude that Hobbes is a mammal.

Here is the general algorithm:

ALGORITHM 13.3.1 *Given a semantic net $\mathcal{S}$, an object* A *and class* X, *and the query*

`instance(A,X)`

1. *Set $\mathcal{C}$ to be the set of all classes pointed to by* `instance` *arcs originating at* A.
2. *If $\mathcal{C}$ is empty, return failure.*
3. *Otherwise, select a class* C *in $\mathcal{C}$. If* C = X, *return success. Otherwise, add to $\mathcal{C}$ all of the classes pointed to by* `subclass` *arcs originating at* C.
4. *Return to step 2.*

It should be fairly clear that this algorithm returns success or failure depending on whether A is an X or not. What's more, the algorithm is extremely efficient: In a graph such as that in our examples, the answer is returned in time linear in the size of the graph. Is this efficiency a result of the use of semantic nets, or is it somehow intrinsic to the nature of the problem that we are trying to solve?

Before we discuss this question, I would like to set it in a wider context. Imagine that we have some universal method of problem solving (such as resolution theorem proving in first-order logic), and a variety of specialized methods (such as Algorithm 13.3.1) that, although not universal, give superior performance where applicable. Now there are two separate ways we might go about solving problems generally:

1. We might begin by checking to see if one of our specialized methods

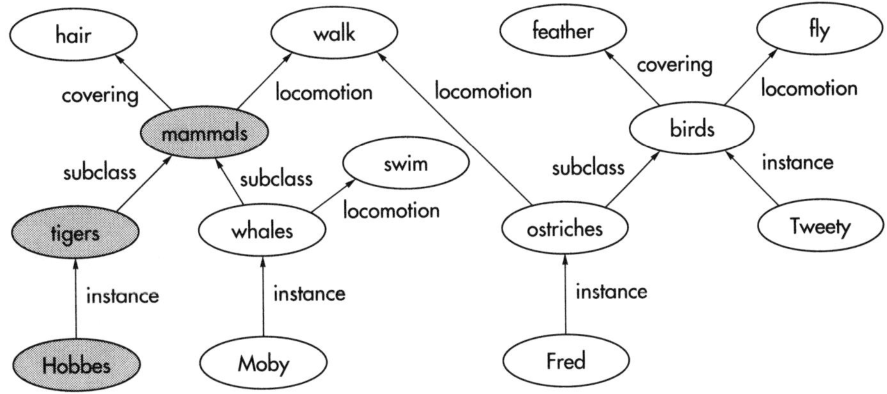

FIGURE 13.6 Proving that Hobbes is a mammal

could be applied, using it if so. If not, we would resort to an application of more general methods.

2. We could work to improve the fundamental efficiency of our general methods, hoping that powerful general techniques would eventually match the performance of the specialized methods where applicable without giving up the generality of the broader approach.

If possible, the second of these approaches is to be preferred for a variety of reasons:

- If the specialized methods fail, it is likely that little will have been learned while attempting them; the general method will probably have to start from scratch. If a single general method is applied, performance on the most difficult problems is likely to be better.
- In some cases, lessons learned from "translating" the specialized methods into the general framework may have implications reaching far beyond the special group of problems for which they were originally developed. Embedding the specialized methods in a general framework may lead to broad performance improvements that would otherwise be missed.

Of course, this is not to say that the goal implicit in the second of the above two options can always be achieved; there are certainly some special-purpose methods that simply do not fit into broader frameworks. But it is always interesting to at least *attempt* to generalize methods as useful as those introduced in this section.

But let's return to Algorithm 13.3.1 and see what it corresponds to in terms of inference. As an example, here is a derivation of the fact that Hobbes is a mammal using resolution:

	Sentence	**Source**
1	`instance(Hobbes,mammal)` $\rightarrow F$	negated query
2	`subclass(x,mammal)` $\wedge$ `instance(Hobbes,x)` $\rightarrow F$	resolve 1,(13.1)
3	`subclass(tiger,mammal)` $\rightarrow F$	resolve 2,(13.8)
4	$T \rightarrow F$	resolve 3,(13.6)

(13.15)

Note how closely this derivation parallels that used by the semantic net. In fact, we can translate Algorithm 13.3.1 generally into the first-order framework, viewing each step of the algorithm as a particular resolution to be performed.

ALGORITHM 13.3.2 *Given an object A and class X, we begin by adding to our database the negated query*

$$\texttt{instance}(A,X) \rightarrow F$$

We now proceed as follows:

1. *Unless* `instance`(A,X) *is in the database, the only available resolution is with (13.1) as in the above example, so we obtain*

   $$\texttt{instance}(A,y) \wedge \texttt{subclass}(y,X) \rightarrow F \qquad (13.16)$$

   as before. (Note that we have reversed the order of the two conjuncts.)

2. *Following the set-of-support strategy, we resolve (13.16) with all possible database facts* **except (13.1) again** *to obtain a set of sentences each of the form*

   $$\texttt{subclass}(C,X) \rightarrow F \qquad (13.17)$$

   for a specific class C of which A is known to be an instance.

3. *We now select one of the sentences of the form (13.17) to work with. If* `subclass`(C,X) *appears in the database, we can derive* T → F *and terminate successfully. If not, we have to resolve with (13.2) to obtain*

   $$\texttt{subclass}(C,y) \wedge \texttt{subclass}(y,X) \rightarrow F$$

   We now follow the set-of-support strategy once again, but **refuse to resolve with (13.2).** *For each sentence of the form* `subclass`(C,D) *in the database, we obtain*

   $$\texttt{subclass}(D,X) \rightarrow F$$

4. *Return to step 3.*

PROPOSITION 13.3.3 *Algorithms 13.3.1 and 13.3.2 are equivalent.*

PROOF This is actually immediate from the descriptions of the two algorithms. If at any point Algorithm 13.3.1 has propagated from the original object *A* to some class *C*, Algorithm 13.3.2 will have derived the goal

$$\texttt{subclass}(C,X) \rightarrow F$$

The converse is true as well, and the individual steps taken by the algorithms match also. ■

We see from this that the efficient semantic net algorithm is really just a specific method for controlling resolution search. The control protocol is a combination of set-of-support and the additional restrictions that appear in boldface in steps 2 and 3 of the description of Algorithm 13.3.2 itself. The boldface restrictions are in fact instances of the following general principle:

PROPOSITION 13.3.4 *Suppose that a resolution theorem prover using the set-of-support strategy has derived the goal*

$$p \wedge q \rightarrow F \tag{13.18}$$

and is considering resolving with $r \wedge s \rightarrow p$ *to obtain*

$$r \wedge s \wedge q \rightarrow F \tag{13.19}$$

Then if $r = p|_\sigma$ *is an instance of* p *and the database contains the fact*

$$s \wedge q \rightarrow q|_\sigma \tag{13.20}$$

the resolution leading to (13.19) need not be performed.

PROOF Suppose that we could derive (13.18) beginning with the resolution leading to (13.19); suppose further that the resolution continues by resolving (13.19) with the sentences $s_1, \ldots, s_n$. Since r is an instance of p, we can equally well resolve (13.18) with the s_i directly.

At some point, the original successful resolution proof must have succeeded in removing all of the atoms preceding s in (13.19), so the modified resolution will have succeeded in removing all of the literals preceding q in (13.18). We can now resolve with (13.20) to recover the result of the originally omitted resolution, continuing as before to derive the desired result. ∎

In Algorithm 13.3.2, we are working from the goal

$$\texttt{instance}(A,y) \wedge \texttt{subclass}(y,X) \rightarrow F$$

so that $p = \texttt{instance}(A,y)$ and $q = \texttt{subclass}(y,X)$. We refuse to resolve with

$$\texttt{instance}(A,z) \wedge \texttt{subclass}(z,y) \rightarrow \texttt{instance}(A,y)$$

Here $r = \texttt{instance}(A,z)$ and $s = \texttt{subclass}(z,y)$; the resolution would produce

$$\texttt{instance}(A,z) \wedge \texttt{subclass}(z,y) \wedge \texttt{subclass}(y,X) \rightarrow F$$

We can justify this by applying the proposition, since

$$\texttt{instance}(A,z) = \texttt{instance}(A,y)|_{y=z}$$

where $\sigma = \{y = z\}$ and our database does contain

$$\texttt{subclass}(z,y) \wedge \texttt{subclass}(y,X) \rightarrow \texttt{subclass}(z,X)$$

The modification in step 3 can be handled similarly, so that we see that Algorithm 13.3.2 is indeed simply set-of-support resolution, modified to take advantage of Proposition 13.3.4.

Notice what has happened here. By examining the special-purpose algorithm that deals with semantic nets, we were able to extend the ideas we developed in Section 9.1. In so doing, we both extended the power of our resolution system generally and ensured that it work as efficiently as Algorithm 13.3.1 when applied to problems that the specialized algorithm is able to solve.

Let me end this section by looking at some problems of a slightly different form. First, suppose that instead of trying to prove

instance(Hobbes,mammal)

we had been trying to find a v for which

value(Hobbes,covering,v)

was true. What is Hobbes covered with?

An algorithm quite similar to Algorithm 13.3.1 can be used to solve problems like this; as before, we work our way up from the node corresponding to Hobbes and stop as soon as we find a node from which we can determine the value of the `covering` slot. Here it is specifically:

ALGORITHM 13.3.5 *Given a semantic net $\mathcal{S}$, an object A and property P, and the query*

value(A,P,v)

where v is a variable:

1. *If there is a value known for* A's P *property, return that value.*
2. *Otherwise, set* $\mathcal{C}$ *to be the set of all classes pointed to by* `instance` *arcs originating at* A.
3. *If* $\mathcal{C}$ *is empty, return failure.*
4. *Otherwise, select a class* C *in* $\mathcal{C}$. *If there is a value known for* C's

P property, return it. Otherwise, add to $\mathscr{C}$ all of the classes pointed to by `subclass` arcs originating at C.

5. *Return to step 3.*

In Figure 13.7, we show the results of applying this algorithm to conclude that

```
value(Hobbes,covering,hair)
```

Finally, let's have a look at problems like that introduced in Figure 13.5. How can we respond to a query such as

```
smaller(Hobbes,Moby)
```

There are a variety of ways in which we might do this; they all have a similar flavor. We begin by marking all of the nodes in the diagram that are instances of `smaller`. Say we mark these nodes with a 1.

We go on to mark with a 2 all of the nodes of which Hobbes is an instance, and mark with a 3 all nodes of which Moby is an instance. Having done this, if there is any node marked with a 1 that has a node marked with a 2 as its first slot and a node marked with a 3 as its second slot, we can conclude (as in Figure 13.8) that Hobbes is smaller than Moby. If not, the conclusion does not follow from the information in the net.

By marking the net in this way, we ensure that we have to determine only once which classes have Hobbes as a member. If we were simply to check each node that is an instance of `smaller` to see if Hobbes was an instances of its `first` slot and Moby an instance of its `second`, a great deal of work might be repeated. The efficient approach to solving problems in semantic nets is often referred to as *marker propagation* or *spreading activation* because a single node such as `Hobbes` has an effect that gradually spreads throughout the network.

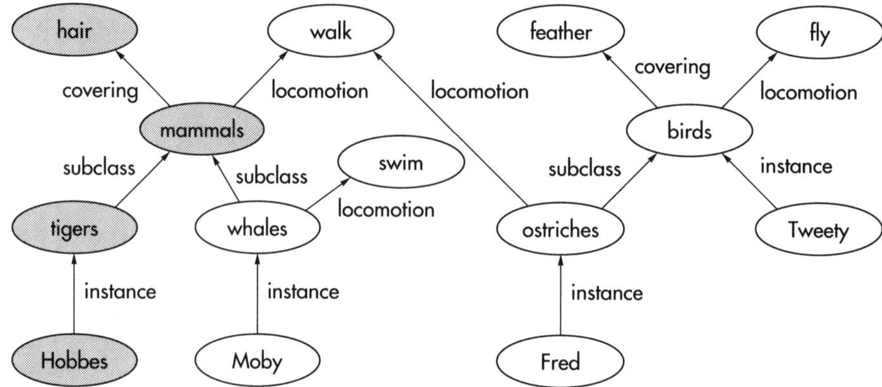

FIGURE 13.7
Hobbes is hairy

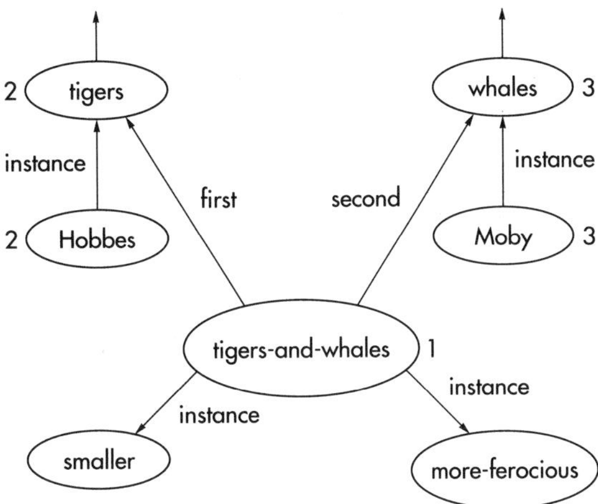

FIGURE 13.8 Hobbes is smaller than Moby

13.4 INFERENCE IN NONMONOTONIC FRAME SYSTEMS

When we add nonmonotonicity to the above discussion, things become much more complicated. As we have seen in Figure 13.3, it is possible that the defaults about a certain object conflict, and we need some way to resolve these conflicts when they occur.

The view that we will take here is that we are going to look for brave extensions of the associated default theory, so that we are allowed to conclude in Figure 13.3 either that

```
value(Nixon,politics,hawk)
```

or

```
value(Nixon,politics,dove)
```

The reason we take this view is that it allows us to continue to use Algorithm 13.3.5; this algorithm works its way up from the original object A and will therefore always use the most specific information available when determining the value to be assigned to any particular property of A.

As an example, if A is `Tweety` and P is `locomotion`, we will notice that there is no explicit information in the database about how Tweety gets around, and therefore move to the node dealing with birds. Birds fly, so Tweety does as well. Had we been interested in Fred instead, we would have stopped when we got to the `ostrich` node, thereby concluding that Fred walks.

The axiomatization in first-order logic needs some modification to deal with default values for slots, however. As a start, there is nothing in our existing axiomatization preventing our concluding that both

$$\texttt{value(Fred,locomotion,walks)}$$

and

$$\texttt{value(Fred,locomotion,flies)}$$

The first thing we need is to say that for any object o and property p, there can be only one value v with value(o,p,v):

$$\texttt{value}(o,p,v) \wedge v \neq v' \rightarrow \neg\texttt{value}(o,p,v') \tag{13.21}$$

The appearance of the inequality in this axiom causes further problems, however. How do we know that walking and flying are different? Just because the objects walks and flies have different names doesn't necessarily mean that they are different objects—after all, the objects "George Washington" and "the first president of the United States" have different names but refer to the same thing.

So we'll need to state explicitly conditions under with one object is different from another. We rewrite (13.21) as

$$\texttt{value}(o,p,v) \wedge \texttt{different}(v,v') \rightarrow \neg\texttt{value}(o,p,v') \tag{13.22}$$

and add the axioms

$$\texttt{different(walks,flies)}$$

$$\texttt{different(walks,swims)}$$

$$\texttt{different(hawk,dove)}$$

We still aren't done, though. Think about Fred for a minute; since he's both an ostrich and a bird, there are two possible extensions in this case. In one, he is a normal ostrich and walks; in the other, he is a normal bird and flies. We want to prefer the extension in which he walks because ostriches are a subclass of birds, but the axiomatization that we have presented thus far does not tell us to do this. Slightly more formally, in the first extension we have

$$E_1 = \{\texttt{ab(Fred,bird,locomotion)}\}$$

since Fred doesn't inherit the usual value of the locomotion slot from the `bird` class. In the other extension, we have

$$E_2 = \{\texttt{ab(Fred,ostrich,locomotion)}\}$$

because Fred doesn't inherit from the `ostrich` class.

We discussed this problem in Section 11.2.2, where we said that there was as yet no general method for preferring one extension to another. In this case, however, there is a reason: Information about subclasses should be preferred to information about superclasses. We can write this as

$$\texttt{subclass}(c_1,c_2) \wedge \texttt{ab}(a,c_1,p) \rightarrow \texttt{ab}(a,c_2,p) \qquad (13.23)$$

In other words, once an object a in a class c_1 is known to be abnormal with regard to a property p, it is assumed to be abnormal with regard to p for all superclasses of c_1.

In our example, the axiom (13.23) adds to E_2 the abnormality `ab(Fred,bird,locomotion)`. But now E_2 is a superset of E_1, so that E_1 is the only extension remaining. This is the extension in which Fred is an abnormal bird and walks.

The discussion that we have presented here only scratches the surface of nonmonotonic frame systems. As you will see in the exercises, there are problems with both Algorithm 13.3.5 and with the formalization that we have presented. Formalizing inheritance, as with many other areas of commonsense reasoning, is much harder than was originally believed. The accessibility and apparent ease of what turn out to be such difficult problems is one of the things that makes AI so interesting.

13.5 FURTHER READING

Frames and semantic nets have a long history in AI; they were introduced to the field by Marvin Minsky [1975]. An excellent (although now somewhat dated) survey article describing them is Brachman [1985]; the articles by Woods [1990a and 1990b] are more up-to-date but less engaging. Brachman was also involved in two of the earliest and most influential frame-based representation languages, KRYPTON [Brachman *et al.* 1983] and its successor KL-ONE [Brachman and Schmolze 1985]; SNePS [Shapiro 1979] was another early language of this type. The languages LOOM [MacGregor 1990] and CYCL [Guha and Lenat 1990] are fairly representative of current work in this area of knowledge representation; the impact of frame-based reasoning is also apparent in the nature of object-oriented programming languages such as Common Lisp [Steele, Jr. 1990].

Nonmonotonic frame systems have occupied the attention of the nonmonotonic reasoning community for some time, and solutions are just now beginning to emerge. Early work on formalizing the nonmonotonic inheritance reasoning done by these systems is the subject of Fahlman [1979] and Touretzky [1984]; unfortunately, there are serious problems with these approaches. Fairly successful special-purpose algorithms that analyze a particular network by considering the paths it contains are introduced by Horty *et al.* [1987] and Horty and Thomason [1988], although more recently Makinson and Schlechta [1991] suggest that there are fundamental problems that this path-based approach is incapable of addressing. A very recent paper by Hector Geffner and Judea Pearl [1992] discusses the inheritance problem as an instance of the multiple extension problem generally; the solution presented there is probably the best one known at the present time. Geffner and Pearl also present an extension of the algorithmic ideas that we discussed in Chapter 11 that implements their theoretical suggestions.

Complexity results concerning the problem of determining whether or not a conclusion is a brave or cautious consequence of a frame system are discussed by Patel-Schneider [1989] and Kautz and Selman [1991].

Finally, I should confess that the description of frames presented here is colored by my desire to have this material mesh with the contents of other chapters; as a result, I have surely not done credit to the substantial literature on applications of nonmonotonic frame systems in a variety of areas in AI:

- Minsky's original paper [1975] suggests applying the idea to problems in perception.
- Natural language applications are discussed by Woods [1975].
- Schank and Abelson [1977] suggest that a slot-and-filler architecture known as *scripts* can be useful in solving planning problems.

13.6 EXERCISES

1. Extend the example used in this chapter to include a new subclass of mammals, bats. Your extension should also include the existence of a specific bat named Dracula. Explain the modifications that would need to be made to all three of the representations discussed (logic, frames, and semantic nets).
2. Extend the example in this chapter so that it includes information about what various types of animals eat using the predicate `food`(C,F) to mean that animals in the class C typically eat the food F. As in the previous exercise, present the extension in all three of the representations discussed.
3. This exercise concerns the extension of the ideas in the text to allow

individuals (in addition to classes) to have slots other than `instance-of`.

(a) What changes would need to be made to frame systems to allow individuals to have other slots?

(b) What would the declarative translations of these axioms be? Is there any point to allowing the translations to be defaults, or should they always be true with certainty?

(c) Extend the example in the text to include mice, a subclass of mammals. Describe a particular mouse, Mighty, that can fly.

4. Suppose that I asked you for a program that translated from frames to semantic nets or vice versa. Develop data structures that you could use to represent frames and semantic nets so that you wouldn't have to write this program at all.

5. Given the axiomatization in Section 13.2.2, can we actually derive `smaller(Hobbes,Moby)`? What can we derive instead?

6. Change the net of Figure 13.5 so that it implies that tigers are smaller than tigers. What is the declarative translation of this net?

7. Give an example of a semantic net where Algorithm 13.3.1 fails to terminate. How can the algorithm be modified to cater to this problem? Can a similar modification be made to a first-order reasoning system?

8. Show explicitly that the omitted resolutions in step 3 of Algorithm 13.3.2 are covered by Proposition 13.3.4.

9. Develop an analog to Algorithm 13.3.2 that deals with queries of the form

`value(`A,P,v`)`

in a way matching Algorithm 13.3.5.

10. (a) Make precise the marker propagation algorithm that was described briefly at the end of Section 13.3.

(b) Develop a resolution control strategy that duplicates this algorithm. Are any new control principles needed, or does Proposition 13.3.4 suffice?

11. Implement Algorithm 13.3.5 and use it to solve the query

`value(Moby,locomotion,x)`

12. Show explicitly that Algorithm 13.3.5 can get either answer when responding to the query

`value(Nixon,politics,x)`

in Figure 13.3.

FIGURE 13.9
African ostriches

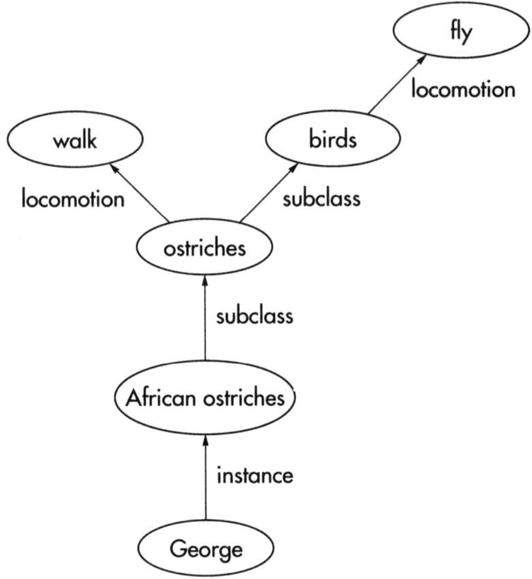

13. Consider the semantic net shown in Figure 13.9.
    (a) What should the response be to the query

    `value(George,locomotion,x)`?

    (b) Are all African ostriches birds? Add an arc to the net in the figure to indicate this.
    (c) Apply Algorithm 13.3.5 to the resulting network. What went wrong?

14. Does our axiomatization including (13.22) also need an axiom

    $$\texttt{different}(x,y) \rightarrow \texttt{different}(y,x)$$

    Why or why not?

15. Suppose that instead of sanctioning a conclusion that holds in *any* interpretation of a semantic net, we want to sanction only those conclusions that hold in all such interpretations.
    (a) What conclusions should we now draw in Figure 13.3?
    (b) Construct a modification to Algorithm 13.3.5 that behaves in this way, only returning conclusions that do not conflict with other information in the network.

PART V

AI SYSTEMS

In this last part of this book, I'd like to focus on some AI problems that have wider scope than those we have discussed thus far. An intelligent artifact will need to examine its environment, decide what actions it should take, communicate with other agents (including us!), and learn from its mistakes. A vision, planning, natural language, or learning system will involve much more than simple knowledge representation. Although ideas from search and knowledge representation underlie almost all other work in the field, much progress has been made on problems in these broader areas. The next few chapters are intended to give you both an overview of that progress and an understanding of the problems that motivated it.

I said back in the introduction that this book's aim was to present to you those ideas that were central to AI. Because so much of AI rests on concepts from search and knowledge representation, it was fairly easy for me to decide what to say about these subfields; in this part of the book, it's harder. Planning *is* central to AI. So is vision. And learning, and natural language understanding, and expert systems. In some cases, however, what is central are not the details of some particular methodology, but the nature of the problems that this methodology is trying to address.

Although easy to understand, many of the problems we'll see in the remainder of the book have proven very difficult to solve, and it would be less than candid for me to present descriptions that made it appear otherwise. But please remember my remarks from the preface: AI is a science in its infancy. And as in any science, the fact that there remains so much progress to be made should be cause for excitement, not embarrassment.

CHAPTER 14

PLANNING

The first of the AI "systems" that we will consider involve *planning*. A planning system is expected to analyze the situation in which an agent finds itself and then to develop a strategy for achieving the agent's goal—presumably by finding a series of actions that can be expected to have a desirable outcome.

Planning is one of a set of problems that are known as *synthesis* problems because they involve the development of a mental object of some form—a plan, a design for a circuit, what have you. Synthesis problems are to be contrasted with the problems that we have considered thus far, which are typically "classification" problems. In a diagnostic system, the aim is to classify the observed behavior of some device in order to determine which component is failing. The small set of possible outcomes (limited by the number of potentially faulty components in a diagnostic example) makes classification problems much easier than synthesis problems. After all, the number of possible circuits is tremendously larger than the number of components out of which the circuits are constructed. The number of possible plans is much greater than the number of single actions that might be taken in any given situation.

This is not to say that planning doesn't involve knowledge representation and search, of course. Information about the domain of action still needs to be communicated to the planning system, and search is still intrinsic to finding a solution to the planning problem. What we are trying to point out here is that the space of possible solutions is much larger for synthesis problems than it is for classification problems.

It is possible, incidentally, to view planning as classification—given the current situation, the aim is only to decide what single action to take next, as opposed to developing a general plan of action that will achieve the desired goal. But solving planning problems in this way seems fruitless—it's not terribly reasonable to store facts of the form, "If you want to get to Boston, the first thing you should do is get to a phone." (To call your travel agent, presumably.) You'll look pretty silly racing to a phone if you happen to be in an airport already (just go to the ticket counter), or if you're already in Boston! In addition, plans often need to be debugged; if you merely classify your situation based on the best action to take next and then something goes wrong, you won't really have any idea of how to fix it.[26]

Before we look at planning specifically, let me point out that there is yet another class of problems that are harder than either classification or synthesis problems—learning problems. By a *learning* problem I mean a problem where the idea is to discover a new and useful concept of some kind, like the *idea* of a "bird" if all you know about is animals, feathers, flying things, and so on.

The reason that learning is so hard is that the space of possible concepts is even larger than the space of possible plans. Roughly speaking, the space of possible solutions to a synthesis problem (for example, plans) grows exponentially in the number of actions one could take. But the number of possible concepts (basically normal-form expressions using existing predicates) grows doubly-exponentially in the size of the domain.

My own view is that classification problems are basically solved, at least in the sense that once we have determined the classification function to be used, the techniques available to implement such functions are well understood. Learning problems, on the other hand, are currently too hard for us because of the enormous search involved. (But there's still lots going on, as we'll see in the next chapter.) Planning problems, however, are "just right." If I had to predict the area of AI research that will make the most progress in the next ten years, I'd pick planning. There are a tremendous number of problems that are both interesting and tractable. Research in planning as a whole should show substantial progress as progress is made on the individual issues that we will discuss shortly.

There are other reasons that planning is interesting. For one thing, it is clearly a fundamental part of intelligent behavior. All of us are capable of developing strategies to achieve our goals, and our artifacts will need to be able to do the same.

Yet another thing that makes planning interesting is how hard it is. It seems like we should be able to write a planning system by just describing the domain to a theorem prover, and then asking it to prove that a plan exists. Since the proof can be expected to be constructive, this would enable us to use our existing declarative methods to solve planning problems.

As an example, imagine that we are trying to plan to achieve some simple goal, like making breakfast in the morning. A proof that we can make pancakes would presumably involve proving that we can get milk and flour, mix them in a bowl, and then cook the pancakes on the griddle—but the discovery of this proof is equivalent to solving the original planning

26 Actually, you won't even be bothered by the fact that something's gone wrong—with only a view of what action should be taken next and no view of why, you won't realize that anything's amiss!

problem. We have seen in a variety of places in Part III that computer-generated proofs tend to be constructive, so it seems as if the universality of first-order logic should imply that a planning system can be constructed in this fashion.

This is a nice idea, but it doesn't work. And the reasons it doesn't work will be the focus of this chapter. I'll spend some time talking about potential solutions to the problems we'll be discussing, but most of the material will be about the problems themselves. After all, I said in the introduction that I'd try to focus on topics that were well established in the AI literature—and in planning, the problems are much better established than the solutions are.

14.1 GENERAL-PURPOSE AND SPECIAL-PURPOSE PLANNERS

Before turning our attention to these general issues, I should spend a little more time on the possible reduction of planning problems to classification ones. Instead of classifying a situation in terms of, which action should I take next?, what if we attempt to classify it in terms of, which plan would allow me to achieve my goal?

A lot of the planning that we do is of just this form. I typically ride my bike to work if it's sunny, but drive if it's raining or cold. Either way, I know the route I expect to take; what I'm doing when I decide how to get to work is determining whether I want to invoke my existing bike-to-work plan or my existing drive-to-work plan.

Sometimes, of course, things aren't so simple. It was sunny last week, but I was having a new floor put in in the kitchen and that meant that the cat was locked in the garage. The cat hates being locked up; if I went to get my bicycle out of the garage, the cat would probably run away. Since my car was parked on the curb, I decided to drive to work instead of bicycling.

In the normal case, I have a simple set of rules that tells me to look at the weather and decide how to get to work. This is what is known as *special-purpose* planning; I invoke a planner that is capable of solving only a very restricted problem and then use the result. In the example involving my cat, I had to invoke a planner with a much deeper understanding of my household domain in order to decide what to do; it's unlikely that the special-purpose planner that I typically use could anticipate my difficulties. Planners that rely on deep knowledge about their domain are called *general-purpose* planners.

Special-purpose planners are classification systems; general-purpose planners are synthesis systems—and it is in general-purpose planning that all the problems show up. Although many special-purpose planners have been built and used in restricted domains, the point of this particular example is to remind you that the need to resort to general-purpose methods—to plan from first principles—is never very far away.

14.2 REASONING ABOUT ACTION

A simple planning problem is shown in Figure 14.1; our goal is to get block B onto block C. We will begin our discussion of planning by examining one of the issues underlying planning—how are we to describe actions themselves?

We start by identifying the vocabulary we will use when working in this domain, which is known as the *blocks world*. We introduce a predicate loc(b,l), indicating that the block b is at the location l. l might be a location on the table, or another block, and so on. Given this, our goal is to achieve loc(B,C).

There is a single action in this domain, that of moving a block to a new location; we denote this action by move(b,l). We will initially take move to be a predicate in our domain, so that move(b,l) means, "The block b has been moved to the location l." We will further assume that the nature of the domain is such that the move action succeeds only if both the block being moved and the target location are clear when the action is attempted.

Let's not worry about the preconditions for a moment, however. How are we to say that the result of moving b to l is that b is at l? It is tempting to write

$$\texttt{move}(b,l) \rightarrow \texttt{loc}(b,l) \tag{14.1}$$

but a moment's reflection shows that this is unsatisfactory. If, for example, we move b first to a location l_1 and then to a new location l_2, we would have

$$\texttt{move}(b,l_1) \wedge \texttt{move}(b,l_2)$$

and we can conclude from this and (14.1) that b is located at both l_1 *and* l_2!

The problem with (14.1) is that we can't really talk about the effects of actions without describing the situations in which the actions take place. So what we really want to say in (14.1) is that if we perform a move action in a situation s, then the result will hold in the next situation:

$$\texttt{move}(b,l,s) \rightarrow \texttt{loc}(b,l,\texttt{next}(s)) \tag{14.2}$$

FIGURE 14.1 Move B to C

Note that we have added a third "situational" argument to the `move` and `loc` predicates.

It will be a bit more convenient if we rewrite (14.2) in a slightly different form. Rather than talk about the "next" situation, we will talk explicitly about the result of performing an action a in a situation s. Rather than the function `next`, we use a function `result`, where `result`(a,s) is the situation that results from performing the action a in the situation s. (14.2) now becomes

$$\texttt{loc}(b,l,\texttt{result}(\texttt{move}(b,l),s)) \tag{14.3}$$

This axiom says explicitly that b will be located at l in the situation that results from moving b to l in s. We've changed `move` to a function here; `move`(b,l) takes a block b and a location l and produces the action of moving b to l. `result` is also a function.

Now: What about the preconditions? Let's introduce a new predicate `clear`, where `clear`(l,s) means that the location (or block) l is clear in the situation s. (14.3) finally becomes:

$$\texttt{clear}(b,s) \wedge \texttt{clear}(l,s) \rightarrow \texttt{loc}(b,l,\texttt{result}(\texttt{move}(b,l),s)) \tag{14.4}$$

If, in some situation s, the block b and the location l are both clear, then b will be at l after we move it there.

Before turning to the problems with this kind of an axiomatization, let me introduce an alternative formulation of it. Rather than introduce a situational argument to all of the predicates in our domain, we can instead reify predicates like `loc`, making objects out of sentences such as `loc`(B,C). Instead of writing

$$\texttt{clear}(b,s)$$

to indicates that b is clear in s, we can write

$$\texttt{holds}(\texttt{clear}(b),s) \tag{14.5}$$

where `clear`(b) is now an object of our domain instead of a sentence. What (14.5) says is that the *object* `clear`(b) holds in the situation s. If we do this, (14.4) becomes

$$\begin{aligned} &\texttt{holds}(\texttt{clear}(b),s) \wedge \texttt{holds}(\texttt{clear}(l),s) \\ &\qquad \rightarrow \texttt{holds}(\texttt{loc}(b,l),\texttt{result}(\texttt{move}(b,l),s)) \end{aligned} \tag{14.6}$$

We have already seen examples of reification in Chapter 13, where we used it to present a convenient description of inheritance hierarchies; (14.5) and (14.6) are another example of this technique.

Finally, let me introduce a little bit of terminology. A description like the one we have given of our domain, involving reified sentences like (14.6), uses what is known as the *situation calculus* because of the appearance of situational arguments in sentences like (14.6). The old predicates (like clear) that are functions in the new formulation are often called *fluents*. Thus clear is a fluent because clear(b) is an object in the reified description.

One difficulty with reification is that since we are treating expressions like clear(b) as objects, we have to be careful to avoid operating on them with logical operators. Thus we cannot write (14.6) as

$$\texttt{holds}[\texttt{clear}(b) \wedge \texttt{clear}(l),s] \rightarrow \texttt{holds}[\texttt{loc}(b,l),\texttt{result}(\texttt{move}(b,l),s)]$$

since conjunction is not defined as an operation on the *objects* clear(b) and clear(l).

One advantage of reification is that it allows us to quantify over the sentences (now objects) being reified. If we want to say that *nothing* holds in some situation s_{wow}, we could write this as

$$\forall f.\neg \texttt{holds}(f,s_{\mathrm{wow}})$$

If we were not to reify the sentences in our domain, this axiom would involve quantification over predicates and would therefore not be a legitimate sentence of first-order logic. We will see a more interesting example of this use of reified sentences in Section 14.3.3.

The frame problem Suppose, then, that we decide to describe the move action using (14.6) or perhaps (14.4). Is this an adequate description?

Not yet. The reason is that we have no way to decide that if we move B to C in Figure 14.1, the block A will stay where it is.

This is a problem that we have already seen in the discussions of Sections 10.2.3 and 11.1.2. We observed there that any description of action needs some way to encode our knowledge that things typically stay the same from one situation to another. Making this observation precise is known as the *frame problem*, and we discuss some solutions that have been proposed in Section 14.3.

The qualification problem Even if we have found some way to address this difficulty, the resulting description is still inadequate, since there are typically "unmentioned" preconditions to most of the actions that we might consider. In our blocks world example, a precondition of move(b,l) is $b \neq l$, since it is impossible to put a block on top of itself. It seems, however, as if this fact should not force us to add a new precondition to the move action; we should be able to derive this precondition from the domain constraint

$$\forall b,s.\neg \texttt{holds}(\texttt{loc}(b,b),s)$$

In other words, given the fact that no block can ever be on top of itself, we should be able to conclude that any attempt to move it there will fail.

This is one aspect of the so-called *qualification problem:*

An action may fail because its success would involve the violation of a domain constraint.

Unfortunately, formalizing this idea precisely turns out to be very difficult.

The qualification problem refers to the fact that actions typically have preconditions that are not an explicit part of the domain description; as we've just seen, one way in which this can happen is when the precondition is a consequence of constraints on the domain in which the planner is working.

Another aspect of qualification is that actions often have preconditions that are unstated simply because they are unlikely to arise in practice. Consider an example from Chapter 11, where we noticed that you won't be able to start your car if someone has stuck a potato in the tail pipe. Is it reasonable to make the absence of the potato an explicit precondition to starting the car?[27]

There are simply too many potential preconditions of this sort for us to enumerate them in advance. Even if we could enumerate them, reasoning through these preconditions in order to decide whether or not a particular action will succeed could never be computationally viable in practice.

This sort of a qualification on the success of an action shares some features with the one mentioned earlier. Since a car with a blocked exhaust cannot run, we can derive the hidden precondition using whatever technique allowed us to realize that the action move(b,b) will always be unsuccessful.

But things are not so simple. Given an action move(b,l), we can presumably tell whether $b = l$ or not; when we go to start our car in the morning, do we know whether or not there is a potato in the tail pipe?

The conventional wisdom is that we nonmonotonically assume that actions succeed once their explicit preconditions have been satisfied. We assume that the action of starting our car in the morning will work, and conclude from that (if necessary) that there is no potato in the tail pipe.

But even this approach has problems. Certainly the conclusion is correct—we *do* assume that our car has no potato in the tail pipe. But what if our car is out of gas? Now the action of starting it has no chance of succeeding, but we still feel justified in concluding that the potato is missing.

We see from this that qualification assumptions such as the absence of

27 In the 1985 film *Beverly Hills Cop*, Eddie Murphy used a banana to block a car's exhaust. But in the 1977 paper "Epistemological Problems of Artificial Intelligence," John McCarthy discusses a potato. We use a potato in the interests of historical accuracy.

a potato are not really assumptions about actions (for example, that the action of starting the car will succeed); they're assumptions about the domain itself (for example, tail pipes are normally potato-free). This doesn't make the problem of identifying and describing these assumptions any easier, however.

The ramification problem Even if the frame and qualification difficulties are addressed, problems still remain. As an example, have a look at Figure 14.1 again. After moving *B* to *C*, how do we know that *B* is no longer located at its initial location?

This is the *ramification* problem; not only is it hard to specify exactly the things that *don't* change as actions take place and time goes by, it's hard to say what *does* change as these things happen. In the example we are considering, not only do we need to say that *B* isn't at its original location any more, we need to say that *C* is no longer clear.

Other examples are more subtle because the ramifications of successful actions can be situation-dependent. The action of moving an object typically doesn't change its color. But what about moving your car into the path of a spray paint gun? Cameras work because moving one object (the shutter) causes *another* object to change color (the film).

These, then, are the three problems in formalizing action:

1. The qualification problem. Describing precisely when actions do or do not succeed is more subtle than one might expect.
2. The frame problem. Describing precisely what stays the same when an action does succeed is more subtle than one might expect.
3. The ramification problem. Describing precisely what changes when an action succeeds is also more subtle than one might expect.

Other than that, no worries.

14.3 DESCRIPTIONS OF ACTION

In this section, we discuss some of the solutions that have been proposed in response to these difficulties.

14.3.1 Nondeclarative Methods

Probably the best-known approach is the one used by an implemented general-purpose planning system known as STRIPS. STRIPS uses a special-purpose data structure to describe actions and then manipulates this description using procedures designed specifically to solve planning problems. Because the planning process is procedural, it is reasonable to think of the STRIPS description as nondeclarative.

The data structure used by STRIPS describes actions in terms of *preconditions*, *add lists*, and *delete lists*. The preconditions of an action are those fluents that must hold in order for the action to be successful. The elements of the add list are the fluents that will hold after the action succeeds; the elements of the delete list are the fluents that cease to hold when the action succeeds. Any fluent not on an action's add or delete list is assumed to persist through the execution of that action. Since STRIPS is not a declarative system, it is free to maintain its description of the domain in any fashion it chooses; the representation used is simply a list of valid fluents. This list is modified destructively as actions occur.

It should be clear from this description that STRIPS makes no attempt to address the qualification problem; all of an action's preconditions need to be stated explicitly. The frame problem is handled via the assumption that unmentioned fluents persist from one situation to another; this is often known as the *STRIPS assumption*. The ramification problem is treated by explicitly listing all of the consequences of any action—both direct and "inferential."

Because the inferential consequences may be situation-dependent, STRIPS needs to split any action with potentially situation-dependent effects into a collection of action subtypes. In the example of the previous section, one would need the following actions:

```
move-car-into-spray-paint
move-car-elsewhere
move-camera-shutter-with-film-in-camera
move-camera-shutter-on-empty-camera
move-other-than-car-or-camera-shutter
```

Things are clearly getting out of hand here; as the domain becomes more complicated, the number of action subtypes can be expected to grow exponentially with its size. Although STRIPS has a computational mechanism for dealing with the ramification problem, this mechanism is unlikely to be able to cope with domains of interesting size.

14.3.2 Monotonic Methods

The fact that the STRIPS representation of action is not declarative also has the consequence that information about actions cannot interact with other available information.

Think about my cat locked in the garage once again. Assuming that I hadn't previously thought about the problem of the cat escaping if I open the door, I won't know that "the cat is out" should be on the add list of the action "open the garage door with the cat locked in the garage."

The difficulty here is a result of the fact that the STRIPS action language is not one in which I can conveniently express all of my other information about the world—in this particular case, information about the fact that my cat hates being locked in the garage and so on.

A general-purpose planner like STRIPS is not as brittle as a special-purpose planner would be. But because STRIPS has no effective access to the declarative information already available to the system, some brittleness remains. Alternatively, since STRIPS makes specific assumptions about the form of the actions being described, it is unable to work with any actions that cannot be described in this way.

Here's another example. Like most other general-purpose planners, STRIPS assumes that the consequences of an action are well-defined. But what are the consequences of playing the lottery? It depends on whether you win or lose—and the planning system will hardly be able to predict this in advance! STRIPS also cannot handle simultaneous actions, actions that take more than a single unit of time to have effect, and so on. Some planning systems address some of these issues; other systems address others. But the limited expressive power of these methods remains.

Instead of trying to give a STRIPS-like description access to declarative information, an alternative approach is to use a legitimately declarative description of action, as we did in (14.4) and (14.6). The universality of first-order logic should now guarantee that we are capable of describing any possible action, and that this description interfaces easily with whatever other declarative information is available.

A description of action using first-order logic might be expected to deal with the ramification problem by saying, for example, that a block can only be in one place:

$$[\mathtt{holds}(\mathtt{loc}(b,l),s) \wedge \mathtt{holds}(\mathtt{loc}(b,l'),s)\ ] \rightarrow l = l' \qquad (14.7)$$

Given this axiom and the fact that the action of moving B to C is successful in Figure 14.1, it is possible to conclude that

$$\neg\mathtt{holds}(\mathtt{loc}(B,l_2),\mathtt{result}(\mathtt{move}(B,C),s_0)) \qquad (14.8)$$

where s_0 is the initial situation shown in the figure and l_2 is B's initial location.

The frame problem is not so simple, however. In order to specify exactly which fluents are preserved through the execution of which actions, one needs to break actions into subtypes as we did in the previous section. As an example, in order to describe situations in which moving an object doesn't change its color, we need to list explicitly exceptions involving cars, paint guns, and so on.[28] Just as the number of action subtypes grew exponentially in the size of the domain for a STRIPS system, so does the size of a monotonic axiomatization.

28 There is no *proof* that monotonic descriptions of action need to be this bad, and researchers continue to search for satisfactory monotonic axiomatizations. Section 14.6 contains pointers to some recent efforts.

14.3.3 Nonmonotonic Methods

What we would *like* to say, of course, is simply that fluents persist from one situation to the next if there is no reason to believe otherwise. So it would seem that nonmonotonic reasoning would be well-suited to the problem of describing action.

When we wanted to say that birds fly if there were no reason to believe otherwise, we wrote

$$\texttt{bird}(x) \wedge \neg \texttt{ab}(x) \rightarrow \texttt{flies}(x)$$

If a bird is not abnormal, it can fly. We then used nonmonotonic techniques to ensure that when possible, we would conclude $\neg \texttt{ab}(b)$ for any particular bird b.

For actions, what we would like to say is that if a fluent f holds in a situation s, then the fluent will continue to hold after we execute an action a:

$$\texttt{holds}(f,s) \wedge \neg \texttt{ab}(a,f,s) \rightarrow \texttt{holds}(f,\texttt{result}(a,s)) \tag{14.9}$$

(14.9) says exactly this: If f holds in s, and a is not abnormal in that it reverses the sense of f in s, then f will hold in $\texttt{result}(a,s)$. Note that the abnormality predicate appearing here has three arguments—whether or not the action causes f to cease to hold might depend on the action taken, the fluent involved, or the situation being considered.

Unfortunately, (14.9) turns out not to work. The rule (14.9) leads to multiple extensions that prevent our drawing all of the conclusions we would expect after a sequence of actions is executed; details of this are the topic of Exercise 5 at the end of this chapter. This difficulty can be addressed, however, by a suitable modification of the frame axiom (14.9); the idea is that it is not a *situation* like "the result of moving B onto C in the initial state" that should appear as an argument to ab, but a *description* of that situation, like "any state in which C is on B, B is on A, and A is on the table." This makes some intuitive sense—the fact that a fluent f is affected by the action a in the situation s should depend not on what s happens to be called, but should instead depend on the set of fluents f' for which $\texttt{holds}(f',s)$ is true.

14.4 SEARCH IN PLANNING

Having solved all of these formal problems in some way, we now need to deal with the huge *size* of the planning search space. In this section, we continue by examining some of the ideas that have been suggested in this regard.

14.4.1 Hierarchical Planning

Imagine that I am trying to get from Stanford to MIT.[29] I construct the tentative plan of driving to San Francisco airport, then flying to Logan (the airport in Boston), and finally driving from Logan to MIT.

The actions in this tentative plan aren't things I can execute directly; driving to San Francisco will involve getting to my car, starting it, and following some route between my starting location and the airport. Why, then, do I bother to form the three-step "high-level" plan that focuses the rest of my analysis?

The reason is exactly that: The high-level problem is far easier to solve than the low-level version that I must eventually confront. Once I have solved the high-level problem, my efforts when working on the low-level one will be simplified by my ability to focus on the intermediate goals of getting to and from the San Francisco and Boston airports.

This is a very general phenomenon; we form hierarchical plans all the time. In the example we are considering, my subplan of starting my car is itself hardly a primitive action. I will need to get the keys out of my pocket, insert them into the ignition, depress the clutch, turn the key, and so on. Depressing the clutch involves moving my foot to a certain location and then exerting a downward force.

One way to think of hierarchical planning is that we first solve an easier, more abstract planning problem and then use the solution to focus our attempts to solve the original problem. As we've described it, the "easy problem" is constructed by using a set of high-level actions to achieve our goal instead of doing so using the primitive actions allowed in our domain. Since the difficulty of a planning problem can be expected to be exponential in the depth of the search (that is, the length of the plan constructed) and each high-level action subsumes a sequence of low-level ones, the high-level plan should be short and constructing it should be easy.

Unfortunately, it is not always possible to flesh out the high-level plan to produce a viable low-level one. In our travel example, my car might be in the shop, there may be no available flights from San Francisco to Logan, or I may be unable to rent a car on my arrival in Boston. Note that the difficulties here are not things that will prevent my *executing* my low-level plan, but problems that will prevent my developing that plan in the first place. If I know my car to be in the shop, I will have difficulty finding a plan for driving to the airport. If there are no flights to Logan or no cars available in Boston, my travel agent will presumably inform me of the difficulty and I will need to modify my high-level plan in some way.

In some cases, it *is* possible to guarantee that the high-level plan has a low-level instantiation; we've already seen examples of this in our discussion of macro operators in Chapter 4. When we decide to flip two of

29 Why anyone would actually want to *do* this escapes me, but imagine it nevertheless.

the cubies in Rubik's cube en route to a solution, we know for sure that it will be possible to do so.

Finally, where does the high-level description of a domain come from in the first place? It can either be supplied by the user of the system or, more interestingly, be developed automatically. There are at least three ways in which this can be done.

In the first approach, the system can construct high-level actions by simply dropping some of the preconditions of lower-level ones. In the blocks world, perhaps we should first find a plan for achieving our goal by assuming that we can move blocks even if their intended destinations are not clear. After all, we can always clear these destinations off, and making this assumption will undoubtedly simplify the problem. This is the approach taken by an early hierarchical planner known as ABSTRIPS, but it appears not to be terribly useful on realistic problems.

The second approach involves examining previous planning efforts in order to identify "chunks" of low-level actions that should be grouped as potential high-level actions in future planning; this is the approach taken by a general problem-solving system called SOAR. However, since this is more a learning issue than a planning one *per se*, we will defer its discussion to the next chapter.

The final possibility is to use default information that is already in our domain to describe the high-level plan. Perhaps we have a default saying that one can typically drive anywhere close or fly between any two large cities; it is now this information that tentatively validates our high-level plan for getting to MIT.

14.4.2 Subgoal Ordering and Nonlinear Planning

Another simple blocks-world problem appears in Figure 14.2, where the goal is to get *A* on *B* and *B* on *C*. Which of these goals should we achieve first?

To a human planner, it's obvious that we have to get *B* on *C* first; towers have to be built from the bottom up. But an automated planner has no such intuition and is as likely to begin by putting *A* on *B* as otherwise.

To see why this is such a problem, imagine that we are trying to construct a larger tower involving the blocks $b_0, \ldots, b_n$. Of the $n!$ possible orders in which we might try to achieve the n subgoals of getting b_{i-1} onto b_i,

FIGURE 14.2 Get *A* on *B* and *B* on *C*

only one will be satisfactory. Is there any way to reduce the size of the search space so that these $n!$ attempts are not examined separately?

There is. Suppose that instead of viewing a "plan" as an ordered sequence of actions, we view it as a *partially* ordered sequence of actions. We don't commit to putting b_2 on b_3 before putting b_1 on b_2 until we realize that is the order in which these subgoals need to be achieved.

In more general terms, suppose that we know that our plan will include the two actions a_1 and a_2. We do not commit to either of these actions being before the other until information about the domain forces us to do so. In this particular example, a_1 would be the action of putting A on B, and a_2 the action of putting B on C. When we realize that the success of a_1 will cause the failure of one of the preconditions to a_2 (that B be clear), we add a constraint that the action a_1 must follow a_2 in the final plan. (Each of these might still be unordered with respect to a third action a_3, of course.)

Completely ordered plans are often called *linear* plans; the approach in which actions are initially unordered and constraints are established to order them is known as *nonlinear* planning.

The most successful nonlinear planning system is David Wilkins's SIPE. Unlike many other general-purpose planning systems, SIPE has been used in a practical application—the control of an Australian beer factory. SIPE's ability to handle the complexities involved in this application are a testimony to the power of nonlinear planning.[30]

In spite of the practical success of nonlinear planning systems, there are some important theoretical arguments against them. The first is that determining the consequences of a nonlinear plan can be NP-hard.

To see this, suppose that we have a nonlinear plan involving n actions and constraints among them. Of the $n!$ possible "linearizations" of the nonlinear plan, some of these will comply with the constraints and others won't. In general, if we want to know if some fluent f holds after the nonlinear plan has been executed, there is no more efficient approach than to work our way through each of the $n!$ possible linearizations and see if f holds after each one that complies with the partial ordering information.

The trade-off here is actually pretty obvious: Nonlinear plans are more expensive to compute with than their linear counterparts, but using them reduces the size of the search space. Whether or not they lead to overall performance improvements is in some sense an experimental question, and Wilkins's success with SIPE shows that the answer is yes in at least one interesting application.

In actuality, however, the technique people appear to use to reduce the size of the planning search space involves not nonlinearity but our ability

30 In order to get SIPE to work in this domain, Wilkins had to develop a parallel version of his planner, which he tentatively named P-SIPE. Wilkins's superiors at SRI, however, realized that "pissup" was Australian slang for a wild, drunken party, and they demanded that the system be called SIPE II instead.

to *debug* plans that fail for some reason. When we are unable to achieve our goal in Figure 14.2 of getting *A* on *B* and *B* on *C* by getting *A* on *B* first, we analyze the *reason* for the failure and use this to focus our subsequent planning efforts.

Planners need to debug the plans they construct whether they are linear or not—when it comes time to execute a plan in a real environment, environmental uncertainty will occasionally cause the plan to fail for an unexpected reason. It will almost invariably be more efficient to address the difficulty by debugging the original plan than by constructing a new one from scratch. Just as nonlinear planners appear to be more effective in practice than their linear counterparts, it seems likely that debugging planners will be more efficient still.

14.4.3 Subgoal Interaction and the Sussman Anomaly

The final problem we will discuss is shown in Figure 14.3; the initial situation is the same as that in some of our earlier examples, but the goal is now to get *B* on *C* and *A* on *B*. Which of these two goals are we to achieve first?

In fact, we can't achieve *either* subgoal first. If we begin by putting *B* on *C*, we'll have to take it off in order to get *A* onto *B*. If we begin by putting *A* on *B*, we'll have to take *it* off in order to get *B* onto *C*. The best plan here is to interleave the plan for getting *B* onto *C* (put it there) with the plan for getting *A* onto *B* (move *C* out of the way and then put *A* on *B*).

This problem is known as the *Sussman anomaly*. In general, it seems that subgoals *do* interact; when they do, we have no trouble achieving our overall goals by interleaving the plans for the subgoals. Automated planners need to behave similarly.

14.5 IMPLEMENTING A PLANNER

The fact that we have described planning in terms of problems as opposed to solutions may have given you the wrong impression; although planning is hard, progress is being made. So I'd like to end this chapter by describing a working planner in some detail. The system we'll present is not declar-

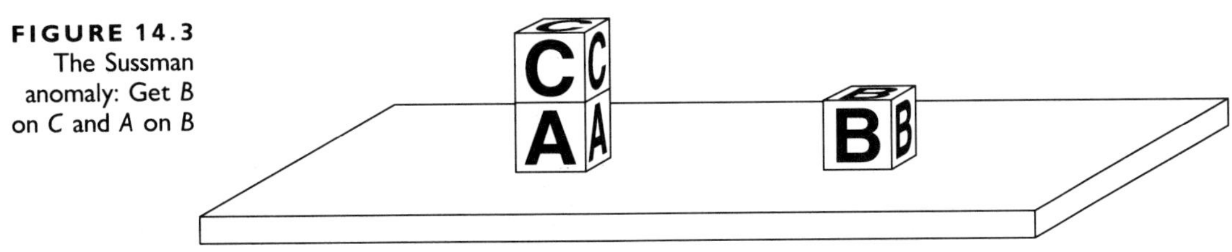

FIGURE 14.3 The Sussman anomaly: Get *B* on *C* and *A* on *B*

ative, or nonlinear, or any of those other fancy things, but it does get the job done.

Following STRIPS, we will describe an action a in terms of a set of preconditions $P(a)$, an add list $A(a)$, and a delete list $D(a)$. A situation S will be described simply by listing those fluents that hold in S. We can now make the following definitions:

DEFINITION 14.5.1 *Given a situation* S *and an action* a, *we will say that the action* succeeds *in that situation if and only if* $P(a) \subseteq S$, *so that every precondition to the action holds in the situation. The* result of executing an action a *that succeeds in the situation* S *is given by the situation*

$$\texttt{result}(a,S) = [S - D(a)] \cup A(a)$$

Given an action sequence $a_1, \ldots, a_n$ *and a situation* S, *we set* $S_0 = S$ *and* $S_i = \texttt{result}(a,S_{i-1})$ *for* $i = 1, \ldots, n$ *so that situation* n *is the result of applying action* a_n *in situation* $n - 1$. *We will say that the* action sequence succeeds *if every individual action succeeds, and that the* action sequence achieves the goal g *if* $g \in S_n$.

Our domain will be the blocks world as we have described it earlier in this chapter. There are two actions in this domain, `move` and `move-to-table`. The action `move(x,y,z)` moves the block x from the location y onto the block z; `move-to-table(x,y)` moves the block x from y onto the table. Here are the formal descriptions:

a	$P(a)$	$A(a)$	$D(a)$

`move(x,y,z)`	`clear(x)`
	`loc(x,y)`
	`clear(z)`
		`loc(x,z)`
		`clear(y)`
			`loc(x,y)`
			`clear(z)`

`move-to-table(x,y)`	`clear(x)` `loc(x,y)`	`loc(x,table)` `clear(y)`	`loc(x,y)`

Note the compromises we have had to make in order to use our simple STRIPS-like language: We have had to split the `move` action into two subactions, since the table is always assumed to be clear and there is no third precondition to the action of moving a block to the table. We have had to specify the blocks' starting locations as well as their ending locations, so that we know to include `clear(y)` in the add list of `move(x,y,z)`, saying that y will be clear after x is moved away. This change has also forced us to add additional preconditions to the `move` actions, saying that the blocks really are starting out where we expect them to be. Finally, we have had to treat `clear` explicitly, as opposed to defining a clear block as one with nothing else on it and letting the system deduce information about `clear` as a ramification of the `move` actions.

Rather than present an algorithm for planning using these ideas, we'll describe the search space associated with planning problems; the ideas of Part II can then be used to construct an implementation.

The nodes in our search space will be labelled with goals that our planner has yet to achieve; we'll construct our action sequences beginning with the last action (which presumably achieves our goal) and working backwards, adding actions that achieve the preconditions of later ones.

It is now tempting to describe the planning search space by labelling a node with a partial action sequence $\mathcal{A}$ and a set Z of still-to-be-achieved goals. Here is a more formal description:

DEFINITION 14.5.2 *Given an initial situation S and a set G of goals, the* STRIPS search space *associated to S and G is as follows:*

1. *The root node of the search space is ([],G), where the first element of the pair is an action sequence (empty, since we haven't thought of any actions yet) and the second element is a list of goals that have yet to be achieved.*
2. *A node $([a_1,\ldots,a_n],Z)$ is a goal node if $Z \subseteq S$, so that all of the remaining goals hold in the initial situation.*
3. *Given a node $([a_1,\ldots,a_n],Z)$, let a be any action that adds an element of Z, so that $A(a) \cap Z \neq \emptyset$. Then a successor node to $([a_1,\ldots,a_n],Z)$ is the node*

$$([a,a_1,\ldots,a_n],Z - A(a) \cup P(a))$$

where a has been added to the front of the action sequence, the goals that a adds have been removed from Z and a's preconditions have been added to Z as new subgoals.

As an example, we show in Figure 14.4 a solution to the planning

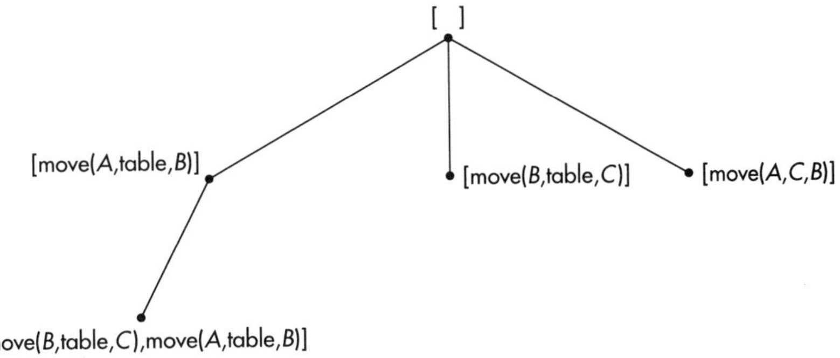

FIGURE 14.4 Solving the problem of Figure 14.2

problem of Figure 14.2. (In the interests of conserving space, only the actions are shown.) We begin with the root node

([],{loc(*A*,*B*),loc(*B*,*C*)})

Now adding the action move(*A*,table,*B*) gives us the node

([move(*A*,table,B)],{clear(*A*),clear(*B*),loc(*A*,table),loc(*B*,*C*)})

where the goal loc(*A*,*B*) has been replaced with subgoals that are the preconditions to the move action. Next, we generate the node

([move(*B*,table,C),move(*A*,table,B)],
{clear(*A*),clear(*B*),clear(*C*),loc(*A*,table),loc(*B*,table)})

in a similar way; since all of the new subgoals actually hold in the initial situation, we return [move(*B*,table,*C*),move(*A*,table,*B*)] as a solution to our planning problem.

Unfortunately, Definition 14.5.2 isn't right! In Figure 14.5, we show another "solution" to this problem that begins by putting *A* on *B*, and then puts *B* on *C* afterwards—but this plan won't work, since the action of moving *B* to *C* will fail if *A* is on top of *B*.

Our description of the problem has failed to take into account the fact that actions also delete things; one of the things they may delete is a solved precondition to another action. We need to modify Definition 14.5.2 as follows:

DEFINITION 14.5.3 *Given an initial situation S and a set G of goals, the* STRIPS *search space associated to S and G is as follows:*

1. *The root node of the search space is ([],G).*
2. *A node* $([a_1,\ldots,a_n],Z)$ *is a goal node if* $Z \subseteq S$*, so that all of the remaining goals hold in the initial situation.*

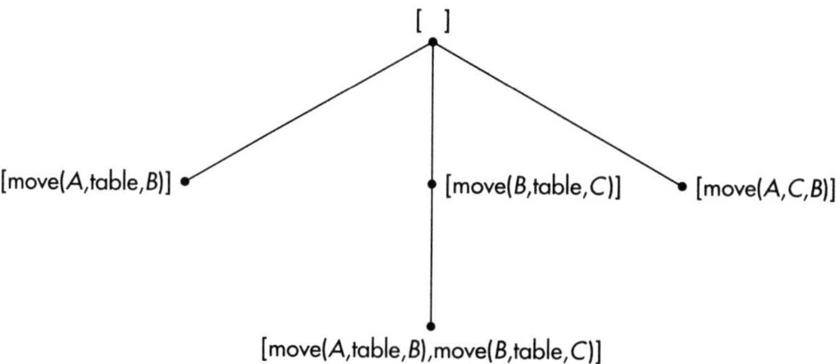

FIGURE 14.5 Not solving the problem of Figure 14.2

3. *Given a node* ($[a_1, \ldots, a_n], Z$)*, let* a *be any action that adds an element of* Z*, so that* $A(a) \cap Z \neq \emptyset$, ***and deletes no goal in*** Z, ***so that*** $D(a) \cap Z = \emptyset$. *Then a successor node to* ($[a_1, \ldots, a_n], Z$) *is the node*

$$([a, a_1, \ldots, a_n], Z - A(a) \cup P(a))$$

where a *has been added to the front of the action sequence, the goals that* a *adds have been removed from* Z *and* a*'s preconditions have been added to* Z.

The effect of the change is to disallow any action that would delete a goal g that we were hoping to achieve earlier in the action sequence (that is, later in the planning process). If we want to take such an action, it must be followed by another action that achieves g.[31]

Given this change, we can no longer "derive" the bad plan of moving *A* onto *B* and then *B* onto *C*. If we make move (*B*, table, *C*) the final action of the plan, we get the search node

$$([\texttt{move}(B,\texttt{table},C)],\{\texttt{clear}(B),\texttt{clear}(C),\texttt{loc}(B,\texttt{table}),\texttt{loc}(A,B)\}) \tag{14.10}$$

and now we cannot add the action `move(`*A*,*B*`)`, since this deletes the subgoal `clear(`*B*`)`. Expanding the node (14.10) will therefore require that we add an explicit action that takes place after move (*A*, table, *B*) and that clears off the top of *B*.

14.6 FURTHER READING

Planning is one of the most active research areas in AI and the amount of material published about it is enormous. Let me see if I can give you pointers to some of the more interesting stuff.

There are two areas of planning that have been left fairly untreated in this chapter: reactive planning and case-based planning. Reactive planners do indeed reduce planning to classification by computing in advance correct responses to any situation in which the planner might find itself; to act, we simply look up our current situation in the database and execute the associated action.

The advantage of this approach is that it is possible to bound the amount of time the system will spend thinking about a planning problem (it's just a database lookup); this is important if the system is to function in the real

31 In terms of conventional planning terminology, the troublesome action is said to *clobber* the goal g. The subsequent action that reinstates g is called a *white knight* [Chapman 1987].

world. The disadvantage is that the number of possible situations is simply too large for these ideas to be useful in practice. A debate on this question can be found in *AI Magazine* [Ginsberg 1989, and the replies to it]; I believe that the view these days is that although some measure of reactivity is needed by intelligent agents, complete prior analysis of all possible situations is impractical in fielded systems.

Related to reactive planning is *dynamic* planning, which concerns the problem of constructing plans that work in environments that change in unpredictable ways (as all real environments do, when it comes right down to it). GUARDIAN, for example, is a system that monitors critically ill medical patients [Hayes-Roth *et al.* 1989]; PHOENIX constructs plans for dealing with fires in Yellowstone National Park [Cohen *et al.* 1989]. TILEWORLD is a program that provides a dynamic testbed environment for researchers in this area [Pollack and Ringuette 1990].

In case-based planning [Hammond 1990], the basic idea is to respond to a planning problem by retrieving a solution from a library of "canned" plans. Although not exactly applicable to the situation in which the planner finds itself, the retrieved plan should at least be close, and is then debugged using domain-specific information to make it usable in the situation that is actually at hand. The problem is that plan debugging is hard and there has been very little progress made on it, at least so far.

With regard to the ideas that we have presented: The situation calculus was introduced by McCarthy and Hayes [1969] and Green [1969]. The frame problem first appears in McCarthy and Hayes [1969]; the qualification problem in McCarthy [1977]. The ramification problem has been around for a while, but is first referred to by this name by Finger [1987]. The blocks world was introduced in Terry Winograd's Ph.D. thesis, later republished [Winograd 1972].

The original reference for STRIPS is Fikes and Nilsson [1971]. The SIPE system, which we also discussed in the text, is described in more detail by Wilkins [1988]; other planning systems of considerable theoretical importance are TWEAK [Chapman 1987] and the work of McAllester and Rosenblitt [1991], both of which present clear formal descriptions of conditions under which fluents hold in nonlinear plans. All of these systems are nondeclarative.

A variety of authors have recently attempted to provide monotonic descriptions of action; the most important papers here are those by Elkan [1990], Reiter [1991], and Schubert [1990]. The basic idea in all of this work is to write monotonic axioms of the form, "If a fluent f has changed value, then an action a must have occurred." It is then possible to reason from the fact that a did not occur to the conclusion that f is unchanged.

Nonmonotonic descriptions of action currently seem the most promising; there was an enormous flurry of activity in the late 1980s when Hanks and McDermott [1987] introduced the "Yale shooting problem," which we describe in Exercise 5 at the end of this chapter. The solution sketched in the text is due to Baker [1991].

Hierarchical planners are introduced in Fikes *et al.* [1972]; recent work on the automatic construction of these hierarchies can be found in Knoblock [1990] and Ginsberg [1991b].

Finally, nonlinear planning began with Sacerdoti's work on NOAH [Sacerdoti 1977], and has continued with TWEAK and SIPE. It is shown in Dean and Boddy [1988b] that determining whether or not a fluent holds after the execution of a nonlinear plan can be exponentially difficult; a variety of authors (SIPE is typical) have dealt with this in practice by restricting the temporal language somewhat so that this determination can be made quickly. A general comparison of the efficiencies of linear and nonlinear planning can be found in Minton *et al.* [1991]. The Sussman anomaly first appears in Sussman [1975].

14.7 EXERCISES

1. Emanuel Lasker was the world chess champion from 1894–1921. When asked how many moves deep he looked when searching for a move, he replied, "Only one. But it's always the best move." Discuss this in the context of planning, game tree search, and classification problems.

2. In the text, we described as a disadvantage of reification the fact that one had to be careful not to use logical operators on the reified predicates; an advantage is that one can quantify over these predicates. What are the analogs of these observations in the reification examples of the previous chapter?

3. Prove that the number of subaction types needed by a STRIPS description of action can grow exponentially with domain size.

4. (a) What axioms are needed to describe the initial situation s_0 that appears in Figure 14.1?
   (b) Prove (14.8) from these axioms and others in the text.
   (c) What similar axioms would you need to conclude that C is not clear after moving B to C in Figure 14.1?

5. Consider a domain that contains two actions, `shoot` and `wait`. There are also two fluents, `loaded` and `alive`. The first of these means that our gun is loaded; the second means that our intended victim is alive.

If the gun is loaded, then shooting it has the intended effect:

$$\texttt{holds(loaded,}s\texttt{)} \rightarrow \neg\texttt{holds(alive,result(shoot,}s\texttt{))}$$

Now suppose that s_0 is an initial situation in which the gun is loaded:

$$\texttt{holds(loaded,}s_0\texttt{)}$$

(a) Assuming that we use the default description of the frame axiom given by (14.9), does

$$\neg\texttt{holds(alive,result(shoot,result(wait,}s_0\texttt{)))}$$

hold in every extension of the default theory? (Hint: You may want to use the result of Exercise 9 in Chapter 11.)

(b) Does this seem intuitively reasonable?

This problem is known as the *Yale shooting problem* and first appeared in Hanks and McDermott [1987].

6. **Conditional planning**

(a) Suppose that instead of a move action, we have two actions `stack`(x,y) and `flip`(x,y). The action `stack` has no preconditions and results in a situation in which either x is on y or vice versa:

$$\texttt{holds[loc(}x,y\texttt{),result(stack(}x,y\texttt{),}s\texttt{)]}$$
$$\vee\ \texttt{holds[loc(}y,x\texttt{),result(stack(}x,y\texttt{),}s\texttt{)]}$$

Meanwhile, the action `flip`(x,y) flips the blocks x and y provided that x is on y when it is attempted:

$$\texttt{holds[loc(}x,y\texttt{),}s\texttt{]} \rightarrow \texttt{holds[loc(}y,x\texttt{),result(flip(}x,y\texttt{),}s\texttt{)]}$$

Prove (using resolution or some other means) that there is a plan to get A onto B. What does this plan correspond to in more conventional terms?

(b) I live in a house with two bathrooms; suppose that a terrorist has planted a bomb in one of them. If I flush the toilet with the bomb in it, the bomb will be defused. I don't have time to flush both toilets, though; if I guess wrong, a timer on the bomb in the other toilet will cause it to explode.

i. Prove that there is a plan consisting of a single action that will defuse the bomb.

ii. Does the plan seem reasonable?

7. **Hierarchical planning and island-driven search.** Island-driven search was discussed in Exercise 11 in Chapter 3.

   (a) Show that hierarchical planning can be viewed as a special case of island-driven search.

   (b) We sometimes do not know that it will be possible to extend a plan from one level of the hierarchy to the next lower one. Is hierarchical planning likely to be computationally effective in these situations?

   (c) Give an example of a planning domain that shows this sort of behavior.

8. **Conjunctive subgoals and the frame axiom.** This problem concerns the blocks world as described by (14.6) and the (admittedly flawed!) frame axiom (14.9).

   (a) In the initial situation s_0, there are three blocks, A, B, and C. They are all clear and are located at locations l_1, l_2, and l_3. Describe this situation using the `holds` predicate.

   (b) Suppose that our goal is to get A on B and B on C. Not realizing that the subgoals interact, we try putting A on B first; it is no longer possible to put B on C.

      i. What axiom do we need to conclude that the second `move` action will fail after we put A on top of B?

      ii. Given the above axiom, what crucial instance of the frame axiom is violated for the action of moving A onto B in the initial situation s_0?

   (c) In general, suppose that we have a conjunctive goal $g_1 \wedge g_2$, and know that we can achieve g_1 because the preconditions $p_1, \ldots, p_m$ hold, and we can achieve g_2 because the preconditions $q_1, \ldots, q_n$ hold. If the action sequence that achieves g_1 is $a_1, \ldots, a_k$, what frame assumptions do we need to make in order to be able to conclude that we can still achieve g_2 after achieving g_1?

9. Imagine that we are trying to bolt two metal parts together and that they need to be positioned precisely relative to one another. If we put the bolt in and tighten it, we will be unable to position the parts after doing so; if we position the pieces first, we won't have a free hand to insert the bolt.

   The typical solution to this is to insert the bolt and tighten it only enough to produce some friction between the parts being connected. They are then positioned carefully and the bolt is tightened the rest of the way.

   What does all of this have to do with the Sussman anomaly?

10. Use Definition 14.5.3 to write a program that accepts as inputs a situation S, a group of action descriptions, an action sequence $\mathcal{A}$, and a

FIGURE 14.6 The fruitcake problem

goal g and determines whether or not the sequence succeeds in achieving the goal. Use the implementation to check a plan that solves the problem in Figure 14.6.

11. In the description of action in Section 14.5, why couldn't we have added `clear(table)` to our domain description and avoided splitting the `move` action in two?

12. Suppose that we were interested in constructing plans forward from the initial situation, instead of backward from our goal. In other words, a planning problem would consist of an initial situation S and a goal g; a node in the search space would be simply a successful action sequence

$$\mathcal{A} = [a_1, \ldots, a_n]$$

The successors to this node are obtained simply by adding a new action to the end of $\mathcal{A}$, where the new action is required to be successful in the situation resulting from executing the sequence $\mathcal{A}$ in the original situation S. A node is a goal node if the associated action sequence succeeds in achieving the goal g.

(a) What is the root node of the search space in this description?

(b) Describe the search space used by this approach to solve the problem appearing in Figure 14.2.

(c) How does the branching factor for this approach compare with that of an approach based on the goal-directed ideas of Section 14.5?

13. (a) Show in detail the search space the planner of Section 14.5 would use to solve the Sussman anomaly shown in Figure 14.3.

    (b) Show a path from the root node to the goal in the search space associated with Figure 14.6.

14. Suppose that the root node in the search space of Definition 14.5.3 is $([], G)$ and that we manage to reach the goal node $(\mathcal{A}, Z)$. Prove that the action sequence $\mathcal{A}$ is successful and that it achieves each goal $g \in G$.

15. (a) Find a goal G and an action sequence $\mathcal{A}$ that achieves it but does not appear in the search space given by Definition 14.5.3.

    (b) Prove that if $\mathcal{A}$ is an action sequence that achieves a goal G, there is always some subsequence of $\mathcal{A}$ that achieves G and does appear in the search space given by Definition 14.5.3.

16. Implement a planner based on the ideas of Section 14.5 and use it to solve some of the blocks-world problems we have described.

CHAPTER

15

LEARNING

The status of learning in AI is like the status of planning, only more so: The problems are harder and recognized solutions are rarer. In an attempt to make some sense of this AI subfield, I am going to break learning down into *discovery learning* and *generalization learning*. By *discovery learning*, I mean the kind of learning that goes on when one leaps to a bold new conclusion, like the physical-symbol system hypothesis. By *generalization learning*, I mean extrapolation from existing information, as in the conclusion that a particular large yellow mushroom is poisonous because all of the large yellow mushrooms you've seen in the past have been.

Generalization learning can be broken into two subtypes. I will call generalization learning that is logically valid *deductive* generalization learning. As an example, suppose that I'm trying to drive to a friend's house; I've never been there before, and a route that looks good on the map turns out not to work because one of the roads is one way. The next time I visit my friend, I shouldn't try to take that route again; I can deduce that the road will still be one way and I'll have the same problem as last time.

Most instances of generalization learning are not deductive, however; consider the mushroom example mentioned earlier. Nondeductive generalization learning is called *inductive*. In this chapter, we will examine each of these approaches to learning.

Deductive or not, all learning is a form of inference—the aim is to start with information about our domain, and to then extend that information in some way. We spent most of Parts III and IV discussing inference of various forms; learning is yet another example. The fact that most learning is nondeductive gives it quite a different flavor from our earlier discussions, but it is inference nevertheless.

15.1 DISCOVERY LEARNING

Roughly speaking, there has been only one successful AI program that attempted to learn new things by discovering them. It's a fairly old piece of work, but an important one; the program was written by Doug Lenat as his doctoral thesis at Stanford, and was called AM.

The inputs to AM were two things: first, a description of some concepts of set theory, in the form of LISP functions that implemented them. AM's initial information included descriptions of things like set union and intersection, the empty set, and so on.

AM's other input was information about "how to do mathematics" that Lenat gleaned from George Polya's book *How To Solve It* (and other sources). An example of the information supplied to AM was that if you had decided that $f(x,y)$ was an interesting function of two arguments, and the arguments could be equal, then the function $f(x,x)$ was likely to be an interesting function of a single argument. Thus if the program managed to "invent" the operation of addition and decided that it was interesting, the function $x + x$ was likely to be an interesting function of a single argument. The hope was that this sort of a rule would lead AM to invent multiplication once it had found addition.

AM's purpose was to develop interesting mathematical concepts, and it did just that. In fact, given just the above information, it "discovered":

- The integers. AM learned fairly early that it was possible to count the elements of any set, and decided that the image of this counting function—the integers—was an interesting set in its own right.

- Addition. Disjoint sets were interesting, and set union was interesting. The image of the operation "take the union of disjoint sets" under the counting function described above is addition.

- Multiplication. This was discovered using a rule such as the one presented above.

  At this point, Lenat stepped in and gave the machine more effective descriptions of addition and multiplication, which were previously described in terms of laborious set-theoretic manipulations. The effect of this was only to make the machine's subsequent deliberations more efficient; no change of substance took place.

- Prime numbers (!). Having discovered multiplication, the machine quickly discovered that numbers could be factored. It was most interested in numbers that had only one factor. The reason is that if there is an interesting function f and an interesting value y in the range of f, the set of x such that $f(x) = y$ is likely to be interesting. Take f to be the function "cardinality of the set of divisors" and y to be the interesting number 1.

  Of course, the only number with only one factor is 1 itself. But the integer 2 is almost as interesting as the integer 1, and the prime numbers are just those that have exactly two factors.

- Goldbach's conjecture (!!). The even number 28 can be written as the sum of the two primes 11 and 17. In 1742, Goldbach conjectured that all even numbers can be written as the sum of two primes; the conjecture is still unproven. AM made a similar conjecture.[32]

- Finally, AM inspired a "new" piece of mathematics. In addition to looking at primes—numbers with as few factors as possible—it examined numbers with as *many* factors as possible, saying that an integer k was "maximally divisible" if k had more factors than any integer less than k. The integer 12 is an example; it has six divisors (1, 2, 3, 4, 6, and 12) and there is no smaller number with as many. The set of maximally divisible numbers had not previously been considered by Lenat or other members of the AI community, although they had been investigated by the Indian mathematician Ramanujan.

What's more, AM did all this discovery overnight.

This is an enormously impressive piece of work, and AM is one of AI's most important early successes. AM is also an almost perfect example of experimental AI—Lenat's work involved producing a program that might exhibit interesting behavior. The program did just that, even surprising its developer in the process!

What lesson are we to learn from AM? What was the future of the program? Did it go on to rediscover all of modern mathematics? Were the ideas applied successfully in other domains? And why was AM so successful in the first place?

The reason that AM was so successful, it turns out, is because of the close connection between LISP and mathematics. In part, AM generated interesting functions by modifying the code describing functions that it already believed to be interesting.

This is hardly likely to be viable in general—arbitrarily modify one line in a long program and you are quite likely to end up with absolute nonsense. But the connection between LISP and mathematics is so tight that arbitrary modifications to very small LISP fragments (such as the ones with which AM was working) in fact *are* reasonably likely to produce interesting results. In some sense, AM was successful because it exploited the insights John McCarthy had when he developed the LISP language itself.

This observation has two obvious consequences. The first is that AM's ability to develop new mathematics should fall off rapidly as the concepts with which it is working become more involved—one is far less likely to be able to modify randomly a long piece of LISP code than a short one. And this has been observed—even with more computational resources, AM never discovered much more than what we have already reported.

32 AM didn't prove it, of course. In actuality, AM never proved anything—it simply noticed that many even numbers could be written as a sum of two primes and speculated from this that all even numbers could be. Lenat was interested in discovery, not automated proof theory.

The other consequence is that techniques such as those used by AM are unlikely to work outside of the domain of mathematics, since other domains are unlikely to exhibit a similarly close connection between bits of code and interesting ideas. This, too, has been observed in practice.

After his work on AM, Lenat went on to develop EURISKO, which was intended to be a generalized version of AM that would discover interesting ideas in arbitrary domains. But in spite of EURISKO's application to a variety of problems, its successes were quite limited.

As an example, EURISKO was used in an attempt to learn how to build three-dimensional integrated circuits. The program did manage to generate a very small integrated circuit on the surface of a Möbius strip, but other than that, it performed poorly.

EURISKO was also used to play a fleet management game, where each player is given a fixed budget and must then build a fleet of ships by providing specifications for the sizes, weaponry, and so on of the ships in the fleet. The fleets then do battle; if either destroys the other fleet, it is the victor.

EURISKO learned to play this game by playing against itself, and then entered the national tournament. It won! But it won by building "mosquito" ships—ships that were very small and fast, but had no armament at all. When EURISKO faced a superior opponent, all of its ships would be destroyed except the mosquito ships, which would continue buzzing around, incapable of doing any damage to the opposing fleet but saving EURISKO from loss because the rules stated that the opponent's fleet had to be destroyed entirely. It was this loophole in the rules that allowed EURISKO to perform so effectively.

There is something in common between this example and the original performance of AM—in both cases, the program needed to exploit a loophole of some sort in order to be successful. In EURISKO's case, the loophole was in the rules of the fleet game. In AM's case, it was in the close connection between LISP and mathematics. It appears that discovery learning that avoids these loopholes will rest on much deeper understandings of the domains being investigated.[33]

15.2 INDUCTIVE LEARNING

Because discovery learning seems to rest on such deep knowledge, the AI community's focus has been almost exclusively on generalization learning, and we turn to this now. We discuss inductive learning first, where a system tries to induce a general rule from a set of observed instances.

33 Alternatively, one can argue that *all* discovery learning—including that performed by humans—works by exploiting loopholes of one sort or another. This is not a debate I wish to consider here.

All problems of this sort have a similar flavor: The input to the program is a set of training instances (which can be selected either randomly or in an attempt to make the learning as effective as possible), and the output is expected to be a method of classifying subsequent instances. An example is that of the introduction to this chapter, where we discussed the possible classification of new mushrooms as edible or poisonous based on the mushrooms one has examined thus far. We will assume that the aim of inductive learning is to solve a binary classification problem—edible versus poisonous or something similar.

15.2.1 PAC Learning

Inductive learning can never be deductively sound. The fact that the last 10,000 yellow mushrooms we saw were all poisonous doesn't *prove* that the next yellow mushroom will be as well; it just gives us good inductive (as opposed to deductive) evidence that it will be. Given this observation, against what framework can we measure the performance of a system that learns inductively?

An answer to this question was developed by Valiant in 1984; he argued that a learning system should be *probably approximately correct*—PAC, for short.

Let's begin by describing what it means for a system to learn a rule that is approximately correct. Since the classification problem we're attempting to solve is binary, there is no way for the answer itself to be approximately correct—it's either right or wrong. The mushroom is either correctly classified or not.

Instead, we will say that a rule like, "All yellow mushrooms are poisonous," is *approximately correct* whenever it gets most of the problems right. A learned rule is approximately correct if it's completely right most of the time.

To make this precise, suppose that we denote by $p(x)$ the binary concept that we're trying to learn—edible or inedible, what have you. Let us also suppose that we denote by $\hat{p}(x)$ the approximation to p that the system actually learns. We will say that $\hat{p}$ is in *error* for x if p and $\hat{p}$ are different, so that `error`(x) is defined to be

$$[p(x) \wedge \neg\hat{p}(x)] \vee [\neg p(x) \wedge \hat{p}(x)]$$

Using $\equiv$ to denote the equivalence of two logical expressions, we can write this slightly more compactly as

$$\neg[p(x) \equiv \hat{p}(x)]$$

The probability that the learned rule is wrong is the same as the probability that `error`(x) is true, and we define:

DEFINITION 15.2.1 *A learned rule* $\hat{p}$ *will be called* approximately correct with accuracy ϵ *if and only if*

$$\text{pr(error)} \leq \epsilon \tag{15.1}$$

where pr *is the probability function.*

In order to use this rule, we need some way to evaluate the probability in (15.1). To do this, we will assume that the object x being classified is taken from some universe U (the set of all mushrooms, for example), and that each element $m \in U$ is chosen with some probability *pr(m)*. Assuming that

$$\sum_{m \in U} \text{pr}(m) = 1 \tag{15.2}$$

so that we know that we will pick some element of U, the probability in (15.1) can be rewritten as

$$\text{pr(error)} = \sum_{\{x|\text{error}(x)\}} \text{pr}(x) \tag{15.3}$$

where we have simply summed the probability over each x for which $\hat{p}$ is in error.

What about *probably* approximately correct? This just means that the system will probably learn rules that are approximately correct!

But probably relative to what? Think about it this way: Learning systems can typically be "fooled" by giving them anomalous training data. Maybe all the yellow mushrooms we looked at were poisonous even though most yellow mushrooms are actually fine. If all the system sees are poisonous yellow mushrooms, we shouldn't really fault it for drawing the wrong conclusion.

To address this problem, we will assume that the training examples used to develop our rules are chosen with the same probabilities that already appear in (15.2). We obtain training examples using the probabilities pr(m) and then apply some learning procedure L to arrive at a learned concept $\hat{p}$. We now make the following definition:

DEFINITION 15.2.2 *A learning procedure* L *is* probably approximately correct (PAC) with confidence δ *if, given a sequence of randomly selected training examples, the probability that* L *learns a rule that is not approximately correct is at most* δ. *Slightly more formally, we require that*

$$\text{pr}[\text{pr(error)} > \epsilon] < \delta$$

There is one additional idea used in PAC learning, and that is the notion of *bias*. In order to make the ideas that we've described more effective, most learning algorithms restrict their attention to learning concepts of a particular syntactic form. Version spaces, for example (an idea we will be examining shortly), assume that the idea is always to learn a conjunctive concept—perhaps big yellow mushrooms are poisonous and all others are not. Other systems make other assumptions. It is typically assumed that both the target concept p and the learned approximation $\hat{p}$ satisfy these syntactic restrictions.

The reason that these assumptions are important is that they restrict the size of the hypothesis space; it should be fairly clear that the larger the size of this space, the harder it will be to learn any particular instance of it. This particular form of bias is known as *restricted hypothesis space bias*.

Now consider the following learning algorithm: Given a set of m training instances, simply return any predicate $\hat{p}$ that both meets the hypothesis space restriction and is in agreement with the reported values on the training examples. Can such a learning procedure be PAC?

If our universe U is finite and m is infinitely large, the answer is obviously yes. For large m, the likelihood is that *all* of the elements of our learning universe U will appear as training examples, so that any predicate $\hat{p}$ that matches the training data will be equivalent to the target concept p. So the real question is: How large do we need m to be for this approach to be PAC?

To answer this, suppose that we have m training examples. What is the probability that we can find a concept $\hat{p}$ that is in accord with these training examples but *not* approximately correct?

To answer *this*, let q be a concept that is selected randomly subject to the condition that it not be approximately correct. The probability that q matches the training data is clearly no greater than $(1 - \epsilon)^m$, since the probability that q succeeds on a single training instance is at most $1 - \epsilon$. If it were any higher, q would be approximately correct.

Given the restricted hypothesis space bias with which we are working, suppose that there are a total of H possible concepts in our language. Since each one has probability at most $(1 - \epsilon)^m$ of both matching the data and not being approximately correct, it follows that the probability that there is *any* such q is bounded by

$$H\,(1 - \epsilon)^m$$

After all, if there is to be such a q it must be one of the H concepts and the probability of the big disjunction (one term for each concept) is bounded by the sum of the probabilities for each disjunct. We have therefore shown:

LEMMA 15.2.3 *Simply returning any sentence consistent with the training data is PAC whenever*

$$H\,(1-\epsilon)^m \leq \delta \tag{15.4}$$

We can rewrite (15.4) in a somewhat more convenient form. Solving for m, we get

$$m \geq \frac{\ln(\delta/H)}{\ln(1-\epsilon)} \tag{15.5}$$

where the sense of the inequality has changed because $\ln(1-\epsilon)$ is negative.

We now claim that

$$\ln(1-\epsilon) + \epsilon < 0 \tag{15.6}$$

for $0 < \epsilon < 1$. To see this, note that (15.6) evaluates to 0 if $\epsilon = 0$, and that the derivative of (15.6) with respect to ϵ is

$$-\frac{1}{1-\epsilon} + 1 = -\frac{\epsilon}{1-\epsilon}$$

which is clearly negative for $0 < \epsilon < 1$. (15.6) now follows, so that $\ln(1-\epsilon) < -\epsilon$ and (15.5) becomes

$$m \geq -\frac{\ln(\delta/H)}{\epsilon} = \frac{\ln(H/\delta)}{\epsilon}$$

THEOREM 15.2.4 *Simply returning any sentence consistent with the training data is PAC whenever*

$$m \geq \frac{\ln(H/\delta)}{\epsilon} \tag{15.7}$$

As an example, suppose that we use the bias that our target and learned concepts are conjunctions in a space with n predicates. Since there are 3^n such conjunctions (each predicate can appear either positively, negatively, or not at all), (15.7) tells us that any acceptable concept will be PAC if

$$m \geq \frac{n}{\epsilon} \ln \frac{3}{\delta}$$

There are two features of Theorem 15.2.4 and (15.7) that are especially important. The first is that it no longer mentions the probability distribution appearing in (15.3); (15.7) holds for *any* such distribution, provided that

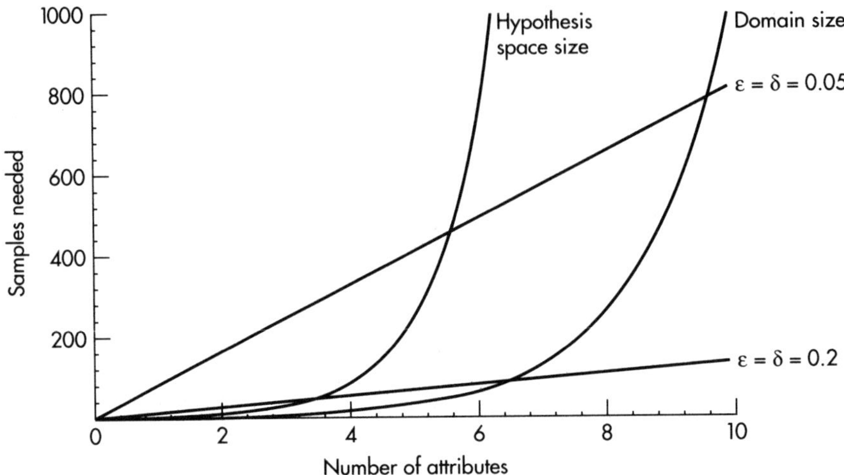

FIGURE 15.1 Number of examples needed in PAC learning

the same distribution is used to both define the error function and to select the training instances used by our learning procedure.

The second thing to realize is that the number of training instances required in Theorem 15.2.4 is growing logarithmically with the number of possible concepts. In Figure 15.1, we return to our conjunctive example, showing the number of possible elements in the domain (2^n, since each predicate can be either true or false), the number of possible concepts (3^n as discussed earlier), and the number of examples needed by a PAC learning system for various values of ϵ and δ.

15.2.2 Version Spaces

But how are we to actually find a concept that matches the data in the training set? It is fairly clear, after all, that examining every syntactically acceptable concept to see whether or not it is a match will in general be completely impractical.

In the case where the concept is assumed to be a conjunction of positive literals, the best-known algorithm for producing an acceptable concept is Mitchell's *version space* algorithm.[34] This algorithm in fact produces a description of all acceptable concepts; when there is only a single description left, we know that the concept has been identified precisely.

The version space idea is best described by an example. Suppose that we are working with a pack of cards, trying to identify some currently unknown conjunctive concept. The predicates in our language are things like "red," "black," "spade," "club," "even card," "odd card," and so on. The diamond eight is an even card, a red card, and a diamond. The training

34 By a conjunction of positive literals, we mean a concept that conjoins the available predicates without negating them. In the example to follow, "nonspades" would not be a legal concept.

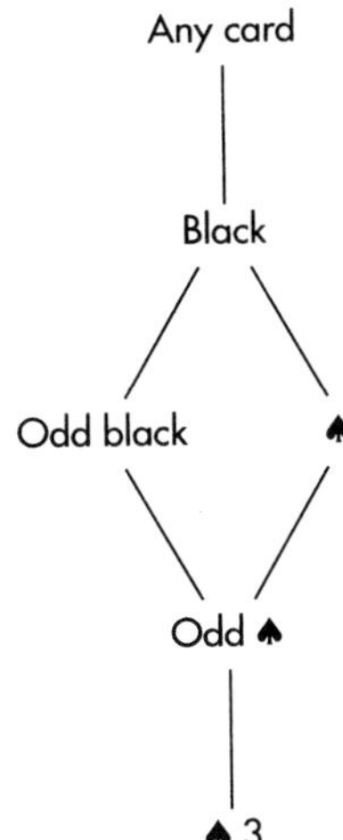

FIGURE 15.2 The specificity ordering on conjunctive concepts

set consists of a collection of cards; for each, we are told whether or not it is in the target set.

The key to the version space algorithm is the observation that the set of conjunctive concepts in this (or any other) domain can be partially ordered by specificity. Thus the concept "black" is less specific (that is, more general) than the concept "odd black" or "spade." The two concepts "odd black" and "spade" are incomparable with one another, since neither is more specific than the other. "Black" is more specific than "any card;" "any 7" is more specific than "any odd card." A partial diagram of the set of all concepts in our domain is shown in Figure 15.2, with less specific concepts higher on the page than more specific ones.

The version space algorithm deals with the training data incrementally. As it works, it retains a list of the most and least specific concepts that are consistent with all of the training instances that have been encountered thus far. Note, incidentally, that if p_1 and p_2 are two conjunctive concepts that are consistent with the data, the conjunction $p_1 \wedge p_2$ is more specific and consistent with the data as well. This means that the "most specific concept consistent with the data" is always unique.

As an example, suppose that our training data is as follows:

Card	In the target set?
A♠	yes
7♣	yes
8♡	no
9♣	yes
5♡	no
K◇	no
6◇	no
7♠	yes

Initially, the most specific concept consistent with the data is the empty set; the least specific concept is the set of all cards. But when we see that the A♠ is in the target set, the most specific concept is the A♠ alone (assuming that "ace" is in our language); the least specific concept is still that of all cards. When we learn that the 7♣ is in, the most specific concept is probably "odd black cards"; the least specific concept is unchanged.

Now we learn that the 8♡ is out. There are two least specific concepts consistent with this—all odd cards and all black cards. As we continue, observed positive instances cause the most specific concept to gradually become less specific (for example, odd black cards instead of only the spade ace). Negative instances cause the least specific concepts to become more specific. If the two sets meet, the result is guaranteed to be the target concept.

Note that the version space algorithm is also useful *before* the two sets meet. Even though the target concept has not been identified uniquely at this point, we have identified a group of concepts matching the training data, and can potentially apply Theorem 15.2.4 to conclude *inductively* that all of these concepts are PAC. When the algorithm has identified the concept precisely, we can conclude *deductively* that the target concept has been found, subject to the validity of our assumption that this concept is a conjunction of positive literals.

In a subtle way, the version space algorithm is tied to the assumption that the target concept is conjunctive. The reason is that disjunctive descriptions can all too frequently be obtained by simply disjoining the known positive instances of a class to get concepts such as "the A♠ or the 7♣ or the 9♣." If there are single terms in our language that allow us to form conjunctions independent of the syntactic bias with which we are working (for example, "the ace of spades" is really a conjunction of the concepts "ace" and "spades"), using the version space algorithm with a disjunctive bias is like attempting to use it with no bias at all. Our language itself appears to be biased in a way that encourages us to consider conjunctive concepts instead of disjunctive ones. And this seems reasonable: It's easier to "think about" conjunctive concepts than disjunctive ones. It's much easier to imagine a blond Republican than to imagine a generic member of the class of people who are either blond *or* Republicans.

15.2.3 Neural Networks

Let's look at another kind of restricted hypothesis space bias. Imagine that the argument x to our predicate is a single real number, and the bias we pick is to assume that $p(x)$ is of the form $x > c$ or $x < c$ for some constant c. By looking at the training data, we can try to pick c. We show a typical example in Figure 15.3, where the concept is all $x > 5.0$ and the indicated training instances are consistent with the hypothesis $x > c$ for any $c \in [4.2, 5.3)$.

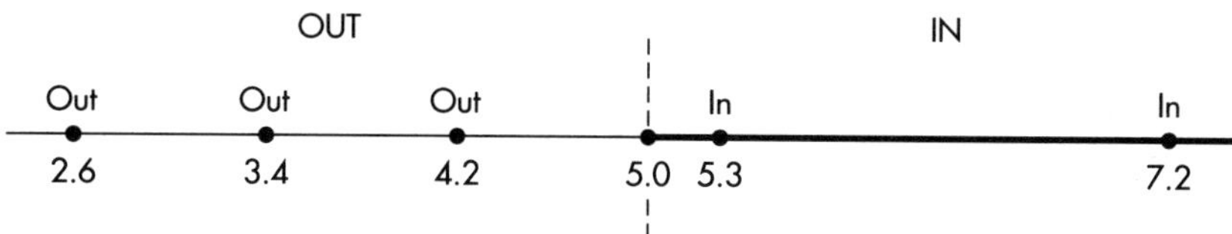

FIGURE 15.3 Learning an inequality

Even though the size of the hypothesis space (H in Theorem 15.2.4) is infinite, provided that we can bound the range of possible input values x, the m randomly selected training examples are likely to do a fairly good job of bracketing the actual transition point c, and an analog to Theorem 15.2.4 can be proven in this instance—it is possible to do PAC learning in this domain.

But what if instead of one feature, we have many? A similar idea can be applied in this case. Instead of dividing a line in two with the point c, we can divide a plane in two with a line. We can divide 3-space in two with a plane, and so on. An n-dimensional space can be split in half with an $n - 1$ dimensional hyperplane.

In general, we can model this geometric computation by describing the hyperplane in terms of n coordinates $(h_1, \ldots, h_n)$ and saying that a point $(x_1, \ldots, x_n)$ is to the "right" of the hyperplane if and only if

$$\sum_i x_i \cdot h_i > \theta \tag{15.8}$$

for some fixed θ. (There is some redundancy in this description; we can multiply both θ and all of the h_i by a positive constant without affecting (15.8).) In Figure 15.4, we have drawn a schematic representation of three inputs being processed in this way to produce a single output that is either 1 or 0 (depending on whether (15.8) holds or not, respectively).

Now suppose that we are trying to learn some function f, and that we assume that it has the specific form given by (15.8). This turns out to be a

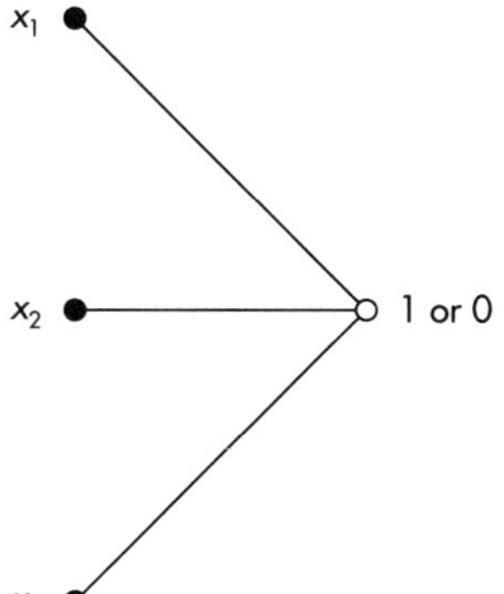

FIGURE 15.4 A single-layer neural network

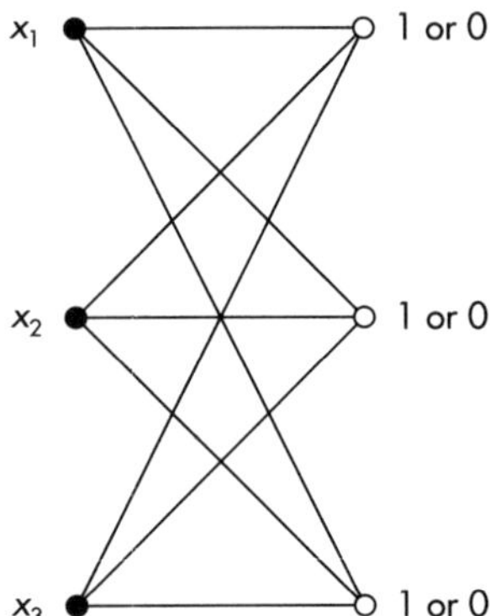

FIGURE 15.5 A more complicated network

substantial bias—there are many functions that cannot be approximated by learned functions of this form.

To get around this, suppose that we process our inputs not once, but many times, as shown in Figure 15.5. The results of the multiple computations can themselves be viewed as inputs to yet another computation of the form (15.8); we have drawn the result schematically in Figure 15.6.

It turns out that the difficulty is now addressed: Every function of multiple inputs *can* be approximated by a function of the form depicted in the figure. What's more, algorithms exist for learning the values to be used for the h_i's and θ's appearing in the various versions of (15.8) that are used in the computation.

So here is the question: Suppose that we have some difficult concept that we want to learn. Perhaps we want to decide whether or not the price of a stock will go up or down based on external information such as the company's profits, the state of the economy, and so on. Can we use a network such as that shown in Figure 15.6 to learn things such as this?

What a wonderful way this would be to solve all of AI's problems! Given sensory inputs, systems could simply learn to classify their potential

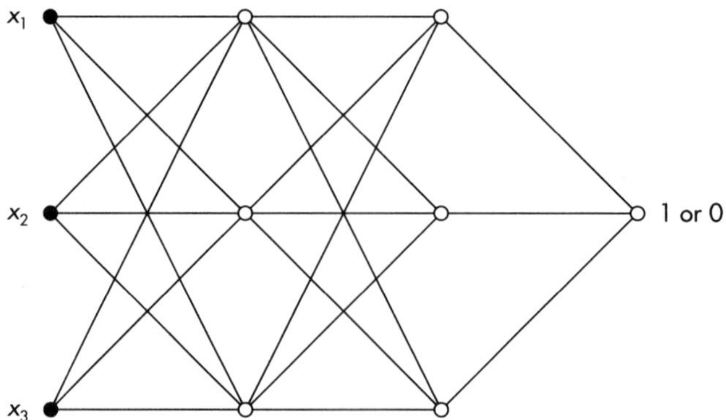

FIGURE 15.6 A three-layer neural network

actions as intelligent or not intelligent—and then act intelligently. Unfortunately, it is not obvious that this approach to AI is going to succeed—in principle it will, but making it work in practice is quite another matter. The dimensionality of the spaces involved may be impractically large, the time needed to learn the concepts may be effectively infinite, there is currently no way to decide how many internal layers a particular network needs, and so on.

What we've been discussing are what are called *neural networks*. The individual calculations such as that appearing in (15.8) and depicted by small circles in the figures are referred to as *thresholding elements*. Each thresholding element has been likened to a single neuron in the human brain, since there seems to be some biophysical analogy between the computation in (15.8) and the behavior of these neurons. (But the neural approach to intelligence will be in serious difficulty if we need 10^{12} thresholding elements!)

Neural networks are not a declarative approach to AI. If we use a large network to learn the concept of intelligence directly, there is no reason to believe that the values computed by the internal nodes will have any relationship to identifiable objects in the system's environment—and this is exactly the assumption of declarativism that we discussed in Section 1.1.2 at the beginning of this book. It is for this reason that we have chosen to devote so little space to neural networks in this text.

15.2.4 ID3

There is one other inductive learning technique that I would like to discuss before moving to deductive methods; it's an algorithm due to Quinlan and known as *ID3*.

The hypothesis space assumption made in ID3 is that the concept being learned can be expressed using a decision tree such as the one in Figure 15.7. In this tree, to classify a particular mushroom m, we begin by determining if m is large or not. If m is large, so that `large`(m) is true, we move to the left side of the tree; if `large`(m) is false, we move to the right side.

FIGURE 15.7
A decision tree

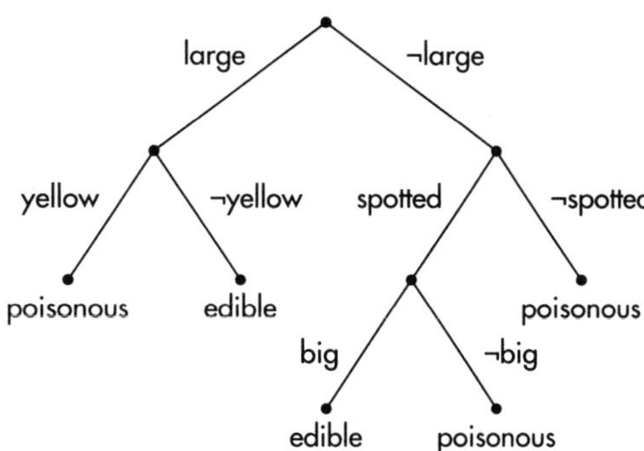

Then we consider either yellow(m) or spotted(m), and so on. When we eventually reach a leaf node of the tree, the mushroom will have been classified as poisonous or not. In the example of the figure, the decision tree is equivalent to rules of inference including

$$\texttt{large}(m) \wedge \texttt{yellow}(m) \rightarrow \texttt{poisonous}(m) \tag{15.9}$$

It is not hard to see that decision trees aren't really biased at all; any concept can be represented using one. The contribution made by ID3 is in realizing that there are effective ways to learn concepts in this form, just as version spaces are an effective means of learning conjunctive concepts. Once we pick the predicates used to label the arcs, it's pretty easy—fringe nodes are easily recognized because the training examples that get to such nodes either all satisfy the target concept or all fail to satisfy it.

In ID3, the arcs are labelled so that they do as effective a job as possible of splitting the training instances at each node into positive and negative instances. This means that we want each test to split the set of training instances roughly in half (if the target concept is "odd spades," there isn't much point in testing for just the spade 7), and we also want the tests to be relevant to the target concept (if the target concept is "odd cards," checking the color of a card is likely to split the training instances evenly but doesn't correlate with the concept we're trying to learn). Is there any way for us to define precisely which attribute should be checked at any point in the decision tree?

There is. The math is a little complicated, so bear with me while we work through some preliminaries.

Suppose that we have a set S of size $|S|$, and that we want to ask yes/no questions about a particular element to determine which it is. S might be the set of integers below 1000, and we would ask about a specific integer x, "Is it above 500? Above 750?" and so on. The minimum number of questions that we will need to ask is clearly $\log_2|S|$, since the best we can reliably do at any point is to split the set of remaining possibilities in half.

Now suppose that S is broken into two subsets, P and N, and I tell you which of these two subsets contains x. How many questions will you need now to determine the value of x?

If $x \in P$, you'll need $\log_2|P|$; if it's in N, you'll need $\log_2|N|$. Assuming that the probability that $x \in P$ is p_p and that $x \in N$ is p_n, the total number of questions you'll need to ask given the additional information about x is, on average

$$p_p \log_2|P| + p_n \log_2|N|$$

It follows from this that the number of questions you *save* by knowing whether x is in P or in N is

$$\log_2|S| - p_p \log_2|P| - p_n \log_2|N| \tag{15.10}$$

But now note that $p_p = |P|/|S|$, so that we can rewrite (15.10) as

$$\begin{aligned}\log_2(S) - p_p\log_2(p_p|S|) - p_n\log_2(p_n|S|) &= \log_2(S) - p_p\log_2(p_p) \\ &\quad - p_n\log_2(p_n) - (p_p + p_n)\log_2(|S|) \\ &= -p_p\log_2(p_p) - p_n\log_2(p_n) \quad (15.11)\end{aligned}$$

This expression will typically be less than one; we can always just ask, "Is x in P or not?" But if the sizes of P and N are vastly different, this would not be an effective use of one of our yes/no questions. (15.11) is telling us the "information content" of knowing whether something is in P or in N.

In a classification problem, of course, our goal is not to decide exactly which element of the set S is being considered, but only whether or not that element x is an instance of the target class T (that is, whether or not a particular mushroom is poisonous). Somewhat more formally, given that we can ask any of a variety of yes/no questions (large or small? yellow or not? ugly or pretty? and so on), we want to ask a question that does the best job of telling us whether or not x is in T. In other words, *we want to ask that question for which there is no expected value of the additional information about whether* x *is in* T.

Suppose, then, that we have a subset $U \subseteq S$; we can partition U into the two subsets $U_+ = U \cap T$ and $U_- = U - T$, where T is the target class. According to (15.11), the information gain if we now learn whether the object being considered is in T is given by

$$I_U = -\frac{|U_+|}{|U_+| + |U_-|}\log\frac{|U_+|}{|U_+| + |U_-|} - \frac{|U_-|}{|U_+| + |U_-|}\log\frac{|U_-|}{|U_+| + |U_-|} \quad (15.12)$$

Now suppose that we have a particular feature f, and the question we are considering asking is whether or not the instance x under consideration satisfies f. If our earlier questions have reduced the set of possible instances to a subset $V \subseteq S$, we will denote by V_{f+} the subset of V that satisfies the feature f, and by V_{f-} the subset of V that does not satisfy f. The expected information gain of learning whether or not x is in T after we use the feature f to split V into V_{f+} and V_{f-} is now given by

$$G_f = \frac{|V_{f+}|}{|V_{f+}| + |V_{f-}|} I_{V_{f+}} + \frac{|V_{f-}|}{|V_{f+}| + |V_{f-}|} I_{V_{f-}} \quad (15.13)$$

The first term corresponds to the information gain if we first learn that $x \in V_{f+}$ (weighted by the probability that this is what we learn when asking about f); the second term corresponds to the information gain if we first learn that $x \in V_{f-}$.

DEFINITION 15.2.5 *Suppose that we are constructing a decision tree, and have reached a node corresponding to a subset* V *of our entire domain. We will say that a feature* f *is* maximally discriminating *for a target concept* T *if it is the feature that minimizes the value of* G_f *appearing in (15.13).*

As an example (it's about time for one!), let's say that we're trying to figure out what question to ask first given that our target concept in the card domain is "odd black cards or the 2♡." The features we could ask about are color, suit, parity, or any rank. Let's consider just the two possible questions: Is the card red? and Is the card a three?

If we ask about the color, there is a 50 percent chance that it's red and a 50 percent chance that it's black. So (15.13) becomes

$$G_{\texttt{color}} = .5\, I_{V_{\texttt{red}}} + .5\, I_{V_{\texttt{black}}} \tag{15.14}$$

Of the twenty-six red cards, one (the 2♡) is in the target class and twenty-five are not. So the additional value of the information about whether or not x is in T is given by

$$I_{V_{\texttt{red}}} = -\frac{1}{26}\log\frac{1}{26} - \frac{25}{26}\log\frac{25}{26} = .235$$

Of the twenty-six black cards, fourteen (the odd ones) are in T and twelve aren't. So

$$I_{V_{\texttt{black}}} = -\frac{14}{26}\log\frac{14}{26} - \frac{12}{26}\log\frac{12}{26} = .996$$

Combining this with (15.14), we get

$$G_{\texttt{color}} = .615$$

If we ask about the card being a three, (15.14) becomes

$$G_3 = \frac{1}{13} I_{V_3} + \frac{12}{13} I_{V_{\neg 3}}$$

Of the four threes, two (the black ones) are in T and 2 are not. This means that $I_{V_3} = 1$. Of the forty-eight non-threes, thirteen are in the set (the twelve remaining odd black cards and the 2♡) and the rest are not. This leads to $I_{V_{\neg 3}} = .843$, so that

$$G_3 = .855$$

and we see from this that asking about the color is more effective than asking if the card is a three. This is as it should be—asking about the color goes a long way toward deciding if the card is an odd black card, while asking if it's a three is fairly pointless.

Once we have the ability to select the most useful question to ask, constructing the decision tree is easy; at any given point, we stop if we've got enough information to determine if an object is in the target class or not. If we don't have enough information, we ask the best question and recur:

ALGORITHM 15.2.6 **ID3** *Given as inputs a set* F *of features, an overall set* S *and a target concept* T:

1. *If every element of the set* S *is in* T, *return "yes." If no element of* S *is in* T, *return "no."*
2. *Otherwise, let* f *be the most discriminating element of* F. *(If there are no features remaining, return failure.) Return a tree whose left branch is* ID3(F − {f},S ∩ f,T) *and whose right branch is* ID3(F − {f},S − f,T). *We are denoting that subset of* S *that satisfies* f *by* S ∩ f *and the subset that fails to satisfy* f *by* S − f.

In practice, of course, our training data will include information not about all of the objects in our domain but only about some of them. Given this, ID3 can be used to construct a PAC description of the target concept.

15.3 EXPLANATION-BASED LEARNING

The last general type of learning that we will examine is called explanation-based learning; the basic idea is to use results from one problem-solving effort to help you the next time around. For this reason, explanation-based learning is often called *speedup* learning. Yet another way to look at this is as a search for lemmas that are useful in your domain—by discovering these lemmas and caching them as new axioms, a system can improve its efficiency on the next problem encountered. Note that the search for lemmas is *deductive* learning—the new information is a legitimate consequence of things we already know.

The ideas behind explanation-based learning can probably be made clearest by an example. Suppose we have the goal of getting to Sun City, a small town near Phoenix. In our database, we have:

$$\texttt{near(Phoenix,Sun-City)} \tag{15.15}$$

$$\texttt{airport(Phoenix)} \tag{15.16}$$

$$\begin{aligned}&\texttt{near}(x,y) \wedge \texttt{holds}(\texttt{loc}(x),s)\\ &\quad\rightarrow \texttt{holds}(\texttt{loc}(y),\texttt{result}(\texttt{drive}(x,y),s))\end{aligned} \tag{15.17}$$

$$\texttt{airport}(z) \rightarrow \texttt{holds}(\texttt{loc}(z),\texttt{result}(\texttt{fly}(z),s)) \tag{15.18}$$

Phoenix is near Sun City and has an airport. If x is near y, we can get to y by driving there from x, provided that we were at x in the first place. Finally, we can get to any city with an airport simply by flying there.

Given these axioms, if our goal is to find some situation s for which

holds(loc(Sun-City),s)

we can prove

holds(loc(Sun-City),result(drive(Phoenix, Sun-City), result(fly(Phoenix),s')))

In other words, we can get to Sun City by flying to Phoenix and then driving to our final destination.

Now suppose that we analyze our result with an ATMS. We will conclude that we used (15.15), (15.16), (15.17) with x bound to Phoenix and y bound to Sun-City, and (15.18) with z bound to Phoenix. The fact that Sun City appears in both the query and the binding list for (15.17) suggests that we attempt to abstract it away to get

holds(loc(x),result(drive(Phoenix,x),result(fly(Phoenix),s')))

This isn't right, though—we can't get to an arbitrary location x by flying to Phoenix and then driving there!

The reason is that Sun City also appears in our database; when we abstract it to the variable x, we need to explicitly record the use of the fact (15.15). This gives us:

near(Phoenix,x) →
  holds(loc(x),result(drive (Phoenix,x),result(fly(Phoenix),s')))

In other words, if x is near Phoenix, we can get to x by flying to Phoenix and then driving. This inference is correct.

Instead of abstracting away Sun City, we could have abstracted away Phoenix to get

near(x,Sun-City) ∧ airport(x) → (15.19)
  holds(loc(Sun-City),result(drive(x,Sun-City),result(fly(x),s')))

In other words, we can get to Sun City by flying to a nearby airport and then driving there. If flying into Phoenix is unsuitable for some reason (perhaps your mother-in-law lives in Phoenix and will be offended if you don't stop in and visit), (15.19) will lead to efficient generation of a plan for getting to Sun City via an alternate airport.

Finally, we could abstract away both Sun City *and* Phoenix in the original derivation, leading to

```
near(x,y) ∧ airport(x) →
        holds(loc(y),result(drive(x,y),result(fly(x),s')))
```

which gives us a plan for reaching any destination near an airport.

This technique is known as *explanation-based learning*, or EBL: the idea is that by automatically generating useful lemmas, subsequent problem solving can be made more efficient. EBL is important because the cached intermediate results are frequently of value in subsequent problem solving. After all, there is at least one example—the problem just solved—for which they are known to be useful; this is at least weak evidence that they will continue to be of use when we address future problems. A variety of additional ideas have been proposed that are aimed at ensuring that rules such as (15.19) generated by an explanation-based system are useful in practice; these ideas are implemented in the SOAR and PRODIGY problem-solving systems.[35]

15.4 FURTHER READING

There are a variety of sources for additional material on machine learning; one excellent one is Dietterich's survey article [1989]. There is also a series of edited volumes describing the field (Michalski *et al.* [1983], Michalski *et al.* [1986], and Michalski and Kodratoff [1988]) and a recent special issue of *Artificial Intelligence* [Carbonell 1989].

Lenat's thesis work is described [Lenat 1982a], and AM and EURISKO are discussed in Lenat [1982b, 1983a, 1983b]. A discussion similar to ours regarding the reasons for the programs' successes can be found in Lenat and Brown [1984]. Polya's famous book on the heuristics used in mathematics is Polya [1945].

Valiant's paper introducing PAC learning is Valiant [1984]. In Blumer *et al.* [1989] and Ehrenfeucht *et al.* [1988], Valiant's results are extended to continuous domains such as those arising in our discussion of neural networks. The impact of bias on PAC learning is discussed by Haussler [1988]. Natarajan [1991] also discusses these ideas.

Version spaces first appear in Mitchell's Ph.D. thesis [1977]; the material also appears in Mitchell [1982].

Single-layer neural networks were introduced by Rosenblatt [1962] and called *perceptrons*. However, Minsky and Papert [1969] showed in the book *Perceptrons* that the expressive power of such networks was very limited; they also speculated that multilayer networks would lack many of the at-

35 SOAR refers to explanation-based learning as "chunking," but the idea is essentially the same.

tractive computational features of the single-layer ones. This speculation essentially killed research on neural networks until effective algorithms for constructing the internal layers were discovered—first in 1974 [Werbos 1974] (but they were again forgotten), and then again in the mid-1980s (LeCun [1985] and Rumelhart *et al.* [1986]). The procedure currently used to solve this problem is Rumelhart's and is known as *backpropagation*. But problems remain: A great number of training examples are typically needed, and there is as yet no way to determine the number of layers that the network should have. Both of these difficulties are the focus of current research.

ID3 is introduced by Quinlan [1986b] and has been extended in a variety of ways. In Quinlan [1987], the algorithm is extended to remove from the decision tree choices that are sanctioned by Definition 15.2.5 but don't turn out to be useful because of the statistically small number of examples considered deep in the tree. This is an instance of a general problem known as *overfitting*: Our interest is not really in finding an exact fit for the training data, but in finding an expression that is likely to be useful in predicting the behavior of future instances. Much recent work on ID3 (and other approaches to inductive learning) has been aimed at solving the overfitting problem.

A version of the ID3 algorithm that processes the training examples incrementally (perhaps they are discovered one at a time) is discussed by Utgoff [1989], and one that deals with noisy data is discussed by Quinlan [1986a].

The two systems that we mentioned as using explanation-based learning are SOAR [Laird *et al.* 1987] and PRODIGY [Minton 1988]. A description of PRODIGY is included in Minton *et al.* [1989], which discusses EBL generally at considerable length. Minton [1990] discusses the problem of ensuring that *useful* generalizations are learned, as opposed to simply any generalizations.

15.5 EXERCISES

1. Suppose that instead of a binary classification, we are trying to divide a group of samples into n distinct subtypes. (As an example, we might be trying to classify furniture as chairs, tables, desks, and so on, as opposed to simply chair/not chair.) Derive an analog to Theorem 15.2.4 in this case.

2. (a) Show that in a language with n predicates, the language consisting of normal-form expressions built from these predicates is of size 2^{3^n}.

   (b) Suppose that we do not restrict our hypothesis space at all. Can you derive an analog to Theorem 15.2.4 in this case?

3. Suppose that the training data received by a learning system is noisy, in that there is some small probability p that any particular training example will be described incorrectly (for example, a poisonous mushroom described as edible). We cater to this by requiring that instead of our learned predicate $\hat{p}$ matching *all* of the training data, it matches only a fraction $1 - \frac{\epsilon}{2}$ of it. Derive an analog to Theorem 15.2.4 in this case.

4. (a) Continue the example of Section 15.2.2, supposing that our language consists of color (red or black), suits (for example, spades), parity (odd or even), and rank (ace through king). At what point is the concept determined uniquely?

   (b) Repeat the example allowing negated concepts, such as "not a 3 and not a spade." Is the version space algorithm still viable?

5. Suppose that we are working in a domain of size 2^n that contains n independent binary features (like red/black, odd/even, and so on) and that there is some conjunctive concept c that we are trying to learn using the version space method.

   (a) How many distinct conjunctive concepts are there in this domain?

   (b) What is the smallest number n such that by carefully selecting n samples, we can guarantee that we can identify the concept in question? Assume that we select each sample after learning the result on the previous one.

   (c) What is the largest number m such that it is possible that we see the results of m randomly selected distinct samples and are still unable to identify the concept exactly?

6. Consider the two neural networks shown in Figure 15.8.

   (a) Show that the expressive power of functions of the form shown in (a), where only a single node appears in the middle layer, is no greater than that of single-layer neural networks.

   (b) Construct an example of a function of the form (b) that cannot be approximated by a single-layer neural network.

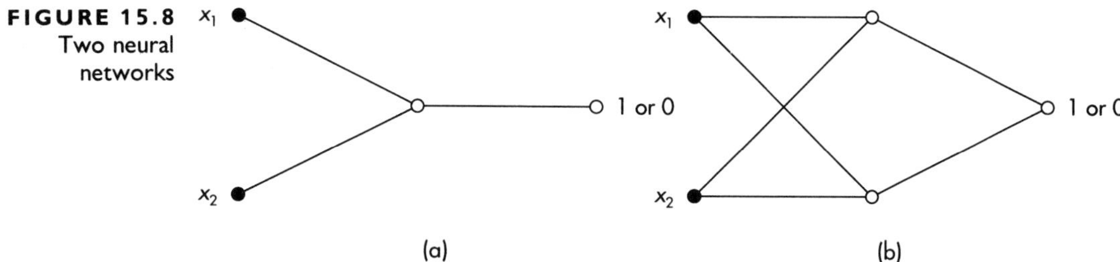

FIGURE 15.8 Two neural networks

7. What other rules of inference like (15.9) are implied by the decision tree appearing in Figure 15.7?

8. Complete the analysis begun in the text, constructing the most effective decision tree to identify elements of the target class, "Odd black cards or the 2♡."

9. Implement Algorithm 15.2.6 and use it to respond to the previous question.

10. Find the smallest decision tree that can be used to represent the concept

$$[p_1(x) \wedge p_2(x)] \vee [p_3(x) \wedge p_4(x) \wedge p_5(x)] \qquad (15.20)$$

Why is this decision tree larger than the expression (15.20) itself?

11. Suppose that you have a query $q(a)$, and that this query follows from the database using the assumptions $p_1, \ldots, p_n$, where the binding needed for p_i is σ_i.

    (a) If we denote by $p_i^{a \to x}$ the result of replacing a with x in p_i, prove that our original database implies

$$\bigwedge_{i=1}^{n} p_i^{a \to x} \to q(x)$$

    (b) Suppose further that the object constant a appears only in the first j of the p_i's, so that $p_{j+1}, \ldots, p_n$ do not mention a. Now show that the original database implies

$$\bigwedge_{i=1}^{j} p_i^{a \to x} \to q(x)$$

    (Note the change in the superscript in the conjunction.)

    (c) What does all of this have to do with explanation-based learning?

12. It has been suggested that explanation-based learning can be extended by looking at partial arguments that are *shared* by multiple invocations of a theorem prover on a variety of different goals, as opposed to simply storing generalizations of arguments that are used only once.

    (a) What might the advantages of this approach be?

    (b) What is the formal analog of this generalization?

    (c) Give an example of a learning situation where this approach is a good idea.

CHAPTER 16

VISION

At some point, AI systems are going to have to do more than reason abstractly with declarative information obtained through some mystical means; they're going to have to process sensory inputs to get this information in the first place. In this chapter, we discuss how machines can be expected to process visual inputs to learn about their domain.

There are other applications of this technology as well. Here are some existing ones.

- Visual inspection of integrated circuits
- Assembly of printed circuit boards
- Document reading
- Analysis of medical or satellite images
- Automated navigation systems

Imagine, then, that we have a photograph such as the one appearing in Figure 16.1, and that we want a computer program to make sense of it. What sort of difficulties can we expect to encounter?

It turns out that vision is hard for at least three reasons:

1. There is a great deal of data involved. We see in the next section that the digitization of a photograph such as that in the figure can easily involve over a megabyte of data, and we see in subsequent sections that each pixel may need to be processed in a fairly complex way. A real-time visual system can also be expected to process multiple images per second (human vision processes some twenty-two images each second, for example).

2. Pictures are noisy. The information in the photograph (not to mention the digital version of the photo) contains many small inaccuracies that do not affect our overall understanding of the image. A spurious value

FIGURE 16.1 Ginsberg while not working on this textbook

taken at a single pixel (or even a small group of pixels) should not make it impossible for us to analyze the remainder of the scene. There are also image variations that occur naturally—fog or smoke can obscure a scene, an image that is sharp on a sunny day may be somewhat diffuse on a cloudy one, and so on.

3. Pictures are ambiguous. When we collapse three-dimensional reality to a two-dimensional image, information is necessarily lost. What is written on the cliff directly behind the airplane? We can't tell if anything is, since this portion of the original image has been occluded. How do we know that the airplane is symmetric? After all, it is possible that the plane is not symmetric at all, but is being photographed from an unusual angle that only gives the impression of symmetry. Our machines will need to disambiguate the outputs of their visual sensors—just as we need to.

A variety of suggestions have been made to address these difficulties; the most conventional approach is to divide the vision process into a group of successive stages:

1. First, the sensor inputs—typically analog—need to be digitized and presented to the machine.

2. Second, a variety of low-level processing needs to be done. Noise in the data needs to be identified or somehow eliminated. Image features that can be identified locally (such as elements of edges) need to be identified.
3. Using these geometric primitives, we can form larger geometric objects (such as complete edges) and thereby identify the general regions that appear in the image—the surface of a desk, a cloud in the sky, and so on. This splitting of the image into regions is known as *segmentation*.
4. At this point, three-dimensional information can hopefully be recovered from the two-dimensional photograph. Having identified the surface regions in the picture, we need to decide how far the surfaces are from the camera and what their orientations are.
5. Finally, we have to actually understand what's going on in the picture. We need to identify the objects we've seen (tanks, cars, elephants, and so on) and to interpret the result (for example, a tank has its turret aimed halfway between a car and an onrushing elephant).

In this chapter, we spend some time examining each of these steps, describing a fairly typical technique used to address each problem assuming that the previous step has completed successfully. Our three-dimensional reconstruction, for example, will use information about connected regions in the scene and will assume that this information is correct. Let me point out now that the techniques we examine are hardly the only solutions known to the problems in question; I have chosen to examine individual ideas in some depth as opposed to sketching a variety of ideas at a shallower level.

Before we turn to these individual ideas, I should also remark that there is a more recent notion that seems likely to address some of the computational problems faced by vision systems. This is known as *active vision* and is the topic of Section 16.5.

16.1 DIGITIZATION

Digitization is the simplest of the steps involved in vision; the idea of translating an analog image into digital form is a well-understood one. CDs do it with music; optical scanners do it with visual images.

As we remarked earlier, the problem is that a single image tends to produce a *lot* of digital data; since the data has to be analyzed (and not just stored and retrieved as in a CD), this can lead to serious computational difficulties.

To see how serious the difficulties are, suppose that we have a single high-resolution image, 1024 pixels on a side. There are therefore about a million pixels involved in the image—but it doesn't end there. Even a black-

and-white image won't have each pixel either "on" or "off" because there are shades of gray that need to be represented. If we say that each pixel has 256 intensity levels, we need to record 1 byte of information per pixel, so the amount of information in our black-and-white picture is 1 megabyte. The result of digitizing a small portion of a black-and-white photograph is shown in Figure 16.2.

Most pictures are color, however. A color photograph can be split into blue, green, and red images (this is how a color TV works), so that we'll need to store not one copy of the input picture, but three. Our single picture now involves 3 megabytes of data! Performing a single computation on each byte will take a full second on a 3 MIP machine; 3 MIP is fairly slow these days, but we potentially need to do many computations on each pixel and to process many photographs per second.

FIGURE 16.2 A portion of Sarah Bernhardt's eye

183	196	199	200	214	215	118	226	98	104
208	194	200	226	157	88	76	157	0	43
209	214	199	182	91	71	59	173	217	177
214	214	175	150	88	71	59	138	217	214
193	215	208	199	113	60	55	52	244	199
138	105	137	152	215	109	71	44	70	168
137	120	105	102	104	157	244	137	75	68
140	123	120	123	105	105	120	137	244	199
138	118	139	109	108	138	138	138	138	168
109	114	121	121	138	119	119	138	138	152

Two possible approaches to dealing with the enormous amount of data processed by vision systems are the following:

1. Massive parallelization. The most obvious approach to dealing with the data is to deal with each pixel in parallel. As we will see, much of the initial analysis is done on a pixel-by-pixel basis, and it is therefore possible to use n processors to speed up the early stages of vision by a factor of n. This is the approach that appears to be taken by the human visual system; unfortunately, we cannot currently duplicate in hardware the enormous parallelization that occurs in biological systems.

2. Hierarchical analysis. We also might analyze a scene hierarchically, using the results of a coarsely-grained analysis to focus our efforts to understand the scene itself. This might alleviate some of the computational problems encountered in solving the finely grained problem that is actually of interest to us. Hierarchical techniques are known to be effective in solving planning problems; perhaps the same idea can be applied to vision also.

16.2 LOW-LEVEL PROCESSING

Once we have digitized an image, we need to analyze it. The first two steps in this process are typically to remove the noise in the visual image and to search the image for specific local features such as edges.

16.2.1 Noise Removal

People are very good at dealing with noisy visual data. If you stand up too quickly and "see stars," your visual system is corrupting the incoming image by adding all manner of noise to it—but you still have no trouble functioning. You may shake your head to clear it, but you won't be tempted to brush the stars away as if they were flies. In a similar way, we have no trouble making sense of fuzzy or damaged photographs.

Sanitizing a digitized picture to remove noise appears to be a local process; roughly speaking, we look at each small region of the image and smooth it so that it matches neighboring regions. On a pixel-by-pixel basis, we might replace the intensity level in each pixel with the average of the intensity levels in the neighboring pixels.

There is a problem with this approach. In deciding to replace the value of each pixel with the result obtained by taking an average over its neighbors, we become incapable of detecting an object that is only one pixel in size. If we average over a wider area (after all, noise may not occur in isolated pixels), we will be unable to detect larger objects.

If we treat noise removal as a local operation, size is the only clue we can use in trying to decide whether a particular intensity variation is noise or an important feature of our domain. As a result, purely local noise removal, although useful, is unlikely to produce a completely clean image.

Subsequent phases of vision therefore need to be able to cope with residual noise in their inputs.

16.2.2 Feature Detection

Having removed the noise from our image (or at least having removed some of it), our next job is to identify small but expected features that appear in our image. This generally means that we want to find the *edges* in the picture—points at which one object ends and another begins. Ideally, we could turn a photograph such as that shown in Figure 16.3(a) into the set of edges shown in Figure 16.3(b). Finding these edges is a natural first step toward identifying the objects that appear in the image itself.

Before continuing, let me make one additional point. Our aim isn't

FIGURE 16.3 Successful edge detection

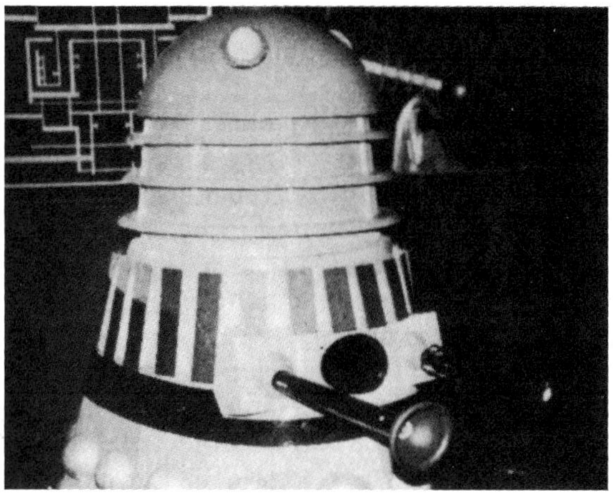

(a)

(b)

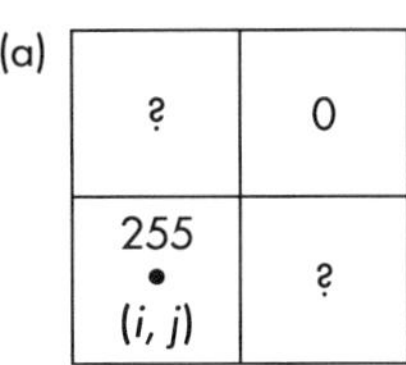

FIGURE 16.4 An edge template

really to find the edges in the *image*, but the edges in the objects the image depicts. In many cases these tasks may be identical—but in others (especially if some noise remains in the image), it will be possible to use information about the expected objects in the scene to make useful distinctions between object features and image features. We will see an example of this in Section 16.3.

Rather than look for complete edges, we begin by looking for small *pieces* of edges; the reason is that we can hopefully detect these locally. As an example, consider the situation shown in Figure 16.4(a).

This looks like an edge. We can't tell if the edge is running from left to right, or top to bottom, or diagonally downward, but the change in intensity between the upper-right and lower-left pixels indicates the presence of an edge. Similarly, the situation in Figure 16.4(b) is also likely to represent an edge; this one might run diagonally up and to the right, however.

Now suppose that we have an arbitrary 2×2 square of pixels; to what extent does the pattern in this square match either of the ones shown in the figure? If we denote the intensity of pixel (i, j) by $f(i, j)$, where i increases from left to right and j from bottom to top, then the situation in Figure 16.4(a) corresponds to a maximum in $|f(i+1, j+1) - f(i, j)|$, while the situation in part (b) of the figure corresponds to a maximum in $|f(i+1, j) - f(i, j+1)|$. To handle both of these possibilities, we define

$$\texttt{edge}(i,j) \equiv \sqrt{[f(i+1, j+1) - f(i,j)]^2 + [f(i+1, j) - f(i, j+1)]^2} \quad (16.1)$$

so that edge(i, j) gives us a local indication of how likely it is that the (i, j)th pixel is part of an edge of some kind.

There is another, similar method for local edge detection. Roughly speaking, we are looking for a large change in intensity between one portion of the image and another, the sort of a feature shown in the center of Figure 16.5(a). But these sorts of large changes correspond to maxima in the first derivative of the intensity,[36] as shown in Figure 16.5(b). Finally, a maximum in the first derivative corresponds to a zero in the second derivative, as shown in Figure 16.5(c). In other words, edges can be identified by looking for zeroes in the second derivative of the intensity of the image.

36 Given a function $f(x)$, the *derivative* of f is the function whose value at a point x is the rate of change in f at that point. Since the function can't be increasing or decreasing at points where it takes a maximal value, the derivative must be zero at those points. The *second* derivative of f is the derivative of the derivative of f.

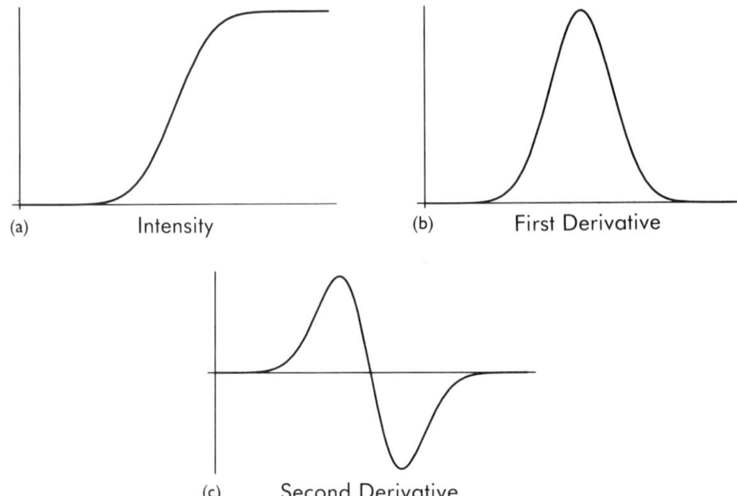

FIGURE 16.5 Edges as zeroes of the second derivative

When we extend these ideas to two dimensions (after all, pictures *are* two-dimensional!), new problems arise. There is no reason to believe that a particular edge will be in either of the standard coordinate directions, so that if the intensity of the image is $f(x,y)$, edges may not correspond to zeroes in the second derivative of f with respect to either of these two variables.

Computational expense can also be saved if the image is processed once to both remove the noise and detect edges, instead of one pass for each of these purposes. This can be accomplished by combining a purely local edge detector like that appearing in (16.1) with one that smooths the image by considering the intensities over some range of coordinate values.

Unfortunately, the mathematics underlying these techniques is considerably beyond what I have assumed elsewhere in this book (multivariate calculus is an absolute minimum); the basic idea is to quantify the ideas we have described in the previous few paragraphs and then to find edge-detection mechanisms that make sensible compromises between the competing needs for speed, accuracy, and the ability to deal with noisy images. The result of applying such a mechanism to an actual image appears in Figure 16.6, where we show a photograph and the output of an edge-detection system when applied to it. Note the difference between Figure 16.6 and the earlier Figure 16.3.

16.3 SEGMENTATION AND THE HOUGH TRANSFORM

The next task that a vision system must address is the need to assemble the pieces of edges it has found into the edges themselves—features that extend over large portions of the image. Roughly speaking, this is a matter of distinguishing legitimate edge segments from spurious ones.

FIGURE 16.6 Realistic edge detection

(a)

(b)

There are a variety of techniques known to be useful here; one can, for example, begin with the portions of edges in which one has the highest confidence (perhaps because edge(i, j) has the highest value) and try to extend these edge elements outward to obtain complete edges. A dual approach is to begin with empty regions in which there are no edges and to try to extend *them* outward, eventually taking the edges to be the boundaries between the regions so constructed.

We focus in this section on a somewhat different approach known as the *Hough transform*.[37] Consider the image in Figure 16.7, which is known to be a photograph taken directly above a group of washers, so that all of

37 Hough is pronounced so as to rhyme with *tough*.

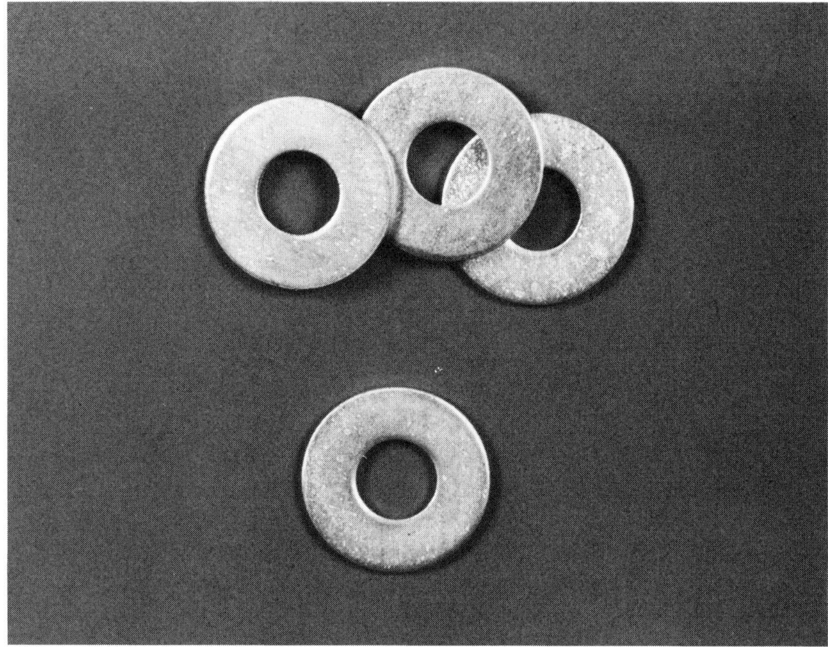

FIGURE 16.7 An image of some washers

the edges in the picture should be circular arcs. How are these arcs to be identified from the information in the function edge(i, j)?

To address this, suppose that there is some point (i, j) that is part of an edge. What circle might such a point be part of?

The circles containing (i, j) are those for which there is an origin point (x,y) and a radius r such that

$$(i - x)^2 + (j - y)^2 = r^2 \tag{16.2}$$

Now suppose that instead of thinking in terms of the coordinates (i, j) where edges appear, we work with those triples (x,y,r) that correspond to those coordinates. More specifically, we take the *Hough transform h* of $f(i, j)$ to be given by

$$h(x,y,r) = \sum_{\{(i,j) | (i-x)^2 + (j-y)^2 = r^2\}} \text{edge}(i, j) \tag{16.3}$$

After transforming the image to "circle space," we can identify the objects in the image because they correspond to maxima in the transformed function $h(x,y,r)$.

An advantage of this approach is that it is able to deal with edges that include gaps. As an example, one of the washers in Figure 16.7 has an outer edge that is broken into two separate arcs by an occluding washer in the picture. In the transformed space, these two edges are combined as evidence for the existence of the single washer in the photo.

Another advantage is that we can easily extend our ideas to include information about the direction of the edge segments. Suppose that instead of a function edge(i, j) that gives us the likelihood of the pixel at (i, j) being part of an edge, we have a function edge(i, j, θ) that gives us the likelihood of there being an edge at (i, j) that is in the direction θ, where θ is an angle from 0 to 180 degrees. (We discuss how such information might be obtained in Exercise 3 at the end of this chapter.)

Information about edge direction allows us to further restrict the sum in (16.3). Examining Figure 16.8, we see that we can additionally require

$$\frac{j-y}{r} = \sin(\theta - 90) = -cos(\theta) \tag{16.4}$$

when transforming edge(i, j, θ) to $h(x, y, r)$ using (16.3).

Finally, note that there is no reason that the Hough transform needs to be used to identify circles only. Any time we can write down an expression like (16.2) for the expected form of the edge, similar ideas can be applied. Thus we can use Hough-like transforms to locate line segments, ellipses, or other curves.

16.4 RECOVERING 3-D INFORMATION

Having identified the complete edges in our image, we next need to remove the ambiguities introduced by our conversion of three-dimensional reality to a two-dimensional image. Which objects are in front of which others? How far away are the objects? What is the orientation of the various surfaces that have been identified?

16.4.1 The Waltz Algorithm

An old solution to part of this problem is shown in Figure 16.9. What we have done is to take a line drawing and, for each edge, determine whether it is on the boundary of the figure, an "outside" (convex) edge or an "inside"

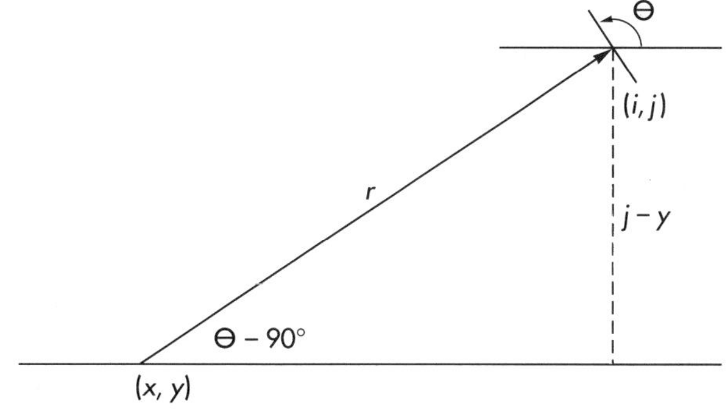

FIGURE 16.8 Directional edge information

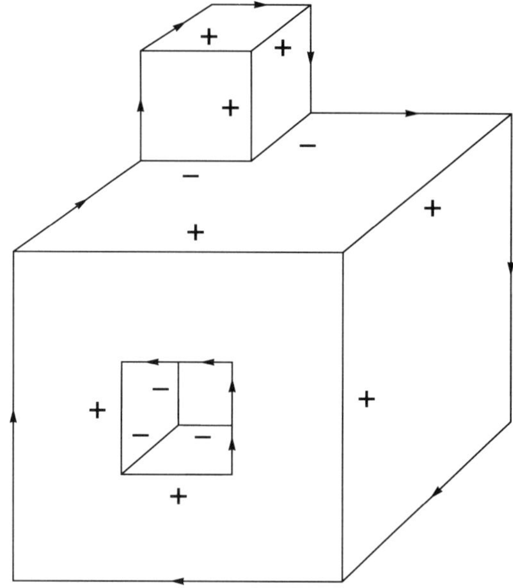

FIGURE 16.9 A labelled line drawing

(concave) edge. The boundary lines are marked with arrows such that if we were to walk in the direction of the arrow, the object would be to our right and open space to our left. We mark the outside edges with + and the inside ones with −. Recovering the three-dimensional information in the image is, in part, a matter of labelling all of the edges with arrowheads, + and −.

The reason that it is often possible to assign a unique labelling to figures such as that in the picture rests on the following observations:

1. It is the *edges* that are labelled, not the vertices. If one vertex is an "out" vertex so that each of its edges is labelled with a +, each edge must have the same label at the vertex at its other end.

2. In a physically realizable object,[38] there are only a limited number of ways in which two or more edges can meet in a vertex. Two edges can meet in an angle, an edge can meet a line in a T, an edge can meet an acute angle to make an arrow, or three edges can meet obtusely to make a fork. Each of these basic patterns is shown in Figure 16.10.

   What's more, each of these patterns can only be labelled in a limited number of ways. It turns out that there are only eighteen possible la-

38 We are making some assumptions here, namely that all edges are straight and that every intersection in the image corresponds to the meeting of at most three planar surfaces in the objects depicted.

FIGURE 16.10 The basic structures appearing in a line drawing

bellings that can arise in a realizable object; these are shown in Figure 16.11.

Given these restrictions, there is frequently only one legal labelling for a line drawing such as the one in Figure 16.9; the fact that both ends of an edge get the same label allows us to generate global information from the purely local information given by the restrictions of Figure 16.11.

The *Waltz algorithm* takes a line drawing like that in Figure 16.9 (but without the labels) and searches for an edge labelling such that all the vertex labels appear as allowed possibilities in Figure 16.11. A node n in the search space is a partial labelling for the figure, and n's children label additional nodes in consistent ways.

Like the crossword-puzzle problem, labelling diagrams using the Waltz algorithm is a constraint-satisfaction problem. In the crossword-puzzle problem, each square had to be filled with a letter such that the words were legal English; in this case, each vertex has to be labelled in a way that is consistent with Figure 16.11 and such that both ends of an edge get the same label. Unlike the crossword-puzzle problem, though, there is typically only one legal labelling for a line diagram such as that shown in Figure 16.9; many line drawings have a unique physical realization.

There are a variety of problems with the Waltz algorithm, however. The first is that it works only in the restricted domain of perfect line drawings. Circles can't be handled; neither can incidences involving more than three edges, such as appear in Figure 16.12. In general, a figure consisting of

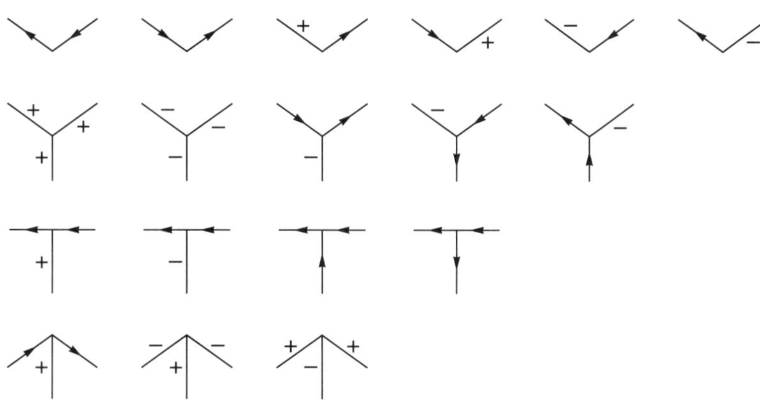

FIGURE 16.11 Possible vertex labels in the Waltz algorithm

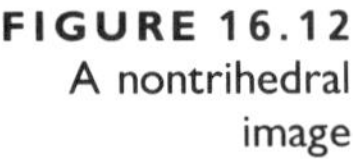

FIGURE 16.12 A nontrihedral image

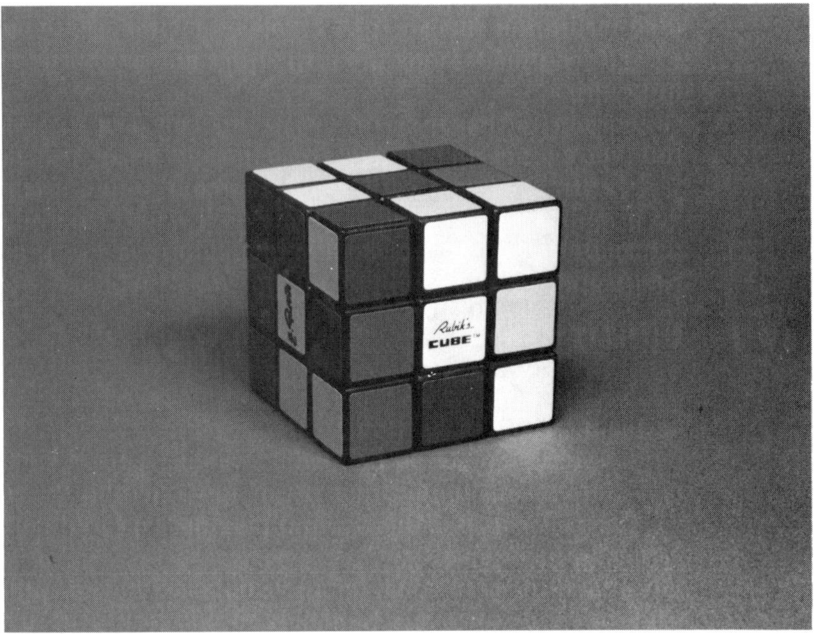

only straight lines and such that every vertex is a meeting point of at most three planes is called *trihedral*; as mentioned in an earlier footnote, the Waltz algorithm only works for images of trihedral objects. What's more, it works only if the image actually *appears* trihedral—if there is a visual coincidence and several vertices overlap, the Waltz algorithm will be unable to cope with the resulting image.

It is because of these drawbacks that the Waltz algorithm has faded in importance as AI vision work has progressed. But there are two insights that remain important:

1. It is possible to obtain global information about an image by considering interactions among purely local phenomena.
2. The local constraints used are the result of analyzing the physical situation that the image depicts.

Even in instances where the Waltz algorithm *per se* cannot be applied, these observations remain valuable.

As an example, consider the object shown in Figure 16.13, called a *three-pronged blivet*. This picture clearly has no real-world manifestation; the reason is that the global constraints generated by the part of the figure below the dashed line and those generated by the part above the line are inconsistent.

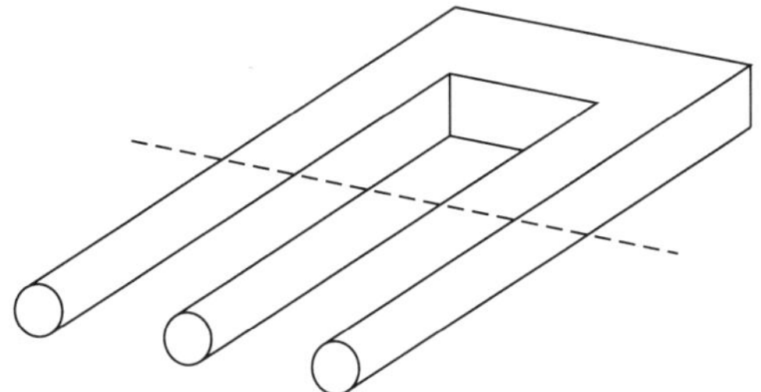
FIGURE 16.13 A three-pronged blivet

What is a vision system to do if it encounters an image for which there is no three-dimensional analog? If the image is a drawing, it may be right simply to recognize the drawing as impossible; if the image is a photograph, something else will need to be done. Perhaps the results of the segmentation process were in error and need to be recomputed; perhaps the assumptions underlying the local constraints need to be reconsidered. As an example, one could easily have a photograph of a *drawing* of a blivet. The lines in the drawing have no three-dimensional reality in this case. The assumption that the image is trihedral might also be in error.

In other cases, there may be *many* valid three-dimensional interpretations of a given scene. This is a much more typical vision problem: disambiguating a scene with multiple allowed interpretations.

In this particular phase of the vision problem, there are some recognized techniques for dealing with ambiguous images. One is to extend the Waltz algorithm to include shading information. In Figure 16.14, we have redrawn

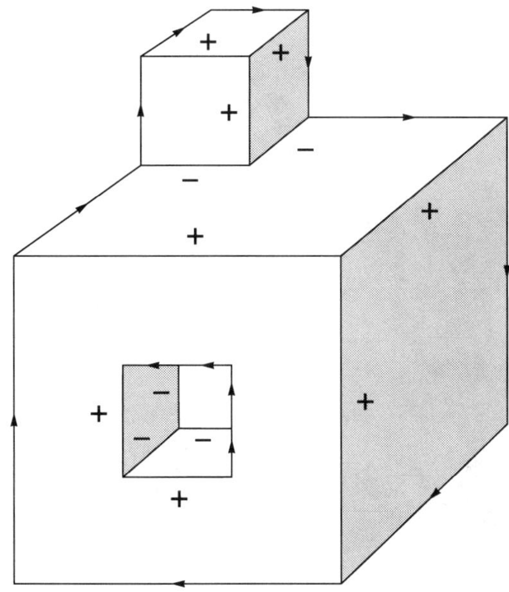

FIGURE 16.14 Figure 16.9, redrawn with shading information

Figure 16.9 to include shading information as if the source of illumination were to the left of the figure. Including this new information produces more allowed vertices of the form appearing in Figure 16.11, but also produces new constraints, since a surface that is shaded at one vertex will typically be shaded at all of the other vertices it includes. As a result, the constraint satisfaction problem involved in labelling a particular line drawing is less likely to be ambiguous if shading information is included.

16.4.2 The $2\frac{1}{2}$–D Sketch

At the end of the last section, we pointed out that it might be possible to recover 3-D information from shading that appears in the image being analyzed. In fact, it's possible to recover this sort of information from a variety of sources.

In a generalized setting (that is, images that are not necessarily trihedral), this process is referred to as constructing a *$2\frac{1}{2}$–D sketch*. This "sketch" includes information about the distances to the objects depicted in the image and about their surface orientations. The sources of this additional information include the following:

Shading As we've already seen, shading information can be used to disambiguate images with multiple interpretations. This can be done either in the restricted setting of the Waltz algorithm or in more general ways. In Figure 16.15, for example, we can tell that the photograph is of a sphere (a ping-pong ball, in fact) because of the shading from left to right.

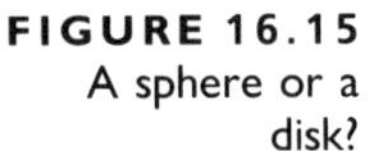

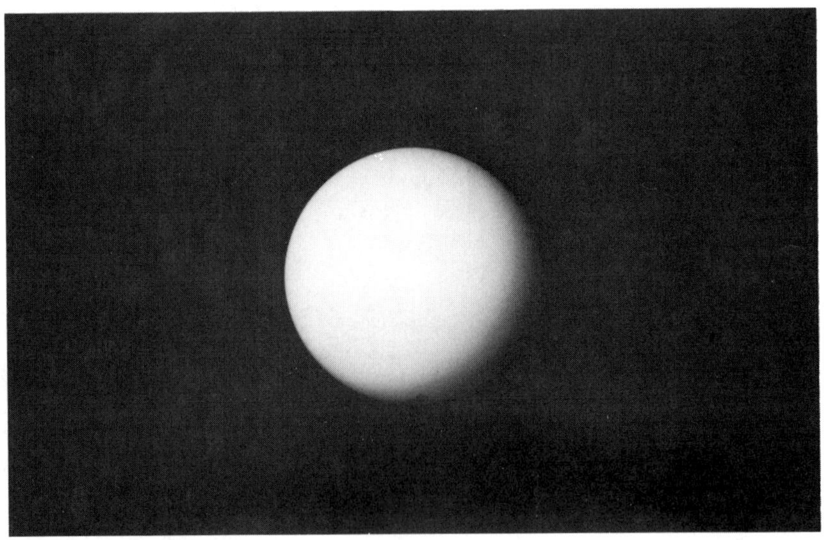

FIGURE 16.15 A sphere or a disk?

Perspective This is another source of $2\frac{1}{2}$–D information. Consider the picture in Figure 16.16(a); the railroad tracks are clearly heading off into the distance. Assuming that we know that Figure 16.16(b) is a picture of some records, we can get orientation information from the fact that records are round and round objects appear elliptical when viewed from an angle.

FIGURE 16.16
$2\frac{1}{2}$–D information from perspective

(a)

(b)

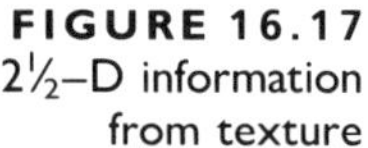

FIGURE 16.17 $2\frac{1}{2}$–D information from texture

Texture What about the image shown in Figure 16.17? The assumption that the dimpling on the surface of the golf ball is uniform allows us to conclude that we are looking at a sphere as opposed to a disk, a football, or some other shape. Similar considerations allow us to continue to interpret the image of a basketball that has had the air let out of it.

Note that there is domain knowledge being used here: When we use perspective to orient the railroad tracks in Figure 16.16(a), we use the fact that railroad tracks are supposed to be parallel. Figure 16.16(b) relies on the fact the records are round; Figure 16.17 on the fact that smooth surfaces are typically made of uniform material.

Multiple perspectives Images can also be disambiguated by comparing two or more similar views of the same object. Even if two images are individually ambiguous, there may be only a single 3-D representation that is consistent with both of them. An example is shown in Figure 16.18, where we can tell that there are three bowling pins in the figure by combining information from the views from the left and right sides of the picture.

One common source of multiple images of a single scene is just this—a stereo vision system, such as the human one. An artificial system can obtain multiple images similarly by using multiple cameras.

Another source of multiple images is motion. The objects that we are examining are often moving in some direction or another; even if we have only one eye or camera, we can get an image that is effectively stereo simply by waiting for the object to move a little bit and examining it afresh.

These two approaches share a common computational problem: Given multiple images of a single scene, how do we decide which line segments in one image match which segments in the other? In Figure 16.18, we have

FIGURE 16.18
Stereo images

(a)

(b)

no trouble realizing that there is one bowling pin in front and two others in back; this depends on our being able to identify the front pin as corresponding to the same object in both parts of the figure. Endowing an automated vision system with this capability is known as the *correspondence problem*.

A variety of techniques are known that bear on this difficulty; the human visual system appears to make crucial use of the "smoothness" assumption that an image doesn't change much from one view to the next. If we see a photograph of a man walking down the street and then another photo of the same man three seconds later, it is reasonable to assume that the man's tie is still around his neck, and hasn't been removed and put around one of his ankles! As we analyze the second image, we make extensive use of the information obtained from the analysis of the first one.

Another important idea is that instead of matching two entire images, we match only those portions of the images that are "interesting," like the tie in the previous paragraph. One way to identify interesting points automatically is as places where the image changes drastically, such as corners or other discontinuities. Unfortunately, these discontinuities are exactly the places at which the smoothness assumption is likely to fail.

Because we cannot effectively combine the two attractive approaches involving the smoothness assumption and the idea of matching only interesting regions in the image, there is currently no completely satisfactory solution to the correspondence problem, and work here is ongoing.

Active sensor techniques Finally, a robot can determine the distance to objects in its domain in an active way, by bouncing things off of those objects. Many robots use sonar for this purpose; some use a laser range finder or some other active method. Yet another approach involves analyzing known geometric details of the illumination to obtain depth information. Needless to say, the human perceptual system is not like this, although there are exceptions (you can measure the size of a cave by shouting and listening to the echo).

16.5 ACTIVE VISION

While the human visual system is not active in the sense that it controls the nature of the light used to illuminate an object, it *is* active in the sense that the vantage point from which objects are examined is controlled by the observer. Human vision is also active in the sense that the focus of the eye is under the observer's control and there is a small area near the center of the visual field with much higher resolution than the rest of the visual system. We continuously refocus our attention on portions of a scene likely to be of interest.

It appears that many of the difficulties we have discussed in this chapter can be at least partially addressed using active techniques similar to these. Here are a few of the reasons:

1. An active vision system can modify its behavior depending on the task being performed. If all we care about when crossing a road is, Is that red Mercedes going to hit me before I reach the other side?, we need to collect different visual data than if our interest is, Where is the baseball that I just threw out into the street?

2. Active systems can use physical search in addition to algorithmic search. If you've ever lost a contact lens, you know how important this can be—finding the lens doesn't involve carefully considering the view you have standing up, but getting down on your hands and knees and looking. This both brings you closer to the object being searched for and makes accessible regions of the visual image that were previously occluded (like the space under the couch in a living room).

3. Active vision systems can use known camera movements to remove spatial ambiguities. Imagine that you're standing in a meadow, and there are two trees in the distance; you want to know which is closer. It's quite natural to move from side to side and use parallax to solve this problem; if moving to the left makes the trees appear closer together, the leftmost tree is closer.

4. Finally, active vision allows computational systems to work with coordinate systems that are centered on the objects in the visual field instead of being centered on the observer. Many of the computational problems arising in vision work are made more tractable by this change in reference.

16.6 OBJECT AND SCENE RECOGNITION

What we've discussed so far is "pure" vision in some sense; we haven't really been concerned with what's in an image so much as we've been trying to understand the general geometric properties of what we see. At some point we need to understand the image in a way that allows us to use what we see; we have to incorporate the information in the image into our overall view of the world. The first step in this is to identify the objects in the image for what they are.

People, for example, can tell the difference between an orange and a watermelon. Oranges are orange. They are a lot rounder than watermelons (but not as round as an orange pool ball), and a lot smaller. When we decide what's in a particular image, we use information about the world in general. This is why this phase of vision is so difficult: It uses results and understanding from the rest of AI. Given that our artificial systems cannot yet reason about commonsense things like oranges and watermelons, how can we expect to pick these same objects out of photographs? The vision problem has been called "AI-complete" in the sense that solving vision isn't any easier than solving all the rest of AI.

Have another look at the picture in Figure 16.1. How is it that you know that the plane is upside down, and not the picture? There are a variety of reasons, all involving the use of outside knowledge. Pictures in books typically are right-side up. The waves breaking against the cliff at the bottom of the picture serve to orient it. Even the shadow on the fuselage helps indirectly by giving us a clue where the light source (the sun, presumably!) is for the photograph.

When the assumptions that we use to interpret visual data are wrong, the results can be very unsettling. As an example, I was visiting Universal Studios a few years ago; the entrance is crowded with wax dummies from a variety of Universal's successful movies. On this particular day, there was also an unemployed actor hanging around. He was dressed in a cowboy outfit that looked like it was straight from a 1950s movie, and would just stand there, not moving a muscle.

Eventually some unsuspecting tourist would come up, carefully inspecting the wax dummies to get a better look at the costumes or something. He'd look at a few dummies and then get to the cowboy. The cowboy would wait until the tourist was about an inch away from him, then stick out his hand and say, "Hi." The tourist (whose visual system had just malfunctioned in a rather serious way) would invariably jump half out of his skin.

One way that we identify objects in a scene (or in the case of the above story, *try* to identify them) is to know in advance what to look for, and to recognize these objects when we see them.

There are other methods as well. Suppose that we're looking in an aerial photograph for a hidden enemy tank, and we find something that looks like it might be a turret. If that's a turret *there*, we reason, then there should be some caterpillar treads *here*. Rather than simply looking for parts of the tank at random, we focus our investigation of one part of the picture using our general understanding of what tanks can be expected to look like. Do you recognize the picture in Figure 16.19 from your trips to the doctor as a youngster?

We can also use general information about an image to help us identify what's in it. A robot whose job is to align labels on wine bottles can make effective use of the fact that the object at which it is looking presumably *is* a wine bottle with a label on it. Analyzing a photograph of an airport is a lot easier once we know whether we're looking at a military or a civilian airfield. Making sense of an X ray requires that we know what part of the body is being depicted. In all of these examples, we use special-purpose knowledge of the domain to help us understand the image being considered.

Even after the objects have been identified, the job of the vision system is still not done—the hard-learned information must be made available to the reasoning system of the agent involved. Any spatial or temporal information in the image needs to be translated into a suitable knowledge representation language and stored. The information needs to be accessible to the components of the agent responsible for reasoning, planning, and acting. Inconsistencies between the agent's beliefs about the world and the output of its perceptual subsystem need to be analyzed and understood. In our wax dummy story, the reason the tourist was so surprised was be-

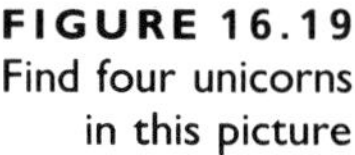

FIGURE 16.19 Find four unicorns in this picture

cause his confidence in the output of his vision system forced him—for a moment—to accept the conclusion that wax dummies can come to life.

16.7 FURTHER READING

The vision literature is not as accessible as it should be; most of the available material is either somewhat outdated or extremely technical. Good general introductions are Ballard and Brown [1982], Brady [1982], and Marr [1982]; Aloimonos and Rosenfeld [1991] is more recent but is also quite short. Finally, you might have a look at the section introductions in Fischler and Firschein [1987]. Both Fischler and Firschein [1987] and Kasturi and Jain [1991b, 1991a] are excellent collections of papers on a variety of vision topics, but the papers are not likely to be accessible without a good deal more preparatory material than has been presented here. Kasturi and Jain [1991a] also contains papers describing the use of computer vision systems in fielded applications from industry, medicine, autonomous navigation, and elsewhere.

Probably the single most influential paper on edge detection is by Marr and Hildreth [1980], which provides the first analytical description suitable for a machine implementation. Marr and Hildreth's work is extended by Canny [1986]. Once again, be warned that the mathematical sophistication used in this work is substantial.

The Hough transform is initially described in Hough [1962]; a more recent paper that both gives a clear description of Hough's original work and extends it in a variety of ways (including the use of directional information as described in the text) is Ballard [1981].

What is known almost universally in AI as the Waltz algorithm was actually discovered by Huffman [1971] and Clowes [1971]; Waltz [1975] observed that the performance of the algorithm could be improved by the inclusion of shadowing information.

Shape from shading is discussed by Ikeuchi and Horn [1981] and Pentland [1988]; shape from texture by Kender [1979]. Active depth-finding methods are discussed by Aloimonos *et al.* [1988] and Bajcsy [1988]. The extension of active methods to deal with visual problems generally is due to Ballard [1991]. That human vision is task-dependent is argued by Yarbus [1967].

16.8 EXERCISES

1. Consider the picture shown in Figure 16.20. What is it? Does the human visual system work hierarchically?

2. Use the edge function in (16.1) to find the edges in Figure 16.2.

3. Suppose that we are looking for the edges in a planar image. Show that every point at which there is a maximum in the edge-detection function (16.1) corresponds to a zero in some direction of the second derivative of the intensity. If the second derivative is zero in the direction $\vec{n}$, what is the expected direction of the edge?

4. Suppose that we have a continuous function $f(x,y)$ giving us the image intensity of the point (x,y), and that we have an image of a disk in which the intensity at a point (x,y) is a function of the distance of (x,y) from the origin, with the exact distribution being as shown in Figure 16.21.

   (a) Show that as $\Delta \to 0$, edges are detected as one would expect in this figure.

   (b) Use the results of the previous exercise to show that the directions of the detected edges are also as one would expect.

5. How should (16.3) be changed if we want to search for straight lines in the figure, as opposed to circles?

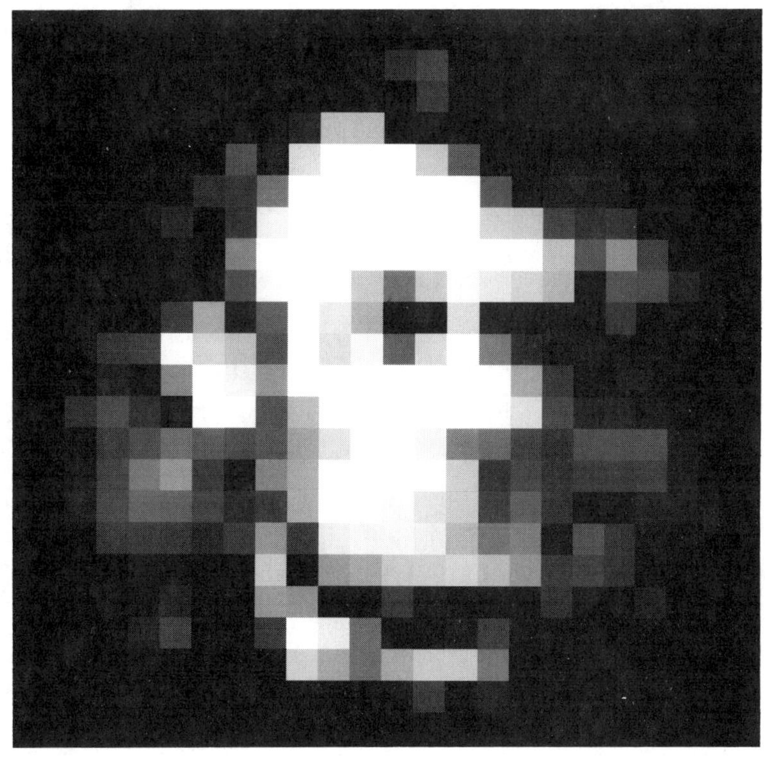

FIGURE 16.20 A coarsely grained image

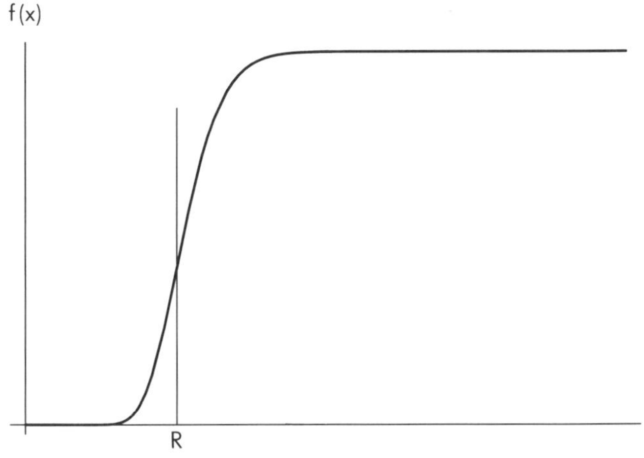

FIGURE 16.21 Intensity as a function of distance from the origin

6. Suppose that we have a perfect image of a circular disk, so that $f(i,j)$ is given by

$$f(i,j) = \begin{cases} 1, & \text{if } i^2 + j^2 < r^2; \\ 0, & \text{otherwise.} \end{cases}$$

   (a) Use (16.1) to compute $\mathtt{edge}(i,j)$.
   (b) Operate on the resulting function using the Hough transform. Interpret the result.

7. There is no possible labelling for a fork in Figure 16.11 that has exactly two edges labelled $-$. Why is this?

8. Does the hole in Figure 16.9 go all the way through the cube?

9. Use the Waltz algorithm to label the drawing in Figure 16.22. Is the labelling unique?

10. Consider the object in Figure 16.23, known as the *Penrose triangle*. Is it possible to find a Waltz labelling for this figure? Why or why not?

11. Consider the stereo image in Figure 16.24, where the penny is known to be ½ inch in diameter. Assuming that the images were taken by two cameras that are 1 foot apart and that the penny is 2 inches in front of the playing card, how far away is the penny?

FIGURE 16.22 A trihedral drawing

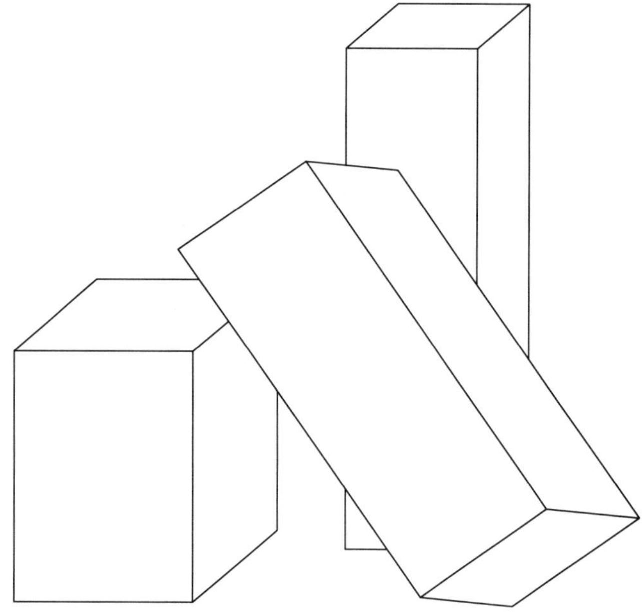

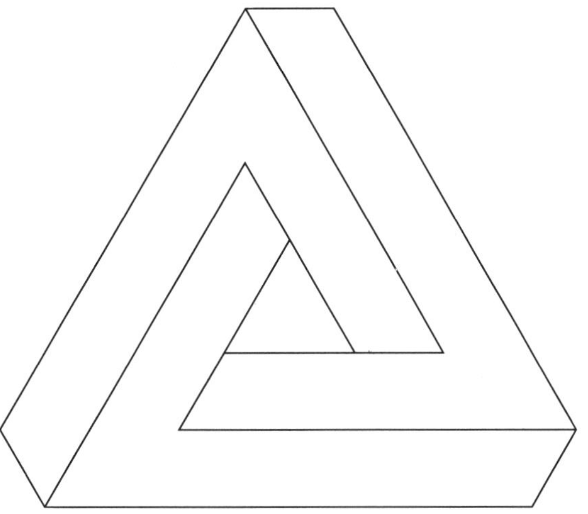

FIGURE 16.23 The Penrose triangle

FIGURE 16.24 Quantitative analysis of a stereo image

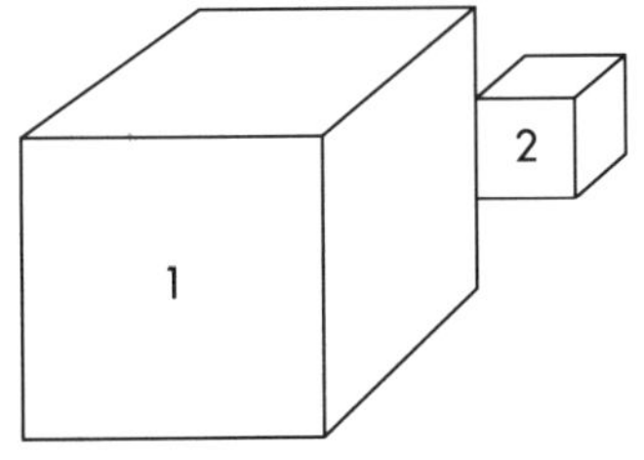

FIGURE 16.25 Another nontrihedral drawing

12. In our description of the Waltz algorithm, we assumed that there were no coincidences such as that shown in Figure 16.25, where the second cube is actually some distance behind the first but appears to be touching it because of the location of the viewer. Can active vision help address this problem?

13. In Section 16.5, we made a statement regarding the use of parallax to determine which of two trees in a field was closer. Prove this claim.

CHAPTER

17

NATURAL LANGUAGE

There are many parallels that can be drawn between vision and natural language understanding. Both processes begin by digitizing an analog signal (visual in one case, acoustic in the other) and conclude by modifying a knowledge base in some useful way. In both cases, the overall process has been broken by the AI community into a sequence of subtasks that are hoped to be fairly independent of one another.

There are differences as well. Human language is a large, artificial construct; the problems involved in natural language processing often depend as much on the structural complexity of language as they do on the computational complexity of the analysis. Perhaps more importantly, language needs to be *generated*. It is not sufficient for an artificial agent to understand sentences; it must produce them as well.

But I'm getting ahead of myself. Just as we separated vision into a sequence of distinct subtasks, here are the subtasks involved in natural language understanding.

- Signal processing
- Syntactic analysis
- Semantic analysis
- Pragmatics

Signal processing is the task of taking a spoken bit of language and turning it into a sequence of words. In many natural language applications, this step can be avoided because the input to the system is already in textual form—consider a machine trying to understand a newspaper article, or trying to translate such an article from one language to another.

Syntax refers to the structure of the sentences being analyzed. The two sentences, "John hit Mary," and "Mary hit John" use the same words. The words mean the same things in each sentence, but the sentences mean different things because the words are in a different order. Syntactic analysis involves parsing sentences to extract whatever information the word order contains; it's related to the sentence diagrams that we all had to deal with in junior high school.

Semantics involves making sense of the resulting parse by examining the meanings of the words it contains. Some disambiguation may be done here; as an example, "pen" has multiple meanings in English. Semantic analysis selects the appropriate one when distinguishing between the two sentences

The pig is in the pen.

and

The ink is in the pen.

Finally, *pragmatics* involves understanding the sentence or other text in the context of our overall knowledge base. "Do you know when the train leaves?" is a request for information if asked of a ticket agent, but a simple yes/no question if asked of a friend planning a trip.

Before turning to details, though, let me mention some of the applications to which a natural language system could be put.

The most obvious involves automatic translation. There was a great deal of work on this in the 1950s and 1960s; the idea was simply to have machines translate books, articles, and so on from one language to another.

Unfortunately, it isn't nearly this simple; the reason is that what a sentence "means" depends on much more than a surface analysis of the words it contains. As an example, a translator was reportedly written that would take an English sentence and return a Russian one, and also one that would work in the other direction. The system was then given an English sentence, which it translated to Russian and back to English. The result was

The liquor is holding out all right, but the meat has spoiled.

This seems reasonable enough until you learn that the sentence that was originally input to the system was, "The spirit is willing but the flesh is weak."[39]

A natural way around this problem appears to be to have a machine do "most" of the translation, and then to have the work checked by a human. The advantage is that the human doing the checking need not be

39 *Harper's* credited this story to Colonel Vernon Walters, Eisenhower's official interpreter, in August of 1962. It is probably something of an urban legend, but the overall sense of the example is realistic.

bilingual; a speaker of the target language can generally determine whether the translation is appropriate or not. The Japanese Information Center for Science and Technology reports that this technique has been used to halve the cost of translating a technical abstract.

Another use to which a natural language system might be put is in the construction of natural language interfaces to existing programs such as database systems. An automated travel agent would be able to deal with queries like, Can you get me a cheap flight to Chicago tomorrow? A payroll system could be asked to list all corporate executives making less than $100,000 per year.

There are other applications as well. Systems that read books for the blind. The physicist Steven Hawking communicates by typing into a synthetic speech device. U.S. Sprint recently introduced a system where the identification number associated with a telephone calling card is spoken into the phone by the caller. If you want to phone home or your office, you can just say, "Call home," or "Call office."

Finally, a natural language system could help with the problems encountered in using declarative systems. Advances in natural language generation would allow these systems to explain their conclusions in normal language instead of via an inference trace of some kind. On a far more ambitious note, rather than hand-coding knowledge about (say) failure modes in jet engines, I could find a book on the topic and just hand it to the machine. Needless to say, we aren't there yet.

17.1 SIGNAL PROCESSING

The problems involved in analyzing an acoustic signal and picking out the words it contains are similar to the problems involved in finding the edges in a visual image. First, the signal needs to be digitized. The acoustic equivalents of edge segments then need to be identified and these segments need to be assembled into words.

With regard to digitization, there is far less data in an acoustic image than in a visual one. Roughly speaking, the information one needs is only the frequency amplitude of the sound as a function of time. Since natural language understanding doesn't require nearly the level of detail needed by a visual system, there is far less information to analyze.

The linguistic equivalent of an edge segment is a phoneme, something like the sound we make when we say the letter *m*. Because of the reduced amount of data in auditory signals, real-time identification of the phonemes in any particular utterance is fairly tractable.

Assembling these phonemes into words is a much more subtle problem. The reason is that English is often ambiguous; there are many sequences of phonemes that may mean one thing or another depending on the context in which they occur. As an example, a foreigner visiting New York once returned to her host and asked what a "nominal egg" was. Somewhat confused, the host asked why she was interested, and was informed that his visitor had overheard a conversation in which one New Yorker complained to another that the apartment he wanted to rent cost a nominal egg.

On the face of it, this interpretation isn't any more or less foolish than the one that was actually intended by the speaker. The moral of all this is:

It's very hard to wreck a nice beach. (17.1)

Say it out loud a few times; you'll see what I mean. We bring a great deal of knowledge to bear when turning a spoken utterance into text.

17.2 SYNTAX AND PARSING

In the remainder of this chapter, we will assume that we are dealing with a sequence of words instead of an acoustic signal directly. Perhaps the problems of the previous section have been solved; perhaps the input to the system is textual. Given a sequence of words, how do we decide what it means?[40]

Sentence understanding has long been of interest to the linguistics community; the accepted approach is to produce a grammar that generates the legal sentences of English. In order to drive our discussion, though, I'm going to try something a bit different from the presentation in the previous chapter. Here, we'll focus on a single sentence as the analysis progresses:

What did Mary give the man of her dreams? (17.2)

Let's warm up with something simpler. The parse we'd like to generate for the sentence, "Mary walks," is the following:

```
(S (MOOD declarative)
   (SUBJ (NP (NAME Mary)))
   (VERB walk) (TENSE present)
   (NUM 3s))
```

The parse is analyzed recursively. We have a sentence S, the mood of which is declarative. The subject of the sentence is a name, *Mary*, and the main verb of the sentence is the verb *walks*. The sentence is in the present tense because its verb is, and is in the third person singular because the

40 I do not mean to imply that phonemes must be assembled into words before syntactic processing can begin. Indeed, it seems that there is an interleaving here, as subsequent analysis is often used to select among competing interpretations of spoken language. This is how we discard (17.1) in favor of the intended, "It's very hard to recognize speech."

subject and verb both are. The subject and verb are required to agree about number and person; there should not be a grammatical parse for a sentence like, "Mary walk."

In some cases, the values taken by attributes may be sets. Here is the parse for "You walked":

```
(S (MOOD declarative)
   (SUBJ (NP (PRONOUN you)))
   (VERB walk) (TENSE past)
   (NUM {2s,2p}))
```

We can't tell if *you* is singular or plural here. The individual verb *walked* can be any person or number; the number is assigned to the overall sentence by taking the intersection of the number of the subject *you* (2s or 2p) and that of the verb *walked* (any of 1s, 1p, 2s, 2p, 3s, or 3p).

We will construct these parses using what are known as *augmented transition networks*, or ATNs. Here is the ATN used to extract the subject noun phrase from "Mary walks":

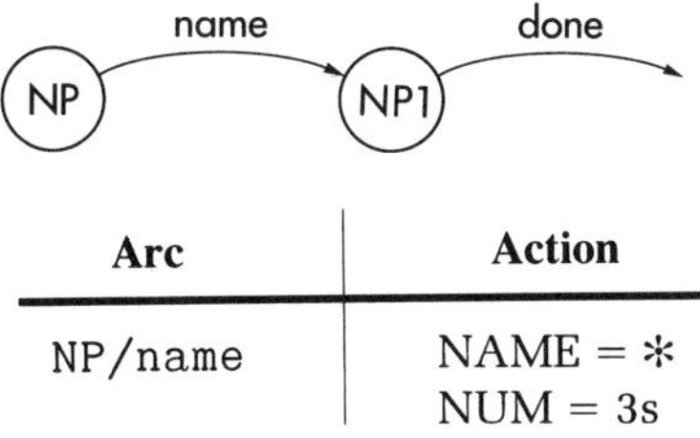

Arc	Action
NP/name	NAME = * NUM = 3s

We enter the ATN at the node marked NP and exit when we traverse the arc done. As we work our way along the arcs, we assign values to various slots in the structure we are building; here there is only one arc, NP/name, and when we traverse it we set NAME to *, the word processed during the traversal (*Mary*, in this case). We also set the number of the noun phrase to 3s, since names are third-person singular. The current word needs to be a name (the label for the arc) in order for the traversal to be successful. More generally, the input token processed by the ATN must be of the category labelled by the arc.

When we encounter the done arc, we exit the ATN, returning a list labelled with the root node of the ATN. Each element of the list is a pair, the first element of the pair being one of the slots that was filled by the ATN (NAME or NUM in this case), and the second element of the pair being its value.

Let's suppose that the entry in our dictionary (often called a *lexicon* in natural language work) for the word *Mary* is the following:

Word	Type
Mary	name

This allows us to traverse the above ATN, since *Mary* is indeed a name. The value returned is

```
(NP (NAME Mary) (NUM 3s))
```

In this simple case, the ATN corresponding to an entire sentence is the following:

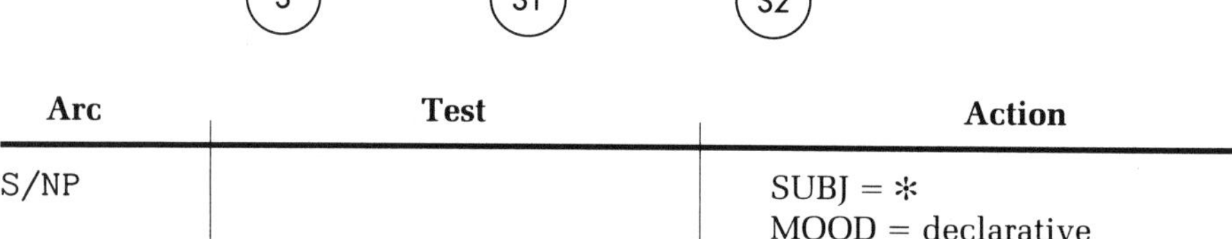

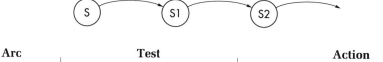

Arc	Test	Action
S/NP		SUBJ = * MOOD = declarative
S1/verb	NUM(SUBJ) ∩ NUM(*)	VERB = * NUM = NUM(SUBJ) ∩ NUM(*)

There are two new features here. The first is that we have labelled an arc not with a word category, but with the identifier of another network (the noun phrase network). To traverse this arc, we invoke this other network and set * to the result.

The second new feature is the inclusion of a test for the arc `S1/verb`. The test means that the arc can be traversed only if the value of the test is not empty—in other words, there has to be some intersection between the number of the noun phrase and the number of the current verb. If there is agreement, the number of the entire sentence is set to the value of the intersection. We remarked earlier that arcs could only be traversed if the word being processed was of the appropriate category. In this more general case, we require that the category be appropriate and that the test be applied successfully.

One final modification and we'll be there. In some cases, grammatical components have optional subfields. The verbs in a sentence can be simple verbs like *gave* or compound verbs such as *could have been giving*. The auxiliary words are optional.

To handle this, we introduce a `jump` arc in ATNs. Traversing a jump arc doesn't use any of the words in the sentence being parsed; provided that any associated tests are satisfied, the arc is traversed and the parse continues.

With these ideas in mind, here are the ATNs needed to parse the sentence, "Mary gave me a new picture."

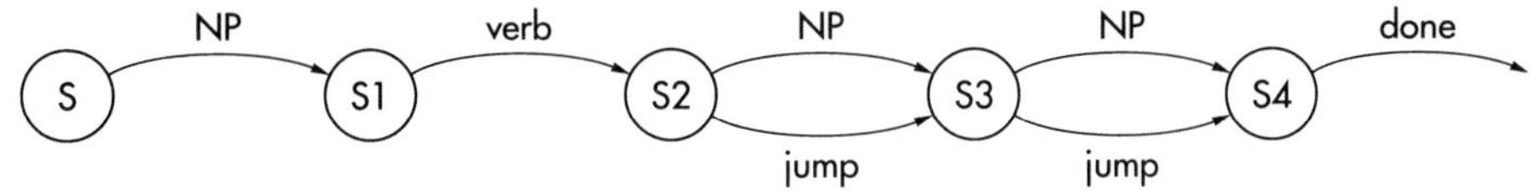

Arc	Test	Action
S/NP		SUBJ = * MOOD = declarative
S1/verb	NUM(SUBJ) ∩ NUM(*)	VERB = * NUM = NUM(SUBJ) ∩ NUM(*)
S2/NP	Transitive(VERB)	OBJ = *
S2/jump	¬Transitive(VERB)	
S3/NP	Bitransitive(VERB)	IND-OBJ = OBJ OBJ = *

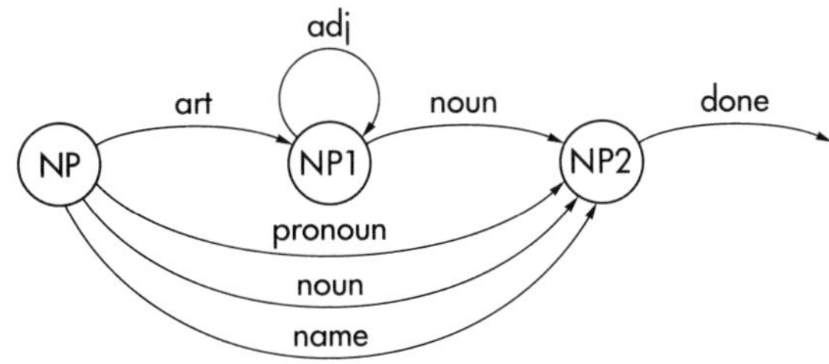

Arc	Test	Action
NP/art		DET = * NUM = NUM(*)
NP/pronoun		PRONOUN = * NUM = NUM(*)
NP/noun	NUM(*) = 3p	NOUN = * NUM = 3p
NP/name		NAME = * NUM = 3s
NP1/adj		ADJS = append(ADJS,*)
NP1/noun	NUM(*) ∩ NUM	NOUN = * NUM = NUM(*) ∩ NUM

We've written Transitive(VERB) to mean that the current value of the VERB variable is transitive and therefore accepts a direct object, and Bitransitive to mean that the verb can also accept an indirect object. The verb *love* is transitive but not bitransitive. Noun phrases include determiners (*a*, *the*, and so on) and arbitrary sequences of adjectives. The lexicon we will be using appears in Figure 17.1.

To execute the parse, we need to keep track of two pointers. One points to our current location in the ATN, and the other to our location in the

FIGURE 17.1 Lexicon for the grammatical examples

word	type	feature	value(s)
what	wh-pronoun	NUM	3s,3p
Mary	name		
did	do verb	TENSE NUM VERB TYPE TENSE NUM	past 1s,1p,2s,2p,3s,3p do transitive, bitransitive past 1s,1p,2s,2p,3s,3p
walks	verb	VERB TENSE NUM	walk present 3s
walked	verb	VERB TENSE NUM	walk past 1s,1p,2s,2p,3s,3p
give	verb	VERB TYPE TENSE NUM	give transitive, bitransitive infinitive, present 1s,1p,2s,2p,3p
gave	verb	VERB TYPE TENSE NUM	give transitive, bitransitive past 1s,1p,2s,2p,3s,3p
me	pronoun	NUM	1s
a	article	NUM	3s
the	article	NUM	3s,3p
her	article	ROOT NUM	she 3s,3p
picture	noun	NOUN NUM	picture 3s
man	noun	NOUN NUM	man 3s
dreams	noun	NOUN NUM	dream 3p
boat	noun	NOUN NUM	boat 3s
of	preposition		

sentence. The ATN pointer is actually a list of pointers, since when we jump from one ATN to another, we need to keep track of our return point in the original ATN.

Initially, the ATN pointer has the value (S); we are at the beginning of the ATN that parses complete sentences. The sentence pointer is in front of the word *Mary*.

The only arc out of the S node is labelled with NP, so we need to invoke the NP ATN. We do this by making the ATN pointer

(NP S)

including information about our return point.

There are four arcs out of the NP node, but only one of them matches the current word in the sentence, which is identified as a name by the information in the lexicon. We update the ATN pointer to

(NP2 S)

and the sentence pointer to *gave*. We also take the steps indicated in the ATN annotations, setting NAME to *Mary* and NUM to *3s*.

Now we come to the done arc in the NP ATN. We pop back to the original ATN, and traverse the NP arc. The value returned by the NP ATN is

`(NP (NAME Mary) (NUM 3s))` (17.3)

where we have attached the name of the noun phrase ATN to a list of the accumulated values. This is the "value" of the arc S/NP, and when we set SUBJ = * as this arc requires, the value of the subject of our sentence is taken to be (17.3).

As we continue this process, here is the detailed parse:

ATN pointer	Sentence pointer	Variables and values
S	Mary	
NP S	Mary	
NP2 S	gave	NAME = Mary
		NUM = 3s
S	gave	* = (NP (NAME Mary) (NUM 3s))
S1	gave	SUBJ = (NP (NAME Mary) (NUM 3s))
		MOOD = declarative
S2	me	VERB = (V (VERB give) (TENSE past) (NUM 1s,1p,2s,2p,3s,3p))

At this point, we have a choice. We can take the jump arc out of S2, or attempt to find a NP that is an object of the verb and use that.

But the `jump` arc has as a condition that the current VERB not be transitive. Since *gave* is identified as transitive by the lexicon, we need to take the NP arc out of S2, and the parse continues:

ATN pointer	Sentence pointer	Variables and values
S2	me	VERB = (V (VERB give) (TENSE past) (NUM 1s,1p,2s,2p,3s,3p))
NP S2	me	
NP2 S2	a	PRONOUN = me
		NUM = 1s
S2	a	* = (NP (PRONOUN me) (NUM 1s))
S3	a	OBJ = (NP (PRONOUN me) (NUM 1s))

Another choice point. It is legal to take the `jump` arc from S3 at this point, but this would put us at S4 with words still remaining to be processed in the sentence. We therefore look for another noun phrase:

ATN pointer	Sentence pointer	Variables and values
S3	a	OBJ = (NP (PRONOUN me) (NUM 1s))
NP S3	a	
NP1 S3	new	DET = a
		NUM = 3s
NP1 S3	picture	ADJS = (new)
NP2 S3		NOUN = picture
		NUM = 3s
S3		* = (NP (DET a) (ADJS (new)) (NOUN picture) (NUM 3s))
S4		IND-OBJ = (NP (PRONOUN me) (NUM 1s))
		OBJ = (NP (DET a) (ADJS (new)) (NOUN picture) (NUM 3s))
Ø		* = (S (MOOD declarative) (NUM 3s)
		(SUBJ (NP (NAME Mary)))
		(VERB (V (VERB give) (TENSE past)))
		(IND-OBJ (NP (PRONOUN me) (NUM 1s)))
		(OBJ (NP (DET a) (ADJS (new)) (NOUN picture))))

All of the purely grammatical information has been extracted at this point. Here is the algorithm that we followed:

ALGORITHM 17.2.1 **ATN-based parsing** *To parse a sentence:*

1. *Set the* ATN *pointer to (S) and the sentence pointer to the beginning of the sentence in question. The current node is always the first element of the* ATN *pointer.*
2. *Select an arc out of the current node. In order to legally traverse the arc, it must satisfy the following conditions:*

   (a) *Any associated test must be satisfied by the current variable values.*
   (b) *If the arc is labelled with a word category, the current word must be a member of that category.*
3. *Execute the actions associated with the arc. In addition, do the following, based on the type of the arc:*
   (a) *If the arc is a word category, update the current position in the sentence by one word and change the current node to the destination of the arc.*
   (b) *If the arc corresponds to another* ATN, *push the starting node of that* ATN *onto the* ATN *pointer.*
   (c) *If the arc is* `jump`, *change the current node to the destination of the arc.*
   (d) *If the arc is* `done`, *pop the current node off of the* ATN *pointer and set* * *to the value returned by this node. If the* ATN *pointer is now empty and all of the text has been processed, return* *. *If the* ATN *pointer is empty and text remains, fail. Otherwise, return to step 2.*

In step 2 of Algorithm 17.2.1, we have to select an arc out of our current node in the ATN; because of this, the algorithm itself must be augmented with a search procedure of some sort. This will ensure that we gradually consider each possible arc selection that might lead to a successful parse of the sentence in question.

As usual, there are many techniques that can be employed here—forward search, backward search, and so on. The ATN representation is especially well-suited to forward search, since we need to choose which arc to explore next, but there are other descriptions that are better suited to backward search or other methods.

The two most important of these other descriptions are structure grammars and first-order logic grammars. In a structure grammar, we write something like

$$\text{S} \rightarrow \text{NP verb} \tag{17.4}$$

to indicate that a sentence can be replaced with a NP followed by a verb. This approach is best-suited to backward chaining, since we select the overall structure of the sentence first and work out the details later. This has been referred to as *top down* parsing; the ATN approach is *bottom up*.

In a first-order logic grammar, the information content of an ATN or a rule such as (17.4) is captured using a description in first-order logic. An advantage of this approach is that the representation is unbiased with regard to the direction of inference; a disadvantage is that the description is probably not as easy to follow as the one we have presented here.

In all of these approaches, the basic ideas remain the same; the overall features of language do not change from one representation to the next. Since the amount of space we can spend on syntactic parsing is limited, I have chosen to describe the ATN approach in some depth as opposed to giving you briefer presentations of a variety of equivalent techniques.

But back to our example involving Mary and the man of her dreams. If we want to extend our syntactic techniques to deal with the original sentence (17.2), there are three additional points that need to be addressed:

1. We need to extend our analysis of verbs to include expressions like "*did* give."
2. We need to include prepositional phrases as in "the man *of her dreams*."
3. We need to modify our description of sentences to include questions.

We begin with the first two; the third is a bit more subtle and we will deal with it separately. Our temporary goal is to find a parse of a declarative version of our original sentence:

$$\text{Mary did give the man of her dreams a picture.} \qquad (17.5)$$

Compound verbs Rather than give a complete description of verb phrases, we present a smaller one that handles *did* expressions only. Here it is:

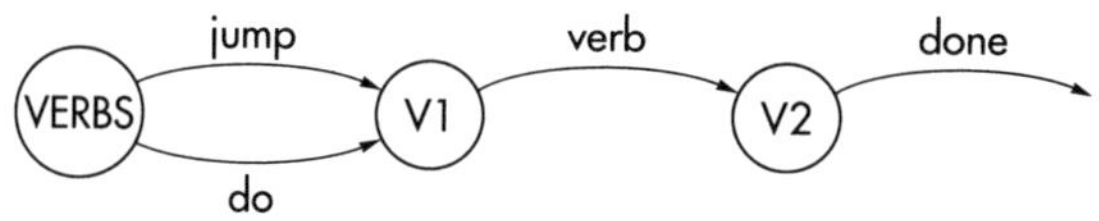

Arc	Test	Action
VERBS/do		AUX = do
		FIRST-V = *
V1/verb	if AUX = do, TENSE(*) = infinitive	VERB = *
	else TENSE(*) = present or past	if FIRST-V = nil, FIRST-V = *
V2/done		TENSE = TENSE(FIRST-V)

The AUX field is used to record the fact that the verb has been modified with *do*; if so, the main verb must be an infinitive. If not, the tense of the main verb must be present or past. FIRST-V is used to record the first verb of the sequence, since it is this verb that has the overall tense information (*Mary did give* is in the past tense, and so on).

Prepositional phrases The structure of a prepositional phrase is straightforward enough; here it is:

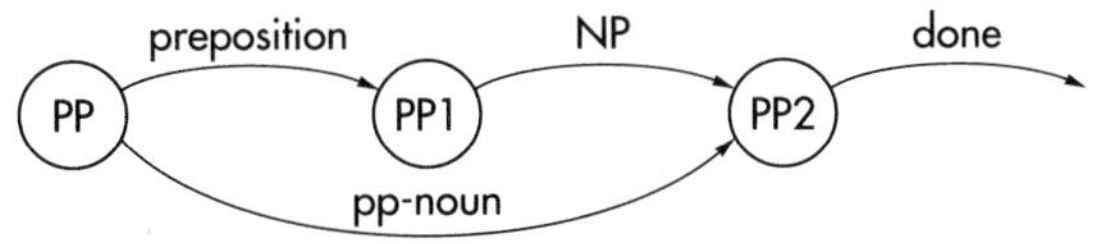

Arc	Action
PP/preposition	PREP = *
PP/pp-noun	PP = *
PP1/NP	OBJ = *

We've included prepositional phrase nouns in the ATN; these are single words that can substitute for prepositional phrases, like *yesterday* in, "I gave him the book yesterday."

Prepositional phrases can modify either noun phrases as in

Mary gave him the picture of the boat.

or entire sentences, as in

Mary gave him the picture on Thursday.

To handle this, we need to add prepositional phrase arcs to node S4 of the sentence ATN and to node NP2 of the noun phrase ATN, both on page 357. In both cases, the arcs return to the same node they originate from. We add a "modifiers" slot to the sentence or noun phrase, and the action to take when encountering a prepositional phrase is

MODS = append(MODS,*)

This adds the prepositional phrase to the list of modifiers.

At this point, the parse of (17.5) proceeds much like the parse of "Mary gave me a picture." When the prepositional phrase is encountered, however, there is ambiguity as to its referent. One possible parse proceeds by finishing the NP *the man*, jumping to node S4 of the sentence ATN, and then treating *of her dreams* as a sentential modifier. This parse fails, however, because we are forced to jump out of the ATN with the two words, *a picture*, still unparsed.

The alternative is to treat the prepositional phrase as a modifier to the NP *the man*. This allows the parse to complete as before.

Handling movement Now for the hard part: constructing the question. What this involves is transforming a declarative "sentence" like

Mary did give the man of her dreams what (17.6)

(which we can already deal with) into the question

What did Mary give the man of her dreams? (17.7)

The transformation involves moving parts of the sentence around; we swap *did* and *Mary* and also move the trailing noun phrase (*what*, the direct object in (17.6)) to the beginning of the sentence. Similar ideas are involved in the construction of yes/no questions like

Did Mary give the man of her dreams a picture? (17.8)

and in the transformation of sentences into the passive voice, as in

John was given a picture by Mary. (17.9)

We can deal with all of these examples by finding some way to reuse our existing grammar but to augment it so that it handles movement in an appropriate way.

The basic idea is the following: When we see the *What* at the beginning of (17.7), we do two things. First, we change the mood of the sentence from declarative to interrogative. Second, we realize that the *what* is taking the place of a NP elsewhere in the sentence, so we store the *what* as a "virtual noun phrase" to be used later. We do this by setting the value of a special variable, HOLD, to the noun phrase *what*.

Moving *did* past *Mary* is a bit simpler. In an interrogative sentence like (17.8) where the subject is not a virtual NP like *what*, an auxiliary verb must precede the NP that is the subject of the sentence. We handle this by explicitly requiring the presence of the auxiliary before the noun phrase can be processed.

The new ATN corresponding to complete sentences is shown in Figure 17.2; we have also incorporated the handling of *do* by the VERBS ATN. Here are the annotations to the network.

FIGURE 17.2 The final ATN for sentences

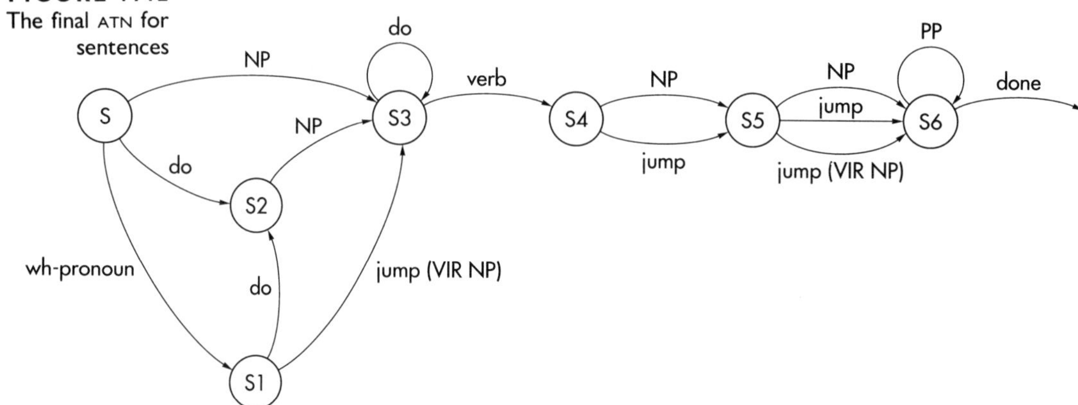

Arc	Test	Action
S/NP		SUBJ = * MOOD = declarative
S/do		AUX = do FIRST-V = * MOOD = yes-or-no
S/wh-pronoun		HOLD = * MOOD = wh-query WH-TYPE = *
S1/do		AUX = do FIRST-V = *
S1/jump (VIR NP)		SUBJ = HOLD HOLD = nil
S2/NP		SUBJ = *
S3/do	AUX = nil	AUX = do FIRST-V = *
S3/verb	if AUX = do, TENSE(*) = infinitive else TENSE(*) = present or past also NUM(SUBJ) ∩ NUM(*)	VERB = * if FIRST-V = nil, FIRST-V = * NUM = NUM(SUBJ) ∩ NUM(*)
S4/NP	Transitive(VERB)	OBJ = *
S4/jump	¬Transitive(VERB)	
S5/NP	Bitransitive(VERB)	IND-OBJ = OBJ OBJ = *
S5/jump (VIR NP)	HOLD and Bitransitive(VERB)	IND-OBJ = OBJ OBJ = HOLD HOLD = nil
S6/PP		MODS = append(MODS,*)
S6/done	HOLD = nil	TENSE = TENSE(FIRST-V)

When we use the virtual NP, we set HOLD to nil to indicate that we have done so; we do not allow the done arc to be traversed unless the held NP has indeed been used by one of the arcs coming out of S1 or S4. This is to ensure that we are unable to parse a sentence like, "What did Mary give the man of her dreams a picture."

The tests on nodes S, S1, S2, and S3 are to ensure that we establish the virtual NP correctly, have at most one auxiliary *do*, and that this auxiliary is in the correct place. The remainder of the ATN is quite like the previous one, except we allow the virtual NP to be the direct object of the sentence and require that HOLD be nil before exiting.

We can now parse (17.7). Initially, we encounter the wh-pronoun, *what*, and move to node S1, determining the overall sentence to be a wh-query.

One possibility is now to jump to node S3, treating *what* as the object of the sentence.

Having done so, if we treat *did* as an auxiliary, we will be unable to process *Mary* in node S3. So we'll need to treat *did* as the main verb of the query, treating *Mary* as its object. (This would make sense if the sentence were something like, "What did the job?")

But now we're stuck anyway, since *give* is a verb and cannot be processed by node S5. So we should have processed the original *did* out of node S1, instead of using the virtual NP at that point.

This allows us to correctly identify *Mary* as the subject of the sentence and *did give* as the verb. The NP beginning with *the man* is the indirect object of the sentence, and the virtual NP *what* is its direct object. But there is an ambiguity: The PP *of her dreams* can modify either the NP *the man* or the sentence itself. Here are the two possible parses:

```
(S (MOOD wh-query)
   (WH-TYPE what)
   (SUBJ (NP (NAME Mary)))
   (AUX do)
   (FIRST-V did)
   (TENSE past)
   (VERB give)
   (NUM 3s)
   (OBJ what)
   (IND-OBJ (NP (DET the) (NOUN man) (NUM 3s)
                (MODS (PP (PREP of)
                          (OBJ (NP (DET her) (NOUN dream)
                                   (NUM 3p))))))))
```

```
(S (MOOD wh-query)
   (WH-TYPE what)
   (SUBJ (NP (NAME Mary)))
   (AUX do)
   (FIRST-V did)
   (TENSE past)
   (VERB give)
   (NUM 3s)
   (OBJ what)
   (IND-OBJ (NP (DET the) (NOUN man) (NUM 3s)))
   (MODS (PP (PREP of) (OBJ (NP (DET her) (NOUN dream)
                                (NUM 3p))))))
```

We know that the first of these should be selected, but syntactic arguments cannot help us do so. After all, the sentence could just as well have been

What did Mary give the man during July?

or the truly ambiguous

What did Mary give the man in her dreams?

17.3 SEMANTICS AND MEANING

The next phase of linguistic analysis involves making use of word meanings to extend and perhaps disambiguate the result returned by the syntactic parse. As a start, let's drop some of the information we won't be using from the parse of our query (17.7), so that the two potential parses become

```
(S (WH-TYPE what)
   (SUBJ (NP (NAME Mary)))
   (VERB give) (TENSE past)
   (OBJ what) (NUM 3s)
   (IND-OBJ (NP (DET the) (NOUN man) (NUM 3s)
                (MODS (PP (PREP of)
                          (OBJ (NP (DET her) (NOUN dream)
                                   (NUM 3p))))))))
```

```
(S (WH-TYPE what)
   (SUBJ (NP (NAME Mary)))
   (VERB give) (TENSE past)
   (OBJ what) (NUM 3s)
   (IND-OBJ (NP (DET the) (NOUN man) (NUM 3s)))
   (MODS (PP (PREP of) (OBJ (NP (DET her) (NOUN dream)
                                (NUM 3p))))))
```

The goal of the semantic phase is to eliminate the second parse as impossible, since *of her dreams* cannot modify *give*, and to produce the following logical expression from the first parse:

$$\begin{aligned}&\texttt{past}(e) \wedge \texttt{action}(e,give) \wedge \texttt{agent}(e,Mary) \wedge \texttt{object}(e,what)\\&\quad \wedge \texttt{recipient}(e,n) \wedge \texttt{definite}(n) \wedge \texttt{singular}(n) \wedge \texttt{man}(n)\\&\quad \wedge \texttt{location}(n,p) \wedge \texttt{plural}(p) \wedge \texttt{dream}(p) \wedge \texttt{owner}(p,her)\end{aligned} \tag{17.10}$$

In other words, there is an event *e* that took place in the past and was a giving event. The agent was Mary, the object given is the object of the query (`what`), and the recipient was *n*. The recipient is singular, definite (*the* man of Mary's dreams as opposed to *a* man of Mary's dreams), and a man located in a place *p*. This place is plural, a dream, and belongs to `her`. We are not yet trying to identify the referent for the possessive pronoun *her*; as we will see in the next section, doing so typically involves an appeal to knowledge beyond that available in the definitions of the words appearing in the sentence.

The above translation will be based on sets of rules. One set translates the overall sentence, another translates noun phrases, and so on. Here is one of the rules used to translate the entire sentence:

Component	**Trigger**	**Result**
S	(TENSE past)	past(*)

The component, S, indicates that the rule is to be applied to entire sentences. The trigger is a list of pairs that must appear in the syntactic parse for the rule to be applicable, and the result is the logical form that is constructed as a result.

Note the appearance of the * in the result. Any particular syntactic structure refers to a single object or event, and when we analyze the structure, we need to name this object. The * should be replaced with the name of the syntactic component being analyzed.

Here is another rule:

Component	**Trigger**	**Condition**	**Result**
S	(VERB give) (SUBJ x)	animate(x)	agent(*,x)

We have added a condition to the rule, saying that the agent performing a giving action must be animate. The variable x here can be bound as appropriate; in the construction of (17.10), x is bound to `Mary`. The condition flags are created by other portions of the semantic analysis:

Component	**Trigger**	**Result**	**Asserts**
NP	(NOUN man)	man(*)	physical-object(*), animate(*)

When analyzing a noun phrase, if the main noun is *man*, the resulting noun phrase is both animate and a physical object.

Other semantic rules are ambiguous; consider the two noun phrases "a day in June" and "the man in the house." If the main noun and the noun phrase that is the object of *in* are both times, the meaning is "during." If the main noun is a physical object and the embedded noun phrase is a location, *in* specifies the location of the object. We can't mix these; "a day in the house" and "the man in June" don't make sense.

Here is the associated rule:

Component	Trigger	Condition	Asserts
NP	(MODS (PP (PREP in) (OBJ x)))	time(*) ∧ time(x) physical-object(*) ∧ place(x)	during(*,x) location(*,x)

There is only one rule, but two potential outcomes depending on the eventual meaning of *in*.

Given rules of this form, the semantic analysis proceeds by applying all of the rules whose triggers are satisfied, accumulating the result as a large conjunction. Note that *all* of the rules must be applied:

> *In a successful semantic analysis, every rule whose trigger is satisfied must be applied. If there is some rule with a satisfied trigger for which every condition is unsatisfied, the semantic analysis fails.*

This is the reason we cannot deal with a phrase like "a man in June." We can't ignore the semantic rule that deals with *in* as part of a noun phrase, and the rule cannot be applied because *man* is not a time and *June* is not a location.

The semantic rules for our running example appear in Figure 17.3. We explicitly exclude a prepositional phrase beginning with *of* as a modifier to *give*; other prepositional phrases are handled as we have discussed elsewhere in this section.

Given these rules, we can assemble the various semantic contributions to obtain (17.10) as the unique meaning of our original query (17.2). Other sentences, such as

What did Mary give the man on her boat? (17.11)

can be handled similarly. In this case, the sentence is legitimately ambiguous and two semantic interpretations are constructed.

The only slight subtlety is that we may need to be careful about the order in which the semantic rules are applied. As an example, we need to realize that *man* is a physical object before applying the semantic rule that deals with the prepositional phrase "of her dreams."

As it turns out, this apparent dependence on rule order is an illusion: Since assertions are accumulated as the rules are processed, we can perform the analysis using a list of "assumed" assertions and check them at the end. As an example, we can process the prepositional phrase "of her dreams" before realizing that *man* is a physical object, recording the fact that the semantic analysis requires the noun phrase to refer to a physical

FIGURE 17.3
Semantic rules

	Trigger	Condition	Result	Asserts
S	(TENSE past)		past(∗)	
S	(VERB x)		action(∗,x)	
S	(VERB give) (SUBJ x)	animate (x)	agent(∗,x)	
S	(VERB give) (OBJ x)	phys(x)	object(∗,x)	
S	(VERB give) (IND-OBJ x)		recipient(∗,x)	
S	(MODS (PP (PREP during) (OBJ t)))	time(t)	during (∗,t)	
S	(MODS (PP (PREP in) (OBJ p)))	place(p)	location(∗,p)	
S	(VERB give) (MODS (PP (PREP of) (OBJ p)))	false		
NP	(DET the)		definite(∗)	
NP	(DET a)		¬definite(∗)	
NP	(DET her)		owner(∗,her)	
NP	(NUM 3s)		singular(∗)	
NP	(NUM 3p)		plural(∗)	
NP	(NOUN dream)		dream(∗)	place(∗)
NP	(NOUN man)		man(∗)	phys(∗), animate(∗)
NP	(NAME x)		∗ = x	phys(∗), animate(∗)
NP	(MODS (PP (PREP of) (OBJ p)))	phys(∗) ∧ place(p)	location(∗,p)	
NP	(MODS (PP (PREP during) (OBJ t)))	time(∗) ∧ time(t)	during(∗,t)	
NP	(MODS (PP (PREP in) (OBJ x)))	time(∗) ∧ time(x)	during(∗,x)	
		phys(∗) ∧ place(x)	location(∗,x)	

object. If it does so after the work is complete, the semantic pass completes successfully. If not, the semantic pass fails. Using this technique, only very limited search need be involved in semantic analysis.

It is also possible to couple the semantic analysis more tightly with the declarative information in our database. Consider again the entry in Figure 17.3 that says that men are animate physical objects:

Component	Trigger	Result	Asserts
NP	(NOUN man)	man(∗)	phys(∗), animate(∗)

More effective would be simply to use the result of the rule, man(∗), and then to combine this with implications such as

$$\text{man}(x) \rightarrow \text{physical-object}(x)$$

$$\text{man}(x) \rightarrow \text{animate}(x)$$

This serves the dual purpose of allowing us to drop the "asserts" field from the semantic rules and coupling these assertions more effectively to our other knowledge about the domain.

Finally, the description that we have given of semantics assumes that the semantic analysis begins when the syntactic analysis is complete. There is no real reason for this, however; we can fire the semantic rules as the syntactic analysis proceeds, if we wish.

The advantage of doing this is that some ambiguous parses can be eliminated early on using semantic considerations. Consider the following:

Visiting relatives can be trying.

This is legitimately ambiguous, and will be parsed as such by the grammar. But

Visiting museums can be trying. (17.12)

is not ambiguous; the adjective *visiting* can only modify animate nouns. Semantic analysis can determine this after only two words have been processed, thereby avoiding the computational expense of constructing one of the two parses of (17.12).

There is also direct evidence that semantic and syntactic analyses occur in parallel. People have no trouble understanding nongrammatical sentences; few of the "sentences" in naturally occurring speech *are* grammatical. It's far more common, I mean, grammar is sort of a luxury in spoken speech. That last sentence sounds natural when spoken, but is likely to be a mystery to most parsers. One way to handle this might be to extend the grammar to deal with these semigrammatical utterances, but it seems far more likely that we analyze them semantically using partially successful parsing information.

17.4 PRAGMATICS

The next phase of analysis uses the knowledge in our domain to remove the remaining ambiguities in our understanding of the sentence and to interpret this sentence in the larger context of what we know. One ambiguity does remain in (17.10): the referent of the possessive pronoun *her*.

In this case, the problem is solved fairly easily; *her* refers to *Mary*, the latest completed noun phrase in the sentence. So we can finally replace (17.10) with

$$\texttt{past}(e) \wedge \texttt{action}(e,\texttt{give}) \wedge \texttt{agent}(e,\texttt{Mary}) \wedge \texttt{object}(e,\texttt{what}) \wedge \texttt{recipient}(e,n) \wedge \texttt{definite}(n) \wedge \texttt{singular}(n) \wedge \texttt{man}(n) \wedge \texttt{location}(n,p) \wedge \texttt{plural}(p) \wedge \texttt{dream}(p) \wedge \texttt{owner}(p,\texttt{Mary}) \quad (17.13)$$

where we have identified the dreams being discussed as Mary's.

The problem of finding the referent of a pronoun is called *anaphora resolution*, and the most straightforward solution is the one mentioned above: Find the most recent possible reference, and use that. We may have to exploit some domain information to do this, of course; consider the two sentences

Mary gave the man his shoe.

and

Mary gave the man her shoe.

In the first, the shoe belongs to the man; in the second, it belongs to Mary. This distinction is based on the fact that *his* cannot refer to a female and *her* cannot refer to a male.

Here is a more subtle example:

> Fred went to the supermarket. He found a bottle of milk in the dairy section, paid for it and left.

The most recent NP before *it* is the dairy section; we need database information to the effect that one does not buy entire portions of supermarkets in order to eliminate it. Once we manage to do so, the bottle of milk is identified as the object Fred bought.

More subtle still is the following example:

> Thelma met Louise at her apartment. They couldn't meet anywhere else because Thelma's car was broken.

In this example, *her* can either be Thelma or Louise; deciding which depends on information in the second sentence. And *they* is even more subtle—it refers to Thelma and Louise together—a concept that doesn't even *appear* in the first sentence!

There are other aspects of pragmatics as well. Let me touch on two here: discourse analysis and plan recognition.

Discourse analysis This part of the book, "AI Systems," is prefaced by a short description of the topics covered. Here's an excerpt.

> A vision, planning, natural language, or learning system will involve much more than simple knowledge representation. Although ideas from search and knowledge representation underlie almost all other work in the field, much progress has been made on problems in these broader areas.

What is the referent of "these broader areas"?

There is no pronoun here, but the problem of reference remains. The most recent viable referent appears to be the areas of search and knowledge representation; how is it that we know the actual referent to be vision, planning, and so on?

The reason we know that the "broader areas" don't refer to search and knowledge representation is that the clause, "Although ideas from search and knowledge representation underlie almost all other work in the field," has a separate focus from the rest of the paragraph.

The first sentence in the quotation focuses our attention on vision, planning, and so on. The second sentence, introduced by *although*, includes a temporary change of focus to search and knowledge representation; when the clause is completed, the focus returns to vision and planning.

This is quite a general phenomenon; identifying the intended focus of a portion of natural language text is an essential component of understanding it. In general, as text is analyzed or as a discussion proceeds, we retain a stack of the previous focal "segments" of the discussion. The word *although* in the original quote indicates that a new segment is being pushed onto the stack, to be removed once the current clause has been processed.

Although isn't the only linguistic marker for a segment change of this sort. *Incidentally* and *by the way* also signal the beginnings of new segments; *anyway* and *getting back to* explicitly mark returns to previous segments:

> **Tom:** Do you have the $20 I lent you last week?
> **Sam:** What $20?
> **Tom:** You remember. I lent it to you for some AI book. You said yesterday you'd have it for me today.
> **Sam:** Oh, yeah. That's right. (*A pause.*) By the way, who won the football game yesterday?
> **Tom:** The 49ers.
> (*Silence.*)
> **Tom:** Getting back to my $20 . . .

Plan recognition Consider the following passage from a short story:

> David needed money desperately. He went to his desk and took out a gun.

When we read this, we draw conclusions that aren't sanctioned by the literal text. David is about to commit a crime, he'll use a gun, and so on. Understanding natural language often involves an analysis of the intentions of the agents speaking or being discussed.

We've already seen another example of this; when we ask a ticket agent, "Do you know when the train leaves?" we expect him to realize that we are asking because we probably want to know as well. This is why, "At two o'clock," is a more appropriate response than, "Yes." If the listener is someone planning a trip, we expect him to realize that we have no real interest in the specific time of departure, and the situation is reversed.

From a formal point of view, this process of plan recognition is not too hard to understand. We have some agent A (David in the first example; the speaker in the second) and need to find a goal g that A might have, and such that A's actions are part of a plan for achieving g. The crucial assumption is that people do not act randomly—they only take actions in furtherance of their goals.

Thus when we learn that David took out a gun, we search for a plan that uses a gun to achieve his known goal of getting money. If the conclusion of the passage had been instead, "He went to the safe and took out the diamond ring that had been in the family for four generations," a different plan would have come to mind. In the train example, the ticket agent is expected to realize that we have no real reason for asking about the train unless we want to know the departure time ourselves. Our trip-planning friend, however, can explain our question in terms of a general concern for his well-being.

The computational problems involved in plan recognition are far more severe than these simple examples indicate. For a start, plan recognition is substantially more difficult than planning is—instead of planning for a specific goal g, we have to in some sense plan for *all* of the agent A's possible goals and then decide which of them would involve taking the observed actions.

As with vision, the line dividing the later stages of natural language processing from the rest of AI becomes fuzzy. Pragmatic analysis often rests on a deep understanding of the dialog generally.

17.5 NATURAL LANGUAGE GENERATION

We still aren't done with Mary and the man of her dreams. Once we have managed to understand the question, we need to respond to it.

In some ways, this is straightforward. We can pass (17.13) to our theorem prover, treating `what` as a variable and returning the binding for the result. In response to the question, we might say, "tickets to the Olympics," or "a headache." These aren't complete sentences, though; perhaps we should say

Mary gave the man of her dreams a headache. (17.14)

Is this really an appropriate response? Probably not; it's hard to imagine a situation in which you are asked (17.2) and respond with (17.14). Much more likely is

She gave him a headache.

Here is one of the principal problems of natural language generation: While the mapping of a sentence into first-order logic may be effectively unique, the construction of a sentence *from* a statement in first-order logic virtually never is. Is the sentence to be in an active or passive voice? Which noun phrases should be replaced by pronouns? And so on.

More subtle problems arise when we remember that the original question often "means" much more than its logical translation. Suppose that we are asked, "What did Mary give her husband?" and know that Mary just got divorced. A logically acceptable response would be to say that she gave him nothing, since the query associated with (17.13) fails. But much more likely would be

Nothing; she just got divorced.

where we also take the time to correct the speaker's misunderstanding. Needless to say, we can't correct the misunderstanding unless we are able to extract the assumptions underlying the original question.

"Do you know when the train leaves?" and "Can you pass the salt?" place even stronger requirements on the listener. Questions such as these are often referred to as *speech acts* because the asking of the question involves an additional action as well. Although on the face of it I am only asking whether you *know* what time the train leaves or *could* pass the salt, in reality I am asking you to tell me the time or pass me the salt.

Other speech acts are more direct. When we say of a new ship, "I christen this vessel the *U.S.S. Lexington*," we are doing more than informing a listener that we hope the vessel is named the *Lexington*—we are actually naming it.

Natural language generation is difficult for a variety of reasons. There is the inherent complexity of understanding the many linguistic conventions with which we work—both the complexity of English grammar and the host of assumptions underlying speech acts are examples. Language generation and understanding are also hard for fundamental AI reasons, requiring as they do good models of other speakers, of their beliefs, and of the domain in which we are working.

17.6 FURTHER READING

Probably the best general reference on natural language processing is by Allen [1987]; there is also a volume of collected readings on the subject by Grosz *et al.* [1986]. An entertaining collection of essays on natural language generally is edited by Pullum [1991].

Much of the work on speech processing was driven by a large government-sponsored project between 1971 and 1976; the systems emerging from this work are described by Lea [1980].

Syntax is discussed in greater depth by Winograd [1983]; Quirk *et al.* [1985] and Sager [1981] attempt to present comprehensive grammars for English. The ATN approach that we have described has actually been superseded by more computationally effective methods, but—as we have remarked—the ideas are essentially unchanged. *Chart parsers* are one important modern technique discussed in Allen [1987] but not in the text.

There are many semantic issues that we have left completely unaddressed. These include the following:

- Logical operators such as quantification and negation. We need to be careful to interpret the sentence, "Every boy does not like Mary," as meaning that every boy dislikes her, as opposed to that not every boy likes her. "Every boy likes a girl," is legitimately ambiguous; do they all like the same girl, or are different girls involved? This problem is discussed by Hobbs [1986].

- Noun-noun phrases like "ball game" cannot be treated by the grammar we have presented. The question of when one noun can be used to modify another is still fairly open; understanding of this issue is needed if one is to make sense of sentences such as

  Time flies like an arrow.

and

Fruit flies like a banana.

- Complex adjectival phrases can also be ambiguous. If I talk about the "light red block," is the block a pale color or is it easy to lift? One typically needs to use domain knowledge to disambiguate constructs such as this; work here, too, is ongoing.

The ideas of discourse analysis that we presented appear first in a paper by Grosz and Sidner [1986]. Plan recognition, on the other hand, has a somewhat wider history.

An old and informal approach is due to Schank and involves the idea of a *script*. Roughly speaking, a script is a description of how a certain sequence of events should go. We might have a script for robbing a bank, involving getting a gun, holding up the bank, and escaping with the money. By comparing this script to what we know about David in the example of the text, we can identify the plan he is about to execute. Scripts are described by Schank and Abelson [1977].

A more recent idea is discussed in Allen *et al.* [1991], where Kautz formalizes our observation that agents only take actions that help to achieve their goals. More precisely, Kautz assumes nonmonotonically that an agent will not take an action a unless that action helps to achieve some goal g to which the agent is committed. Given that David has taken out a gun and the fact that David's only explicit goal is to get some money, Kautz is able to derive the fact that David intends to use the gun to obtain money illegally.

A somewhat less formal approach appears in Pollack [1988]; the ideas there can be used without making the restrictive assumptions needed by Kautz's method. Discourse analysis and plan recognition are both discussed by Grosz *et al.* [1989].

Question answering is discussed by Webber [1987]; as we have already seen, answering a question effectively often depends on constructing a model of the asker's beliefs. Formal models of belief are outside the scope of this textbook; work in this area is typically based on the possible world semantics developed by Kripke [1971] and discussed by Hughes and Cresswell [1968]. Situations where a speaker and a listener come to *share* beliefs are discussed by Halpern and Moses [1984].

A survey of work on natural language generation is McDonald [1992]. Natural language generation is also the topic of a recent special issue of *Computational Intelligence* [Pattabhiraman and Cercone 1991].

Finally, let me give you pointers to some successfully implemented natural language systems. Probably the most famous are Winograd's thesis work SHRDLU[41] [Winograd 1972] and ELIZA, a program that didn't really understand much of anything but used simple syntactic techniques to give the impression that it did [Weizenbaum 1966]. Other examples are LIFER, an interface to naval command-and-control databases [Hendrix *et al.* 1978], LUNAR, an interface to a database of information about the moon rocks brought back by the Apollo astronauts [Woods 1977], and the more recent TEAM, a general interface tool initially used with a database of geographical data [Grosz *et al.* 1987].

17.7 EXERCISES

1. Show the results of parsing (or attempting to parse) the following sentences:
   (a) Mary gave me a pictures.
   (b) Mary gave me the pictures.
2. In English, the first noun phrase following a verb might be either the direct or indirect object of the verb; you can't tell which until later in the sentence (when you either encounter another noun phrase or don't). How is this handled by the ATN in Figure 17.2?
3. Show in detail the parse of "Mary gave the man of her dreams a picture."
4. Show in detail the parse of "What did Mary give the man of her dreams?"
5. Show explicitly that the ATN of Figure 17.2 will not parse "What did Mary give the man of her dreams a picture?"
6. In Figure 17.2, there is no arc between S4 and S5 labelled `jump (VIR NP)` because we do not want to allow the use of a virtual noun phrase to replace the indirect object of a sentence.
   (a) Explain why the indirect object should not be virtual.
   (b) Is the desired effect actually achieved by the ATN in the figure? Give an example of a sentence whose direct object is virtual but that cannot be parsed as shown.
   (c) Modify the ATN to handle this difficulty.
7. Present as many parses as possible for the sentence, "Albert hit the man on the chest with the hammer."

41 The full name of the system is ETAOIN SHRDLU. This apparently meaningless acronym is in fact simply the twelve most commonly used letters in the English language.

8. (a) Modify the ATN for noun phrases so that it can handle possessives such as "Mary's picture," "his picture," and "Mary's friend's picture."
   (b) Modify the semantic rules in Figure 17.3 so that they deal with this extension.
9. Figure 17.3 includes the following rule:

Component	Trigger	Condition
S	(VERB give) (MODS (PP (PREP of) (OBJ p)))	false

   Why is this rule needed? Could we have simply omitted it?
10. Show in detail the semantic analysis for the two sentences (17.2) and (17.11).
11. Extend the semantic rules so that they can successfully handle

    Mary gave the man a picture of her boat.

    but not

    Mary gave the man a picture of her dreams.
12. (a) Use the suggestion following (17.11) to construct a semantic analysis algorithm that is equivalent to the method described in the text but is independent of the order in which the semantic rules are applied.
    (b) Can the algorithm be applied if we modify the semantic rules to appeal to declarative information in the database instead of using explicit assertions?
    (c) Does your answer to (b) continue to hold if the underlying database is nonmonotonic?
13. (a) Select a suitable search method and implement Algorithm 17.2.1. Use the implementation to parse the usual (17.2).
    (b) Implement a semantic analysis system based on the ideas in the text. Use it to construct (17.10) from the result of (a).
14. When resolving the anaphoric reference in, "What did John give the president of his company?" why isn't the referent of *his* determined to be *the president*?
15. Consider the following telephone dialog from Allen [1987] between an expert **E** and an apprentice **A**:

    E: Now attach the pull rope to the top of the engine. By the way, did you buy gasoline today?

A: Yes. I got some when I bought the new lawn mower wheel. I forgot to take the gas can with me, so I bought a new one.

E: Did it cost much?

A: No, and we could use another anyway to keep with the tractor.

E: OK, how far have you got? Did you get it attached?

Explain how referents can be determined for the following:

(a) *Some* and *one* in the apprentice's initial response.

(b) *It* in "Did it cost much?"

(c) *It* in the expert's final question.

CHAPTER

18

EXPERT SYSTEMS

Expert systems are AI's commercial showpiece. More than any other area, they show the potential impact that our field can have on a wide variety of problem-solving tasks. My main goal in this chapter is to give you a feeling for this technology: why it works, what the advantages of expert systems are, and how they can be developed in practice.

But I have another goal as well, and that is to discuss an ongoing debate within the AI community about the eventual role that expert systems will play in the construction of a generally intelligent artifact. Expert systems' commercial successes have been so great that some AI researchers have suggested that AI has now been reduced to engineering—to a matter of extending expert systems technology to ever wider areas.

Has intelligence been reduced to an engineering problem, or are there still difficult scientific issues to be addressed? Section 18.4 is intended to give you a feeling for the arguments underlying this debate, as in my attempt in Chapter 12 to give you a feel for the arguments surrounding the question of whether or not probability theory was the "correct" way to solve knowledge representation problems.

18.1 EXAMPLES AND HISTORY

Expert systems attempt to use declarative techniques to capture the domain knowledge of experts in specific fields.

Perhaps the most famous expert system is MYCIN, developed by Ted Shortliffe at Stanford to diagnose and treat bacterial blood infections. MYCIN's performance is quite similar to that of the experts whose knowledge it uses—given a patient, MYCIN requests lab tests and then analyzes the results using rules such as

IF:

1. The gram stain of the organism is gramneg, and
2. The morphology of the organism is rod, and
3. The aerobicity of the organism is anaerobic

> THEN there is suggestive evidence (.6) that the identity of the organism is bacteroides. [Buchanan and Shortliffe 1984, p.71][42]

MYCIN also prescribes treatment using rules like

> IF:
> 1. The therapy under consideration is one of: cephalothin clindamycin erythromycin lincomycin vancomycin, and
> 2. Meningitis is an infectious disease diagnosis for the patient
>
> THEN the therapy under consideration is not a potential therapy for use against the organism. [Buchanan and Shortliffe 1984, p. 82]

The interesting thing about MYCIN isn't the rules it uses, but the performance of the system—MYCIN has been tested on a variety of sets of patient data, and its performance is comparable to that of experts in the field. It easily outperforms both medical students and general practitioners. A sample MYCIN consultation appears in Figure 18.1.

Another well-known expert system is known as R1; the domain of application here is the configuration of Digital Equipment's VAX computers.

Before R1 was developed, individual Digital salesmen configured VAXes; there were a variety of problems with this. The first was that a customer would describe his intended application, and the engineer would then design a system using (say) one CPU, one back plane, two busses, one printer, and so on. A price would be computed and supplied to the customer; if the engineer made a mistake and left something out, Digital would have to supply it at no charge. The second problem with the engineers' designs was that they tended to be highly idiosyncratic—one engineer would often have trouble maintaining and repairing a system that another engineer had configured. By standardizing the configuration process using R1, Digital was able to save itself millions of dollars annually.[43]

---

42 This is not the internal form of the MYCIN rule, of course. Buchanan and Shortliffe [1984] report that the implemented version of this rule is the following:

```
PREMISE: ($AND (SAME CNTXT GRAM GRAMNEG)
               (SAME CNTXT MORPH ROD)
               (SAME CNTXT AIR ANAEROBIC))
ACTION: (CONCLUDE CNTXT IDENTITY BACTEROIDES TALLY .6)
```

43 The name R1 is a result of R1's developer, John McDermott, saying, "Six months ago, I didn't know anything about expert systems, and now I are one."

There are other apocryphal stories about the names of expert systems. Shortliffe's current research involves ONCOCIN, a system that grew out of the MYCIN work and is used in selecting chemotherapy protocols for cancer patients. (The study of cancer is called oncology, hence the name.) His license plate even reads "ONCOCIN."

Now, the one thing you need to understand about Ted Shortliffe is that he is absolutely as straight as an arrow. This is a man who is less likely to use drugs than he is to swim across the Atlantic Ocean. But after buying gas one day, the attendant gave Shortliffe a sly grin while he was writing ONCOCIN on the credit card slip. The reason? He was interpreting Shortliffe's license plate as meaning "on cocaine."

FIGURE 18.1
Excerpts from a consultation with MYCIN

```
1) Patient's name: (first-last)
** FRED BRAUN
2) Sex:                                                        (Questions 1-3 request
** M                                                           background patient data.)
3) Age:
** 55
4) Are there any cultures for Fred Braun which may be related to
   the present illness, and from which organisms have been grown
   successfully in the microbiology laboratory?
** Y

   --------CULTURE-1--------
5) From what site was the specimen for CULTURE-1 taken?
** BLOD
=BLOOD                                          (System corrects typing error.)
6) Please give the date and time when CULTURE-1 was obtained.
   (mo/da/yr time)
** JUN 20, 1977
The first organism isolated from the blood culture of 20-JUN-77
(CULTURE-1) will be referred to as:

   --------ORGANISM-1--------
7) Enter the laboratory-reported identity of ORGANISM-1:
** UNKNOWN                                  (Typically identity is not yet known.)
8) The stain (gram or Ziehl-Neelsen acid-fast) of ORGANISM-1:
** NEG                                 (Preliminary lab results give some clues.)
9) Is ORGANISM-1 rod or coccus (etc.):
** ROD
10) What is the form of the individual organisms (e.g. lancet-
    shaped for cocci, fusiform for rods, etc.)?
** FUSIFORM

               (. . . more questions follow in order to gather sufficient information
               to infer the identity and significance of the infecting organisms . . . )

23) What is the suspected portal of entry of the gramneg rod from the
    blood culture of 20-JUN-77 (ORGANISM-1) into this sterile site?
** GI (6)                           (User indicates the uncertainty of his response.)
24) Is Fred Braun a burn patient?
** N
25) Is Fred Braun a compromised host (e.g. alcoholic,
    sickle-cell-disease, immunosuppressed)?
** N
26) Is Fred Braun febrile?
** Y

                    (. . . after about 50–60 questions, MYCIN prints the diagnostic
                    hypotheses on which therapy will be based . . . )

My therapy recommendations will be designed to treat for organisms that are either very
likely or, although less likely, would have a significant effect on therapy selection if they
were present. It is important to cover for the following probable infection(s) and
associated organism(s):

INFECTION-1 is BACTEREMIA

  <ITEM-1> E.COLI [ORGANISM-1]
  <ITEM-2> KLEBSIELLA [ORGANISM-1]
  <ITEM-3> ENTEROBACTER [ORGANISM-1]
  <ITEM-4> KLEBSIELLA-PNEUMONIAE [ORGANISM-1]
```

The last expert system I want to describe is one that was developed by Teknowledge, Inc., on behalf of the French oil giant, Elf-Aquitaine.

Elf-Aquitaine drills offshore oil wells (among other things); it turns out that when you are drilling for oil in the ocean, the drill bit sometimes gets stuck. It also turns out that there are about three people in the world who know how to unstick drill bits that are stuck in this fashion.

So, when Elf-Aquitaine had this problem, they would have to find one of these three experts and call him up. Assuming that he was available (and not working on some other oil rig), he would then have to be flown out to the rig that was having the problem, where he could bring his expertise to bear and correct the difficulty. This was an expensive proposition, since the rig in question would be down for a matter of days while a suitable expert was found.

What Teknowledge did was build a system that captured the knowledge of these experts in an expert system, which could then be used to unstick drill bits without the associated platform being idle for days. Interestingly enough, the experts themselves were also pleased with this approach. For one thing, it guaranteed them a sort of immortality, as their knowledge would continue to be used to address these sorts of problems. For another, they could focus their efforts on only the most challenging stuck drill bits—those that required principles and techniques not included in the expert system. The novel situations in which experts would continue to be consulted were those that were the most interesting for the experts themselves.

How many successfully fielded expert systems are there? It depends on whom you ask. Of the three that we have mentioned, R1 and the oil-well tool were successfully delivered to their corporate sponsors; MYCIN has not been put into actual use. Ed Feigenbaum will tell you that there are on the order of five thousand successfully fielded expert systems; Hubert Dreyfus, one of AI's leading critics, has said that there are about five fielded systems, and only four of those make money. One hundred thirty-nine implemented expert systems are listed in Feigenbaum *et al.* [1988].[44]

Before turning to general issues, let us take one more look at MYCIN. We remarked above that it hasn't been put into actual use. Why not?

One reason is legal. Suppose that some general practitioner is using MYCIN to decide how to treat a patient, and that MYCIN suggests giving the patient a particular drug. The doctor does this, and the patient dies. Is Ted Shortliffe legally responsible? What if the doctor ignores MYCIN's advice and the patient dies? Is the doctor now responsible? The legal and ethical issues here are quite subtle—and this is one reason why expert systems are making inroads only very slowly (if at all) into life-critical domains.

---

44 In some sense, this disparity may reflect differing opinions on what constitutes an "expert system." To Dreyfus, it is a stand-alone system like R1 or MYCIN; to Feigenbaum, it may well be a small expert system embedded in a larger application.

How does one write an expert system? It's like writing any other piece of software; you write a preliminary version and then debug it until it works:

1. Examine the domain to ensure that expert-system technology is appropriate.
2. Interact with an expert to capture the relevant knowledge.
3. Build a prototype system.
4. Validate its performance by using it on new instances of the problem class.
5. Debug the knowledge base and return to step 2.
6. Handle interface issues.

A few of these steps bear some additional discussion.

Capture the knowledge As with any declarative project, this involves the selection of a knowledge representation scheme and a language in which to work, as well as the actual knowledge capture. This is quite an interesting problem—the person responsible for getting the knowledge into the computer (a "knowledge engineer") needs to acquire enough expertise in the domain to be able to interact with the experts, but obviously doesn't want to spend so much time on the domain that he becomes an expert himself.

Interface issues The users of a typical expert system cannot be expected to be computer literate (think of the average worker on a drilling platform), but they must be able to interact with the system effectively. The most typical approach to this in the expert-system community is to engineer the interface after the internals of the expert system are complete, although this is at odds with current thinking in computer-human interaction, which suggests that systems should be built around the interface from the beginning.

Is the technology suitable? What MYCIN and the two other expert systems we have described have in common is the following:

1. A limited domain of expertise.
2. A field in which expertise exists.
3. A problem that takes a human expert between five minutes and five hours to solve.

In MYCIN, for example, the limited domain of expertise is that of blood diseases. Expertise exists in the form of human doctors or specialists who deal with these infections. And a human doctor does indeed typically take between five minutes and five hours to deal with a single patient. Similar remarks can be made about configuring computer systems or unsticking oil well drill bits.

As far as the *reasons* for these commonalities, the first has to do with the fact that we are currently unable to describe large bodies of commonsense knowledge in a declarative way—consider the problems we have seen in nonmonotonic reasoning or in planning. As a result, we are unlikely to be able to construct an expert system in any domain that needs a broad commonsense understanding of how the world works; typical here might be a legal expert system that could handle liability claims. The amount of damage suffered because of a broken hand is likely to be different depending on whether the victim is a pianist or a professional wrestler; the way in which we evaluate claims like this appeals to a great deal of general knowledge.

Second, there must be recognized expertise. The people who unstick oil drill bits are really *good* at it; that's why they used to be awakened at 3 a.m. and asked for help. But there are no such recognized experts on (for example) Wall Street, so there isn't going to be an expert system for stock trading. Perhaps there are a few people who are marginally better than the rest of the pack, but marginally better is as good as they get.

Finally, there are restrictions on how hard the problem can be. If a human can solve it in less than five minutes, the problem can typically be attacked using conventional programming techniques; if it takes more than five hours, the problem is probably too hard for a declarative system, especially given the primitive state of our ability to control reasoning. Diagnosing a blood disease given test results is on the easy end of this spectrum; configuring a computer system is on the hard end.

Although these three conditions appear to be necessary to the development of a successful expert system, they are not sufficient. The industrial community has had a great deal of hard experience attempting unsuccessfully to construct expert systems in domains that meet these conditions. One example—and there are many—involved an attempt to automate the process of writing up the service order when you bring your car in for maintenance. The domain is restricted (good!), expertise exists (there are people whose job this is, after all), and the task takes about five minutes. Unfortunately, this task also involves a preliminary visual inspection that is beyond the scope of any expert system. (Are the directionals failing because the switch is broken or because of an internal fault?) Obvious in retrospect, but a considerable amount of effort went into this particular project before it was eventually abandoned.[45]

45 My remarks here are based on discussions with some of the individuals involved in this project. It is unfortunate that experimental failures are never documented as well as are the successes.

But let me end this section on an upbeat note. One of the most interesting things about expert systems is that they work at all—that the combinatorics involved in declarative systems do not overwhelm us as these systems come to contain a thousand pieces of information or more. This may be the most profound lesson learned by the expert systems community: That by modelling human problem solving, systems can be built that solve interesting problems in large domains. Szolovits' description of expert systems as "an attempt to build systems that achieve intelligence by approximating difficult computations in ways inspired by observation of human behavior" is a fair one.[46]

18.2 ADVANTAGES OF EXPERT SYSTEMS

There are also good technological reasons why expert systems have generated such excitement. We describe three such reasons here—the nature of declarative information, interface aspects of declarative programming, and an expert system's ability to explain its conclusions to the user.

Declarative information Programming an expert system isn't like writing a conventional computer program; it is more a matter of capturing the knowledge used by the experts in question.

This observation has important practical consequences. One is an outcome of the fact that knowledge is modular. If an expert system under development fails to draw a certain conclusion, it is generally possible to understand the failure in terms of a piece of missing knowledge, which can then be added to the system. If an erroneous conclusion is drawn, it is often possible to isolate and replace a faulty statement in the database. It is typically *not* necessary to rewrite large pieces of code or to consider the subtleties of how the new knowledge will interact with the old; if each piece of knowledge provided to the system is accurate, its conclusions should be as well.

Another result of the declarative nature of knowledge is that maintaining an expert system is a matter of keeping the knowledge current as opposed to modifying code. An expert system, once developed, can often be maintained and updated by its users. The key contribution of the original knowledge engineer is not a large body of code but a choice of ontology and representation scheme. This choice can be expected to be far more stable as time passes than is the knowledge itself.

Interface issues Because the inferences drawn by an expert system are intended to be similar to the inferences drawn by the experts themselves,

46 Peter Szolovits, personal communication.

the overall behavior of the system is naturally user-friendly; have another look at the dialog in Figure 18.1 for an example.

We have already touched on one consequence of this, the fact that the users of the system can often maintain it as well. Another advantage is that the knowledge that is missing from the system can be obtained in a natural way—when MYCIN requests that a lab test be performed, it is doing little more than asking the user for help in supplying a specific piece of declarative information. Figure 18.1 contains a variety of examples.

An elegant exploitation of this observation is to modify the declarative database so that it includes the information the user will eventually provide, but to flag these sentences so that the system must retrieve them by querying the user instead of accepting them as they appear in the database. We might include in our database the sentence

$$\forall xy.\mathtt{gender}(x,y) \tag{18.1}$$

(apparently indicating that every person is all genders), but tagged so that the user is queried when an instance of (18.1) is needed.

Explanation The most important property of expert systems, however, is their ability to explain their conclusions. We discussed the theory underlying this in Chapter 10, where we showed that conclusions could be defended in terms of the database sentences that were used to derive them.

The explanation mechanism can be taken further. When MYCIN or another expert system asks its user a question, the user can ask why MYCIN is interested. Once again, the response is clear from a declarative point of view—the system can indicate the path back to the original query in the resolution proof space. An example combining both of these explanatory properties is shown in Figure 18.2.

The details of the explanations in the figure show a difference between MYCIN's style of explanation and the ATMS-based ideas we discussed in Chapter 10. We computed the entire set of database sentences needed to justify a particular conclusion; MYCIN only displays the database sentence used "most recently" in the argument.

From a semantic point of view, this is meaningless—whether or not a set S of sentences entails a particular query q does not depend on the order of the elements in the set. But the distinction is useful from a practical point of view; MYCIN's responses in the figure seem to match our intuition about a natural ordering to the elements of the justification. Where does this ordering come from?

It comes from the syntactic form of the database. Suppose that the database is Horn, and that we have used Algorithm 10.1.1 to show that a query q follows from a set S. Since our resolution proof begins by adding $q \rightarrow F$ to the database, there must be some sentence in the database that

FIGURE 18.2 MYCIN explains itself

```
34) Was penicillinase added to this blood culture (CULTURE-1)?
** WHY

[i.e. WHY is it important to determine whether penicillinase was added to
CULTURE-1?]

[3.0] This will aid in determining whether ORGANISM-1 is a contaminant.
  It has already been established that
    [3.1] the site of CULTURE-1 is blood, and
    [3.2] the gram stain of ORGANISM-1 is grampos
  Therefore, if
    [3.3] penicillinase was added to this blood culture
  then
    there is weakly suggestive evidence (.4) that ORGANISM-1 is a
contaminant [RULE039]

** WHY

[i.e. WHY is it important to determine whether ORGANISM-1 is a
contaminant?]

[4.0] . . . In order to determine whether there is significant disease
  associated with this occurrence of ORGANISM-1.
  It has already been established that
    [4.1] this blood culture was taken from a sterile source
  Therefore, if
    [4.2] ORGANISM-1 is not a contaminant
  then
    there is strongly suggestive evidence (.9) that there is
    significant disease associated with this occurrence of ORGANISM-1
  [RULE032]

** WHY

[i.e. WHY is it important to determine whether there is significant
  disease associated with this occurrence of ORGANISM-1]

[5.0] . . . In order to determine the organisms which require therapy.
  It has already been established that
    [5.1] the infection is known, and
    [5.2] the identity of ORGANISM-1 is known
  Therefore, if
    [5.3] there is significant disease associated with this occurrence
    of ORGANISM-1
  then
    it is definite (1.0) that ORGANISM-1 is one of the organisms which
    require therapy
  [RULE090]

** HOW 5.2

[i.e. HOW was it established that the identity of ORGANISM-1 is known?]

Question 9 was asked, but you weren't sure; so the following was used:

    [5.5] RULE084 was used to conclude that the identity of ORGANISM-1 is
    streptococcus-group-a (.29).
```

resolves with this sentence, so that the Horn database contains a sentence of the form

$$a_1 \wedge \cdots \wedge a_m \rightarrow q \tag{18.2}$$

A sentence of the form (18.2) must be in the explanation S as well.

Given the appearance of (18.2) in S, we can explain the conclusion of q in terms of (18.2) and the collection of a_i; since (18.2) is in the explanation for q, we know that each of the a_i's must be a consequence of the database as well.

As an example, let us return to John the lawyer and his big house. That John's house is a lot of work to maintain is supported by

$$\texttt{big}(h) \wedge \texttt{house}(h,p) \rightarrow \texttt{work}(h) \tag{18.3}$$

We therefore report the reason for the conclusion work(house-of(John)) as (18.3), together with the facts that John's house is big and that it is a house. Note that we use the variable instantiations generated by the proof when we construct the explanation.

DEFINITION 18.2.1 *Given a database* S, *we will say that an* expert explanation *of a sentence* p *is a minimal set* T *of sentences with the following properties:*

1. $\mathrm{T} \models \mathrm{p}$.
2. $\mathrm{S} \models \mathrm{T}$.
3. *There is a subset* $\mathrm{S}' \subseteq \mathrm{S}$ *such that* $\mathrm{S}' \models \mathrm{p}$ *but* $\mathrm{S}' - \mathrm{T} \not\models \mathrm{p}$.

The first two clauses of the definition should be clear; we require that the explanation entails the sentence being explained and that the explanation is itself a consequence of the information in the database. The third clause is a bit more subtle.

What we are saying here is that there is some subset S' of S that needs at least one fact in T in order to entail p. Consider the following example:

$$p_1 \rightarrow q \tag{18.4}$$

$$z \rightarrow p_1 \tag{18.5}$$

$$z \tag{18.6}$$

$$p_2 \rightarrow q$$

$$p_2$$

There are two separate derivations of q here. One uses p_1 and z; the other uses p_2. The third clause in the definition is to allow us to take the set

$$T = \{p_1 \to q, p_1\} \tag{18.7}$$

as an expert explanation for q. More specifically:

1. $T \models q$. This is clear.
2. $S \models T$. Also clear; the first element of T appears explicitly in the database, and the second is a consequence of (18.5) and (18.6).
3. For the third clause, we take S' to be (18.4)–(18.6). This set continues to imply q but we've removed the information underlying the second explanation. If we now remove the elements of (18.7) from S', we remove (18.4) so that $S' - T \not\models p$.

PROPOSITION 18.2.2 *Let S be a Horn database in normal form. If a sentence*

$$a_1 \wedge \cdots \wedge a_m \to p \tag{18.8}$$

appears in an explanation for a query q, *then*

$$T = \{a_1 \wedge \cdots \wedge a_m \to p, a_1, \ldots, a_m\} \tag{18.9}$$

is an expert explanation for p.

PROOF That $T \models p$ is obvious. To see that $S \models T$, let E be the explanation of q that includes (18.8). The first element of T is in E, and therefore in S. For the various a_i, suppose there is some a_k such that

$$S \not\models a_k$$

It must now be the case that we could remove (18.8) from E without affecting our ability to derive q; the rule is effectively useless because one of its premises is not a consequence of the database. But the set E is assumed to be a minimal explanation for q. This contradiction means that a_k must be a consequence of S; the second condition of Definition 18.2.1 is proved.

The third condition is actually easy—we can just take $S' = E$. ∎

Explanation is important for a variety of reasons. First, it helps the user understand the conclusions drawn by the system. If these conclusions are questionable, the user may be able to evaluate the system's performance by examining the viability of the supporting knowledge in the application instance being considered. If the system is still under development, the programmer may be able to use the explanations to help debug the knowledge that has been entered.

Explanation is also important because it is a practical contribution that AI can truly claim as its own. An expert system's unique ability to explain its conclusions is a direct consequence of the similarities between the inference steps taken by a declarative system and those taken by the expert being modeled.

18.3 CYC AND OTHER VLKB PROJECTS

As work on expert systems has progressed, the knowledge bases with which these systems deal have gotten progressively larger. This leads to the following question:

> *Can a large enough expert system exhibit general intelligence and pass the Turing test?*

Might it be possible to lift the three restrictions on the technology being suitable that were discussed at the end of Section 18.1?

Five minutes to five hours This restriction will surely be lifted as declarative techniques and computing technology improve. There isn't anything *wrong* with solving easy problems declaratively; it just tends not to be worth the effort. And as work on control of reasoning progresses and hardware becomes ever faster, it should be possible to attack increasingly difficult problems using declarative methods.

Expertise exists This particular restriction may never be lifted, but lifting it has no bearing on the Turing test. After all, there are *plenty* of agents that are expert at being human—about five billion of them, in fact. An expert system doesn't need to be a whiz on Wall Street to pass the Turing test.

Restricted domain Here, the Turing test is completely relevant; people perform admirably in commonsense domains that depend on broad knowledge of the world. If expert systems technology cannot behave similarly, the ideas as a whole will eventually be of little fundamental interest to AI.

Expert systems are among the most brittle examples of modern technology. Not only do they not function outside their restricted domains of expertise, they have absolutely no idea when these limits have been reached. If MYCIN is asked to diagnose a frog, it will still ask for the frog's temperature and blood pressure. It may well ask the frog if it has a stomach ache. Elf-Aquitaine's project is no better. If you attempt to use it to remove the $\frac{3}{32}$ inch drill bit that has gotten stuck while installing a curtain in your bedroom, you may well be advised to pour 200,000 gallons of water on the fixture in question.

Can these difficulties be surmounted? Can expert-systems technology be extended to broad knowledge?

I think not, at least not in its current form—expert reasoning and commonsense reasoning are too different. From a formal point of view, commonsense reasoning is far the more difficult of the two. Building an enormous knowledge base that covers commonsense domains is like trying to build a ladder to the moon: You can keep adding steps, but it just isn't going to work. John McCarthy has said it much more eloquently:[47]

> *Fundamental progress cannot be achieved through incremental advances in existing technology.* [McCarthy, personal communication]

Others would disagree. To Feigenbaum, intelligence *is* just engineering at this point. He believes that a sufficiently large knowledge base will be capable of generally intelligent behavior. This belief has led him and others to embark on *very large knowledge base* (VLKB) projects.

At Stanford, Feigenbaum is encoding all of our knowledge about electromechanical devices (from microwave ovens to fighter aircraft, presumably). The idea is to capture in a single knowledge base all that we know about objects of this kind, and to then use that knowledge to assist in the processes of designing, building, and maintaining these devices.

Doug Lenat, the author of AM, is working on a still more ambitious project at MCC in Texas. The project is CYC, a system that is intended to capture all of the knowledge—both implicit and explicit—in a hundred randomly selected articles in the EnCYClopaedia Britannica. The interest is primarily on the underlying information that is assumed by the authors of the Britannica articles—things that they assumed without feeling a need to tell them to their readers.

As an example, suppose we read in the encyclopedia that Wellington learned of Napoleon's death. We can conclude from this that Napoleon never learned of Wellington's death, but doing so involves an appeal to a great deal of implicit information: That you only die once, that you stay dead once you die, that you can't learn of anything after you die, that time is a total order without loops, and so on. But none of this information is made explicit to the reader. Lenat expects that the implicit knowledge underlying his selection of one hundred articles will be, roughly speaking,

---

47 This is, of course, just McCarthy's and my opinion. It is also our preference, if the truth be known. The fundamental problems facing AI—nonmonotonic reasoning, planning, understanding causality, and so on—strike us as *fun*. If AI has already been reduced to an engineering discipline, to the construction of an enormous artifact using existing technology, McCarthy and I will find that both uninteresting and disappointing. Surely intelligence is more magical than that!

all the implicit knowledge assumed by the authors of the encyclopedia, so that a computer program with access to this implicit knowledge will be able to read and make sense of the rest of the encyclopedia without further human intervention.

CYC is an ambitious project; it is expected to take about ten years and to cost some fifty million dollars. Much of the money pays Lenat's "knowledge enterers," who are responsible for identifying the knowledge assumed by the Britannica's authors and then translating it into CYCL, the knowledge representation language used by the CYC project.

There are at least three problems that any VLKB project must face. The first is a result of the size of the database itself—as we remarked in Section 6.5, a reasoning technique of complexity $o(n^2)$ is likely to be valueless when applied to a database containing a million facts or more.

To address this, some sort of control knowledge is needed. An interesting approach taken by CYC is to have the system's knowledge be available in two separate forms—an epistemological form (used for entering the knowledge, examining it, and so on) and a heuristic form (used for reasoning with the knowledge and including special-purpose modifications to make this process more efficient).

The second problem faced by VLKB projects is that of maintaining and modifying the knowledge base itself. What if the program uses its million-fact database to conclude that Napoleon might have learned of Wellington's death after all? Now the need for an explanation mechanism is crucial; we may well also want some sort of browsing tools so that we can ask the machine to tell us everything that it knows about Napoleon in the first place. CYC includes both of these facilities. The bottom line is that a VLKB must be developed in a *principled* way; it is insufficient simply to enter facts as they are thought of and hope to get much useful out at the end of the day.

The last problem faced by VLKB designers is that they have to find the knowledge somewhere. There are at least three possibilities:

1. The knowledge can be hand-coded, with individual facts being entered by individual scientists.

2. The knowledge can be obtained by reading. We remarked in the previous chapter how efficient it would be to explain failure modes in jet engines to a system like Feigenbaum's simply by giving the program a book on the topic.

3. Finally, the computer could discover the knowledge itself.

According to Lenat, things can be expected to go just this way. Initially, hand-coded knowledge must be entered into a system until it contains the knowledge assumed by the authors of the books it wants to read. Then it reads the books until it knows most of what's been understood by humans generally, and then it analyzes this information to find connections and principles that we have not yet discovered. An ambitious project indeed—with CYC's role being to bridge the gap between hand-coded knowledge and knowledge obtained by reading.

Is the experiment worth the money? If it succeeds, certainly. But if there is a substantial amount of science left to do in AI, the CYC project will succeed only in demonstrating the shortcomings of one approach to the VLKB enterprise. The leaders of the CYC project themselves describe the following outcome as a good one:

> Although not directly built on and widely used, the CYC research might still provide some insights into issues involved in building large commonsense knowledge bases. Perhaps, it would give us an indication about whether the symbolic paradigm is flawed and, if so, how. It might also yield a rich repertoire of "how to represent it" heuristics and might at least motivate research issues in building future AI systems. [Guha and Lenat 1990, p. 57]

Fifty million dollars is a high price for such information.

Lenat and Feigenbaum [1991] would argue that in spite of the uncertainty in the eventual success of the project, it is worth the money. Their argument is based on broad assumptions that they make about the state of AI generally, and I would like to turn to those next.

18.4 AI AS AN EXPERIMENTAL DISCIPLINE

According to Feigenbaum and Lenat, there are three lessons to be learned from the work that has been done in AI so far:

- **The knowledge principle** Performance is achieved in large systems via the use of domain-specific information. Difficult problems typically cannot be solved using general-purpose methods.
- **The breadth hypothesis** Declarative systems use broad knowledge to ensure that their performance degrades gracefully as they reach the limits of their domain-specific knowledge.
- **The empirical inquiry hypothesis** AI is currently an experimental discipline as opposed to a theoretical one.

As an example, suppose that I find myself at home but in desperate need of some ice cream. I have a great deal of specialized knowledge about Palo Alto and navigating therein; I'll presumably just drive to the local Häagen-Dazs and be done with it.

If I'm visiting my mother, I'm not quite so well off. I'll probably end up generating a plan that relies on less specific information about the town—I know how to get from Mom's house to the downtown area, so I'll likely just do that and hope I can find an ice cream shop from there. In a strange town, I can resort to still more general techniques by asking the manager of the hotel in which I might be staying, by looking in a phone book, or by asking a local.

If the strange town I'm in happens to be Paris, things are worse still because I don't speak French. Now I'll need to resort to quite general knowledge, perhaps trying to get a resident to give me directions to a restaurant. In all of these cases, I resort to more and more general methods as the situation becomes one with which I am less and less familiar.

Let's examine each of Feigenbaum and Lenat's three lessons in a bit more detail.

The knowledge principle The conclusion that we use domain-specific knowledge to solve difficult problems is based partly on the theoretical observation that general-purpose methods use brute force to address the combinatorics of the problems they face. Consider the number of wrong turns I will doubtless make and the number of restaurants I will likely visit in my attempt to find some ice cream in Paris! More important is the experimental observation that the performance of systems can often be improved dramatically by giving them access to more knowledge.

The example cited by Feigenbaum and Lenat involves DENDRAL, an expert system that was developed to determine the three-dimensional structure of complex organic molecules. Given the chemical makeup of such a molecule, there are a variety of sources of information one can use to prune the number of structures considered—everything from the valences of the molecular atoms to the results of nuclear magnetic resonance. The size of the search space after applying each of these knowledge sources is as follows:

Knowledge source	Size of space
topology	42 million
valences	15 million
mass spectrometry	1.3 million
first-principles chemistry	1.1 million
nuclear magnetic resonance	1

The more knowledge used, the smaller the size of the space that needs to be investigated.

The breadth hypothesis The evidence for this is simple: Every subarea of AI appears to be AI-complete. We can solve simple vision problems easily but there are always cases where we need to resort to general knowledge about the domain. We can parse most sentences, but not all of them. It's hard to wreck a nice beach. And so on.

The empirical inquiry hypothesis The evidence for this is that the surprises in AI are in the results of experiments and that for a discipline like AI, it is the surprises that lead to progress.

I agree with Feigenbaum and Lenat about their first two conclusions, but disagree here. It is not always the case (in AI or elsewhere) that experimental results drive theoretical ones; sometimes the reverse occurs. Einstein's work in developing general relativity was motivated almost purely by theoretical concerns. After the theory was developed, he was able to use it to make specific predictions (about the deflection of starlight by the sun, for example) that were then validated experimentally.

In AI itself, consider nonmonotonic reasoning. Given the tremendous success of the formalization of *monotonic* reasoning earlier this century, it was generally assumed in the AI community that machine and human reasoning, when formalized, would be similar in nature. The realization in the late 1970s that this was wrong was a tremendous surprise, and a theoretical one at that. (You don't need an "experiment" to realize that commonsense reasoning is nonmonotonic, just common sense.)

This theoretical surprise has impact across all of AI; most every algorithm we have presented fails if the underlying database is not monotonic. There are profound philosophical implications as well—just as we often change our minds when dealing with real-life problems (the practical manifestation of the nonmonotonicity), so we can expect our artificial agents to do the same.

Contrast this to the experimental surprises that came out of the work on AM. Yes, AM is a tremendously impressive piece of programming. Yes, its results are fascinating. But what fundamental insight does it give us about the nature of intelligence?

Very little. When the reasons for AM's success were finally understood, they had much more to do with the relationship between mathematics and LISP than they had to do with intelligence itself. The observation that commonsense reasoning is nonmonotonic, on the other hand, does indeed tell us something fundamental about the nature of intelligence.

Feigenbaum and Lenat seem right in their belief that experimental surprises are more common than their theoretical counterparts. But the theoretical surprises, when they occur, are likely to be much more important. The lessons that they teach us are likely to be more fundamental. In addition, they are more likely to be reproducible.

Consider Hanks' and McDermott's observation that the "obvious" nonmonotonic solution to the frame problem doesn't work, as we discussed in Exercise 5 (and elsewhere) in Chapter 14. As soon as their result was circulated, researchers elsewhere were able to reproduce the problem themselves and to try to find a solution to it. So reproducible was the Hanks-McDermott difficulty that three solutions to it were presented before Hanks and McDermott even described the problem at the national AI conference in 1987!

When AM surprised Lenat, the situation was far less useful. Certainly, he could report the surprise to the AI community as a whole. But if another researcher wanted to duplicate the result, he was unlikely to be able to do so. He could (perhaps) obtain and run Lenat's code, but that isn't the same as actually repeating the experiment. Surprises arising out of the CYC work are going to be even less reproducible, since no other research group is likely to be able to afford the fifty-million-dollar ante.

This lack of reproducibility means that CYC has to justify its price tag by its own experimental results, as opposed to the value it will add to experimental work elsewhere. When particle physicists build superconducting supercolliders, their experiments can be expected to drive theoretical physics for a decade; can CYC make the same claim?

I suspect not, for two reasons. First, the physicists are asking much sharper questions than CYC is; the answers are therefore more likely to be of compelling theoretical interest. Second (and this is a related point), it may well not even be clear what the results of the CYC experiment *are*. CYC itself will doubtless be neither as successful as its developers hope nor as fruitless as its critics predict, but what sense is the AI community to make of partial success, especially for an irreproducible experiment? The lack of a solid theoretical background makes it unclear that CYC is asking *any* specific questions, let alone a fifty-million-dollar one.

The bottom line, I think, is that Feigenbaum and Lenat are alchemists. But I do not mean this in a pejorative way—the analogy between AI and alchemy has always struck me as a good one, and work of this sort may be necessary to make progress.

Alchemy was, after all, a completely necessary precursor to chemistry and most of the rest of modern science. What made alchemy so difficult was that the people in the field were trying to solve a tremendously hard problem—that of turning lead into gold—without being able to identify any manageable subproblems whose solutions would clearly contribute to their overall goals. AI may well be in the same state.

The alchemists of the seventeenth and early eighteenth centuries eventually decided that heat was an essential part of the transmutation process (as we in AI have generally decided that declarative knowledge plays a crucial role in intelligence), and this focus led them along the path from a prescientific discipline to a scientific one. The interest in heat led them to study burning, and it was "discovered" that objects burned by releasing a substance, called phlogiston, into the air around them. The reason that a candle goes out if you cover it with a glass is that the air in the glass becomes saturated with phlogiston, unable to absorb any more.

This observation led the alchemists to produce "dephlogisticated air," air with all the phlogiston removed. Of course, we now know dephlogisticated air to be oxygen; in a very real sense, chemistry was born in the late 1700s when the French scientist Lavoisier proposed that burning is a matter of absorbing oxygen instead of releasing phlogiston. The ensuing debate—with telling points scored on both sides—is one of the most interesting in the history of science.

Where in the spectrum between science and prescience is AI? It's probably too early to tell. There is certainly some good science going on in our discipline; it is equally certain that the field lacks the cohesion and rigor that typify more mature enterprises. Given this, it seems to me that both approaches should be pursued. Surely there is room in a field as exciting as ours for both the prescientific work exemplified by CYC and other VLKB projects and for the scientific work exemplified by results in theoretical knowledge representation.

18.5 FURTHER READING

There is a great deal of material on expert systems and expert-system development; most of it appeared in the early 1980s when expert systems were in their heyday. An informal and extremely optimistic book on the importance of the technology is by Feigenbaum and McCorduck [1984]; the opposite point of view is presented by Dreyfus [1979].

A slightly more technical overview of the field can be found in Harmon and King [1985] or Hayes-Roth [1984]. More recently Scott *et al.* [1991] discuss knowledge engineering specifically, while Hendler [1988] discusses human interface issues.

MYCIN is the topic of Buchanan and Shortliffe [1984]; a discussion of its performance can also be found in Yu *et al.* [1979]. Fikes *et al.* [1991] describe the Stanford VLKB project on electromechanical devices, and a good description of CYC is Guha and Lenat [1990].

As mentioned in the text, our philosophical discussion of the eventual applicability of expert systems to the Turing test begins with the arguments of Feigenbaum and Lenat [1991]. The analogy between AI and alchemy is originally made by Dreyfus [1965]; an excellent discussion of the general transition from prescience to science can be found in Kuhn [1962].

18.6 EXERCISES

1. We commented in the text that one of the strengths of the expert systems paradigm is the modularity of declarative knowledge. Is this true if the underlying knowledge representation scheme is nonmonotonic? Would you expect this to be a problem in implemented systems?

2. We discussed a modification to the conventional lookup procedure so that some sentences can be flagged as user queries. Develop a resolution control protocol that defers these lookups where possible, avoiding querying the user if an alternative line of reasoning could be used in-

stead. Can you combine this with the set of support and ordering protocols of Chapter 9?

3. (a) Prove the following result, similar to Proposition 18.2.2:

PROPOSITION 18.6.1 *Let S be a database in normal form. Then if a sentence*

$$a_1 \wedge \cdots \wedge a_m \rightarrow b_1 \vee \cdots \vee b_n$$

appears in explanation for a query q *where* $b_k = q$, *then*

$$T = \{a_1 \wedge \cdots \wedge a_m \rightarrow b_1 \vee \cdots \vee b_n, a_1, \ldots, a_m, \\ b_1 \rightarrow q, \ldots, b_{k-1} \rightarrow q, b_{k+1} \rightarrow q, \ldots, b_n \rightarrow q\}$$

is an expert explanation for q.

(b) Find an example showing that the requirement that S be in normal form is necessary.

(c) In the statement of the proposition, we require $b_k = q$, so that the result can only be used to explain the original query. Produce an example showing that this restriction is also necessary.

4. (a) Use Proposition 18.2.2 to give a MYCIN-like response to the query, Why is John's house a lot of work to maintain? in the running example of (8.39).

(b) Continue to use the proposition to give expert explanations for each of the intermediate sentences generated during the proof.

5. (a) Extend the lookup modification described in the text so that it can explain why a certain question was asked. Make sure that you can support multiple levels of why questions, as in Figure 18.2.

(b) What happens if the user keeps asking why in these situations?

6. (a) Implement the ideas in the previous exercises and use the resulting system to respond to the query, What is a lot of work to maintain? that was discussed at length in earlier chapters.

(b) Modify the implementation so that

```
lawyer(John)
```
(18.8)

must be obtained by querying the user. Specifically, modify the database so that any query of the form

```
lawyer(x)
```

is resolved by asking the user.

7. Extend the implementation of the previous exercise by reifying the `lawyer` predicate, so that instead of (18.10), one writes

```
occupation(John,lawyer)
```

   Assume that queries about any particular person's occupation are handled by asking the user.

8. Construct a database containing the knowledge needed to derive the conclusion that Napoleon never learned of Wellington's death from the statement that Wellington *did* learn of Napoleon's death. Present a resolution proof demonstrating the completeness of your solution.

9. (a) Write a commercially viable expert system.

   (b) What went wrong?

CHAPTER

19

CONCLUDING REMARKS

In these final few pages, I'd like to say just a few more things about AI's status as a discipline. Everything here is completely and utterly my opinion; whether you end up sharing these opinions or not, I hope that you will at least consider the issues because I feel them to be important ones.

Roughly speaking, there are three things that can go wrong with any scientific enterprise. It can be misperceived, in that the public can have unrealistic views and expectations of the field's current state. It can be misunderstood, in that the field's long-term goals may not be understood by the public at large. And finally, it can be misapplied, as benign technology is put to malignant uses. AI has suffered from all of these problems, and it is my responsibility—and yours as well—to try to reduce the extent to which this happens in the future.

Let me also point out that this responsibility is yours whether you view AI as a participant or as a spectator. Just as scientists must work to keep the public informed, so must the public work to keep *itself* informed.

19.1 PUBLIC PERCEPTION OF AI

The claims that were being made by AI folks around 1960 were extraordinary. Give or take a few years, AI was going to be done by now. Robots would be vacuuming our houses and writing sonnets. The claims in 1980 were somewhat tempered, but tremendously optimistic nevertheless.

One particular instance of this was the autonomous land vehicle (ALV) project. This was an attempt to get the crew out of a tank, to create a land vehicle that could navigate over difficult terrain and carry out tactical military missions without risking human lives to do it.

The project was an almost complete failure. The best that the ALV ever managed was to negotiate a paved road with brightly painted yellow boundaries at about eight miles an hour. There's nothing wrong with failing, of course—unless you've promised your funders that you're going to succeed.

The U.S. military invested heavily in the ALV project based on early promises of success, and was predictably disappointed when the project failed.

As a result, funding for *all* aspects of AI has contracted as the field has earned a reputation for not delivering on its claims. In the late 1980s, a Ph.D. in AI would get you multiple offers at prestigious academic institutions. By 1992, the same institutions were receiving hundreds of applications for each position they advertised.

Funding reductions are bad for science in other ways. When money is tight, individual scientists are tempted (and sometimes forced) to modify their research agendas to match the interests of their funders. This is hardly as it should be: Scientists should examine the problems that *they* find interesting, not those that their funders do.

Another consequence of broken promises is that funders tend to monitor their contractors much more closely. This is also a shame: Science should not be done under a microscope. What would have happened if after producing the special theory of relativity in 1905, Einstein had been asked in 1910, Well, special relativity is pretty good stuff, but what have you done for us lately? General relativity didn't appear until 1915; Einstein really had no choice but to sit and mull things over for the intervening ten years. Neither the government nor the public has this kind of patience for work in AI these days.

This is a shame, because there isn't really any reason to believe that AI is any easier than theoretical physics is. But by *claiming* that it is, by claiming, for example, that the CYC project will have computers reading the general literature in a decade, we ourselves have volunteered to be measured by standards appropriate to engineering disciplines in which uniform progress can be expected. It is high time that AI's funders and the public understood just how hard AI's problems are and how slow progress on them may be. Needless to say, doing this can be most unnerving for scientists who are competing for funds with less responsible researchers.

19.2 PUBLIC UNDERSTANDING OF AI

Even if we manage to sort out what the public thinks of the current status of AI, we will still have problems with its perception of AI's long-term ambitions.

To see why this can be a problem, let me try to draw an analogy between AI and genetic engineering. In some incredibly weak sense, we have potentially similar goals: the construction of an artifact with capabilities greater than our own.

This is a tremendously *scary* goal; witness the public perception of work on genetic engineering, even though their stated goals are much less the creation of a superior intelligence than ours are. The only saving grace in our case is that we seem to be a little further from success than they are.

The reason that this matters is that as we make progress toward our goals and come to grapple with the difficult ethical issues that AI can be expected to raise, AI's research agenda will inevitably be restricted by public legislation. This is as it should be; if public ethics prohibit the genetic or other enhancement of human beings, that is the public's right.

What matters is that the decisions that the public makes be informed ones. As an example, a bacterium was engineered recently that, if injected into strawberries, would help to protect them from frost. This work was completely out of the public eye until it came time to test the bacterium on a real strawberry patch north of San Francisco, at which point there was an enormous hue and cry about the dangers of the experiment. Sweeping laws were proposed that involved blanket bans against the release of *any* artificial organism into the environment. The decision on whether or not to pass this law was made by a public that had very little idea of the real risks and potential benefits involved.

The public, of course, has the right to pass whatever laws it wants. Our responsibility is to make sure that their legislative decisions are based on fact instead of fiction.

AI has a mixed track record in this regard; consider the *Terminator* movies. The fascinating moral issues raised in these films are dealt with thoroughly and well, while today's technological limitations are hardly touched upon. Other books and films are similar.

Artistic license is important. And the *use* of artistic license is important: By firing the public imagination and by exploring the moral questions raised by modern technology, the entertainment community does artificial intelligence and science generally a tremendous service. But the scientists also have a role to play; it is our responsibility to ensure that the public comes to a realistic understanding of the challenges, limitations and current technical status of the field itself.

19.3 APPLICATIONS OF AI

Finally, there is the issue of the uses to which AI technology will be put.

Because the bulk of AI's funding comes from military sources, some of these applications will be military. This strikes me as inevitable: Military men have always used scientific progress to further their abilities to destroy one another. The discovery of quantum mechanics led inevitably to the development of atomic weapons.

I expect that it would be fruitless to attempt to fight this trend. What we *can* do is to make as clear as possible the peaceful applications of our technology, and there are many. There is, after all, little difference between an autonomous tank and an autonomous pizza truck.

AI's most immediate applications *are* peaceful: Intelligent interfaces that make computers easier to use for everyone, such as telephones where you can talk in German but listen on the other end in English. Household robots will vacuum our houses some day (not soon, but some day); AI generally holds the promise of freeing us from the drudgery that we can hope to delegate to our machines.

AI is a field with tremendous potential and with tremendous risks—as is any other scientific discipline. The problem—indeed, the very *idea*—of constructing an intelligent artifact is sure to capture the public interest. We must be sure that our zeal and enthusiasm is confined to our research, and does not damage our abilities to honor the responsibility that we all have to keep the public well informed of the nature of scientific activities.

Bibliography

Abramson, B., and M. Yung. Divide and conquer under global constraints: A solution to the n-queens problem. *J. Parallel and Distributed Computing,* 61:649–662, 1989.

Allen, James. *Natural Language Understanding.* Menlo Park, CA: Benjamin Cummings, 1987.

Allen, James, James Hendler, and Austin Tate. *Readings in Planning.* San Mateo, CA: Morgan Kaufmann, 1990.

Allen, James F., Henry A. Kautz, Richard N. Pelavin, and Josh D. Tenenberg. *Reasoning about Plans.* San Mateo, CA: Morgan Kaufmann, 1991.

Aloimonos, Yiannia, and Azriel Rosenfeld. Computer vision. *Science,* 253:1249–1254, 1991.

Aloimonos, J. Y., I. Weiss, and A. Bandyopadhyay. Active vision. *Intl. J. Computer Vision,* 1:333–356, 1988.

Anantharaman, Thomas, Murray S. Campbell, and Feng hsiung Hsu. Singular extensions: Adding selectivity to brute-force searching. *Artificial Intelligence,* 43: 99–109, 1990.

Bajczy, R. Active perception. *Proc. IEEE,* 76:996–1005, 1988.

Baker, Andrew B. Nonmonotonic reasoning in the framework of situation calculus. *Artificial Intelligence,* 49:5–23, 1991.

Ballard, Dana H. Animate vision. *Artificial Intelligence,* 48:57–86, 1991.

Ballard, Dana H. Generalizing the Hough transform to detect arbitrary shapes. *Pattern Recognition,* 13:111–122, 1981.

Ballard, Dana H., and Christopher M. Brown. *Computer Vision.* Englewood Cliffs, NJ: Prentice-Hall, 1982.

Bayes, T. An essay towards solving a problem in the doctrine of chances. *Phil. Trans.,* 3:370–418, 1763.

Bell, Eric Temple. *Men of Mathematics.* New York: Simon and Schuster, 1937.

Berliner, Hans J. Backgammon computer program beats world champion. *Artificial Intelligence,* 14:205–220, 1980.

Berliner, Hans J., and Don F. Beal. Special issue on computer chess. *Artificial Intelligence,* 43:1–123, 1990.

Birnbaum, Lawrence. Rigor mortis: A response to Nilsson's "Logic and artificial intelligence." *Artificial Intelligence,* 47:57–77, 1991.

Blumer, A., A. Ehrenfeucht, D. Haussler, and M. K. Warmuth. Learnability and the Vapnik-Chervonenkis dimension. *J. ACM,* 1989.

Bobrow, Daniel G., and Patrick J. Hayes. Artificial intelligence—where are we? *Artificial Intelligence*, 24:375–415, 1985.

Bond, Alan H., and Les Gasser. *Readings in Distributed Artificial Intelligence*. San Mateo, CA: Morgan Kaufmann, 1988.

Boyer, R. S. *Locking: A Restriction of Resolution*. Ph.D. thesis, University of Texas at Austin, Austin, TX, 1971.

Brachman, Ronald J. "I lied about the trees" or, defaults and definitions in knowledge representation. *AI Magazine*, 6(3):80–93, 1985.

Brachman, Ronald J., Richard E. Fikes, and Hector J. Levesque. KRYPTON: A functional approach to knowledge representation. *IEEE Computer*, 16:67–73, 1983.

Brachman, Ronald J., and Hector J. Levesque. *Readings in Knowledge Representation*. San Mateo, CA: Morgan Kaufmann, 1985.

Brachman, Ronald J., and James G. Schmolze. An overview of the KL-ONE knowledge representation system. *Cog. Sci.*, 9:171–216, 1985.

Brady, J. Michael. Computational approaches to image understanding. *ACM Computing Surveys*, 14:3–71, 1982.

Buchanan, B. G., and E. H. Shortliffe. *Rule-Based Expert Systems: The MYCIN Experiments of the Stanford Heuristic Programming Project*. Reading, MA: Addison-Wesley, 1984.

Campbell, A. N., V. F. Hollister, R. O. Duda, and P. E. Hart. Recognition of a hidden mineral. *Science*, 217:927–929, 1982.

Campbell, Douglas M., and John C. Higgins, editors. *Mathematics: People, Problems, Results*. Belmont, CA: Wadsworth, 1984.

Canny, John F. A computational approach to edge detection. *IEEE PAMI*, 8:679–698, 1986.

Carbonell, Jaime G. Special volume on machine learning. *Artificial Intelligence*, 40:1–395, 1989.

Chang, C. L., and R. C. T. Lee. *Symbolic Logic and Mechanical Theorem Proving*. New York: Academic Press, 1973.

Chapman, David. Planning for conjunctive goals. *Artificial Intelligence*, 32:333–377, 1987.

Charniak, Eugene. Bayesian networks without tears. *AI Magazine*, 12(4):50–63, 1991.

Charniak, Eugene, and Drew McDermott. *Artificial Intelligence*. Reading, MA: Addison-Wesley, 1985.

Cheeseman, Peter. An inquiry into computer understanding. *Computational Intelligence*, 4, 1988.

Clocksin, W. F., and C. S. Mellish. *Programming in Prolog*, 3d ed. Berlin: Springer-Verlag, 1987.

Clowes, M. B. On seeing things. *Artificial Intelligence*, 2:79–116, 1971.

Cohen, Paul R., Michael L. Greenberg, David M. Hart, and Adele E. Howe. Trial by fire: Understanding the design requirements for agents in complex environments. *AI Magazine*, 10(3):34–48, 1989.

Cox, R. Probability frequency and reasonable expectation. *Am. J. Phys.*, 14:1–13, 1946.

Craig, John J. *Introduction to Robotics*. Reading, MA: Addison-Wesley, 1989.

Darwiche, Adnan Y., and Matthew L. Ginsberg. A symbolic generalization of probability theory. In *Proceedings of the Tenth National Conference on Artificial Intelligence*, pages 622–627, 1992.

Davis, Ernest. *Representation of Commonsense Reasoning*. San Mateo, CA: Morgan Kaufmann, 1990.

de Kleer, Johan. An assumption-based truth maintenance system. *Artificial Intelligence*, 28:127–162, 1986.

de Kleer, Johan. Choices without backtracking. In *Proceedings of the Fourth National Conference on Artificial Intelligence*, pages 79–85, 1984.

de Kleer, Johan, Alan K. Mackworth, and Ray Reiter. Characterizing diagnoses and systems. *Artificial Intelligence*, 56:197–222, 1992.

de Kleer, Johan, and Brian C. Williams. Diagnosing multiple faults. *Artificial Intelligence*, 32:97–130, 1987.

Dean, Thomas, and Mark Boddy: An analysis of time-dependent planning. In *Proceedings of the Seventh National Conference on Artificial Intelligence*, pages 49–54, 1988a.

Dean, Thomas, and Mark Boddy. Reasoning about partially ordered events. *Artificial Intelligence*, 36:375–399, 1988b.

Dechter, Rina, and Itay Meiri. Experimental evaluation of preprocessing techniques in constraint satisfaction problems. In *Proceedings of the Eleventh International Joint Conference on Artificial Intelligence*, pages 271–277, 1989.

Deming, W. E., editor. *Two Papers by Bayes*. New York: Hafner, 1963.

Dempster, A. P. A generalization of Bayesian inference. *J. Roy. Stat. Soc. B*, 30: 205–247, 1968.

Dietterich, Thomas G. Machine learning. Technical Report 89-30-6, Oregon State University Dept. of Computer Science, Corvallis, OR, 1989.

Doyle, Jon. A truth maintenance system. *Artificial Intelligence*, 12:231–272, 1979.

Doyle, Jon, and Ramesh S. Patil. Two theses of knowledge representation: Language restrictions, taxonomic classification, and the utility of representation services. *Artificial Intelligence*, 48:261–297, 1991.

Dreyfus, Hubert L. *What Computers Can't Do: The Limits of Artificial Intelligence*. New York: Harper & Row, 1979.

Dreyfus, Hubert L. *Alchemy and Artificial Intelligence*. Santa Monica, CA: Rand Corp., 1965.

Duda, R. O., P. E. Hart, and N. J. Nilsson. Subjective Bayesian methods for rule-based inference systems. In *Proceedings 1976 National Computer Conference*, pages 1075–1082. AFIPS, 1976.

Ehrenfeucht, A., David Haussler, M. Kearns, and Leslie Valiant. A general lower bound on the number of examples needed for learning. In *Proceedings of the 1988 Workshop on Computational Learning Theory*, pages 110–120. San Mateo, CA: Morgan Kaufmann, 1988.

Elkan, Charles. Incremental, approximate planning. In *Proceedings of the Eighth National Conference on Artificial Intelligence*, pages 145–150, 1990.

Enderton, H. B. *A Mathematical Introduction to Logic*. New York: Academic Press, 1972.

Escalada-Imaz, Gonzalo, and Malik Ghallab. A practically efficient and almost linear unification algorithm. *Artificial Intelligence*, 36:249–263, 1988.

Fagin, R., J. D. Ullman, and M. Y. Vardi. On the semantics of updates in databases. In *Proceedings Second ACM Symposium on Principles of Database Systems*, pages 352–365, Atlanta, Georgia, 1983.

Fahlman, Scott E. *NETL: A System for Representing and Using Real-World Knowledge*. Cambridge, MA: MIT Press, 1979.

Feigenbaum, Edward A., and Douglas B. Lenat. On the thresholds of knowledge. *Artificial Intelligence*, 47:139–159, 1991.

Feigenbaum, Edward A., and Pamela McCorduck. *The Fifth Generation: Artificial Intelligence and Japan's Computer Challenge to the World*. New York: New American Library, 1984.

Feigenbaum, Edward A., Pamela McCorduck, and H. Penny Nii. *The Rise of the Expert Company: How Visionary Companies are Using Artificial Intelligence to Achieve Higher Productivity and Profits*. New York: Random House, 1988.

Fikes, Richard, Tom Gruber, Yumi Iwasaki, Alon Levy, and Pandu Nayak. How things work project overview. Technical Report 91-70, Knowledge Systems Laboratory, Stanford University, Stanford, CA, 1991.

Fikes, Richard, Peter E. Hart, and Nils J. Nilsson. Learning and executing generalized robot plans. *Artificial Intelligence*, 3:251–288, 1972.

Fikes, R. E., and Nils J. Nilsson. STRIPS: A new approach to the application of theorem proving to problem solving. *Artificial Intelligence*, 2:189–208, 1971.

Finger, Jeffrey J. *Exploiting Constraints in Design Synthesis*. Ph.D. thesis, Stanford University, Stanford, CA, 1987.

Fischler, Martin A., and Oscar Firschein. *Readings in Computer Vision*. San Mateo, CA: Morgan Kaufmann, 1987.

Gardenförs, Peter. *Knowledge in Flux: Modeling the Dynamics of Epistemic States*. Cambridge, MA: MIT Press, 1988.

Gaschnig, John. Performance measurement and analysis of certain search algorithms. Technical Report CMU-CS-79-124, Carnegie-Mellon University, 1979.

Geffner, Hector. *Default Reasoning, Minimality and Coherence*. Ph.D. thesis, UCLA, Los Angeles, CA, 1990.

Geffner, Hector, and Judea Pearl. Conditional entailment: Bridging two approaches to default reasoning. *Artificial Intelligence*, 53:209–244, 1992.

Genesereth, Michael R., Matthew L. Ginsberg, and Jeffrey S. Rosenschein. Cooperation without communication. In *Proceedings of the Fifth National Conference on Artificial Intelligence*, pages 51–57, 1986.

Genesereth, Michael R., and Nils J. Nilsson. *Logical Foundations of Artificial Intelligence*. San Mateo, CA: Morgan Kaufmann, 1987.

Gentzen, Gerhard. Investigations in logical deduction. In M. E. Szabo, editor, *The Collected Papers of Gerhard Gentzen*. Amsterdam: North-Holland, 1969.

Ginsberg, Matthew L. Dynamic backtracking. Technical report, Stanford University, 1992.

Ginsberg, Matthew L. Computational considerations in reasoning about action. In *Proceedings of the Second International Conference on Principles of Knowledge Representation and Reasoning*, Boston, MA, 1991a.

Ginsberg, Matthew L. The computational value of nonmonotonic reasoning. In *Proceedings of the Second International Conference on Principles of Knowledge Representation and Reasoning*, Boston, MA, 1991b.

Ginsberg, Matthew L. Universal planning: An (almost) universally bad idea. *AI Magazine*, 10(4):40–44, 1989.

Ginsberg, Matthew L. *Readings in Nonmonotonic Reasoning*. San Mateo, CA: Morgan Kaufmann, 1987.

Ginsberg, Matthew L. Counterfactuals. *Artificial Intelligence*, 30:35–79, 1986.

Ginsberg, Matthew L., Michael Frank, Michael P. Halpin, and Mark C. Torrance. Search lessons learned from crossword puzzles. In *Proceedings of the Eighth National Conference on Artificial Intelligence*, pages 210–215, 1990.

Ginsberg, Matthew L., and Donald F. Geddis. Is there any need for domain-dependent control information? In *Proceedings of the Ninth National Conference on Artificial Intelligence*, 1991.

Ginsberg, Matthew L., and Will D. Harvey. Iterative broadening. In *Proceedings of the Eighth National Conference on Artificial Intelligence*, pages 216–220, 1990.

Ginsberg, Matthew L., and David E. Smith. Reasoning about action I: A possible worlds approach. *Artificial Intelligence*, 35:165–195, 1988.

Godel, K. Über Formal Unentscheidbare Sätze der Principia Mathematica und Verwandter Systeme I. *Monatshefte für Mathematik und Physik*, 38:173–198, 1931.

Green, C. C. Theorem proving by resolution as a basis for question-answering systems. In B. Meltzer and D. Michie, editors, *Machine Intelligence 4*, pages 183–205. New York: American Elsevier, 1969.

Grosz, Barbara J., Douglas E. Appelt, Paul A. Martin, and Fernando C. N. Pereira. TEAM: An experiment in the design of transportable natural-language interfaces. *Artificial Intelligence*, 32:173–243, 1987.

Grosz, Barbara J., Karen Sparck Jones, and Bonnie Lynn Webber. *Readings in Natural Language Processing*. San Mateo, CA: Morgan Kaufmann, 1986.

Grosz, Barbara J., Martha E. Pollack, and Candace L. Sidner. Discourse. In Michael I. Posner, editor, *Foundations of Cognitive Science*. Cambridge, MA: MIT Press, 1989.

Grosz, Barbara J., and C. Sidner. Attention, intention, and the structure of discourse. *Comp. Linguistics*, 12, 1986.

Guha, Ramanathan V., and Douglas B. Lenat. CYC: A midterm report. *AI Magazine*, 11(3):32–59, 1990.

Halpern, Joseph Y., and Ronald Fagin. Two views of belief: Belief as generalized probability and belief as evidence. *Artificial Intelligence*, 54:275–317, 1992.

Halpern, Joseph Y., and Yoram Moses. Knowledge and common knowledge in a distributed environment. In *Proceedings of the Third ACM Conference on Principles of Distributed Computing*, 1984.

Hammond, Kristian J. Explaining and repairing plans that fail. *Artificial Intelligence*, 45:173–228, 1990.

Hanks, Steve, and Drew McDermott. Nonmonotonic logics and temporal projection. *Artificial Intelligence*, 33:379–412, 1987.

Harmon, Paul, and David King. *Expert Systems: Artificial Intelligence in Business*. New York: Wiley, 1985.

Hart, P., N. Nilsson, and B. Raphael. A formal basis for the heuristic determination of minimum cost paths. *IEEE Trans. on SCC*, 4, 1968.

Haugeland, John. *Artificial Intelligence: The Very Idea*. Cambridge, MA: MIT Press, 1985.

Haussler, David. Quantifying inductive bias: AI learning algorithms and Valiant's learning framework. *Artificial Intelligence*, 36:177–221, 1988.

Hayes-Roth, Barbara, Richard Washington, Rattikorn Hewett, Michael Hewett, and Adam Seiver. Intelligent monitoring and control. In *Proceedings of the Eleventh International Joint Conference on Artificial Intelligence*, pages 243–249, 1989.

Hayes-Roth, Frederick. The knowledge based expert system: A tutorial. *Computer*, 17(9):11–28, 1984.

Heckerman, David. Probabilistic interpretations for MYCIN's certainty factors. In Laveen N. Kanal and John F. Lemmer, editors, *Uncertainty in Artificial Intelligence*. Amsterdam: North-Holland, 1986.

Hendler, James A., editor. *Expert Systems: The User Inferface*. Norwood, NJ: Ablex, 1988.

Hendrix, G. G., E. Sacerdoti, D. Sagalowicz, and J. Slocum. Developing a natural language interface to complex data. *ACM Trans. Database Systems*, 3:105–147, 1978.

Hobbs, Jerry R. Resolving pronoun references. In Barbara J. Grosz, Karen Sparck Jones, and Bonnie Lynn Webber, editors, *Readings in Natural Language Processing*. San Mateo, CA: Morgan Kaufmann, 1986.

Hodges, Andrew. *Alan Turing: The Enigma*. New York: Simon and Schuster, 1983.

Hofstadter, Douglas R. *Godel, Escher, Bach: An Eternal Golden Braid*. Harmondsworth, England: Penguin, 1979.

Hopcroft, J. E., and J. D. Ullman. *Introduction to Automata Theory*. Reading, MA: Addison-Wesley, 1979.

Horty, John F., and Richmond H. Thomason. Mixing strict and defeasible inheritance. In *Proceedings of the Seventh National Conference on Artificial Intelligence*, pages 427–432, 1988.

Horty, John F., Richmond H. Thomason, and David S. Touretzky. A skeptical theory of inheritance in nonmonotonic semantic networks. In *Proceedings of the Sixth National Conference on Artificial Intelligence*, pages 358–363, 1987.

Horvitz, Eric J., John S. Breese, and Max Henrion. Decision theory in expert systems and artificial intelligence. *Int. J. Approx. Reasoning*, 2:247–302, 1988.

Hough, P. V. C. Method and means for recognizing complex patterns, 1962. U.S. Patent 3069654.

Huet, G. P. A unification algorithm for typed lambda-calculus. *Theor. Comput. Sci.*, 1:27–57, 1975.

Huffman, D. A. Impossible objects as nonsense sentences. In B. Meltzer and Donald Michie, editors, *Machine Intelligence 6*. Edinburgh: Edinburgh University Press, 1971.

Hughes, George E., and M. J. Creswell. *An Introduction to Modal Logic*. London: Methuen, 1968.

Ikeuchi, K., and B. K. P. Horn. Numerical shape from shading and occluding boundaries. *Artificial Intelligence*, 17:141–184, 1981.

Kasturi, Rangachar, and Ramesh C. Jain, editors. *Computer Vision: Advances and Applications*. Los Alamitos, CA: IEEE Computer Society Press, 1991a.

Kasturi, Rangachar, and Ramesh C. Jain, editors. *Computer Vision: Principles*. Los Alamitos, CA: IEEE Computer Society Press, 1991b.

Kautz, Henry A., and Bart Selman. Hard problems for simple default logics. *Artificial Intelligence*, 49:243–279, 1991.

Kender, J. R. Shape from texture: An aggregation transform that maps a class of textures into surface orientation. In *Proceedings of the Sixth International Joint Conference on Artificial Intelligence*, 1979.

Kirkpatrick, S., Jr., C. D. Gelatt, and M. P. Vecchi. Optimization by simulated annealing. *Science*, 220:4598, 1983.

Kirsh, David. Special volume on foundations of artificial intelligence. *Artificial Intelligence*, 47:1–346, 1991.

Knoblock, Craig A. Learning abstraction hierarchies for problem solving. In *Proceedings of the Eighth National Conference on Artificial Intelligence*, pages 923–928, 1990.

Korf, Richard E. Depth-first iterative deepening: An optimal admissible tree search. *Artificial Intelligence*, 27:97–109, 1985a.

Korf, Richard E. Macro-operators: A weak method for learning. *Artificial Intelligence*, 26:35–77, 1985b.

Kowalski, R., and D. Kuehner. Linear resolution with selection function. *Artificial Intelligence*, 2:227–260, 1971.

Kraus, Sarit, and Daniel Lehmann. Automated negotiator. Manuscript, 1988.

Kripke, Saul A. Semantical considerations on modal logic. In L. Linsky, editor, *Reference and Modality*, pages 63–72. London: Oxford University Press, 1971.

Kuhn, T. S. *The Structure of Scientific Revolutions*. Chicago: University of Chicago Press, 1962.

Laird, John E. Allen Newell, and Paul S. Rosenbloom. SOAR: An architecture for general intelligence. *Artificial Intelligence*, 33:1–64, 1987.

Langley, Pat. Systematic and nonsystematic search strategies. In *Artificial Intelligence Planning Systems: Proceedings of the First International Conference*, pages 145–152. San Mateo, CA: Morgan Kaufmann, 1992.

Lea, Wayne A. *Trends in Speech Recognition*. Englewood Cliffs, NJ: Prentice-Hall, 1980.

LeCun, Y. Une procedure d'apprentissage pour reseau a seauil asymetrique. In *Proceedings of Cognitiva 85*, pages 599–604, 1985.

Lee, Kai-Fu, and Sanjoy Mahajan. The development of a world class Othello program. *Artificial Intelligence*, 43:21–36, 1990.

Lenat, Douglas B. EURISKO: A program that learns new heuristics and domain concepts. The nature of heuristics III: Program design and results. *Artificial Intelligence*, 21:61–98, 1983a.

Lenat, Douglas B. Theory formation by heuristic search. The nature of heuristics II: Background and examples. *Artificial Intelligence*, 21:31–59, 1983b.

Lenat, Douglas B. AM: Discovery in mathematics as heuristic search. In Randall Davis and Douglas B. Lenat, editors, *Knowledge-Based Systems in Artificial Intelligence*. San Francisco: McGraw-Hill International Book Company, 1982a.

Lenat, Douglas B. The nature of heuristics. *Artificial Intelligence*, 19:189–249, 1982b.

Lenat, Douglas B., and John Seely Brown. Why AM and EURISKO appear to work. *Artificial Intelligence*, 23:269–294, 1984.

Levesque, Hector J. Making believers out of computers. *Artificial Intelligence*, 30: 81–108, 1986.

Levy, David, and Monty Newborn. *How Computers Play Chess*. New York: Computer Science Press, 1987.

Loveland, D. W. *Automated Theorem Proving: A Logical Basis*. New York: North-Holland, 1978.

Luce, R. Duncan, and Howard Raiffa. *Games and Decisions: Introduction and Critical Survey*. New York: Wiley, 1957.

MacGregor, Robert. Loom user's manual. Technical Report ISI/WP-22, USC/Information Sciences Institute, Los Angeles, CA, 1990.

Makinson, David, and Karl Schlechta. Floating conclusions and zombie paths: Two deep difficulties in the "directly skeptical" approach to defeasible inheritance nets. *Artificial Intelligence*, 48:199–209, 1991.

Malachi, Y., Zohar Manna, and Richard Waldinger. TABLOG—The deductive tableau programming language. In D. DeGroot and G. Lindstrom, editors, *Logic Programming: Functions, Relations and Equations*, pages 365–394. Englewood Cliffs, NJ: Prentice-Hall, 1986.

Marr, David. *Vision: A Computational Investigation into the Human Representation and Processing of Visual Information*. San Francisco: W. H. Freeman, 1982.

Marr, David. Artificial Intelligence—A personal view. *Artificial Intelligence*, 9:37–48, 1977.

Marr, David, and E. Hildreth. Theory of edge detection. *J. Roy. Soc. B*, 270:187–217, 1980.

Martelli, A., and U. Montanari. An efficient unification algorithm. *ACM Trans. Program Lang. Syst.*, 4:258–282, 1982.

Martins, Joao P., and Stuart C. Shapiro. Reasoning in multiple belief spaces. In *Proceedings of the Eighth International Joint Conference on Artificial Intelligence*, pages 370–373, 1983.

McAllester, David A. Reasoning utility package user's manual. Technical Report AIM-667, MIT, 1982.

McAllester, David, and David Rosenblitt. Systematic nonlinear planning. In *Proceedings of the Ninth National Conference on Artificial Intelligence*, pages 634–639, 1991.

McCarthy, John. Circumscription—a form of non-monotonic reasoning. *Artificial Intelligence*, 13:27–39, 1980.

McCarthy, John. Epistemological problems of artificial intelligence. In *Proceedings of the Fifth International Joint Conference on Artificial Intelligence*, pages 1038–1044, Cambridge, MA, 1977.

McCarthy, John, and Patrick J. Hayes. Some philosophical problems from the standpoint of artificial intelligence. In B. Meltzer and D. Michie, editors, *Machine Intelligence 4*, pages 463–502. New York: American Elsevier, 1969.

McCorduck, Pamela. *Machines Who Think*. New York: W. H. Freeman and Company, 1979.

McDonald, D. D. Natural language generation. In Stuart C. Shapiro, editor, *Encyclopedia of Artificial Intelligence*, pages 983–997. New York: Wiley, 1992.

Michalski, Ryszard S., Jaime G. Carbonell, and Thomas M. Mitchell, editors. *Machine Learning: An Artificial Intelligence Approach*, vol. 2. Los Altos, CA: Morgan Kaufmann, 1986.

Michalski, Ryszard S., Jaime G. Carbonell, and Thomas M. Mitchell, editors. *Machine Learning: An Artificial Intelligence Approach*. Palo Alto, CA: Tioga Publishing Company, 1983.

Michalski, Ryszard, and Yves Kodratoff, editors. *Machine Learning: An Artificial Intelligence Approach*, vol. 3. Los Altos, CA: Morgan Kaufmann, 1988.

Minsky, Marvin. A framework for representing knowledge. In Patrick Winston, editor, *The Psychology of Computer Vision*, pages 211–277. New York: McGraw-Hill, 1975.

Minsky, Marvin, and Seymour Papert. *Perceptrons*. Cambridge, MA: MIT Press, 1969.

Minton, Steven. Quantitative results concerning the utility of explanation-based learning. *Artificial Intelligence*, 42:363–391, 1990.

Minton, Steven. *Learning Search Control Knowledge: An Explanation-Based Approach*. Boston: Kluwer, 1988.

Minton, Steven, John Bresina, and Mark Drummond. Commitment strategies in planning: A comparative analysis. In *Proceedings of the Ninth National Conference on Artificial Intelligence*, 1991.

Minton, Steve, Jaime G. Carbonell, Craig A. Knoblock, Daniel R. Kuokka, Oren Etzioni, and Yolanda Gil. Explanation-based learning: A problem solving perspective. *Artificial Intelligence*, 40:63–118, 1989.

Minton, Steven, Mark D. Johnston, Andrew B. Philips, and Philip Laird. Solving large-scale constraint satisfaction and scheduling problems using a heuristic repair method. In *Proceedings of the Eighth National Conference on Artificial Intelligence*, pages 17–24, 1990.

Mitchell, Thomas M. Generalization as search. *Artificial Intelligence*, 18:203–226, 1982.

Mitchell, Thomas M. *Version Spaces: An Approach to Concept Learning*. Ph.D. thesis, Stanford University, Stanford, CA, 1977.

Moore, Robert. Semantical considerations on nonmonotonic logic. *Artificial Intelligence*, 25:75–94, 1985.

Myers, Karen L., and David E. Smith. On the persistence of derived beliefs. In *Proceedings of the Seventh National Conference on Artificial Intelligence*, 1988.

Natarajan, Balas K. *Machine Learning: A Theoretical Approach*. San Mateo, CA: Morgan Kaufmann, 1991.

Newell, Alan, and Herbert A. Simon. Computer science as empirical inquiry: Symbols and search. *Communications ACM*, 19, 1976.

Nilsson, Nils J. Logic and artificial intelligence. *Artificial Intelligence*, 47:31–56, 1991.

Nilsson, Nils J. Probabilistic logic. *Artificial Intelligence*, 28:71–87, 1986.

Patel-Schneider, Peter F. Undecidability of subsumption in NIKL. *Artificial Intelligence*, 39:263–272, 1989.

Paterson, M. S. and M. N. Wegman. Linear unification. *J. Comput. Syst. Sci.*, 16: 158–167, 1978.

Pattabhiraman, T., and Nick Cercone. Special issue on natural language generation. *Computational Intelligence*, 7, 1991.

Pearl, Judea. *Probabilistic Reasoning in Intelligent Systems: Networks of Plausible Inference*. San Mateo, CA: Morgan Kaufmann, 1988.

Pearl, Judea. *Heuristics: Intelligent Search Strategies for Computer Problem Solving*. Reading, MA: Addison-Wesley, 1984.

Pearl, Judea. A solution for the branching factor of the alpha-beta pruning algorithm and its optimality. *Comm. ACM*, 25(8):559–564, 1982.

Pentland, Alex. Shape from shading: A theory of human perception. In *Proc. 2nd Intl. Conf. on Computer Vision*, Tampa, FL, 1988.

Phipps, Geoff, Marcia A. Derr, and K. A. Ross. Glue-Nail: A deductive database system. *SIGMOD Bulletin*, pages 308–317, 1991.

Pollack, Martha E. Plans as complex mental attitudes. In Philip R. Cohen, Jerry Morgan, and Martha E. Pollack, editors, *Intentions in Communication*. Cambridge, MA: MIT Press, 1988.

Pollack, Martha E., and Marc Ringuette. Introducing the tile-world: Experimentally evaluating agent architectures. In *Proceedings of the Eighth National Conference on Artificial Intelligence*, pages 183–189, 1990.

Polya, George. *How to Solve It: A New Aspect of Mathematical Method*. Princeton, NJ: Princeton University Press, 1945.

Poole, David. Normality and faults in logic-based diagnosis. In *Proceedings of the Eleventh International Joint Conference on Artificial Intelligence*, pages 1304–1310, 1989.

Poole, D., R. Aleliunas, and R. Goebel. THEORIST: A logical reasoning system for defaults and diagnosis. Technical Report, University of Waterloo, 1985.

Pople, H. E. On the mechanization of abductive logic. In *Proceedings of the Third International Joint Conference on Artificial Intelligence*, pages 147–152, 1973.

Pullum, Geoffrey K. *The Great Eskimo Vocabulary Hoax, and Other Irreverent Essays on the Study of Language*. Chicago: University of Chicago Press, 1991.

Quinlan, J. Ross. Simplifying decision trees. *Intl. J. Man-Machine Studies*, 27:221–234, 1987.

Quinlan, J. Ross. The effect of noise on concept learning. In Ryszard S. Michalski, Jaime G. Carbonell, and Thomas M. Mitchell, editors, *Machine Learning: An Artificial Intelligence Approach*. Los Altos, CA: Morgan Kaufmann, 1986a.

Quinlan, J. Ross. Induction of decision trees. *Machine Learning*, 1:81–106, 1986b.

Quirk, Randolph, S. Greenbaum, G. Leech, and J. Svartik. *A Comprehensive Grammar of the English Language*. London: Longman, 1985.

Reichenbach, Hans. *The Theory of Probability, An Inquiry into the Mathematical Foundations of the Calculus of Probability*. Berkeley, CA: University of California, 1949.

Reiter, Raymond. The frame problem in the situation calculus: A simple solution (sometimes) and a completeness result for goal regression. In Vladimir Lifschitz, editor, *Artificial Intelligence and Mathematical Theory of Computation: Papers in Honor of John McCarthy*, pages 359–380. Boston: Academic Press, 1991.

Reiter, Ray. Nonmonotonic reasoning. *Annual Reviews of Computer Science*, 2: 147–187, 1987a.

Reiter, Ray. A theory of diagnosis from first principles. *Artificial Intelligence*, 32: 57–95, 1987b.

Reiter, Ray. A logic for default reasoning. *Artificial Intelligence*, 13:81–132, 1980.

Reiter, Raymond, and Giovanni Criscuolo. On interacting defaults. In *Proceedings of the Seventh International Joint Conference on Artificial Intelligence*, pages 270–276, 1981.

Reiter, Raymond, and Johan de Kleer. Foundations of assumption-based truth maintenance systems: Preliminary report. In *Proceedings of the Sixth National Conference on Artificial Intelligence*, pages 183–188, 1987.

Rich, Charles, and Richard C. Waters. *Readings in Artificial Intelligence and Software Engineering*. San Mateo, CA: Morgan Kaufmann, 1986.

Rich, Elaine, and Kevin Knight. *Artificial Intelligence*. New York: McGraw-Hill, 1991.

Robinson, J. A. *Logic: Form and Function*. New York: North-Holland, 1979.

Robinson, J. A. Computational logic: The unification computation. In B. Meltzer and D. Michie, editors, *Machine Intelligence*, vol. 6. Edinburgh: Edinburgh University Press, 1971.

Robinson, J. A. A machine-oriented logic based on the resolution principle. *JACM*, 12:23–41, 1965.

Rosenblatt, Frank. *Principles of Neurodynamics: Perceptrons and the Theory of Brain Mechanisms*. Washington, DC: Spartan Books, 1962.

Rosenschein, Jeffrey S., and Michael R. Genesereth. Deals among rational agents. In *Proceedings of the Ninth International Joint Conference on Artificial Intelligence*, pages 91–99, 1985.

Rumelhart, David E., Geoffrey E. Hinton, and R. J. Williams. Learning internal representations by error propagation. In David E. Rumelhart and James L. McClelland, editors, *Parallel Distributed Processing: Explorations in the Microstructure of Cognition*. Cambridge, MA: MIT Press, 1986.

Russell, Stuart, and Eric Wefald. *Do the Right Thing: Studies in Limited Rationality*. Cambridge, MA: MIT Press, 1991.

Russell, Stuart, and Eric Wefald. On optimal game-tree search using rational metareasoning. In *Proceedings of the Eleventh International Joint Conference on Artificial Intelligence*, pages 334–340, 1989.

Sacerdoti, Earl D. *A Structure for Plans and Behavior*. New York: American Elsevier, 1977.

Sager, Naomi. *Natural Language Information Processing: A Computer Grammar of English and Its Applications*. Reading, MA: Addison-Wesley, 1981.

Schank, Roger C., and Robert P. Abelson. *Scripts, Plans, Goals, and Understanding: An Inquiry into Human Knowledge Structures*. Hillsdale, NJ: Lawrence Erlbaum, 1977.

Schubert, Lenhart K. Monotonic solution of the frame problem in the situation calculus. In Henry E. Kyburg, Jr., Ronald P. Loui, and Greg N. Carlson, editors, *Knowledge Representation and Defeasible Reasoning*, pages 23–67. Boston: Kluwer, 1990.

Scott, A. Carlisle, Jan E. Clayton, and Elizabeth L. Gibson. *A Practical Guide to Knowledge Acquisition*. Reading, MA: Addison-Wesley, 1991.

Searle, John R. Minds, brains, and programs. *Behavioral and Brain Sciences*, 3: 417–424, 1980.

Selman, Bart, Hector Levesque, and David Mitchell. A new method for solving hard satisfiability problems. In *Proceedings of the Tenth National Conference on Artificial Intelligence*, 1992.

Shafer, Glenn. *A Mathematical Theory of Evidence*. Princeton, NJ: Princeton University Press, 1976.

Shapiro, Stuart C. The SNePS semantic network processing system. In Nicholas V. Findler, editor, *Associative Networks: Representation and Use of Knowledge by Computers*, pages 179–203. New York: Academic Press, 1979.

Shekhar, Shashi, and Soumitra Dutta. Minimizing response times in real time planning and search. In *Proceedings of the Eleventh International Joint Conference on Artificial Intelligence*, pages 238–242, 1989.

Shortliffe, Edward H. *Computer-based Medical Consultations: MYCIN*. New York: American Elsevier, 1976.

Shrobe, Howard E. *Exploring Artificial Intelligence: Survey Talks from the National Conferences on Artificial Intelligence*. San Mateo, CA: Morgan Kaufmann, 1988.

Slate, D. J., and L. R. Atkin. *Chess 4.5—The Northwestern University Chess Program*. New York: Springer-Verlag, 1977.

Smith, David E. Controlling backward inference. *Artificial Intelligence*, 39:145–208, 1989.

Smith, David E. *Controlling Inference*. Ph.D. thesis, Stanford University, August 1985.

Smith, David E., and Michael R. Genesereth. Ordering conjunctive queries. *Artificial Intelligence*, 26(2):171–215, 1985.

Smith, David E., Michael R. Genesereth, and Matthew L. Ginsberg. Controlling recursive inference. *Artificial Intelligence*, 30:343–389, 1986.

Stallman, R. M., and G. J. Sussman. Forward reasoning and dependency-directed backtracking in a system for computer-aided circuit analysis. *Artificial Intelligence*, 9(2):135–196, 1977.

Steele, Guy L., Jr. *Common Lisp: The Language*, 2d ed. Billerica, MA: Digital Press, 1990.

Steen, Lynn Arthur, editor. *Mathematics Today: Twelve Informal Essays*. New York: Springer-Verlag, 1978.

Stefik, Mark. *Introduction to Knowledge Systems*. San Mateo, CA: Morgan Kaufmann, forthcoming, 1993.

Sterling, Leon, and Ehud Shapiro. *The Art of Prolog: Advanced Programming Techniques*. Cambridge, MA: MIT Press, 1986.

Stickel, Mark E., and W. Mabry Tyson. An analysis of consecutively bounded depth-first search with applications in automated deduction. In *Proceedings of the Ninth International Joint Conference on Artificial Intelligence*, pages 1073–1075, 1985.

Sussman, Gerald Jay. *A Computational Model of Skill Acquisition*. New York: American Elsevier, 1975.

Touretzky, David S. Implicit ordering of defaults in inheritance systems. In *Proceedings of the Fifth National Conference on Artificial Intelligence*, pages 322–325, 1984.

Treitel, Richard, and Michael R. Genesereth. Choosing directions for rules. *Journal of Automated Reasoning*, 1987.

Turing, Alan. Computing machinery and intelligence. *Mind*, 59:434–460, 1950.

Ullman, Jeffrey D. *Principles of Database and Knowledge-Base Systems, Volume II: The New Technologies*. Rockville, MD: Computer Science Press, 1989.

Utgoff, Paul E. Incremental induction of decision trees. *Machine Learning*, 1989.

Valiant, Leslie G. A theory of the learnable. *Comm. ACM*, 27:1134–1142, 1984.

Waltz, David. Understanding line drawings of scenes with shadows. In Patrick H. Winston, editor, *The Psychology of Computer Vision*, pages 19–91. New York: McGraw-Hill, 1975.

Webber, Bonnie L. Question answering. In Stuart C. Shapiro, editor, *Encyclopedia of Artificial Intelligence*. New York: Wiley, 1987.

Webber, Bonnie Lynn, and Nils J. Nilsson. *Readings in Artificial Intelligence*. San Mateo, CA: Morgan Kaufmann, 1981.

Weizenbaum, J. ELIZA. *Comm. ACM*, 9:36–45, 1966.

Wellman, Michael P. Qualitative probabilistic networks for planning under uncertainty. In John F. Lemmer and Laveen N. Kanal, editors, *Uncertainty in Artificial Intelligence*, vol. 2. San Mateo, CA: Morgan Kaufmann, 1988.

Werbos, P. J. *Beyond Regression: New Tools for Prediction and Analysis in the Behavioral Sciences*. Ph.D. thesis, Harvard University, Cambridge, MA, 1974.

Wilkins, David E. *Practical Planning: Extending the Classical AI Planning Paradigm*. San Mateo, CA: Morgan Kaufmann, 1988.

Wilkins, David E. Using patterns and plans in chess. *Artificial Intelligence*, 14:165–203, 1980.

Winograd, Terry. *Language as a Cognitive Process. Volume 1: Syntax*. Reading, MA: Addison-Wesley, 1983.

Winograd, Terry. *Understanding Natural Language*. New York: Academic Press, 1972.

Winslett, Marianne. Reasoning about actions using a possible models approach. In *Proceedings of the Seventh National Conference on Artificial Intelligence*, 1988.

Winston, Patrick Henry. *Artificial Intelligence*, Reading, MA: Addison-Wesley, 1992.

Woods, William A. The KL-ONE family. Technical Report TR-20-90, Harvard University Center for Research in Computing Technology, Cambridge, MA, 1990a.

Woods, William A. Understanding subsumption and taxonomy: A framework for progress. Technical Report TR-19-90, Harvard University Center for Research in Computing Technology, Cambridge, MA, 1990b.

Woods, William A. Lunar rocks in natural English: Explorations in natural language question answering. In Antonio Zampolli, editor, *Linguistic Structures Processing*. Amsterdam: Elsevier North-Holland, 1977.

Woods, William A. What's in a link: Foundations for semantic networks. In Daniel G. Bobrow and Allan Collins, editors, *Representation and Understanding*. New York: Academic Press, 1975.

Wos, Larry. *Automated Reasoning: Introduction and Applications*. Englewood Cliffs, NJ: Prentice-Hall, 1984.

Yarbus, Alfred L. *Eye Movements and Vision*. New York: Plenum, 1967.

Yu, V. L., B. G. Buchanan, E. H. Shortliffe, S. M. Wraith, R. Davis, A. C. Scott, and S. N. Cohen. Evaluating the performance of a computer-based consultant. *Computer Programs in Biomedicine*, 9:95–102, 1979.

Zadeh, Lotfi A. A review of *A Mathematical Theory of Evidence*. *AI Magazine*, 5(3):81–83, 1984.

Zadeh, Lotfi A. Fuzzy logic and approximate reasoning. *Synthese*, 30:407–428, 1975.

Author Index

SUBJECT INDEX